IRELAND SINCE THE RISING

Ireland since the Rising

TIMOTHY PATRICK
COOGAN

PALL MALL PRESS

Published by The Pall Mall Press Ltd.
77-79 Charlotte Street, London, W.1

FIRST PUBLISHED 1966

© *1966 Timothy Patrick Coogan*

MADE AND PRINTED IN GREAT BRITAIN BY
THE GARDEN CITY PRESS LIMITED
LETCHWORTH, HERTFORDSHIRE

CONTENTS

v

ILLUSTRATIONS

The photographs for Plates 1, 2 and 3 are provided by courtesy of the National Library of Ireland.

*To the memory of
my father and in tribute to
my mother and to Cherry, my wife*

ACKNOWLEDGEMENTS

I AM indebted to so many people for help and advice in the preparation and writing of this book that I hardly know where to begin. Perhaps I should start by paying tribute to my colleagues of the *Evening Press* for the fortitude with which they endured the effects of creativity on my never very angelic temper.

I should like to express particular gratitude to the following for allowing me to interview them: Captain Terence O'Neill, MP, prime minister of Northern Ireland; Mr Frank Aiken, TD, Tanaiste and minister for External Affairs; Mr George Colley, TD, minister for Education; Mr Charles Haughey, TD, minister for Agriculture; Mr Brian Lenihan, minister for Justice; Dr Simms, archbishop of Dublin; Dr Lucey, bishop of Cork; Dr Browne, bishop of Galway; Dr Birch, bishop of Kilkenny; His Honour Judge Conroy; Senator Gerald Boland; Mr Liam Cosgrave, SC, TD; Mr Declan Costello, SC, TD; Mr Edward McAteer, MP; General Richard Mulcahy; Mr Joseph McGrath; Mrs Kathleen Clarke; Mr Martin Wallace; Colonel Eamonn Broy; Colonel David Neligan; Mr Maurice Twomey; Mr George Gilmore; Mr Edward Lawler; Mr Ernest Blythe, director of the Abbey Theatre; Mr Vincent Grogan, SC; Mr Cathal Shannon; Professor David Greene; Breandan OhEithir Uas; Mr Michael MacInerney; Mr Sean Cronin; and Dr Noel Browne.

For their continuing kindness in giving advice and information as this book was being written, I should like to thank Dr David Thornley, fellow of Trinity College, Dublin; Mr Donal Nevin, research officer of the Irish Congress of Trade Unions; and Dr Cruise O'Brien.

Publishers as a class I do not approve of, but I must make honourable exception of Mr Derick Mirfin of the Pall Mall Press for his help and understanding. The staff of the National Library and of Dun Laoghaire Public Library deserve my most sincere thanks for their co-operation and courtesy. I am also indebted to the Trinity College Library Authorities and to the Irish Central Library for Students. There are also a number of people, who must remain anonymous, whose advice and help was of great benefit to me; I express to them my warm thanks.

The opinions expressed in the book are, of course, entirely my own responsibility.   T. P. C.

INTRODUCTION

TO anyone born and reared in Ireland since 1916, analysis of the Easter Rising and its aftermath is like dissection of the Mass by a layman. Any shift in emphasis is heretical, any criticism near-blasphemy.

There are understandable reasons for this. Out of the Rising modern Ireland was begotten. Through it Eamon de Valera, Michael Collins, Cathal Brugha, Harry Boland, Richard Mulcahy, W. T. Cosgrave and most of the great figures in Irish political life of this century were brought on to the national stage. The wave of emotion following the dramatic events of 1916 was to carry Cosgrave and de Valera through the by-elections which swept them triumphantly into the political arena where each was to win the leadership of the country. But, tragically, the unity of the patriots of Easter Week was eventually to crack apart. Cosgrave and de Valera with their followers were sundered in the hour of Ireland's triumph by the Karma of nationhood: Civil War.

The fires of Easter Week burned with phoenix flames, out of which emerged the Ireland of today. But it is not the Ireland the men of 1916 died for. Her thirty-two counties are divided into two separate entities: the Republic of Ireland and Northern Ireland—the one an independent sovereign state, the other a self-governing part of the United Kingdom. And their dream of an Ireland which—in the words of their leader, Patrick Pearse—would be 'not free merely, but Gaelic as well', has not been realised. Ireland is not the Irish-speaking state they hoped for.

Yet it is becoming an Ireland they could be proud of. The enemies today are not the British, but prejudice and poverty. The challenge is not the assertion of the right to nationhood, but the imperative of adjusting to the political and economic implications of the new Europe.

Ireland has passed through her period of revolution and the turbulent aftermath, and her long hard climb to economic prosperity is nearing success. She has reached a watershed in her development wherein the emphasis is no longer on political or constitutional transformation but on economic and social change. Her wounds have healed, or nearly so. She is now able to see herself for what she is: a small nation with much to be proud of, particularly in the field of international affairs; a nation not afraid to face up to its problems.

An important governmental committee charged with making recommendations on the needs of Irish industry in the EEC era typified the new spirit which is at work in Ireland when it said: 'Searching, uninhibited and objective surveys are the only kind worth having'. For too long Ireland has suffered from being given either a whimsical, leprechauny image, quite unlike her real self, or else a hostile, denigrating depiction from émigré writers and foreign observers. I have approached my task in writing this book in the spirit of the words cited above. I have throughout tried to be objective—some possibly will say too uninhibitedly so; and I have certainly been searching.

In Ireland anecdotes are more easy to come by than facts. This is not simply the plaint of a lazy journalist. I have been able to draw on many useful books; these are indicated in the Bibliography. But to weigh impartially conflicting evidence and to gain a clearer insight into the motivation of men and events, I have had to repair to something more than books. My debt to the people whom I may formally thank is expressed in the Acknowledgements. But other sources of information were not so easily obtained. I had to get the figures on the Civil War from a friend in the secret service. The information about Communism came partly through private sources, and some of the information in the 'State and Economy' chapter was obtained through the courtesy of deputies who asked questions in the Dail.

There were, moreover, the little local difficulties. I rang up one marvellous veteran of the stirring years to ask him for an interview, saying I wanted 'to get his attitude towards Ireland today'. He replied: 'You'll have to define what you mean by attitude, what you mean by Ireland, and what you mean by today'. Having endeavoured to satisfy him on these points, I obtained an interview at which *he* took shorthand notes. I was near to gibbering with fright at the thought of what would happen if I made the least variation from his verbatim report in my use of the interview material. But after a while, he put away the pad and produced the decanter. The evening turned out to be one of the most pleasant I have ever spent. His attitude towards Ireland was wholly admirable, though we never got round to today.

Happily I can report that Ireland herself is now very much concerned with the present, and increasingly so.

1. REVOLT

Prelude to Revolt: *New Movements; The Fenian Tradition;*
Preparation for Revolt · The Rising

AT the time it occurred, the Rising in Easter Week 1916 was the most
unpopular event in Dublin since the arrival of Oliver Cromwell.
Today its survivors still marvel at the complete change in the public
attitude to them and their rebellion. Yells of abuse and disgust were flung
at them from the crowds watching them pass through the Dublin streets
to the reeking hold of the cattle-boats that took them to England and
imprisonment. A year later they returned, to meet a surging welcome from
the same Dublin crowds.

The Rising was the work of a small group of men. The call to arms was
answered only by some 1,200 Volunteers and members of the Citizen
Army—and even this figure is the subject of debate. The dead and
wounded among the insurgents, British soldiers, police and civilians
amounted all told to 1,351. Damage to the city is estimated at some £2½
million, and 100,000 people had to be given public relief. With half of
Sackville Street* in ruins, workplaces shut down and utter disruption in the
supply of the necessities of life, the immediate reaction of most Dubliners
was bitter revulsion against the extremists whose attempted coup had
unleashed open war in the city.

In calling for help for the victims of the 'partially socialistic and partially
alien outbreak', the *Irish Catholic* for April 29 said:

> The movement which has culminated in deeds of unparalleled blood-
> shed and destruction of property in the capital of Ireland was as
> criminal as it was insane. Only idiots or lunatics can ever have supposed
> it could prove successful. Traitorous and treacherous as it undoubtedly
> was, it was most traitorous and treacherous to our native land.

The same issue of the *Irish Catholic* also carried reports of condemnations
of the Rising by five members of the Catholic hierarchy, one of whom—

---

* Renamed O'Connell Street in memory of the great leader of Irish nationalism, this
beautiful street became a symbol of Ireland's national torment. Its lower half was destroyed in the fighting between revolutionaries and British in 1916; six years later its
upper half was devastated in the battling of Irishmen against Irishmen.

Dr Kelly, bishop of Ross—termed it 'a senseless, meaningless debauch of blood'. The Protestant archbishop of Dublin wrote to *The Times* a letter, printed May 4, urging the government to take 'the sternest measures' against the rebels. 'This is not the time for amnesties and pardons; it is the time for punishment, swift and stern.'

It was the immediate aftermath of the Rising which changed the climate of opinion. The execution of the leaders—particularly of James Connolly, the Labour leader, who was so badly wounded that he had to be propped up in a chair to be shot—shocked and embittered countless Irishmen who, deploring the Rising, had yet been moved by the courage and patriotic idealism of the insurgents.

PRELUDE TO REVOLT

In 1916, Ireland seemed to be in a strange limbo between disaffection and tranquillity. There was widespread poverty—Dublin had some of the worst slums in Europe—but Irish farmers were getting excellent prices for their cattle because of the war against Germany. And under the political pressure of the Home Rule movement, the worst aspects of British rule had been mitigated.

The country was still linked to the United Kingdom under the Act of Union of 1800, passed by the British parliament and the self-extinguishing Protestant legislature in Dublin during the alarmist aftermath of Wolfe Tone's rebellion of 1798. Wolfe Tone's movement failed, but he created a tradition of blood and Republicanism which was carried on by nationalist successors: Robert Emmet in 1803, the Young Irelanders of 1848 and the Fenians of 1867. These movements failed in their turn, but they played their part in the process of historical gestation which culminated in the birth of the Irish Republic in the bloody labour ward of the General Post Office on Easter Monday, 1916.

Under the Act of Union, Ireland lost the right to legislate for herself under the British Crown. The hundred or so members she sent to West-minster could (until Parnell's time in the late nineteenth century) make little impression in an assembly of 670 on legislation affecting their country's interests. During the eighteenth century Irish trade and industry were systematically discriminated against in favour of the predominant 'partner'. The effects of this—economic backwardness and the stifling of the spirit of enterprise—continue to be felt today. The Irish system of land tenure, with the parcelling out of land into minute peasant holdings and the rack-renting pressure of landlords, many of them absentees, produced the conditions for disaster in the 1840s when the potato, the staple food of the peasantry, was struck by blight. A 'population explosion', the land supersede British justice, an Irish Civil Service, Stock Exchange and Bank. But Arthur Griffith—a superb journalist who could have been a wealthy man had he renounced his idealism to accept the offers made by American interests—was neither a revolutionary nor a republican. His political views were greatly influenced by Deak, a Hungarian, and he wrote a series of articles which created considerable stir when they appeared in book form in 1904 under the title *The Resurrection of Hungary*. Griffith drew a parallel between Hungary and Ireland, observing that Hungary had won its independence by refusing to send members to the imperial parliament in Vienna and by rejecting that parliament's claim to legislate for internal Hungarian affairs. He advocated a Dual Monarchy similar to that of Austro-Hungary, and envisaged the British monarch as king of England and king of Ireland, with separate legislatures in both countries. This in effect amounted to restoring Grattan's Parliament.

Griffith called his newspaper *The United Irishman*, giving it the same name as that of the paper edited by John Mitchel who had called Ireland to revolt in 1848 and who, though unsuccessful, had bequeathed a tradition of separatism and the strategy of striking at England while she was engaged in a European war. In his economic views, Griffith was a disciple of List, the German protectionist, and advocated tariffs to foster native Irish industries. He became generally disliked by Irish Labour leaders because of his capitalist outlook and his condemnation of strikes and labour disputes. One of Griffith's earliest collaborators was Sean T. O'Kelly, later to be president of Ireland.

None of these nationalist movements planned armed rebellion. But all of them to a greater or lesser extent were being infiltrated by an organisation which did: the Irish Republican Brotherhood.

The Fenian Tradition

It was the Irish Republican Brotherhood which brought about the Rising. The IRB had been founded on Saint Patrick's Day 1858 by James Stephens and Thomas Clarke Luby, following the suppression of the Phoenix National and Literary Society. This had been set up by Jeremiah O'Donovan, famous in the history of Irish nationalism as O'Donovan Rossa, called thus from his birthplace at Roscarberry. O'Donovan's organisation was more political than literary. Working among the members of the suppressed Phoenix Society and helped by £90 sent from America by survivors of the 1848 revolt, Stephens and Luby set about re-igniting the fire of insurgency. The IRB's members eventually became known as 'Fenians', following a suggestion of John O'Mahony, the organisation's leading figure in America. A man with literary tastes, he was recalling the Fianna of Irish legend who were a cross between the Knights of the Round

Table and the Samurai. In America, the IRB was more generally known as Clan na Gael (Family of the Gaels). The Clan's leader, John Devoy, was to be the channel through which passed most of the emigrant money that financed the 1916 Rising.

The Fenians were bound by oath. Because of this and of the fact that the Catholic hierarchy upheld the Union during the nineteenth century (except for a short period when Parnell seemed to be making headway), the Fenians were condemned by Church leaders in Ireland, although many of the younger clergy were sympathetic to them. The form of the oath used in 1916 was:

> In the presence of God, I . . . do solemnly swear that I will do my utmost to establish the national independence of Ireland and that I will bear true allegiance to the Supreme Council of the Irish Republican Brotherhood and Government of the Irish Republic and implicitly obey the Constitution of the IRB and all my superior officers and that I will preserve inviolate the secrets of the organisation.

The activities of the Fenians included an attempted invasion of Canada in 1867, the rescue of a group of prisoners from Western Australia in 1876, and the commissioning of the first American submarine, designed by John P. Holland and launched in 1881. They were also associated in the public mind of Britain with the murder of Lord Frederick Cavendish, newly appointed Chief Secretary for Ireland, on May 6, 1882: an outrage which perhaps more than any other embittered British attitudes towards Irish nationalism. But this crime was not committed by the Fenians as such, its perpetrators being an independent group called the 'Invincibles'. What was indisputably the work of the Fenians—and their major activity— was the Dynamite Campaign. The campaign was an offshoot of the American organisation of the IRB, Clan na Gael. The philosophy behind it could be summed up in a phrase of O'Donovan Rossa's: to get the British out of Ireland he would employ 'Dynamite, Greek fire, or Hell fire if it could be had'. The dynamiting began in the spring of 1883. A series of explosions were organised throughout England, culminating in simultaneous explosions at the Tower of London, Westminster Hall and the House of Commons on January 24, 1885. It was not a highly developed movement politically, but this—the forerunner of the IRA bombing campaign against England in 1939—was the political nursery of the man who, in a sense, fathered the 1916 Rising: Thomas Clarke.

Clarke, born in England of Irish parents in 1858, had been captured in 1883 and sentenced to penal servitude for life on a charge of treason felony. Not wanting the British to know his real name, he spent the first five years in prison under the name of Hammond Wilson and without his family's knowing where he was.* Released in 1898 by an amnesty, he went to New York where in 1901 he married Kathleen Daly, the niece of a fellow prisoner. The couple became American citizens, but returned to Ireland in 1907 because Clarke, foreseeing the war between Britain and Germany, had decided, following Mitchel's philosophy, that England's difficulty might be Ireland's opportunity.

Meanwhile the IRB in Ireland had become almost moribund, its leaders having grown old. There was a ripple of nationalist enthusiasm in 1898: the centenary of Wolfe Tone's Rebellion. Two papers—the *Shan Van Vocht* (The Poor Old Woman) run by Alice Milligan in the North, and the *Workers' Republic* edited in the South by James Connolly, the Labour leader—preached separatism. But that was about all the IRB activity there was at this time. The Fenian movement as a whole became afflicted with the *morbus Hibernicus*: heroic nostalgia. They still administered the Fenian oath to their children, but their zeal for the cause was retrospective, not active.

In the North, however, a group of younger IRB men led by Bulmer Hobson (a Quaker who was later to organise the gun-running that gave teeth to the 1916 Rising) and by Denis McCullough (a young Belfast businessman) had decided that something more activist was called for. They set about forming their own groups in the North—Wolfe Tone societies called the Dungannon Clubs—and made contact with kindred spirits in the South, like Dr Pat MacCartan and the Boland brothers, Gerald, Harry and Ned. Some of their seniors, like John Daly in Limerick, Thomas Clarke and Terence MacSwiney (whose death in 1920 after seventy-four days on hunger-strike profoundly moved public opinion in Ireland and Britain), gave encouragement to them. But, generally speaking, the older generation of IRB men resented them.

However, with the revered figure of Clarke on their side, the 'young squirts' (as McCullough called his fellow spirits) routed their elders, and in 1910 founded a new paper, *Irish Freedom*, which had an uncompromisingly separatist policy. Articles contributed by Padraic Pearse, Thomas Mac-Donagh, Hobson and others outlined a policy which, based on Wolfe Tone's republicanism, was a blend of non-recognition of British institutions à la Sinn Fein, of asperity towards (but resigned support of) the Irish Parliamentary Party, of unequivocal support of the workers during strikes, and of strict non-sectarianism. Dublin being a tightly knit community,

* Clarke described his prison experiences in *Glimpses of an Irish Felon's Prison Life*, published as a book in 1922: one of the most remarkable pieces of prison literature ever written. In quiet, emotionless prose it details a fifteen-years' struggle against insanity. A Catholic by birth and upbringing, he seems to have become lukewarm to the faith after a chaplain had refused to intercede for a fellow prisoner who had gone mad and taken to eating broken glass.

some of them were well known socially, but not politically. Part of the success of the independence struggle after 1916 was caused by the detonation in the public consciousness of the realisation that an unknown group of men who had been sneaking in and out of backrooms had achieved what two generations of ardent nationalists had vainly sought for, proclaiming to the sound of gunfire the Republic of Ireland.

In 1916 Denis McCullough was chairman of the Supreme Council of the IRB. When collecting material for this book, I called on him at his large comfortable house in Rathgar, adorned with pictures of the leading figures of the stirring years. His hospitable wife, Agnes, is a member of a notable Irish family whose history mirrors the split which fissured Irish life during and after the Civil War. Her sister Min married General Mulcahy, the man responsible for the military prosecution of the Free State's war against the Anti-Treaty side. Another sister, Phyllis, married Sean T. O'Kelly, later to be president of Ireland and a supporter of de Valera, leader of the Anti-Treaty side; and one of her brothers, James, became a minister under de Valera. McCullough himself supported the Free State side, and their home was blown up during the Civil War. Mrs McCullough pointed to a mahogany cabinet. 'That's all I was able to save', she said.

McCullough talked in a strong voice, telling me how he had gone the previous month to see his old friend Bulmer Hobson 'before either of us dies'. After the Civil War destruction, four friends got him backing from a bank and he built up a large musical instrument business in Dublin. 'I never had any trouble making money.' He and his friends could serve as an object-lesson for anyone who doubts the power of nationalism. They all knew a great deal of history and were familiar with Griffith's writings, devouring each article as it appeared. In their teens and early twenties—many of them at their jobs from 7 a.m. to 11 p.m.—they made time to meet late at night or in the early morning to plan and dream and spark off a revolution.

He is still quaintly nationalistic. In pulling up a chair rather clumsily I mentioned that I'd injured a shoulder playing rugby. 'Serves you right! Rugby's one of the greatest denationalising influences in the country.' Then he relented. 'You're all right, boy. Have another biscuit.' He is realistic about his part in the Rising. 'I know my worth. I was there all the time, working and building up the IRB. But the actual Rising was the work mainly of four men—Pearse, MacDermott, Connolly and Clarke.'

Preparation for Revolt

Of the three men who shared with Clarke the main responsibility for the Rising, James Connolly was the most 'political' in the accepted sense. He succeeded James Larkin as leader of the Irish Transport and General Workers Union when Larkin left for America after his failure to beat the lock-out of 1913. Connolly had worked as a dustman and as a baker in Edinburgh, his birthplace, before he got a job in a factory. He gave this up to stand as a socialist candidate in Saint Giles division, but was defeated. Jobless and dispirited, he was on the point of going to Chile to take up farming when a socialist friend, John Leslie, urged him to go to Ireland. There in 1896 he founded the Irish Socialist Republican Party, but this made so little progress that in 1903 he emigrated to America, where he was a founder of the International Workers' League ('The Wobblies'). Symbolically—though unconnectedly—his return to Dublin coincided with the launching of *Irish Freedom*.

After the Dublin lock-out of 1913, Connolly controlled the only irregular force in Ireland south of the Boyne: the Citizen Army, created originally as a protection for the workers by Captain Jack White, the sailor son of a British field marshal. This Citizen Army was to be the spearhead of the Easter Week coup. Connolly was a sensitive and enthusiastic feminist. He won the friendship of Countess Constance Markievicz, who ran soup-kitchens for the workers during the battle with the employers and was to be one of the leading figures in the Rising. Born Constance Gore Booth of Lissadell, County Sligo, the countess was an important link between industrial and nationalist radicalism in Ireland. She was the founder of Fianna Eireann, an organisation of boys who ran messages for the revolutionaries. To this day it has served to attract lads into the IRA.

Patrick Henry Pearse, a schoolmaster and a Gaelic enthusiast, became—thanks to his writings and oratory—the heart of the revolution and its outward symbol in the minds of the people. He had interesting educational theories, but was such an impractical man of affairs that, after his execution, his school was found to be heavily in debt. A man of many contrasts, he preached violence and bloodshed but could hardly bring himself to handle a knife to cut a loaf. Off the platform he was shy and gentle, but we find him writing in 1915: 'The last sixteen months have been the most glorious in the history of Europe. . . . The old heart of the earth needed to be warmed with the red wine of the battlefields.' He was sharply reproved by James Connolly in *The Irish Worker*: 'No, we do not think that the old heart of the earth needs to be warmed with the red wine of millions of lives. We think anyone who does is a blithering idiot.' In the face of the reality of suffering, however, Pearse was the soul of compassion, spending whole nights sitting beside a sick pupil in his school, and later, during the siege of the General Post Office, watching over a wounded British soldier.

Sean MacDermott was Thomas Clarke's best friend. (He signed himself MacDiarmada, but his friends in conversation with me always called him

MacDermott.) He had worked as a barman before being sworn into the IRB by Denis McCullough. He travelled the country on a salary of £150 organising the revolutionary movement. A humorous smiling man, he limped to his execution uncomplainingly, still showing signs of the polio he had contracted in 1912. He is remembered in Dublin with affection.

As the most prominent of the revolutionaries, Clarke was, of course, heavily shadowed. Often as many as seven political detectives were on duty outside his little tobacconist shop in Parnell Street.* Even so, he managed to continue his plotting unhindered. His most serious setback occurred six months before the Rising when, practising revolver shooting in Ballybough outside Dublin, he was accidentally wounded in the elbow by a friend, Sean McGarry, who became secretary of the Volunteers after the Rising.† His friends were fearful of taking him to the nearest doctor or hospital since this might have put the police on his trail, and so he was forced to spend a night of agony walking his room with a splintered elbow. In the morning arrangements were made to have him treated in the Mater Hospital which was always sympathetic to nationalists. Thereafter he had to practise shooting with his Texas .45 in his left hand.

All this preparatory activity took place in the greatest secrecy. No one in any of the other Irish organisations or on the British side knew anything about the plans for a rebellion. The IRB were almost completely overlooked in the mounting pressure of political crisis.

By 1914 the North-Eastern counties of Ireland and the Conservative Party in Britain had coalesced into a militant intransigence which transformed the entire scene at Dublin, Belfast and Westminster. The reasons for the Protestant revulsion against Home Rule will be discussed later, in the chapter on the North. Here it is sufficient to say that, in reaction to the proposal to place them under a parliament in Dublin, the Northerners had taken three major steps of resistance.

1. The Ulster Covenant was drawn up, signatories to which undertook to employ 'all means which may be found necessary to defeat the present conspiracy to set up a Home Rule Parliament in Ireland'. It was signed by 471,414 people, including police and soldiery. These subsequently formed the Ulster Volunteer Force. 2. The Ulster Unionist Council set up a 'Provisional Government', and this was given support by some of the most prominent figures in British political and military life. 3. In April 1914 the

* His shop was much patronised by British soldiers, not because of any ecumenical welcome they got therein but because both they and the prostitutes with which the city abounded were confined to one side of the street. Both species of outsider were free to walk down Sackville Street on their correct side, but neither was allowed to penetrate as far as fashionable Grafton Street.

† During the Civil War, McGarry's home was fired and his seven-year-old son died of burns.

Unionist Volunteers landed 35,000 rifles at Larne in Antrim. This gun-running exploit came a month after officers of the British garrison at The Curragh, near Dublin, had declared their unwillingness to obey orders which would involve them in taking action against the Ulster Volunteers.

The incipient mutiny at The Curragh was dealt with, but the Liberal government in Britain refrained from taking firm action against the Ulstermen, for two basic reasons. One was its fear that decisive action against the Ulster Volunteers might spark off open battle not only between the Crown and its Ulster subjects but also between Englishmen supporting the government and Englishmen supporting Ulster. The second reason was that, even if actual fighting could be avoided, it doubted whether it had a strong enough base in English opinion to coerce a minority which claimed the right to remain part of the United Kingdom. Asquith's government found itself in an excruciating dilemma. Possibly a more vigorous action against the developments taking place in Ulster might have crushed the nettle of defiance. Winston Churchill, at that time First Lord of the Admiralty, indeed urged his colleagues to threaten a naval bombardment of Belfast if the Unionists did not give way. But the cabinet continued to handle the situation with kid gloves, believing that somehow 'common sense' would prevail. To many in Southern Ireland, however, it seemed that the government's indulgent attitude to the Ulster rebels made a mockery of its pledges to Redmond. With the opponents of Home Rule preparing to resist it by force, the initiative in the South—though no one realised this at the time—passed to the IRB.

Eoin MacNeill, professor of Early Irish History at University College, Dublin, suggested in an article in a Gaelic paper that an Irish Volunteer force be formed. The suggestion was eagerly taken up by the IRB, and he was persuaded to become president of the Irish Volunteers' executive committee and its chief of staff. The committee was a highly respectable body with no apparent connection with the IRB, but with Pearse, Mac-Dermott and Eamonn Ceannt on it, the committee was in fact well and truly infiltrated by militant nationalism. A meeting was held on November 25, 1913, at the Rotunda in Dublin in protest at the policy of 'one of the great English parties to make a display of military force and the menace of armed violence the determining factor in the future of relations between this country and Britain'.

The Irish Volunteers—a response to the Ulster Volunteers—were intended by MacNeill purely as a defensive body.* The organisation

* Mingled with the Volunteers' indignation, there was, in a very Irish way, a feeling of admiration for the Ulstermen's audacity. When Denis McCullough took up arms in 1916, his detachment was equipped with rifles he had bought from an Ulster Volunteers' arms store.

mushroomed to such an extent that Redmond became alarmed. Exerting all his influence he secured a controlling position in the Volunteers in June 1914—much to the disgust of the extremist minority. A split within the organisation became inevitable when, with the outbreak of war in August 1914, Redmond's Nationalist Party at Westminster joined with Liberals and Conservatives in agreeing to postpone the implementation of Home Rule for the duration of hostilities. Redmond was convinced that Ireland's full co-operation with Britain in the war would bind the existing and any future government to Irish autonomy.* The IRB were convinced that 'England's difficulty was Ireland's opportunity'. The extremist wing broke decisively with Redmond when he made a speech in favour of recruiting at Woodenbridge in September 1914. The section controlled by the IRB mustered (unknown to MacNeill) between ten and twelve thousand men. The Redmondite section numbered about 170,000.

The Volunteers were engaged in gun-runnings of their own at the end of July and the beginning of August, at Howth, County Dublin—where Erskine Childers sailed a consignment in his yacht *Asgard* right through a British squadron—and at Kilcoole, County Wicklow. A total of 1,500 rifles had been landed. Ulster gun-running met with no opposition from the forces of the Crown, but the Howth affair ended in shooting. An ill-trained regiment, the Scottish Borderers, fired on a jeering crowd at Bachelor's Walk, killing three and wounding thirty-two. The contrast between this and the official toleration of Ulster gun-running had an inflammatory effect on public opinion.

Her cabinet preoccupied with a mighty war against Germany, Britain reacted in a series of ineptitudes throughout 1915 which were of incalculable benefit to the IRB. Redmond was still the major power in Irish affairs. His nominees controlled the local government authorities and many of the Irish state appointments. As we have seen, the great majority of the Volunteers were under his influence. At the outbreak of war he told the House of Commons that they could safely withdraw all British troops from Ireland and leave the defence of the country to the Volunteers. Whatever its attitude to England, Irish sentiment had been profoundly shocked by the German invasion of Belgium. But Southern Irishmen, who enlisted in their thousands (27,000 of them were to be killed in the war), were grossly mishandled by the War Office, being treated with open suspicion and refused permission to form their own regiments. Redmond's son was refused a commission. Yet in the North, where a little earlier they had

---

* Weighing heavily against Redmond's position was the fact that on July 8 the Lords had passed an amending bill providing for the exclusion of the six North-Eastern counties from the operation of the Home Rule Act. Partition as a 'solution' had thus become a distinct possibility.

been threatening civil war, Ulstermen were allowed to form their own regiments under officers of their choice (a boon which seemed less cherishable after the bloody massacres on the Somme).

Sinn Fein threw all its weight against recruiting. At the same time James Connolly was making incitements to revolt and the IRB were making evident preparations for trouble. The British government met this situation with pinpricking closures of nationalist newspapers and arrests under the Defence of the Realm Act (DORA). All this elicited more and more sympathy for Sinn Fein, which now had become a generic term to describe advanced nationalist elements and the group in the Volunteers which did not support Redmond. The formation in May 1915 of a coalition cabinet which included such powerful Conservative enemies of Home Rule as Bonar Law, Walter Long and Edward Carson—'King Carson' of the Ulster Volunteers—was all grist to the IRB's mill.

THE RISING

In January 1916, the Supreme Council of the Irish Republican Brotherhood decided on a rising for April 23, and empowered a military council to plan it. The council contained, among others, MacDermott, Pearse, Clarke and Joseph Plunkett. Word was sent to John Devoy in New York to get a message to the Germans, as arranged two years earlier, to despatch a promised consignment of arms between April 20 and 22. Roger Casement was already in Germany trying, with little success, to raise a force from among captured Irish prisoners of war to fight against England in Ireland. MacNeill and those officers of the Volunteers who were known to be against the use of arms so long as the British did not attempt to disarm them, were told nothing of all this. Connolly was a problem of a different kind for the IRB. He had been continually threatening to take action with his Citizen Army, and it was feared he might ruin everything by a premature show of force. Accordingly, Connolly was kidnapped and brought to a three-day meeting with Pearse, the upshot of which was that the Labour boss was co-opted into the leadership of the insurrection. With Joseph Plunkett, a mystic and a poet, he worked out the plan for the Rising.

The capture by the British of arms sent from Germany—20,000 rifles, ten machine guns, explosives and 1,000,000 rounds of ammunition—was largely the fault of the Irish Volunteers, who changed their plans after the *Aud* had set sail from Lübeck with instructions to land the arms on the Kerry coast between April 20 and 22. The ship carried no wireless, and a message from Devoy to Pearse warning him of the *Aud*'s sailing never reached the insurgents. It was intercepted and decoded by the British Admiralty. The revolutionaries, at the last minute, decided they wanted the arms to land on the night of April 23 (Easter Sunday) and not as originally agreed. They reckoned that April 24, being a Bank Holiday, would find the officers and many of the men of the Dublin garrison at the races, safely out of the way when the balloon went up. And so, when the *Aud* arrived off the Kerry coast as instructed, the German skipper found no one to meet him. He was eventually captured by a British warship. Escorted to Queenstown (now Cobh) he scuttled his ship just outside the harbour.

Roger Casement, landed from a German submarine near Banna Strand, also in Kerry, was soon captured. Not realising that the date for the Rising had been definitely fixed, he had come from Germany to use his influence to call the whole thing off because the Germans had refused to send officers as promised. It is an indication of the attitude of the people at the time that the farmer who found the abandoned boat straightway informed the police. Austin Stack, in charge of the Volunteers in Kerry and the man who was supposed to oversee the landing and distribution of arms, went to Tralee barracks, where Casement had been sent, to find out what was happening. The police gratified his curiosity by putting him behind bars.

Meanwhile in Dublin, learning at last of the plans for the Rising and the German arms, MacNeill on April 21 called it off. But Pearse and Mac-Dermott succeeded in getting him to rescind the order on the ground that the arms were already on their way. When the next day he learned of Casement's arrest, he decided there was no hope. Clarke and the others argued they must strike now since the events in Kerry made their arrest a near-certainty. MacNeill contended that in the circumstances it would be suicidal for the young, unprepared Volunteer Corps to go into action. He sent messages throughout the country definitely countermanding insurrection. In addition, he put a notice in the *Sunday Independent*, then the largest Sunday newspaper in Ireland, which firmly said that 'no parades, marches or other movements of Irish Volunteers were to take place'. But MacNeill's efforts came too late. On Easter Sunday, April 23, the military council of the IRB met in Liberty Hall and voted in favour of rebellion. Some disagreed with Pearse, Connolly, Clarke and MacDermott, but no one voted against the Rising. It was a democratic vote in favour of death. Pearse issued the mobilisation order.

The next morning, Easter Monday, April 24, the handful of Volunteers who had answered the call, together with the tiny Citizen Army (numbering only a hundred or so), marched out from Liberty Hall, the trade union headquarters, to occupy their positions in the city. Connolly said as he went down the steps: 'We're going to be slaughtered'. The plans made for the insurrection in Dublin alone called for something over double the forces available. The Rising was less a military venture than a blood-sacrifice to the gods of Irish nationalism, unappeased by the ameliorative legislation of recent years and the halting steps towards Home Rule.

Several strong points in the city were seized, the most important being the General Post Office. Here the revolutionary headquarters were set up, the green, white and orange flag hoisted, and from its steps was issued the Proclamation of the Irish Republic. Thus began Modern Ireland.

Poblacht na h-Eireann
The Provisional Government
of the
IRISH REPUBLIC
To the people of Ireland

Irishmen and Irishwomen: In the name of God and of the dead generations from which she receives her old traditions of nationhood, Ireland, through us, summons her children to her flag and strikes for her freedom.

Having organised and trained her manhood through her secret revolutionary organisation, the Irish Republican Brotherhood, the Irish Volunteers and the Irish Citizen Army, having patiently perfected her discipline, having resolutely waited for the right moment to reveal herself, she now seizes that moment and, supported by her exiled children in America and by gallant allies in Europe, she strikes in full confidence of victory.

We declare the right of the people of Ireland to the ownership of Ireland and to the unfettered control of Irish destinies, to be sovereign and indefeasible. The long usurpation of that right by a foreign people and government has not extinguished the right, nor can it ever be extinguished except by the destruction of the Irish people. In every generation the Irish people have asserted their right to national freedom and sovereignty; six times during the past three hundred years they have asserted it in arms. Standing on that fundamental right and again asserting it in arms in the face of the world, we hereby proclaim the Irish Republic as a Sovereign Independent State, and we pledge our lives and the lives of our comrades-in-arms to the cause of its freedom, of its welfare and of its exaltation among the nations.

The Irish Republic is entitled to, and hereby claims, the allegiance of every Irishman and Irishwoman. The Republic guarantees religious and civil liberty, equal rights and equal opportunities to all its citizens, and declares its resolve to pursue the happiness and prosperity of the whole nation and of all its parts, cherishing all the children of the nation equally, and oblivious of the differences, carefully fostered by an alien government, which have divided a minority from the majority in the past.

Until our arms have brought the opportune moment for the establishment of a permanent National Government, representative of the people of Ireland, and elected by the suffrages of all her men and women, the Provisional Government, hereby constituted, will administer the civil and military affairs of the Republic in trust for the people. We place the cause of the Irish

Republic under the protection of the Most High God, Whose blessing we invoke upon our arms, and we pray that no one who serves that cause will dishonour it by cowardice, inhumanity or rapine. In this supreme hour the Irish nation must, by its valour and discipline, and by the readiness of its children to sacrifice themselves, prove itself worthy of the august destiny to which it is called.

Signed on behalf of the Provisional Government

THOMAS J. CLARKE

SEAN MAC DIARMADA	THOMAS MACDONAGH
P. H. PEARSE	EAMONN CEANNT
JAMES CONNOLLY	JOSEPH PLUNKETT

Cut off from the rest of the country, with no support, no artillery, their rifles dating from the Franco–Prussian war, and with only the crudest of home-made bombs, the insurgents fought with great gallantry. They held out for nearly a week against troops supported by artillery, and by the end of the fighting were outnumbered by twenty to one.*

As noted earlier, the revolutionaries were highly unpopular throughout Dublin. After saying that, of course, the British must not make martyrs of the rebels, an editorial in the *Irish Independent* on May 10 observed that some leaders (meaning MacDermott and, especially, Connolly) were still awaiting sentence. 'When, however, we come to some of the ringleaders, instigators and fomenters not yet dealt with, we must make an exception. If these men are treated with too great leniency, they will take it as an indication of weakness on the part of the Government. . . . Let the worst of the rebels be singled out and dealt with as they deserve.' The tone of this leader was a legacy of the bitterness of the 1913 lock-out. Both the *Independent* and the *Irish Catholic* (quoted at the beginning of this chapter) were owned by William Murphy, the leading figure on the employers' side in the struggle to break Larkin's and Connolly's Transport and General Workers Union. Larkin was out of reach in America, but Connolly was in prison. . . .

In comparison with the political repression and brutality of the last fifty years, the British retaliation against the insurgents was restrained. Firing squads shot fourteen in Dublin and one in Cork; one man in London was hanged, Roger Casement, executed in August, when all danger from the Rising was over. Those executed in Dublin included all the signatories of the Proclamation and also Pearse's brother, Willy. Though he fought

---

* Of the many courageous acts, we may take that of The O'Rahilly (an hereditary Irish title) as typifying the spirit which animated this hopeless rebellion. The O'Rahilly sped through the South distributing MacNeill's countermand. Having covered six counties in twenty-four hours, he returned to Dublin to join the revolutionaries in the besieged Post Office. 'I've helped to wind up the clock,' he said. 'I might as well hear it strike.' He was killed in the escape from the burning building at the end of the week.

in the Rising, Willy Pearse played such an insignificant part in planning it that it must be assumed he was shot simply because he was the elder Pearse's brother. Joseph Plunkett had left a nursing home, where he was recovering from an operation, to join the Rising. He was married in his cell on the night of his execution: another faggot on the pyre of emotion. Sean MacDermott had escaped earlier screening, but was recognised by a G-man (so called because belonging to the G division, the political security section at Dublin Castle) as he was walking to the boat among those to be deported. The man beside him was not touched: an oversight which later cost the G-man his life, for MacDermott's neighbour was Michael Collins. Another incident witnessed by Collins also was to lead to the death of a G-man. Clarke was taken out in front of the rest of the prisoners and maltreated. The man responsible for this, Detective Lee, subsequently became an inspector in the Royal Irish Constabulary. Collins had him shot four years later in Wexford. But vengeance lay in the future. Clarke was executed five days after the surrender. The next day his brother-in-law, Ned Daly, a commandant in the Volunteers, was also shot. The gruesome details of Connolly's execution (a man suffering from gangrened wounds, propped up to be done to death) probably did more than anything else to identify the Dublin poor with the insurgents in the aftermath of the Rising —most of whose leaders were 'bourgeois nationalists'. Connolly was potentially the most constructive force in Irish nationalism. Whereas Pearse drew his inspiration from the 'dead generations', the Labour leader was moved to battle on behalf of the living slum-dwellers. His view of Irish history as revealed in his writings was coloured by the classical Marxist interpretation of the class war. He was, however, a Catholic; and a viewpoint which gave such emphasis to social grievances might have given a healthy dose of reformist pragmatism to the child of the Rising, Independent Ireland.

Bishop O'Dwyer of Limerick became the post-Rising hero of the nationalists when he refused General Maxwell's demand for the dismissal of two priests who had shown sympathy with the insurgents. On May 17 he wrote to the press an open letter to the general. 'You took care that no plea for mercy should impose on behalf of the poor young fellows who surrendered to you in Dublin. The first intimation which we got of their fate was the announcement that they had been shot in cold blood. Personally I regard your action with horror, and I believe it has outraged the conscience of the country.' The bishop proved an accurate prophet. He had hitherto been noted for his antipathy towards the separatists, but soon, as the 'conscience of the country' changed, his photograph began to appear in shop windows framed in tricolour ribbon. The conversion of public sentiment was under way.

For several months after the rebellion, Clarke's widow held together the broken threads of nationalism by administering a fund to aid the prisoners' dependants. When I met her in connection with this book, Kathleen Clarke was living alone in a comfortable two-storey house in Ballsbridge. A lady of eighty-six, she still drove a car and tended the garden. Her voice was steady and clear, and when occasional lapses of memory occurred, she paused calmly until the spell passed and then resumed where she left off. She had had a somewhat controversial career in politics, arousing strong criticism—ironically—when she refused to associate herself with a parliamentary vote of sympathy at the death of George V. She became a senator and twice lord mayor of Dublin. Her eyes were like large faded sapphires and it was hard to look straight at them without flinching. There is no record of her ever having flinched from anything. The night before her husband's execution she was in the Castle in detention with some other women.

I thought that in the morning we were likely to be brought before the commanding officer, so I had taken off my blouse and skirt and hung them up so that I wouldn't look too bad. There were six of us and we had only one blanket over us. We had been very annoyed at some young British soldiers coming to flirt with us. It was outrageous. Then an officer came and said I had permission to see my husband. 'My God, Kathleen,' said one of the girls, 'what does that mean?' 'It means death', I said. 'Oh no', said the girl; Marie Perolz was her name. 'Look', said I, 'do you think that if the British government were going to send my husband on a journey any shorter than to the next world that they'd get an officer and a car out at midnight to go for me?' 'You're a stone', said the girl. I was.

We were stopped several times. There were snipers on a lot of rooftops and I didn't think we'd be let go on. But the officer showed his pass and we got through. Kilmainham was terrible. The conditions! There was a monk downstairs. He told me that my husband had put him out of the cell. There was no light in it, only a candle that a soldier held. 'Why did you surrender?' I asked Tom. 'I thought you were going to hold out for six months.' 'I wanted to', he said, 'but the vote went against me'. We talked about the future the whole time. I never saw him so buoyed up. He said that the first blow had been struck and Ireland would get her freedom but that she'd have to go through hell first.

I didn't cry. He had to face the ordeal by himself in the morning. If I broke down, it might have broken him down. I said, 'What did you do to that priest down there?' 'That damn fellow came in here', he said, 'and told me he'd give me confession if I'd admit that I was wrong and that I was sorry. I'm not sorry. I told him that I gloried in what I'd done.' I was expecting a baby but didn't tell him that in case it might upset him.

I asked an officer to have his body sent to me. He hemmed and hawed and

THOMAS J. CLARKE

PATRICK H. PEARSE

ARTHUR GRIFFITH

JAMES CONNOLLY

PLATE 1

KEVIN O'HIGGINS' WEDDING, 1921
Eamon de Valera, Kevin O'Higgins, Rory O'Connor (best man), Irene
O'Higgins, Mrs Kevin O'Higgins (*née* Bridget Cole), Molly Cole

EAMON DE VALERA, *at the time of his first administration, 1932*

PLATE 2

said he'd had no instructions about it. In the end he promised to do something. But they wrote to me afterwards that I couldn't have the body for burial. I walked home by myself from the Castle to Fairview. There was a smell of burning in the air. I had to walk in the middle of the road because things were falling off the roofs. In O'Connell Street a big policeman stopped me. When I told him who I was and where I was going, he said, 'You'd better go down Fairview, ma'am. There's some soldiers up at Parnell's monument and they're not very nice.' I had to climb over a big pile of rubble in North Earl Street. The bricks were still hot. I never met a sinner all the way home.

I had sent the children down to Limerick and there was no one in the house. I don't drink but I had whiskey and brandy in the house in case any wounded were brought in. Now, I thought, I'll have one twenty-four hours of oblivion; and I took out a bottle of port and filled myself out a glass. I thought it would be strong. But I was awake again in an hour.

My sister came up from the country, and that night a lorry came and took us to Kilmainham to say goodbye to my brother. I heard it coming before any of them and I said, 'It's coming to take us to Ned. He's going to be shot.' They thought I was going off my head. But a few minutes later we all heard it. Then it stopped outside the house. My sister didn't want me to go but I insisted. My brother was in uniform. He looked about eighteen. There was a group of officers outside the cell. They seemed to have some spite against him. The soldier holding the candle had been in my husband's firing party. He said that my husband was the bravest man he'd seen. I lost the baby about a week later. I don't know if it was a boy or a girl. I worked at the prisoners' fund even when I was in bed. It saved me from going mad. God must have put the idea into my head.

In the years that followed, Mrs Clarke's home was raided several times a week, sometimes as often as three times in one night, by armed men— soldiers, Black and Tans, Auxiliaries—often inflamed by drink or the death of a comrade. She and her three children, one of them semi-invalid, lived alone during this time. Hers was the kind of experiences that tempered the next phase of the struggle. One night after we had been talking, I asked her before I said goodnight if she were satisfied with the way things had gone since in Ireland. 'No', she said, 'I am not. There isn't enough love. Not enough charity.'

When the prisoners began to be released the work of fund-raising was reorganised. It was decided to hand over the job to a paid secretary: Michael Collins.

2. *AFTERMATH*

War of Independence: *Truce and Treaty*
Civil War: *The Reckoning*

THE period following the Rising until April 30, 1923—when hostilities in the Civil War were officially declared to have ended—was one of the most important, most exciting and certainly most cruelly heart-breaking in Irish history.

Ireland lay under martial law until the recall of the British commander, General Maxwell, in November 1916. But by that time parliamentarianism had lost its appeal. Attention focused on the prisoners in English gaols. De Valera, the last commandant in the Rising to surrender, was sent to Dartmoor where he was chosen as leader of the Irish prisoners there.

Everyone in Ireland was avid for news of the prisoners. Martial law made British rule even more irksome. Recruiting for the Great War fell off. Demands for the release of the prisoners were voiced from the press and in town and county council meetings. Most of them were released by the end of 1916, although de Valera and the hard core were kept in gaol until June 1917. Sinn Fein became a political hold-all in which went every kind of Republican and nationally minded person. The movement soon had a

success to spur it on. In February 1917, Count Plunkett, father of the Rising leader, was elected as Sinn Fein candidate for Roscommon, defeating the representative of Redmond's Irish Party by a two to one majority. There was no question of his taking his seat: Sinn Fein was pledged to recognise an Irish parliament and no other.

A National Council of all the Irish nationalist organisations—Sinn Fein, Cumann na mBan, the Gaelic League and so on—was formed on April 19. It declared Ireland a separate nation and resolved that after the war it would seek for Irish representation at the peace conference. The National Council chose one of the prisoners in Lewes Gaol, Joseph McGuinness, as its candidate for a by-election which fell due in Longford. Using posters showing a man in convict clothes, young nationalists appealed to the electorate to 'put him in to get him out'. He was put in on May 9 by a margin of thirty-seven votes. (At first it was announced that he had lost, but after some slight signs of a mass inclination to homicide on the part of the crowd gathered outside the counting hall, another bundle of McGuinness votes was discovered.) Before the Longford poll, members of the hierarchy and other leaders of opinion had issued a manifesto rejecting Partition. The Irish Parliamentary Party put the issue to its supporters as being a choice between a self-governing Ireland and—as Joseph Devlin, speaking at Longford on May 6, said—'a hopeless fight for an Irish Republic'.

All-embracing as the movement was, Sinn Fein now stood against Partition and for a Republic. The rest of the prisoners arrived back on June 18, 1917 amid scenes of wild enthusiasm. De Valera was elected for Clare in July and Cosgrave for Kilkenny in August. The struggle was now on! The authorities replied with arrests under the Defence of the Realm Act. Offences like flying the nationalist tricolour, or 'making speeches calculated to cause disaffection', filled up the prisons afresh. One of those arrested, Thomas Ashe, died under forcible feeding while on hunger strike. He and Richard Mulcahy had commanded the only successful action of 1916, at Ashbourne, County Meath, where the Volunteers over-powered a large party of the Royal Irish Constabulary. His death caused a public outcry which further benefited Sinn Fein.

Noting all this, Lloyd George (who had become prime minister of Britain's wartime coalition after the ousting of Asquith on December 6, 1916) set up an Irish Convention to draw up proposals for Irish self-government within the British Empire. It met on July 25, 1917. Sinn Fein and Labour boycotted it on the grounds that its membership was repre-sentative neither of Sinn Fein nor of post-Rising sentiment and aspiration. The Northern and Southern Unionists sent delegates, but from different motives. The Southern Unionists wanted to retain the *status quo* in Irish–British political relations, or at least dilute Home Rule to the greatest possible extent. They were opposed to Partition since they were fearful of being overwhelmed in a predominantly Catholic South. The Northern contingent's only concern was whether six or nine counties were to be excluded from the new Irish state.

Ignoring this Convention, a Sinn Fein 'Ard-Fheis', or convention, was held at the Mansion House in Dublin on October 25, 1917. De Valera was elected president of Sinn Fein. It is here possibly that we should look for the origins of the Civil War. In the Sinn Fein Convention, widely divergent views were represented. There were ultra-rightwing nationalists who sought control of taxation and business under a native parliament; there were those who simply wanted the British out with not much concern about the form of government to succeed them; and cheek by jowl with these were several varieties of socialists, including Marxists. Such a situation contained within itself the seeds of disunity. But for the moment there was amity. It was resolved that the Volunteers would declare war if any attempt were made to enforce conscription.

The report of the official Irish Convention on April 5, 1918, proposed a limited version of Home Rule. But any favourable effect this might have had on Irish opinion was nullified by the passing on April 16 of a Conscription Act in the British parliament. The Irish Party in protest withdrew from the House of Commons: a step which represented a tremendous rent in the fabric of political relations between Britain and Ireland. Two days later Sinn Fein, the Irish Parliamentary Party and Labour drew up an anti-conscription pledge, signed with unprecedented solidarity at church doors the following Sunday. The Catholic hierarchy also denounced conscription.

From the military point of view, conscription undoubtedly made good sense to the British government, the situation on the Western Front being what it was. But in post-Rising Ireland it was the equivalent of throwing a can of petrol over the banked fires of Irish nationalism. Lloyd George's Convention seemed to be intended only as a sort of smokescreen while conscription was pushed through.

On May 18, 1918, on the grounds of frustrating what proved to be a mythical German plot, many of the principal leaders of Sinn Fein, including Griffith and de Valera, were arrested. But Michael Collins escaped the net. He had built up a tremendous influence through his reorganisation of the IRB, undertaken both in prison after the Rising and as he went through the country in connection with the Easter Week prisoners' fund. From the time of the Sinn Fein Convention of April 1918, Collins controlled key posts in every phase of the national movement, and he was also Sinn Fein's director of intelligence. The 'German plot' arrests meant that, when the First Dail met in January 1919, thirty-six out of the seventy-three Sinn Fein members of it were in gaol.

The general election of December 1918—the Khaki Election which saw in Britain the return to power of Lloyd George supported by Conservatives and 'Coalition' Liberals—was in Ireland an epoch-making triumph for Sinn Fein, which won seventy-three out of 105 seats. The Unionists, principally in the North-East, won twenty-six.* The old Irish Nationalist Party of Redmond was well-nigh extinguished, gaining only six seats. Labour, so as not to split the national front, did not contest the election. It has since attributed its failure to win a greater representation in Irish political life to this gesture of self-abnegation. But, in fact, from the moment Connolly's powerful personality was committed to the Rising, there was no chance of any force other than nationalism ever gaining dominance. His successors in the Labour leadership did not attain to his stature.

Presided over by Cathal Brugha, the First Dail met on January 21, 1919.

---

* Three Unionists were returned outside the North-East: one for Rathmines, a Dublin suburb, and two for Dublin University. One of the latter was an Independent Unionist.

Its members were the Sinn Fein deputies elected to Westminster, convened in a revolutionary parliament of their own—which the British, of course, refused to recognise. It declared unequivocally for a Republic, elected de Valera as president, appointed delegates to the peace conference at Versailles, and adopted a democratic programme based on the Proclamation of Easter Week. It was intended by William O'Brien and Thomas Johnson, the Labour leaders, to be a good deal more 'democratic' than it proved to be in its final form. Their draft contained two paragraphs which aroused the strong opposition of Michael Collins.

> The Republic will aim at the elimination of the class in society which lives upon the wealth produced by the workers of the nation but gives no useful service in return, and in the process of accomplishment will bring freedom to all who have hitherto been caught in the toils of economic servitude.
>
> It shall be the purpose of the Government to encourage the organisation of the people into trade unions and co-operative societies with a view to the control and administration of the industries by the workers engaged in the industries.

All good syndicalist socialism! But Collins and the IRB would have none of it, and pressed that the programme should not be put to the Dail at all. Sinn Fein's executive protested against this. The national front was showing signs of cracking. As a compromise, Sean T. O'Kelly redrafted it, leaving out the two most socialistic paragraphs. This done, the programme was passed. But the effect was to reduce the standing of Connolly and exalt that of Pearse in the Valhalla of Irish nationalism.

As the Dail was sitting, but in entire unconnection with it, a number of Volunteers carried out an ambush at Soloheadbeg in County Tipperary in which two policemen were shot. This ambush was not sanctioned by the Sinn Fein executive, which did not order the first 'authorised' execution—that of Detective Inspector Hunt—until June 23, 1919. But guerilla warfare developed from then onwards. While the Dail was meeting, Collins and Harry Boland were in England arranging for de Valera's escape from Lincoln prison where he had been held since the 'German plot' arrests. After the escape, de Valera returned to Ireland until June, when Collins smuggled him aboard a liner to America where he engaged in propaganda work and fund-raising.

As we have said, de Valera in his absence was elected president by the Dail. Ministers appointed by it were: Arthur Griffith, Home Affairs; Count Plunkett, Foreign Affairs; Cathal Brugha, Defence; Countess Markievicz, Labour; Eoin MacNeill, Industry; William Cosgrave, Local Government; Michael Collins, Finance; Richard Mulcahy, chief of staff of the Republic's armed forces. Collins was directed to organise a 'national loan' of £250,000. He succeeded in raising the money while conducting a guerilla warfare campaign with a price on his head.

On June 11, 1919 President Wilson informed Irish representatives in Paris that Ireland could not be admitted to the peace conference.* The Dail was proscribed by the British on September 10, and 1919 ended with the introduction of Lloyd George's Partition Plan (the Government of Ireland Act) providing for a separate parliament for the six North-Eastern counties.

WAR OF INDEPENDENCE

In the three-year period 1917–19, there had been 12,589 raids on private homes by Crown forces. By the end of the struggle, the yearly average increased to over 4,000 a month. Men had died on hunger-strikes and there had been several cases of British troops shooting Volunteers. The revolutionary Dail in this period tried to establish its authority wherever it could. On April 16, 1918, the IRA raided a police barracks in Kerry; in mid-June two policemen were shot in a chance encounter in Tralee. The next year, 1919, saw the Soloheadbeg ambush, the shooting of Inspector Hunt and, on July 31, the killing of Detective Patrick Smith in Dublin. The real guerilla war began in August 1919, followed by the suppression of the Dail. Up to this point the tempo of the struggle had been slow and almost casual: all told there had been less than half a dozen deaths. But from the middle of 1920 battle was joined in earnest, with attacks on police barracks, capturing of equipment, prison-breaks and ambushing of soldiers.

The failure of the Versailles mission was a bitter disappointment to Sinn Fein. Ever since Count Plunkett's election success in April 1917, to win the cause by securing international endorsement of Ireland's independence had been an article of faith with the nationalist movement. Hope, dashed at Versailles, now centred on the military front. Apart from de Valera's publicity work in America—where he was like a one-man million-dollar agency in nullifying the effects of British propaganda—the nationalists had, outside Ireland, no other card than the Versailles conference to play which could trump the ace of British influence.

But inside Ireland! Sinn Fein now proceeded to make Ireland ungovernable for Britain. In the municipal and urban district elections of January 1920, its candidates won a majority in every large town except Belfast. The

---

* The peace credentials taken to Paris by Sean T. O'Kelly seem to have had a curiously unpeaceful existence. After the failure at Versailles, they vanished from sight until, on June 10, 1931, in a raid on an IRA arms dump near a place in the Dublin mountains appropriately called the Hell Fire Club, they were discovered nestling among diverse assorted bombs and machine guns.

results in the North-East were particularly significant, for in the nine counties of the historic province of Ulster, twenty-three towns voted for Sinn Fein as against twenty-two for the Unionists. Of the six counties in which the Unionists claimed to have a majority and which by the operation of the Partition Act finally became separated from the rest of Ireland, two counties—Tyrone and Fermanagh—voted for Sinn Fein, leaving the Unionists with a majority in only four: Armagh, Antrim, Derry and Down. These urban elections put a larger sector of local government in Sinn Fein hands. The rural elections of June 1920 completed the movement's mastery of the democratic levers of power.

Sinn Fein also achieved juridical control of the country. In May 1920 it set up arbitration courts to deal with land agitation in the West where landowners were appealing for the Dail to enforce the law and order the British could no longer guarantee. Lawlessness spread through the country until, by July, Sinn Fein were dealing not only with agrarian crimes but also with such offences as burglary and drunkenness. The Crown's courts lost their litigants, the verdicts of the Sinn Fein courts being accepted even in cases where 'prison' was ordered. The convicted offenders were taken to some out of the way place, many of them refusing to be rescued by the police. Parallel with the Sinn Fein initiative, Labour organised transport strikes to hinder the movements of British troops.

The general unit of operations of the Volunteers—or Irish Republican Army (IRA) as it began to be called—was the 'flying column': a group of men who lived on the move, wearing no uniform, armed with rifles and revolvers. These columns operated mainly in the home areas of their members, supported by the local people. They were the invention of Dick McKee, officer in command of the Dublin brigade.* Under generals like Liam Lynch and Tom Barry, the columns sometimes banded together to fight large-scale engagements involving up to 100 men, but ordinarily their plan of operation was to ambush military lorries or attack installations, seizing equipment and escaping before troops arrived. The most deadly unit of all was 'The Squad' under Collins' personal direction. It consisted of twelve men operating on a full-time basis and paid £4 10s a week. These twelve apostles of death were responsible for most of the dramatic killings in Dublin which finally crippled the British Intelligence system, blinding its Cyclops-eye by the removal of particularly dangerous G-men, secret service agents, spies and common informers. And uncommon ones, like Alan Bell, an elderly magistrate appointed to question bank managers with the power to inspect their accounts. His activities jeopardised the

---

* McKee worked as a printer at Gills, the Catholic publishing house. He had a firing range in the firm's basement with a full-length portrait of George V as the target. He was shot in Dublin Castle for complicity in the events of Bloody Sunday. (See below, page 30).

Dail loan for he began to discover how the money was being manipulated through the accounts of various businessmen. Two members of The Squad took Bell off a tram at Elm Park Golf Club and shot him in broad daylight. In this and some other cases, Collins was given the tip-off by contacts in the police.

These police contacts were invaluable to Collins. One of them, Eamonn Broy, a clerk in the G-division, smuggled Collins into police headquarters one evening. He spent the night in the offices of the detective division going over records. It was an experience which gave him a piercing insight into the strength and operational methods of the Royal Irish Constabulary. (The Dublin Metropolitan Police Force, it should be mentioned, was a normal police body and quite distinct from the RIC. Unlike the latter's, its members were given the option of joining the new Garda Siochana—Civic Guard—when the Free State was set up.) Broy was arrested six months before the Truce. An IRA meeting in Clontarf decided that it would be too dangerous to attempt a rescue.

But another detective, David Neligan (the only one to remain at liberty throughout the war), revealed to Collins that the officer in charge of preparing the case against Broy attended daily mass at Mount Argus in Harold's Cross. Collins bicycled over to Mount Argus that night and told the priest in charge that when the officer showed up he was to be told that, if he did not destroy the evidence, he would be shot. Meeting the priest in the morning on arriving with his family for the eight o'clock mass, the officer was delighted when the priest singled him out among the worshippers for particular attention—until he got the message. Every document connected with Broy was destroyed. Neligan was a double agent. Like many other young Irishmen, he had joined the RIC because there were no other openings available. When the Sinn Fein movement became active after the Rising, he offered his services to one of its main organisers, who turned him down. He resigned from the RIC and went home. Collins, hearing about this, tore pieces from the organiser, arranged to meet Neligan, and persuaded him to rejoin the RIC—who welcomed him back gladly! Working for Collins, Neligan was also a G-man and a member of the British Secret Service: a position which had drawbacks, apart from the strain. One day he casually mentioned to Collins that he was meeting a police sergeant called Roche for a drink that afternoon. To his horror, members of The Squad turned up and shot Roche dead before his eyes. Neligan was unaware that Roche was on the IRA's wanted list. It may not actually have been his remark which led to the man's death, but to this day Neligan prays for him every night.

In addition to his police contacts, Collins built up a network in the Post Office, the civil service and inside shipping companies, so that the IRA were able undetected to open or transmit any letter or parcel they wished.

Exact figures of IRA combatants are not known. It would seem there were scarcely more than 15,000 Volunteers in the spring of 1920, and not more than 3,000 of these were in action, because of lack of arms. On the British side the war was carried on by approximately 50,000 men armed with tanks, artillery, armoured cars and machine-guns. In addition they recruited two supplementary forces known as the 'Black and Tans' and the 'Auxiliaries'. The Black and Tans—so called because they were dressed in khaki tunics and black trousers—landed in March 1920 on instructions to 'make Ireland hell for the rebels'. They were paid ten shillings a day. The British government was at its wits' end to know how to cope with the attacks of revolutionary irregulars, and hit on the idea of countering with its own irregulars. The Auxiliaries were ex-officers and were paid £1 a day. These special forces could not be tried before the civil courts for their misdemeanours, which were many. The period from the Auxiliaries' landing until the Truce came into force on July 11, 1921, is known in Ireland as 'the Tan War'.

Before the guerilla campaign began, rural Ireland was a gentle country-side where the chief pastimes were playing cards and visiting neighbours' houses at night, to 'cuaird', have a cup of tea and a chat. There were few telephones or motor cars and almost no electricity. Crossroads dancing was general. The turbulent days of the Land War were only a memory. The coming of the Black and Tans—generally out-of-work servicemen—to what to them was a hateful, hostile countryside, where death spoke from behind the hawthorn bushes, transformed this pastoral scene. The struggle took on a religious hue when the British began their policy of burning creameries and the homes of the people living in the vicinity of IRA ambushes for, to counter-act this, the IRA burned the mansions of wealthy Unionist sympathisers. These were generally Protestant. Though the retaliation was directed against property, not religion, some Protestants were shot because, as sympathisers with the old regime, they had supplied the authorities with information about IRA activities in their area.

In reprisals against the IRA, the Black and Tans imputed collective guilt against the communities in which attacks occurred. Twenty-five houses and a small factory in Balbriggan were burnt in reprisal for the killing there of a Black and Tan. On the night of September 20, 1920, Black and Tans revenged themselves on Cork for an ambush in the area by setting property alight, the flames from which burned out a large part of the central area, including the City Hall. In Mallow, a wrecking raid of reprisal caused damage to the extent of £200,000. Over 100 rural creameries were destroyed.

Both sides shot prisoners as reprisals. Inquests were abolished. Incidents like the hanging, after brutal treatment, of Kevin Barry—an eighteen year old medical student—and the death of Terence MacSwiney after seventy-four days on hunger-strike, focused world attention on the struggle. And, as the struggle continued, accounts of unbelievably atrocious conduct horrified a Europe which thought it had supped its fill of barbarity during the Great War. Black and Tans seized six Volunteers near Cork city and killed them all. When the bodies were found the heart had been cut out of one, the tongue from another, the nose from a third. The skull of a fourth had been battered in, and the bodies of the two others were identifiable only by their clothes. In the West, the bodies of two brothers were found tied together in a bog, their legs partially roasted away. In Meath, Black and Tans trailed a live Volunteer behind a fast-driven lorry until he was literally smashed to pieces. Some Volunteers were just as degenerate. In Tralee, two Black and Tans were thrown into a flaming gas-retort alive. In Miltown-Malbay, Clare, the execution of a resident magistrate was bungled. Still alive, he was buried up to his neck on a beach. Finding that they had buried him above the high-water mark, Volunteers returned the next day, dug him up and reburied him farther down the beach where he could watch the tide advance before it drowned him. By the time the Tan War had ended, and Ireland underwent the agony of Civil War, some Irishmen had learned their lesson of savagery only too well.

The bloodiest incidents of all took place on November 21, 1920—'Bloody Sunday'. In the morning of that day, the IRA's Dublin brigade, aided by The Squad, forced their way into the homes of a number of British undercover agents who had been responsible for the deaths of several of Collins' men, thereby coming near to destroying his intelligence system. Fourteen men were shot dead, some in the presence of their wives and children. That afternoon a detachment of Black and Tans went to a football match at Croke Park to look for IRA gunmen. Accounts differ as to whether the IRA or the Black and Tans fired first; however, there is little doubt but that the latter fired indiscriminately into the crowd. Their commander, General Crozier, states that one of his officers reported to him that they opened fire on the crowd without reason. Twelve men and women were shot dead and sixty wounded by bullets. One of the dead was a player on the field. Dick McKee, commander of the Dublin brigade, was captured that night with Volunteers Clune and Clancy in a raid on Vaughan's Hotel, one of Collins' meeting places. They were taken to Dublin Castle and were dead a few hours later.

Between the sitting of the First Dail and the Truce, Irish casualties are estimated to have been 752 killed and 866 wounded; British casualties were about 600 killed and 1,200 wounded. These figures pale into insignificance in comparison with the death-crop of an hour on the Western

Front; but spread over two years after the end of the 'war to end all wars' and in a country under martial law where burnings, raids and reprisals were almost daily occurrences, the cumulative effect of these killings was horrible. In retrospect, one can see that the British campaign of counter-terror was doomed both as a military action and as a weakener of morale. It was indeed a campaign of half-measures, for the British were fearful of the effect which a full-scale military operation—as urged by Sir Henry Wilson, chief of the Imperial General Staff—would have on world opinion.

From October 1920, peace moves flickered on and off. Elections were held under the Better Government of Ireland Act which came into force on May 3. The incongruity of having an election while the country was going up in flames stemmed from Lloyd George's double policy. While assenting to tactics of terrorism by British forces, he was seeking to allay Orange fears by the offer of Partition and at the same time make provision for Nationalist demands. Unionists continued obdurate, but pressure in Britain for a settlement grew stronger. Pro-Irish sentiment was encouraged by the work of the Peace with Ireland Council formed by Lord Henry Cavendish-Bentinck. (Its secretary was Sir Oswald Mosley!.) The dark side of Lloyd George's policy was exposed in scathing polemics by Chesterton, Belloc and Shaw.

Under the 1920 Act, by which Northern Ireland is still governed, the South was to send thirty-three members to Westminster and have 128 members in a Dublin parliament. The North was to send representatives to Westminster and have its own parliament. Both Irish parliaments were to have senates. The Dail refused recognition to the elections for the Southern Senate since the Act entitled the Crown to nominate some members. It regarded the elections for the lower house as being held for the Second Dail, not for the Dublin parliament. In the South, the 124 Sinn Fein candidates were returned unopposed, the only non-Nationalist candidates being the four unopposed Senate members for Trinity. Only the Trinity representatives and the Crown-nominated senators turned up when the 'Dublin parliament' was opened on June 28. They met for exactly fifteen minutes and were adjourned *sine die*.

In the North, things were different. An election campaign marked by sectarian rioting returned forty Unionists and ten Nationalists. Incited by Unionist and Orange speeches, pogroms broke out all over the North; Catholics were driven from their homes and jobs; property was destroyed —all without intervention from the military. The pogroms were organised by Carson's Ulster Volunteers, and were intense in Bangor, Lisburn and Banbridge. But Belfast was the place worst affected. Here, in intermittent rioting between July 1920 and June 1922, a total of 455 people were killed, of whom 267 were Catholics and 185 Protestants, and 2,000 were wounded. Five thousand Catholics were driven out of the shipyards.

Truce and Treaty

Peace, however, was getting nearer: coming slowly, but coming. Rejecting a 'hard line' speech drawn up for him under Unionist influence, George V prepared with General Smuts of South Africa another version, and delivered it at the opening of the Northern parliament on June 22, 1921:

> . . . I speak from a full heart when I pray that my coming to Ireland today may prove to be the first step towards the end of strife among her people, whatever their race or creed. In that hope I appeal to all Irishmen to pause, to stretch out the hand of forbearance and conciliation, to forgive and forget, and to join in making for the land they love a new era of peace, contentment and good will. It is my earnest desire that in Southern Ireland, too, there may, ere long, take place a parallel to what is now passing in this hall; that there a similar occasion may present itself, and a similar ceremony be performed. For this the Parliament of the United Kingdom has in the fullest measure provided. For this the Parliament of Ulster is pointing the way.

Inconclusive peace moves had been going on since the previous October, when General George Cockerill had written to *The Times* suggesting a conference between 'untrammelled' plenipotentiaries. But the king's speech brought matters to a head.

Lloyd George and de Valera met at last in London on Tuesday, July 12, 1921, with reports still coming in of another 'Bloody Sunday' two days earlier, in which fifteen Catholics had been killed in Belfast and 160 Catholic homes burned. Lloyd George asked de Valera what was the Irish word for 'Republic'. The Sinn Fein leader told him that Saorstat had been preferred to Poblacht by the linguists. He explained to the prime minister that the literal translation of Saorstat was 'Free State'. The Welshman smiled and said the name would not need to be changed. But despite these linguistic amenities, the conference broke down on July 20. The British offered Dominion status with autonomy in taxation and finance generally, but stipulated for a form of settlement which would allow for 'full recognition of the existing powers and privileges of the Parliament of Northern Ireland, which cannot be abrogated save by their own consent'.

The Dail rejected this stipulation on August 10, de Valera explaining to General Smuts: 'An Ireland in fragments nobody cares about. . . . To the principle of self-determination our people are devotedly attached. . . . The

Republic is the expression of that principle.' Lloyd George gave his response three days later. The British government could not acknowledge 'the right of Ireland to secede from her allegiance to the king'. The British Empire had not yet advanced to the stage where the services to anti-colonial nationalism of men like Dr Nkrumah were to be rewarded by their being among the first to be informed of royal pregnancies. By 1921 the Conservative-Unionist section had become the dominant partner in the Coalition.

Against a background of threats to renew the war from the British side and of outbursts of sporadic disorder in Ireland, the sparring continued during August and September. Finally, on the last day of September, de Valera accepted the prime minister's invitation for a second conference on October 11 'with a view to ascertaining how the association of Ireland with the Community of Nations known as the British Empire may best be reconciled with Irish national aspirations'. Neither side had given anything away in the preliminaries to this conference, though the *Morning Post* (since subsumed within the *Daily Telegraph*) commented sourly: 'De Valera may well condescend to the favour which he has granted, for he will come to the conference as one who has already gained his point. Even the elementary condition that he should acknowledge the sovereignty of the Crown has been waived.'

De Valera did not, in fact, figure in the Irish delegation, which was led by Arthur Griffith and Michael Collins, accompanied by George Gavan Duffy, Eamonn Duggan and Robert Barton as representatives. Its secretaries were Erskine Childers, Finian Lynch, Diarmuid O'Hegarty and John Chartres. Austin Stack and Cathal Brugha refused to go. De Valera said that, as head of state, his place during the crisis was at home, adding that, having already rejected a British offer, it would be better if someone with a reputation for more moderation led the Irish negotiating team. If the talks broke down, he would be in a better position to try for a renewal of them. Griffith and Collins went with extreme reluctance. Collins felt that he was a soldier, not a negotiator, and he only accepted the task as a soldier accepts an unpalatable order.

In London the delegates stayed at two houses, one in 22 Hans Place, the other close by at 15 Cadogan Gardens. The latter accommodated the secretaries and attendants: young men fresh from ambushes, the terror of death and a life on the run. They frolicked with muscular abandon. Joseph McGrath (later one of the richest men in Ireland) had the unenviable task of 'looking after' the delegation. He went around inspecting the daily toll of damage, shaking his head and muttering: 'This is going to have to be paid for'. Something else would have to be paid for too. The rent also

fell due on the expensive camping site near the stars on which the First
Dail had pitched its tent.

On December 6, 1921 in the early hours of the morning the Treaty was
signed. At a crucial point in the negotiations which were to have such a
dire outcome there had been a moment of pure farce. The British delegates
—Lloyd George, Austen Chamberlain, Winston Churchill, F. E. Smith
(Lord Birkenhead), Hamar Greenwood, Gordon Hewart and L. Worthing-
ton-Evans—had hastened from the conference room to hunt for a pair of
Lloyd George's trousers! The prime minister had left in a pocket of a
particular pair of nether garments a letter containing a promise from
Griffith to the effect that independent Ireland would grant the six Ulster
counties the right to be separated within twelve months from the jurisdiction of an all-Ireland parliament. Griffith had made this concession—
which was in effect a recognition of the inevitability of Partition—in
response to a request from Lloyd George that he have something to this
effect in writing, purely for use as a ploy in his manoeuvrings: an earnest
of the reasonableness and good faith of the South. However, when the
trousers were found and the letter was produced by Lloyd George as a
definite commitment to be embodied in the Treaty, Griffith honoured
publicly what he had intended as a private assurance. The affair of the
trousers was not the only piece of Lloyd Georgian drama. The Irish
delegates were informed that a destroyer was waiting to convey news of
their decision to Ulster. Refusal to sign the Treaty would be the signal for
'immediate and terrible war'.

Since the preceding May, the British had made it known that full-scale
action against Sinn Fein would involve martial law over the whole country,
with direct government control of all transport, newspapers and civil
courts. There were to be other measures; as outlined by Churchill these
would entail the introduction of 100,000 troops and putting the three
Southern provinces of Leinster, Munster and Connacht under a network
of barbed wire and blockhouses. Collins realised that his band of guerillas
was now, after a long truce, deprived of its most effective weapon:
secrecy. The military struggle had lost its momentum. The Irish people
had taken the Truce as marking the end of the war and the beginning of
negotiations for freedom. Moreover, the evidence seems to show that
Collins was confident that the boundary commission provided for by the
Treaty would reduce the excluded Northern counties from six to four.
Griffith signed because he had given his word; the other three—Barton,
Duffy and Duggan—because the issue put to them was peace or war. The
British insisted that there would be no Treaty unless each delegate signed
it. No one wanted to bear single responsibility for war.

During the negotiations the Irish delegates had to contend with the psychological and physical strain of separation from Dublin. There were exhausting journeys by rail and boat between the two capitals, plunging them at either end into hard bargaining and arguing. Before the actual signing, they were given a little time to return to Hans Place to confer. Why in that time they failed to make use of the telephone to Dublin is still a mystery. Their credentials as plenipotentiaries 'from the elected Government of the Republic of Ireland' certainly empowered them 'to negotiate and conclude on behalf of Ireland with the representatives of George V a Treaty or treaties of settlement, association and accommodation between Ireland and the community of nations known as the British Commonwealth'. But these credentials were accompanied by a sort of safety-catch document which said it was 'understood' that, before anything binding was signed, the proposals 'would be referred back to Dublin'.

It cannot have been clear how Dublin would react to the Treaty. Collins, however, was under no illusion. The night before he signed the Treaty, he said: 'I am signing my own death warrant'. The day after it was signed, he took Joseph McGrath into a quiet corner of Hans Place, away from the crowded rooms where all was elation at the war's ending. The two of them went over the list of Dail deputies, trying to estimate who would be in favour and who against. Events were to prove both of them wrong in their forecasts.

The Treaty set up the Irish Free State as a self-governing dominion of the British Empire, according Ireland the same constitutional status as Canada, Australia, New Zealand and South Africa. The representative of the Crown was to be appointed in the same way as a Dominion governor-general, and the members of the Irish legislature were to take an oath of allegiance to the Constitution of the Irish Free State which pledged them to 'be faithful to His Majesty King George V, his heirs and successors'. The Treaty provided for the right of Northern Ireland to withdraw from the jurisdiction of the Dublin parliament. The Free State had to assume responsibility for part of the public debt of the United Kingdom, yield certain defence facilities to British forces, and in time of war give whatever assistance might be required by HM government. But it was the Oath, Partition and the office of governor-general which formed the main points of objection by opponents of the Treaty.

Eamonn Duggan brought the terms to Dublin on the evening of December 6, ahead of the rest of the delegation. Hitherto the leaders in Ireland had only had newspaper reports of the agreement. The next day de Valera, Brugha, Stack and Cosgrave met. De Valera pressed the other three to repudiate the Treaty and remove its signatories from the Republican cabinet. Brugha and Stack agreed, but Cosgrave insisted that the delegates should be heard first. The following day, December 8—the delegates having returned from London—it was decided by four votes to three to put the Treaty to the Dail for voting. In favour of this were Collins, Griffith, Cosgrave and Barton; against were de Valera, Stack and Brugha. There was a plot by some IRA commandants to arrest the Treaty signatories and have them charged with treason. De Valera and Brugha scotched this, but issued a letter to the press on December 8 in the former's name:

A Chairde Gaedheal:

You have seen in the public Press the text of the proposed Treaty with Great Britain.

The terms of this Agreement are in violent conflict with the wishes of the majority of this nation as expressed freely in successive elections during the past three years.

I feel it my duty to inform you immediately that I cannot recommend the acceptance of this Treaty either to Dail Eireann or to the country. In this attitude I am supported by the Ministers for Home Affairs and Defence.

A Public Session of Dail Eireann is being summoned for Wednesday next at 11 o'clock a.m. I ask the people to maintain during the interval the same discipline as heretofore. The members of the Cabinet, though divided in opinions, are prepared to carry on the public services as usual.

The Army as such is, of course, not affected by the political situation and continues under the same orders and control.

The greatest test of our people has come. Let us face it worthily, without bitterness, and above all without recriminations. There is a definite constitutional way of resolving our political differences—let us not depart from it, and let the conduct of the Cabinet in this matter be an example to the whole nation.

The next day a letter from Griffith was published:

I have signed the Treaty of peace between Ireland and Great Britain.

I believe that this Treaty will lay the foundations of peace and friendship between the two nations.

What I have signed I will stand by, in the belief that the end of the conflict of centuries is at hand.

The lines of division were now drawn. During the Dail debate, de Valera produced a compromise document—'Document Number 2'—which sought to sugar over the pill of the obnoxious clauses. But the Pro-Treaty side was averse from tearing up the signed Treaty to submit the

Michael Collins

William T. Cosgrave

Plate 3

SEAN F. LEMASS, *Taoiseach of the Republic of Ireland*

TERENCE M. O'NEILL, *Prime Minister of Northern Ireland*

PLATE 4

compromise for fresh negotiation with the British. After a fruitless debate, de Valera withdrew it. It has been since argued that had the debate not dragged on for so long the Anti-Treaty party might have carried the day; but the Christmas recess gave the IRB time to operate.

CIVIL WAR

The Treaty was ratified by the Dail on January 7, 1922 by sixty-four votes to fifty-seven. On January 10, an administration was formed under the leadership of Arthur Griffith. Led by de Valera, the Anti-Treaty group left the Dail in protest. With him went, among others, Erskine Childers, Austin Stack, Cathal Brugha and Robert Barton—the last-named allegedly persuaded by Childers, his cousin, to renounce his original endorsement of the Treaty. Those disposed to accept the Treaty included the Collins-Griffith group within the Dail and a strong element in the ranks of fighting nationalists, many of whom were IRB men. By Fenian tradition, Collins was, as head of the IRB, head also of the whole nationalist movement.

It should be borne in mind that, throughout the country as a whole—which, by the nature of the struggle against the British, was often cut off from Dublin—not Collins or Griffith or de Valera or Brugha or any of the political leaders had figured so large in the eyes of the rank and file of the IRA as had their own brigade officer or the headquarters officers with whom they came into contact: men like Gearoid O'Sullivan, adjutant-general; Diarmuid O'Hegarty, chief of organisation; and, above all, Richard Mulcahy, chief of staff. These three, all IRB leaders, were Pro-Treaty men. The IRB was in control of much of the Republican Army and of the public service. Also aligned with the Pro-Treaty side were those elements which wanted not so much a Republic or a Free State as peace. These included church leaders of all denominations in the South; big business interests; Labour led by Thomas Johnson, William O'Brien and Cathal O'Shannon; the Southern Unionists; and a large and uncoördinated section of the general public. Of the IRA men who took the Treaty side, it should be noted that the average young IRA man had gone into battle either to achieve a Republic or die in its cause. During the struggle most of them thought they would never see the former, for this implied defeating the mighty British Empire; but nevertheless they were prepared to face the latter in the cause of Ireland's freedom. But the Truce had a curious psychological effect on many of them. When it came, and the then still united Sinn Fein Party started to build up a paid national army, they suddenly found themselves with uniforms, pay and an increased life-expectancy. This new and unexpected circumstance decided many IRA men in favour of accepting the Treaty.

4—ISTR

On the political wing of the Anti-Treaty side, the great figure was, of course, de Valera. He was backed up by Childers, Brugha, Stack and the deputies who had left the Dail after the vote ratifying the Treaty. Later supporters included Barton and Gavan Duffy—who had originally signed the Treaty—and the celebrated women deputies: Countess Markievicz; Mme Maud Gonne MacBride; Mrs O'Callaghan, whose husband, the mayor of Limerick, had been murdered by Black and Tans; Mary Mac-Swiney, sister of Terence MacSwiney; and Mrs Kathleen Clarke, widow of the hero of Easter Week. The women's organisation, Cumann na mBan, under Countess Markievicz, was also solidly Anti-Treaty. On the military side, there were leaders like Liam Lynch; Tom Barry; Rory O'Connor; Liam Mellows; Joseph McKelvey; Seumas Robinson; Earnan O'Malley; Sean Moylan and Tom Hales. Anti-Treaty feeling was particularly strong in southern areas, notably Cork and Kerry. The Anti-Treaty side also embraced many who were politically to the left of those on the political and military wings who opposed the Treaty purely and simply because it denied the Republic, recognised the Crown and enshrined Partition. To the leftwing group, the Treaty was objectionable not only for these reasons but also because it made more difficult of realisation their dream of a Workers' Republic. Prominent on this wing were Countess Markievicz and Liam Mellows. Of all the IRA leaders, Mellows stood closest to Connolly's philosophy. A set of notes which he smuggled out of Mountjoy prison after his capture in the Civil War set out his social theories. They fell into his opponent's hands and were given communist-scare treatment in the press. Other leading IRA men who shared his beliefs and later became prominent in the IRA during the 'twenties and 'thirties were Peadar O'Donnell and George Gilmore. (See chapter 10.)

On January 14, 1922, in pursuance of the Treaty's requirements, the 'Southern Parliament' was convened. This was composed of the sixty-four Pro-Treaty members of the Second Dail elected in May 1921, together with four representatives of Trinity College. The parliament elected a provisional government for the twenty-six counties and confirmed the provision of the Treaty whereby the provisional government was to evolve into the Government of the Irish Free State a year after the signing of the Treaty. The constitutional position was therefore somewhat intricate since the administration formed under Griffith immediately after the Treaty vote was technically responsible to the Dail, while the provisional government was created by and responsible to the Southern Parliament. The Dail had in theory been the parliament for all Ireland; the Southern Parliament was, in fact as well as theory, the parliament for Ireland-less-Ulster. Although to the outsider it might seem there was no significant difference between the two legislatures (men who were ministers in the Dail becoming ministers of the provisional government), there was a very clear distinction between the two bodies in the minds of the Anti-Treaty Party—or Cumann na Poblachta as it was now styled following its withdrawal from the Dail after the Treaty vote. Its attitude to the provisional government was defined by de Valera thus: '. . . We would not be actively hostile to the setting up of the Government though we do not and cannot admit its right as the Government of this country until the Irish people have spoken'.

Trouble flared up in Limerick when Pro- and Anti-Treaty sections of the IRA seized parts of the town from the evacuating British troops. This was overcome by mediators, and on March 26 a Convention was held in the Mansion House in Dublin in an effort to come to terms between the contending factions. The attempt proved fruitless.

Then, on April 13, came the dramatic seizure of the Four Courts, the former seat of British justice, by a group of Volunteers led by Rory O'Connor. This group wrote to the Dail stating a number of conditions on which agreement could be reached. These included: 'maintaining the existing Republic'; putting the army under the control of an 'independent electoral representative'; and the stipulation that 'no elections on the issue at present before the country be held while the threat of war with England exists'. The Four Courts garrison issued a further letter to the Dail on April 25, 'in order to give that body an opportunity of taking this matter out of the hands of the Cabinet, of saving the country from Civil War now threatened by those who have abandoned the Republic'. The insurgents held themselves responsible solely to an executive council elected by themselves. They began to direct military operations from this centre. These consisted principally of a boycott against Belfast; trains coming from the North were held up and their freight seized. Banks were raided to pay, it was alleged, for this section of the IRA's bills to tradesmen. A certain amount of violent private enterprise was engaged in as bands of young men flitted around the country on various ventures, the military significance of which was apparent only to themselves.

A peace conference was convened at the Mansion House under the auspices of Archbishop Walsh of Dublin and Laurence O'Neill, the lord mayor. Labour continued efforts to mediate between the political sections of the two sides (Griffith refused to negotiate with the Four Courts men). But the conference broke down on April 25. Griffith and Collins were adamant that an election must be held on the issue of the Treaty. The Republican nationalists objected to this on the grounds that the general desire for peace would result in a vote favourable to the Treaty, but such a vote could not be taken as deciding the issue of Free State versus Republic. For one thing, de Valera and Brugha argued, an electoral decision in favour of the Treaty would be immediately repudiated by the militant Republican wing. Moreover, the electoral register was unrevised and a large number of young Republican sympathisers were thus disenfranchised. Postponement of the election, they contended, would allow for the democratic revision of the register.

The Pro-Treaty insistence on holding an election stemmed from the state of the country. Atrocities in the North continued—despite a pact between Collins and Sir James Craig guaranteeing the territorial integrity of the North pending the findings of the Boundary Commission. Worse things than expulsion from home and workplaces were being done: Catholic families were beaten to death and parents shot in front of their children. Moreover, the British were getting restive. In the Conservative-Unionist camp, the Treaty had been regarded as unduly generous: so much so that all those who signed it on the British side were out of office within a year. There were 60,000 British troops in the North—apparently to safeguard the Border by crossing it, if a pretext could be found. Sir Henry Wilson, in particular, was urging that action be taken against the Four Courts garrison. The day before the building was seized, Churchill had underlined the British position thus: 'If a Republic is set up, that is a form of government in Ireland which the British Empire in no circumstances whatever can tolerate or agree to'.

Towards the end of April 1922, an outbreak of shootings in Cork claimed the lives of ten Protestants the week after a Catholic IRA man had been killed by, it was believed, a Protestant. The shootings were roundly condemned by nationalists, but they raised fears of sectarian violence in the South as well as the North. In fact, Collins and Lynch had made an agreement which, if it had come to light, would have had incalculable repercussions: in order to assist the Catholics in the North, Collins was supplying the Anti-Treaty Lynch with guns for use against the Orangemen. At this stage, when pressure from London was mounting, Collins was not altogether averse from having the Four Courts held by Republicans against the Pro-Treaty government, for this enabled the IRA's operations in the North to be attributed to 'freelance' associates of Rory O'Connor.

Under the pressure of the worsening situation, Collins and de Valera, with the intermediation of Harry Boland, negotiated at the end of May a compromise arrangement regarding elections. This almost saved the situation. Up to this point, both sets of politicians in the Dail, whether for or against the Treaty, were members of Sinn Fein. The terms of the Election Pact were that, still under the common banner of Sinn Fein, those in favour of the Treaty would nominate sixty-six candidates and those against it fifty-eight. Thus voters would still be voting for Sinn Fein and keeping the government in Sinn Fein control whatever the stand taken by their representatives over the Treaty. Under the system of proportional representation (introduced by the British in 1920 with the aim of weakening Sinn Fein, but welcomed by Griffith who was a staunch advocate of PR), a Pro-Treaty voter was supposed to give his first preference to the Pro-Treaty Sinn Feiner and his second preference to the Anti-Treaty Sinn Feiner; the Anti-Treaty voter was to do the reverse. The administration and the presidency of the legislature were to be appointed on an agreed basis between the two sides.

The Pact could only be justified in face of the grave situation developing, for it cut across the interests of Labour, the newly formed Farmers' Party, the Southern Unionists and the Independents. From the date of its announcement, the evacuation of British troops—which had been proceeding according to the Treaty's provisions—was halted, and the defences of the six North-Eastern counties were strengthened. The Unionists saw the Pact as a clear breach of the Treaty. Influenced by the increasingly menacing tones coming from London, Collins changed his position. In a speech at Cork he told the electorate to 'vote for the candidate you think best of'. This was regarded by the Anti-Treaty side as a breach of the Pact.

Voting took place on June 16, 1922. As may be imagined, the election campaign was a torrid affair. Liam Pilkington, the IRA commandant for Sligo (who afterwards became a Jesuit), proscribed a meeting in that town at which Griffith was to speak. Griffith made his will, set out from Dublin, and spoke; Pro-Treaty forces were fired on and gun-battles ensued. In Castleblayney, Collins was speaking from an open lorry when an audacious Anti-Treatyite got into the cab and drove off; shooting again followed. In Cork, while the votes were awaiting the count, the armed guard outside the College of Art was circumvented by a band of Anti-Treatyites who got in through the roof and altered 4,000 ballots, changing first preferences for Collins into fourth preferences. The forgery was easily spotted, however, since they used the wrong type of pencil.*

The results of the election were: fifty-eight Sinn Fein deputies for the Treaty; thirty-six Sinn Feiners who were against it; seventeen Labour; all others seventeen. Of the total of 128 seats, thirty-seven were unopposed because of the Pact. If the votes of the Labour, Farmers' Party, University and Independent candidates are taken with those of the candidates supporting Collins and Griffith as representing Pro-Treaty support, the national voting figures on the Treaty question were: *For* 486,419; *Against* 133,864.

---

* The Republicans in Cork were resourceful but at times a trifle naïve. Instructed to write Republican slogans on all available surfaces, one election worker took his order literally and regaled the city with the oft-repeated scrawl: 'Up the Republic wherever a small space presents itself'.

However, by the time the new Dail was due to meet, the question of a coalition cabinet had lost meaning, for the situation in the country had deteriorated beyond the point where a peaceful solution was possible. The event which turned a bitter political struggle into Civil War came on June 22, 1922: the assassination of Sir Henry Wilson on the steps of his London home. Asquith had called him 'that poisonous though clever ruffian'. The Irish had reason to call him something worse. His hostility to Irish nationalism was intense, and its supporters regarded him as their most insidious enemy in the Establishment in England. He had opposed the Truce, and ever since 1916 had favoured the strongest measures of repression against the South. His murder occurred at the time of brutal action against the Catholics in the North-East, for which he, as military adviser to the Ulster government, was held responsible.*

With Britain seething with horror and anger, the government in London contemplated mounting an attack by British forces on the Four Courts, centre of the extremist IRA movement; but were dissuaded by General Macready, commander-in-chief of the British forces in Ireland. The British cabinet delivered a strong protest to the provisional government on June 26. That same day, armed men attached to the Four Courts insurgents seized a number of cars to make up a convoy to go to Belfast and help the Catholics there. The officer in charge was captured; in reprisal, the men from the Four Courts kidnapped the Free State's deputy chief of staff, General 'Ginger' O'Connell. Next morning, June 27, the Four Courts got an ultimatum to surrender from the provisional government. They ignored it and were shelled with field guns borrowed from the British.

De Valera, Lynch, Boland and Brugha and, indeed, most of the leading Republicans outside the Four Courts had continually urged the garrison there not to provoke an armed clash because, few in number and poorly

---

* His killers were Reginald Dunne and Joseph O'Sullivan, both of whom had fought in the British army in the Great War—O'Sullivan losing a leg at Ypres. They made no attempt to escape and were executed in August. At the trial Dunne declared they had shot Wilson in the same cause for which they had fought in France: 'The rights of small nationalities'.

The surprising thing is that there were not more assassinations of prominent enemies of Irish independence. Several times during the struggle plans were laid to kill this or that British politician. Indeed, a scheme was hatched to shoot the entire cabinet, and a group of IRA men travelled to London for that purpose. But while they waited, their nerve steadily deteriorated. The scheme was eventually dropped, but one man among them told me that, realising he would have to take part in shootings when he returned to Ireland, he decided to test his nerve by seeing if in fact he could have got near enough to kill his intended victim, Arthur (Lord) Balfour. The papers told him Balfour would be in Oxford on a particular day. The IRA man went there and met his quarry walking along in a group of women. He asked the great man for directions. 'I'm going there myself', said Balfour. 'I'll show you.' The two of them walked side by side for over a hundred yards. 'I could have done it after all', my informant said.

armed as they were, they would be militarily outclassed by the Pro-Treatyites. Yet, with the same hopeless gallantry with which The O'Rahilly had returned to Dublin to join with the men in the GPO in 1916, the Anti-Treaty leaders took up arms when their comrades were attacked.

By this time, the Pro-Treaty side had formed a war council. The Second Dail was never dissolved; the new parliament was summoned, not as the Third Dail, but as 'The House of Parliament to which the Provisional Government is to be responsible'.* This parliament was prorogued on July 13, 1922 by a notice signed by fifteen men, only seven of whom were members of the Dail cabinet: a proceeding which was afterwards unsuccessfully assailed by constitutional experts. The fifteen men were: Arthur Griffith, Ernest Blythe, W. T. Cosgrave, George Gavan Duffy, E. J. Duggan, Desmond Fitzgerald, Michael Hayes, P. J. Hogan, Michael Collins, Finian Lynch, Richard Mulcahy, Joseph McGrath, Eoin MacNeill, Kevin O'Higgins and J. J. Walsh. The war council consisted of: Michael Collins, commander-in-chief; Richard Mulcahy, chief of staff and minister for Defence; Eoin O'Duffy, general commanding the South-Western division; and Diarmuid O'Hegarty, commandant general.

From the shelling of the Four Courts on June 28, 1922 until May 24, 1923, when the Civil War officially ended, terrible things were done by both sides. It was a war without frontiers, a struggle in which eighteen-year-old youths became colonels. The ordinary processes of law broke down and with them the law of nature. In Terenure a group of Free State troops raiding a house shot a suspect: the son of the officer of the raiding party. At Knocknagoshel, County Tipperary, an Anti-Treaty group set a booby-trap which killed five Treatyites. In reprisal a group of captured Anti-Treaty soldiers were chained together and set to dismantle a barricade at Ballyseedy, County Kerry. It had been mined and they were blown to pieces. In a prison in the West men were castrated during interrogations, to die years afterwards in asylums without ever recovering their sanity.

The experiences of many Irish families is typified by those of a family I am familiar with. By chance it was one which sympathised with the Anti-Treaty side. But what happened arose, not from political beliefs, but from a

---

* The situation by this time had become incredibly complicated. There were no less than six 'governmental' authorities and four armed forces exerting influence to a greater or lesser extent on Irish affairs. There were the 'Parliament of Southern Ireland' (the abortive Dublin Parliament of the British Act), the Parliament of Northern Ireland, the Provisional Government of the Treatyites, the Dail, the Irish Republic of the Anti-Treatyites, and the British government. In the South there were the Pro- and Anti-Treaty sections of the Irish Republican Army, with detachments of British forces in the 'Treaty ports'; in the North there were considerable numbers of British troops together with the armed police of the Royal Ulster Constabulary. In addition to these more or less regular bodies, there were groups of armed men and individuals carrying out private operations.

neighbours' quarrel. The mother took in a party of hunted 'irregulars', as they were known by the Free State authorities. (The Anti-Treaty forces called themselves Republicans.) It was an act motivated by kindliness more than political allegiance. Like the bulk of the people, they had no clear idea of what a 'Republic' was and what a 'Free State', and were mainly moved by personal loyalties. A vindictive neighbour told the authorities of the fugitives' whereabouts and the house was raided. A gun went off accidentally and in the ensuing fusillade one of the hunters and two of the hunted were killed. A boy of thirteen and a girl of sixteen belonging to the family were taken into custody. The girl spent six months in prison. The troops believed the boy could give them information about the leader of a flying squad, and tortured him to force him to speak. The boy, in fact, did not know anything, but he remained silent. After a beating he still refused to speak, even though a priest pleaded with him and, as he told me, he quite expected to be turned into a *pucán* (a young goat) for his refusal. He was then made to kneel by an open grave with a rifle at his head. The boy still kept silent, even when red-hot pokers were pressed on his feet and he was beaten unconscious. His obduracy did not spring merely from loyalty to a friend; his resistance was also to giving information to *anyone* in authority. This spirit was a legacy of British rule in Ireland where authority was always 'them against us'.

On October 25, 1922, de Valera was elected president of 'The Irish Republic' by the Anti-Treaty side. The members of the IRA supporting this side were instituted as the army of the Republic.

Liam Lynch, leader of the military arm of the Anti-Treaty section, issued an order to the effect that any deputy who had voted for the Treaty, and every member of the Free State army above the rank of lieutenant, was to be shot. One deputy, Sean Hales, was killed and his companion, Padraic O'Maille, deputy-president of the Dail, was wounded. As a reprisal four leading members of the Four Courts garrison—Rory O'Connor, Liam Mellows, Dick Barrett and Joseph McKelvey—were executed that same night, December 8, 1922. They had been in gaol since June. It made no pretence to be a legal act; it was an attempt to meet terror with terror. In this it was successful. No more deputies were shot. At this time members of the provisional government were all living in government buildings, sleeping with revolvers by their beds. These men were called on to play an heroic but dreadful role. They fulfilled it with a ruthless efficiency which the disorganised Republican forces could never equal. In all, seventy-seven men were executed, generally in the area from which they came. Relatives of prisoners never knew when reports of a Republican attack might be followed by word of an execution. The 'seventy-seven prisoners' have hardly yet left the Irish political lexicon.

The death of Liam Lynch, fatally wounded in a skirmish on the Knock-mealdown mountains in County Tipperary, broke the heart of the Republican resistance. The Anti-Treaty forces stopped military operations a month later—on May 24, 1923. Lynch had been an outstanding Irish commander in the war of independence with Britain. His men had practically no arms save those captured from the British. He had had no military training, barring study of texts, one of which, by Robert Emmet, dated from 1803. Yet, though the terrain in his area of operations was one of the most difficult in the whole country for fighting over, his Southern Division was probably the most successful in the war against the British. Lynch was a deeply religious man, and General Mulcahy, whose troops shot him, described him to me as 'a glorious character'.

The Reckoning

The Civil War took a heavy toll. Cathal Brugha refused to surrender when the Gresham Hotel was captured in the O'Connell Street fighting after the bombardment of the Four Courts. He came out of a doorway with two revolvers blazing into the muzzles of over a hundred rifles. Brugha was one of the bravest men of all of them. During the Rising he had been wounded seventeen times and left for dead in hospital. Born Charles Burgess, the son of a Carlow man, Brugha was deeply religious, as befitted the owner of a firm making church candles. While the decision was still in the balance whether to introduce conscription in Ireland, he lived in London with a squad of Volunteers. Had conscription been enforced, he was to have taken the squad into the House of Commons and raked the front bench with machine guns. To judge from his record, it seems that the decision not to enforce conscription saved the lives of a number of British politicians.

Erskine Childers, captured by Free State troops in the home of his cousin, Robert Barton, was executed by firing squad. For all his heroism in sailing the guns in for Easter Week, he was so hated for his publicity work on the Republican side that some of the Pro-Treaty side regarded him as an agent provocateur. The night before he was executed, he wrote to his wife: 'I die full of an intense love for Ireland'. He shook hands with each member of the firing squad. Harry Boland was wounded in an accidental flurry when the hotel where he was staying in Skerries was raided. He died in hospital on August 2, 1922. He was a close friend both of Collins and de Valera, and had helped to bring about the Pact between them. Although an IRB man, he had voted against the Treaty. Ten days later, Griffith—the great national journalist whose political writings had laid the powder train ignited by the Rising in Easter Week—died of a heart attack brought on by overwork and physical strain. He had never fired a shot himself. And on August 22, Michael Collins was killed in an ambush at Beal na Blath in his native Cork. The deaths of Collins and Boland—close companions against the British—on opposite sides in the Civil War epitomise the Irish tragedy. They were deeply attached to each other; their companionship running the war against the British had had almost a schoolboy zest.

Ever since Collins' death rumours have circulated that he was murdered. But in fact when the Pro-Treaty authorities investigated the affair, they were satisfied that there was no conspiracy in the killing of Collins. Five Republicans on the brow of a hill saw a cavalcade coming and fired at it. There need have been no casualties had not Collins decided to halt and make a fight of it. The last shot fired struck him. The man who fired it was a rank-and-file Republican of no political importance and he did not know whom he had shot. The identity of this man is known to a small circle, one of whom was Collins' brother Sean (he died in 1964) who is known to have forgiven the man and kept his name secret.

Abrasive-tongued, Collins had scant respect for the dividing line between his own and his colleagues' areas of responsibility. As a guerilla fighter, he would have had little to learn from Mao Tse-tung. Many of his colleagues did not agree with his use of extremist propaganda and uninhibited methods of warfare against the British. It can indeed be argued that the sanction of patriotic necessity given by him to IRA terrorist actions against the British goes far to explain the grievous facility with which both sections of the IRA ferociously slaughtered opponents in the Civil War. For Collins, the way to run a revolution was to leave a row of dead enemies. He resolved on eliminating the British intelligence corps because 'Britain can always replace her army; no one can step into the shoes *and* the knowledge of a spy'. Yet, ruthless as he was in pursuing war against the British, his operations against the Anti-Treaty side in the Civil War were conducted with much greater moderation. In many cases he observed a distinction between British and Irish opponents which was not observed by some of those who had been his disciples in the War of Independence. He delayed the attack on the Four Courts several times because of his unwillingness to shoot old comrades. One of his cabinet colleagues told me: 'He made it very hard for us to start the Civil War'.

Why the British never managed to capture Collins is one of the mysteries of the War of Independence. He never wore disguise, and went every day on a bicycle between his several Dublin offices. The Castle had no photograph of him, and it never seems to have dawned on them there to seek to trace him in Sinn Fein circles through his strong Cork accent. Men were proud to kill and to die for him. With his sunshine and thunder personality, his sharp intelligence and his enormous energy, Michael Collins emerges in Irish history as a Celtic Mars who could have been the Prometheus of his country, bringing benison out of fire, had he lived. He was thirty-two when the bullet struck him down at Beal na Blath.

Born at Clonakilty, County Cork, in 1890, he was the son of a small farmer: a remarkable man who spoke Irish and French, wrote Latin and Greek, diverted himself with mathematics and begot his famous son at the age of seventy-five. Young Collins passed his Civil Service examination when sixteen and entered the Post Office in London. His experience of the administrative machine stood him in good stead when he was made minister of Finance in the First Dail. I have seen private letters of his to his fiancée. It is an extraordinary experience to read things like: 'Darling, I'm terribly sorry I couldn't write you a longer letter, but Lloyd George kept us busy all day. Will write you a proper letter tomorrow,' He never missed sending his betrothed a letter every day during the negotiations, as regular in this as in his daily attendance at Mass.

From September 1922 to July 30, 1923 (the only period for which figures are available) Civil War casualties were approximately 665 killed and 3,000 wounded. Ireland had been hard hit economically by the war with the British; the Civil War brought the country to its knees. Hundreds of thousands of acres went out of cultivation. Of the total population of 2,750,000 in the Free State, 130,000 were unemployed. Damage to Irish property amounted to £30 million; and on top of this came the bill for the prosecution of the war.

Perhaps even graver were the psychological effects. These have bedevilled Irish life to the present day. It is only very recently that welcome signs have appeared of their weakening. The Anti-Treaty side and its sympathisers (over 130,000 people to judge from the voting figures in the 1922 election) regarded the Free State government as an unlawful junta and its army and police as instruments of a party rather than of the nation. When the Anti-Treaty side eventually formed a government, the other side in turn regarded all governmental activity with similar suspicion. This intensified the existing hostility to authority which, as has been mentioned, was a legacy of British rule. In the six months between August 1923 and January 1924—the immediate aftermath of the cessation of Civil War hostilities—lawlessness was widespread, and over 1,502 cases of arson and armed robbery were reported to the police.

The restoration of civil order was the greatest single problem of the new state. A new unarmed Civil Guard was founded. Initiated under circumstances of extreme difficulty, it was to become one of the finest police forces in Europe. The difficulties its founders had to cope with—in addition to a 'crime explosion' in the country—are in part illustrated by this report of my father's. (For obvious reasons I have left out names, dates and places.)

Copy of Inspection Minute s/Commer. Coogan,
Garda Station ———1923

Visited Station in conjunction with Divisional Tour. Sgt —— and Station party present. When I arrived at the Station, the Sgt sat glowering at me and refused to call the party to attention. I called the party to attention myself. Garda —— tried to rise but fell into the fireplace. I asked the Sergeant to account for the state of affairs existing at the Station but he replied in such a manner as would do more justice to the worst cornerboy in the slums of London.

I searched the barracks and found that a seizure of poteen (three gallons) made on the previous day had been almost consumed by the Station party. The Barrack servant sat with a baton in her hand, protecting the remainder of it and refused to move. She also had possession of the Station books and records and she refused to allow me to inspect them. In my examination of the Barracks I found that the w.c. was filled with Station records, apparently used by the Station party on their visits there. I heard noises coming from the rear of the cells. When I went to investigate I found three young ladies there. I took statements from them and they complained that when passing the Barracks they were forcibly taken in by Sgt —— and Gardas —— and ——, for a purpose better imagined than described.

In the Station kitchen I found Garda ——. He caught me by the uniform and would not let me go until I promised to refund him a fine of £5 imposed on him and have record of the same erased. When I returned to the front of the Barracks I found the Sergeant urinating from the front door into the street and he started to argue with me on the footpath with his person exposed.

On leaving the Station I was approached by a local trader who demanded that I make the Station party pay some of their mess debts for the preceding months, now amounting to some £70.

The whole situation at —— Garda Station, County —— was disgraceful. I returned to —— and had all the Station party at —— suspended immediately. I hope that the Divisional Officer will ensure that these men discharge their local debts before they are themselves discharged from the force.

Vendettas were settled murderously. Young Volunteers who had spent the previous four years with their lives depending on their nerves and their guns, took to drink during the inactivity of the Truce period. As a result newspapers were filled with death reports. These became so common a feature that little space was devoted to individual shootings. Typical were three-line items like: 'John Smith ... missing from home three days ... found shot'.

For over forty years after the Civil War, two attitudes hung stagnant and blighting, like the shadow of the Upas tree, over Ireland's political life. Each side tried to fix blame on the other. Against the Pro-Treatyites it was said that their determination to uphold the Treaty against the wishes of their fellow countrymen was the cause of the grief. Collins was blamed for signing the Treaty in the belief that, through the IRB, he could stifle all opposition and enforce a peaceable settlement through conspiratorial methods.

The Pro-Treaty side laid the blame at de Valera's door, condemning him for splitting the nation with his letter rejecting the Treaty before the case for it had been heard and fully discussed; for withdrawing from the Dail; and for making what became known as his 'wading through blood' speeches. In one of these, on March 17, 1922, he had warned what would happen if the Treaty were accepted. 'If the Volunteers of the future attempted to reach the goal which the Volunteers of the past had fought for, they would have to wade through Irish blood, through the blood of the soldiers of the Irish Government, and through, perhaps, the blood of some members of the Irish Government, in order to get Irish Freedom.' His supporters subsequently contended that he had spoken in the same spirit as had Lincoln when on the eve of the American Civil War he had warned the Republican State Convention that 'unless a change is made in our present course, blood will flow and brother's hand will be raised against brother'.

The personal antipathies of the leaders—men living under terrible strain—have been fixed in memory and kept vivid in arguments. Brugha's, Stack's and Childers' dislike of Collins; Griffith's and Collins' dislike of Childers (whom the Pro-Treaty side have always loathed for inducing his cousin, Robert Barton, to repudiate the Treaty); the fact that Mulcahy and Collins had disagreements with de Valera over military policy; the fact that, from the time of the 'German plot' arrests in 1918 to his return from America in December 1920, de Valera was out of touch with those at home; the fact that Brugha had dismissed Mulcahy as chief of staff even before the final break came; the split between the IRB and the IRA—all these things have been incorporated into the respective viewpoints in whatever way they best suited the antagonists.

Both views are, of course, arguable. They have been argued for forty years, and will be argued for as long as Ireland lasts. But personal animosities and this or that misjudgement or folly do not, of themselves, explain the causes of the Civil War. A split of some kind was inevitable when Sinn Fein came to life again after the Rising—not as a well-planned political party, but as a many-toned echo reverberating from the shots of the firing squads which executed the Rising's leaders. The pressure of subsequent events held the disparate elements together; but with the conclusion of peace with the British, the pressure relaxed and each group felt itself free to seek whatever Grail, holy or unholy, it had cherished throughout the struggle.

And while the politicians argued for one form of government against another, the issue ceased to be one of constitutional questions and centred on the question of whether the men in the Four Courts should have the right to decide if elections were to be held or not. Inevitably, once the people had recorded their votes, the problem became one of how to get the armed men out of the Four Courts: by discussion or gunfire. Sir Henry Wilson's murder (even though Rory O'Connor's men had nothing to do with it) and the kidnapping of General O'Connell made only one answer possible.*

A little time ago, I spent an evening talking to an old man who had been a prominent opponent of the Anti-Treaty side both in the fighting and in its subsequent political incarnation. He was a most courteous and generous-tempered man. But as we dwelt on the Civil War, layer after layer of restraint peeled away. He banged on the table and denounced de Valera. 'Far greater wrong was done this country by de Valera than by Lloyd George', he said as he ushered me to the door. The strength of his emotional intensity overwhelmed me.

Leaving the house, I glanced back at the lighted window of his study where he sat amid the wraiths of his dead friends and enemies. I promptly bumped into a girl on the pavement. She probably worked in one of the nearby office blocks built since my host and Mr de Valera had retired from parliamentary life. She wore a Beatle cut and twinkled along cheerily on high heels. I looked after her. How much, I wonder, did she and those like her care about the Civil War?

* The grim irony of it all is that it had been intended to call off the killing of Wilson, as in the case of the plans made to kill Balfour and other leading anti-Irish figures. But in the rush of events the countermand did not reach London. Had Wilson not been shot, and since the Dail was due to meet in a little over two weeks' time, the Four Courts garrison (already somewhat divided among its members) could very easily have been ejected peaceably; they had very little food.

3. COSGRAVE ERA 1923-32

Problems of the New State: *Army Mutiny of 1924; Partition and Agreement of 1925; Rise of Fianna Fail*

THE Free State began with bitter agrarian conflict raging in Waterford and the thunder of the Civil War dying away in spasmodic outrages. In May 1923, agricultural labourers in the South-East, in protest against the reduction of their wages to the level obtaining under the British, spiked meadows, destroyed crops and ambushed troops. The farmers struck back and wrecked the homes of some of the trade union officials in the area. Among acts of Civil War vengeance was the murder of Noel Lemass, a brother of the present prime minister. During the Civil War he went to the Isle of Man. He returned to Ireland in July 1923, but was kidnapped and found dead in the Dublin mountains three months later.

There were just over 12,000 Anti-Treaty sympathisers in gaol, including de Valera. These were released over a period of two years, de Valera being one of the last to be freed, in July 1924. At the end of 1927, Cosgrave said that the Dail session then concluded had been the first which could be said to have been unmarked by military strife.

Neither then nor in the turbulence of the 'thirties, the isolation of the 'forties and the stagnation of the 'fifties did social and economic questions hold a dominant position in Irish politics. Some progress was made in these fields, but the main preoccupations—apart from the Shannon Scheme (see below)—were with constitutional matters or in problems arising from the Civil War.

In the administrations which controlled the Free State from September 19, 1923, until the handing over of power to de Valera in 1932, the outstanding personalities were: W. T. Cosgrave, president of the Executive Council (prime minister)*; Kevin O'Higgins, vice-president and minister for Home Affairs; and Patrick Hogan, a solicitor from the West. As minister for Agriculture, Hogan—who favoured free trade—initiated legislation which set standards for farm produce, grappled with the flooding problem and set up a new industry, sugar making, in the beet-

---

* The title 'An Taoiseach' for the head of the administration dates from the new Constitution of 1937.

processing factory at Carlow. Above all, he was responsible for the great Land
Act of 1923 which sought to complete the process of creating a system of
peasant proprietors begun under the British, and at the same time to
eliminate the uneconomic dwarf holdings in the West. The act went a long
way towards dealing with the conditions which gave rise to the Waterford
land agitation.

Kevin O'Higgins was the most admired and most hated figure of the
administration.* He was responsible for the public safety measures, and
under him Home Affairs covered a wide spectrum, embracing matters
proper to the Local Government and Justice departments. As vice-
president of the Executive Council, he also carried the ball when crises
like the Army Mutiny of 1924 blew up. He had a temper like the wrath of
God and a cutting edge to his tongue which flayed opponents or subordin-
ates who crossed him. A certain awfulness hung about his name. He did
not let the fact that Rory O'Connor was a close friend (indeed, best-man
at his wedding) stand in the way of his approving the execution of the
leader of the Four Courts rebellion.

An opponent once called him the 'National Apostate'. At a subsequent
election meeting, in reply to an eulogy by a Fianna Fail speaker of the
great gifts of purity and probity enjoyed by the Irish people, O'Higgins
read a list of the current statistics for rape and venereal disease, 'revealing
them in my capacity as National Apostate'. He even went so far as to
introduce legislation aimed at reducing the number of public houses and
at restricting the sale of drink. He banned the sale of alcohol on Saint
Patrick's Day and broke up the long sitting after lunch by making bars
shut for the 'Holy Hour' from 2.30 to 3.30 p.m. (His insight into the drink
problem dated from his student days when he used to imbibe fairly heavily,
notably at the *Dropping Well* at Milltown outside Dublin.)

Like most of the other senior politicians on both sides, O'Higgins had
tremendous physical courage. In a raid on a county council office in Naas
during the Tan War, he and Cosgrave were among a group of suspects
seized by British Auxiliaries. They had been conducting illegal local
government business in an attic while the county council proper went on
with its work downstairs. The Auxiliaries, however, were deceived by the
Irishmen's false identity papers and eventually released them. O'Higgins
afterwards said that it was his most terrifying moment of the war. Had they
been unmasked, he and Cosgrave would certainly have been shot, after the
customary beating up 'while attempting to escape'. But throughout the
raid, with that imperturbable sangfroid of his, he kept an irritating smile

---

* During the Civil War, O'Higgins' father was killed in the presence of his wife and
children by his son's enemies, though it seems that this killing (which took place during a
raid on his house) was an unpremeditated act, not a planned murder.

on his face. Enraged, the officer in charge—a man six feet six inches tall known as 'Tiny', an Auxiliary with a particularly terrifying reputation— shoved a revolver in his ribs and roared: 'If you don't take that smirk off your puss, I'll give you six bullets in the belly'. O'Higgins replied: 'Sure I won't feel the last one anyhow'.

When some of his own countrymen murdered him on July 10, 1927, as he walked to twelve o'clock Mass, they made such a botch of the shooting that he felt all the bullets. Though they emptied their revolvers into him, he lived for several hours. Dying in great agony, he said he forgave his murderers, none of whom was ever brought to justice. By a grim quirk of fate, O'Higgins' cabinet colleague, Eoin MacNeill, was walking to Mass at the same church when O'Higgins was attacked. He heard several shots and saw three men together and a fourth falling to the pavement. With great courage he ran to the attacked man's assistance, and found to his horror that it was his colleague in government. By a further eerie turn of fate, the man rumoured by some to have been the driver of the get-away car was afterwards fatally injured in a road accident. As he lay dying by the roadside, he was attended by a passing doctor: a brother of Kevin O'Higgins.*

As a politician Cosgrave was fundamentally a conservative. Sincerely religious, he expected visitors to his home in Templeogue, County Dublin, to join in the saying of the Rosary if they arrived while it was in progress. He showed in conversation a humorous, almost cynical disillusionment. A profile of him in the *Irish Times*, on January 29, 1955, said:

> He was probably, when it came to handling men, the ablest of them all. The team he picked for the organisation of the new Civil Service would be regarded as the most outstanding single contribution of the President. Without Gregg, Brennan, Coogan [the author's father], Merrick and McElligot, the Civil Service could easily have become both corrupt and inefficient.

It is said that Cosgrave talked Collins out of tearing up the Treaty. Though he supported the stern line taken by his side in its successful prosecution of the Civil War, it is unlikely that he would, if a free agent, have initiated such a policy. Using the expertise gained from his experience in municipal administration as a Dublin city councillor, he headed, with O'Higgins, the team which in the post-1916 struggle removed the pith of effectiveness from local government, leaving the British with the husk of empty authority. But though immensely popular, Cosgrave lacked the

---

* What I believe to be the most likely solution to the mystery of O'Higgins' murderers is given in chapter 11, page 261.

dynamism to sustain his party, Cumann na nGaedheal, after the blow it suffered in the assassination of O'Higgins. Moreover, acceptance of the Treaty had postponed, not abolished, the idea of a Republic. The 'dynamic initiative' in politics lay with the Republicans, as de Valera was to grasp.

The greatest contribution to Ireland of Cosgrave's administration (albeit it was the regime which first introduced censorship) lies in its making it possible for the forms of democracy to develop in a country torn by the hatred and violence of Civil War, and in its preventing the emergence of either a police state or a military dictatorship. Sectarian strife was also kept at bay. For example, in 1931 the Mayo County Council objected to the appointment of a Miss Dunbar-Harrison as county librarian on the grounds that she was a Protestant. The government insisted she be installed and when the Council proved obdurate, dissolved it.

The style of Cosgrave's administration was conservative and mildly protectionist (despite Hogan, who was more energetic than radical). In a series of economies during 1924 by which the budget was finally balanced, one shilling a week was struck off pensions for the blind. One minister, Patrick McGilligan, replying in a Dail debate to the charge that the government was failing to provide jobs, said: 'It is no function of government to provide work for anyone'. (In fact he did provide thousands of jobs in promoting the Shannon Scheme: see below.) Cosgrave and his colleagues on the whole dealt with day-to-day problems in an orthodox fashion and in terms of their inheritance of Sinn Fein policies. With one notable exception they were averse from any radical departures.

This exception was the Shannon Scheme: the most constructive venture, and one of the biggest political controversies, of the 'twenties. It entailed the creation of the first of the great state corporations which, with the state companies, are today an integral and distinctive feature of the Irish economy. (See chapter 7.) It was initiated by Dr T. A. MacLaughlin. He came back in 1923 from Berlin, where he had been working as an engineer for Siemens-Schuckert, with a plan for harnessing the Shannon to provide 110 million units of electricity a year. At that time the total production of electricity in the whole country was forty million units a year. Large centres like Sligo, Kilkenny, Drogheda, Tralee and Athlone had no electricity at all. Only about a third of Dublin, a quarter of Cork and a tenth of Limerick had electric power. Such electric power as there was came from privately operated generating stations. In 1923 movements were afoot proposing that the Liffey be developed by a group of businessmen as a source of power. These interests opposed the Shannon Scheme, which advocated the postponement and eventual amalgamation of their scheme within the bigger Shannon project.

MacLaughlin toured Ireland to compute the possible demand, carefully noting down the capacity of any machine he found providing power in every town and sizeable village of the country. His enquiries convinced him that the Shannon Scheme was practicable and he succeeded in getting sufficient support from the government (which, to its credit, did not need much persuading) for a group of experts from Sweden, Norway and Switzerland to be employed to make a report. This report bore out his findings. The project was first put to the Dail by Joseph McGrath; after his resignation in 1924 it was carried through by Patrick McGilligan, who as a parliamentarian ranks as one of the great vitriolics. Through the long hot summer of 1925, he excoriated the opposition to the scheme. This opposition was based on three main grounds: *cost* (£5 million—which in those days for a newfangled idea like electricity was thought wildly excessive); *chauvinism* (the whole thing was a German plot); and *impracticability* (Ireland could never use so much electricity; it wouldn't pay; it couldn't be done). Ranged with McGilligan and the forward-looking group was Gordon Campbell, secretary of the Department of Industry and Commerce, who drew up the white papers for the project. Probably the scheme's greatest single adversary was the Senate's first and most outstanding chairman, Lord Glenavy—Gordon Campbell's father.

After his resignation from the government (see below, page 57), Joseph McGrath became director of labour for the scheme. The construction work took four years. In the beginning it was marked by a strike in which the IRA intervened. But after a good deal of by-play—more notable for muscle than mediation—the strike was ended and the unprecedentedly large number of 4,000 men found employment on a single project, albeit at very low wages based on the current rate for road-workers. Some of the men got as little as 17s 6d a week.

The act setting up the Electricity Supply Board became law in 1927, and the scheme became operative on October 29, 1929. In 1964, 2,375·947 million units of electricity were used by 678,054 consumers. The Electricity Supply Board's capital had increased to £140 million, with an annual revenue of £22 million, and it employed over 9,000 people.

PROBLEMS OF THE NEW STATE

The Constitution which was born to the sound of gunfire was based, to quote Cosgrave, 'on the fundamental principle that all authority, legislative, executive and judicial, is derived from the people'. Presented to the electorate on the day before the election of 1922, the Constitution provided for a second house of the Oireachtas (parliament) to meet the demands of the Unionists in the Free State—who could roughly be defined as the old Protestant landlord and wealthy class. This second chamber, the Senate,* had the power to delay for up to nine months bills from the lower house (Dail), other than those defined as 'money bills', and to force a referendum in certain cases. It consisted of sixty members, many of whom had had their homes burned or been threatened with death during the Civil War. W. B. Yeats and Oliver Gogarty were original members of an assembly whose level of excellence since their day to our own (when one trusts it has reached its nadir) has shown a steady downward course.

In addition to the general desire of the people for peace, and the support it had from the Church, the new regime had a further vital asset in the quality of the civil service. The Free State was fortunate in being able to take over intact the system of British administration in Ireland, and from the start its civil service was modelled on British lines. Very few civil servants, relatively speaking, left at the change-over.

Nineteen twenty-four was a make or break year for the new administration. The government enjoyed a wide measure of confidence, as evidenced by the fact that a national loan of £40 million, floated in January 1924, opened at 95 and closed at 99. But the general economic situation in this year was so bad that the *Annual Register* estimated conditions in Connemara to be at their worst since 1879. The harvest was poor and turf supplies scanty because of the wet weather. The government sought to ease the situation by distributing supplies of turf and by giving food to schoolchildren. The cattle trade was restricted because of an outbreak of foot-and-mouth disease in England. Wage rates were deplorably low. Labour deputies in the Dail protested at the employment on County Council works of demobilised Free State soldiers on the grounds that this was resulting in other workers having to take cuts in pay of from 42 to 28 shillings a week. A similar 'economy measure', the reducing of the size of the army, was to confront the government with perhaps its greatest crisis.

The Army Mutiny of 1924

At the time, the full significance of the Army Mutiny, the existence of which was confirmed to the public by an official army communiqué on March 8, 1924, was appreciated by only a very small circle. Yet at times during its development, this crisis threatened to equal the Civil War in gravity. Before it finally blew over, the crisis had led to the resignation of two ministers and eight deputies, and to the removal of three of the most senior officers from the Army Council (though not from the army itself). It was also marked by a particularly ugly shooting incident.

The pot boiled over in March. The government had embarked on the

* The Irish term 'Seanad' did not come into use until after 1937.

process of cutting down the army from its peak Civil War strength of 55,000 troops and 3,300 officers to 18,000 men and 1,300 officers. March 7 marked the completion of the process by the demobilisation of 1,900 officers. The communiqué from army headquarters stated that two officers had been charged with mutiny but that the situation in the army was normal apart for incidents at Gormanston, Clonmel, Baldonnel and Roscommon, involving a small number of desertions and loss of arms. The government appointed the chief of police, General Eoin O'Duffy, as head of the armed forces. On March 11, the Dail was told that Joseph McGrath, minister for Industry and Commerce, was resigning. Cosgrave read out an ultimatum from the mutineers addressed to him.

Sir: On behalf of the IRA Organisation we have been instructed to present the following ultimatum to the Government of Saorstat Eireann:

Briefly our position is this. The IRA only accepted the Treaty as a means of achieving its objects—namely to secure and maintain a Republican form of Government in this country.

After many months of discussion with your Government it is our considered opinion that your Government has not these objects in view and that their [sic] policy is not reconcilable with the Irish people's acceptance of the Treaty.

Furthermore, our interpretation of the Treaty was that expressed by the late Commander-in-Chief, General Michael Collins, when he stated 'I have taken an oath of allegiance to the Irish Republic and that oath I will keep, Treaty or no Treaty'. We claim Michael Collins as our leader and again remind you that even after the Treaty was signed that drastic action was taken against enemies of the unity and complete independence of our country. Both in oath and honour bound, it is our duty to continue this policy, and therefore present this ultimatum, to which we require a reply by 12 noon, 10th March, 1924.

We demand a conference with representatives of your Government to discuss our interpretation of the Treaty on the following conditions:

(a) The removal of the Army Council;
(b) The immediate suspension of army demobilisation and reorganisation.

In the event of your Government rejecting these proposals we will take such action that [sic] will make clear to the Irish people that we are not renegades or traitors to the ideals that induced them to accept the Treaty.

Our Organisation fully realises the seriousness of the action that we may be compelled to take, but we can no longer be party to the treachery that threatens to destroy the aspirations of the nation.

LIAM TOBIN, Major-General, President of the Executive Council

C. F. DALTON, Col., Secretary to Executive Council

In the ensuing Dail debate, McGrath made a statement in which he launched a veiled attack on the handling of the whole affair by the Ministry for Defence. He said that he proposed to announce the full facts. But, *mirabile dictu*, the next day the Dail learned that a government proposal for an inquiry had not only apparently satisfied McGrath but also the mutineers. A letter from them was read which said that they were now satisfied that they had 'brought the matter sufficiently before the people and will consider [their] object achieved if, as a result of [their] action the Army situation is righted'. The opposition and the press clamoured for details, but though Kevin O'Higgins (who had taken over direction of affairs from Cosgrave, whose health had given way) admitted that the crisis had not burst on the government overnight, the opposition had to be content with a promise that the inquiry would 'lance the abscess'.

What had happened was that on March 11, the day after the affair had become public, the government and the mutineers, with McGrath acting as intermediary, had come to terms. These included the setting up of an inquiry into army administration. The existing members of the Army Council were to be replaced by neutral officers. Men with active service records were to be placed in jobs; there was to be no victimisation; officers and men who had deserted were to return to their posts with their arms; arrests and raids were to stop. The government seemed to have climbed down.

But at nine o'clock on March 16, troops surrounded a Dublin public house, Devlin's in Parnell Street, which had been one of Collins' rendezvous, and remained there until four in the morning. Joseph McGrath appeared on the scene and telephone conversations took place between him, Cosgrave and O'Higgins. McGrath bought drinks for a group of mutineering officers inside. Ten of these were arrested but the government forces failed to capture the ringleaders. The raid could have precipitated a bloodbath. Of the men inside the pub, several had been members of The Squad and all were armed. It was alleged afterwards that the raid had been made with the intention of provoking bloodshed. In the circumstances, McGrath's round of drinks seems to have been one of the most soothing purchases in Dublin pub history. On March 19, General Mulcahy resigned as minister for Defence. Apparently the Parnell Street raid was made without his authority.

Two days later, on March 21, came the ugly side of the affair. A party of unarmed British soldiers from Spike Island—one of the 'Treaty forts'—were coming ashore on leave at Cobh. Four men in Free State army uniforms who had been waiting, Chicago-fashion, in a large yellow car opened fire on them with submachine guns. They killed an eighteen-year-old private and wounded twenty-four civilians and army personnel. A £10,000 reward failed to bring any information about the murderers, who were described by an onlooker as 'four poor desperate rum-runners'. The government apologised to the British and compensated relatives.

The Mutiny had in fact been in preparation a long time before it broke to the public. The mutineers had seen Cosgrave and Mulcahy about their grievances as early as June 21, 1923. Since that time O'Higgins had built up the intelligence system which was ultimately to give the government control of the situation. Of the mutineers, the most notable were Liam Tobin and Tom Cullen, both major-generals in the Free State Army. Tobin had been a tailor's cutter before the War of Independence, and Cullen had worked as a grocer's assistant. Both developed a talent for intelligence work under Collins and were devoted to him.* With Collins dead, they were rudderless and objected to practically everything the government was doing. They strongly resented the 'Trucers': men who had joined the army during the Truce period or after it and had gained promotion. This category included well-trained officers formerly in the British forces; it also included the usual riff-raff who drift into every army after a revolution. They and their supporters fumed with indignation at the government's 'inaction' over Partition, and were zealous for a resumption of conflict with the British and for driving the Orangemen out of the North. The Cobh shooting was intended to start up again the fight against the British, though by then the mutineers had lost the initiative.

The government's handling of the crisis was at times inept. O'Higgins had to contend with the fact that both the cabinet and the ruling party were split over how the problem should be handled. And all the time the authorities knew that there was hovering in the wings another army (the IRA) made up of nationalist enthusiasts who had not surrendered their arms at the ending of the Civil War. The government first of all tried to re-create the Irish Republican Brotherhood as a powerful cabal within the army to counter the malcontents now bound up with the Irish Republican Army.

---

*They were likeable and popular, but living for years on their nerves had left its mark on them. Pictures of them with Collins showed three strained young men, all looking as though they slept in their clothes and badly needed a rest. One night in a raid on Vaughan's Hotel, Tobin and Cullen had escaped the Black and Tans by dangling by their fingertips from a windowsill for twenty minutes while their room was searched. They had taken part in the arrangements for prominent shootings, like those of Sir Henry Wilson and Alan Bell.

Failing in this, it seems then to have decided to resort to Fabian tactics until it could curb the mutineers effectively. The mutineers saw how things were going, and their ultimatum of March 6 was an attempt to force the issue. Possibly had the administration been more generous with demobilisation pay, the Mutiny might not have occurred. The awards were three months' pay with a supplementary grant of £250 to each demobilised officer with pre-Truce service. (I have been told by people in a position to know that, in fact, larger sums than these were paid to some officers, and that this finally allayed the mutinous spirit.)

With the withdrawal from the Dail of a group of eight deputies in a confused gesture of solidarity with the mutineers, the affair came to a peaceable close in October. These eight deputies seem to have been the main losers. In those days, work was hard to find; and, because of their loyalty to their friends, these unemployed former parliamentarians found themselves a drug on the labour market for some years afterwards. Tobin had better fortune. After leaving the army, he ran the Gresham Garage behind O'Connell Street, near to the spot where Cathal Brugha was shot. Later he took a post on the staff of the Dail. When he died in 1964, old Republican and Free State comrades walked together at his funeral.

The Mutiny affair had an interesting sequel. Some time before his assassination, O'Higgins bought some documents from an agent, including the originals of communications received from the mutineers during the crisis. They were in the handwriting of one of his government colleagues.

Partition and Agreement of 1925

As the army crisis died away, the Boundary Commission row blew up. According to the Treaty, the border between North and South was to be defined by a commission charged with delineating the frontier 'in accordance with the wishes of the inhabitants'. This would have meant, had a vote been taken, that at least two whole counties claimed by the Belfast government (Fermanagh and Tyrone) and portions of three others (Londonderry, Down and Armagh) would have gone to the South because of the predominance of Catholics in these areas. There were lively hopes in the Free State that the removal of these areas from Belfast's jurisdiction would eventually force the North to come under an all-Ireland legislature.

Following the royal signature of the Constitution of the Irish Free State Act on December 5, 1922, the North had acted on the provision in the Treaty that the powers of the Irish Free State should no longer extend to Northern Ireland provided that an address be presented to the king by both houses of the Northern parliament. The address was duly presented. The next step provided for by the Treaty was the setting up of the Boundary Commission composed of a representative from each of the Irish governments under a British-nominated chairman. But the North refused to nominate its representative. It was not until Ramsay MacDonald, then the British prime minister, and Cosgrave signed an agreement amending the Treaty (August 4, 1924) that the deadlock was broken—by the device of the British appointing a representative for the North. The commissioners were: chairman, Judge Feetham of South Africa; for the North, J. R. Fisher, an Ulsterman of clear Orange hue and a former editor of the *Northern Whig*, perhaps the strongest organ of Unionism; for the South, Dr Eoin MacNeill, minister for Education.

Nothing much was heard from the Boundary Commission for twelve months beyond reports that it was taking evidence. Then on November 7, 1925 the *Morning Post* published a forecast of the commission's findings to the effect that the Border would remain substantially as it was at the time of the Truce—save that the South would lose a portion of Donegal. Public opinion in the Free State was instantly inflamed. Though MacNeill resigned from the Boundary Commission a fortnight later, announcing that its findings would be indefensible, it was widely felt that he should have declared himself and Dublin have acted earlier. MacNeill gave up his ministerial portfolio. To the Anti-Treaty party, the whole affair was further proof that the Treaty was a disaster, and there were loud voices calling for renewal of the struggle. From the North Sir James Craig, the Ulster prime minister, offered his meed of sweetness and light by announcing that he was ready then, as he had been in 1914, 'to fight in the open against our enemies who would take away the loved soil of Ulster from any of the loyalists who want to remain there'. (*Belfast News Letter*, November 16, 1925.) All this, in conjunction with sabre-rattling on both sides of the Border by Republican and Orange extremists, created a tense atmosphere in which bloodshed seemed inevitable.

But a meeting convened in London on December 3 under the auspices of the British government reached an understanding and a clash was avoided. The Border Agreement was signed, for the British, by Baldwin (as prime minister), Churchill, Joynson-Hicks, Leo Amery and Lord Birkenhead (all members of the British cabinet); for the Free State, by Cosgrave, O'Higgins and Blythe; for Northern Ireland, by Craig and Charles Blackmore (secretary of the Ulster cabinet). Under its terms the Border stayed as it was, while the Free State was bound to make various contributions to the United Kingdom's public debt and to the payment of pensions to former members of the Royal Irish Constabulary.

The Agreement provoked enraged reactions from the Anti-Treaty side and the Irish Labour movement. Labour issued a statement condemning the Border settlement as 'an unmitigated betrayal', and upbraided the section relating to the war costs of the struggle for independence as a 'tacit admission that Ireland had no right to fight that war'. (The British asked for the cost of maintaining the forces which had shot Irishmen and burned Irish towns!) De Valera's party denounced the settlement as enshrining Partition. He and all members of his party who had been elected to the Dail (except four who were either abroad or in prison) signed a statement recording 'unalterable opposition to the partitioning of our country'. But as the Anti-Treaty deputies were still boycotting the Dail, the Border Agreement was passed easily, by seventy-one votes to twenty, on August 10, 1926. Stripped of all emotion, the Border Agreement meant that the Free State settled for less than the area which it and the Catholic population in the North had hoped for. Cosgrave and his colleagues bowed to it because there was no means short of bloodshed whereby the Orangemen would have given up the disputed areas.

The Army Mutiny and the Boundary Commission crisis left their marks on Irish politics. McGrath and the eight members of Cumann na nGaedheal who resigned from the Dail over the Mutiny were all defeated when they stood in subsequent by-elections as candidates of the National Party.* Mr Magenniss, a professor of metaphysics, split away from the government party over the Border Agreement and was supported by the National Party. He drew with him two members of the Dail and one senator. But neither fate nor metaphysical powers conspired to further his policy, which in fact merely consisted of being firmly 'agin the government'. His party, Clann Eireann, became an orphan of the political storm at the first election it contested.

In other sections of political affairs, more important developments were taking place. By an act of March 1925, in the civil service, in local government and in a wide variety of professional and other occupations, employment was made dependent on signing a declaration of allegiance to the Free State Constitution. The allocation of government grants to local authorities was also made conditional on their giving jobs on road repair and similar work to former Free State soldiers. The lines of division among Irishmen, drawn in battle, hardened under discriminatory practices as the government strove to keep the Free State free from subversion.

Rise of Fianna Fail

At the end of 1925 there came an open breach between the Irish Republican Army and de Valera. Finding his policy lacking the action it desired, the Convention of the IRA on November 14 withdrew support from him and from what might be called the 'constitutional wing' of the Anti-Treaty

---

* This is not to be confused with the National League, mentioned later, which sought to revive the traditions of the old Redmondite Irish National Party.

movement. It set up an army council and became an exclusively military organisation, devoted to ending Partition by force of arms. This development left de Valera and his supporters, still operating under the banner of Sinn Fein, with the choice either of continuing to refuse the Oath and thereby excluding themselves from public life, or of finding some way round the obstacle of the Oath and working through constitutional methods to secure its abolition.

A meeting with this latter end in view was held on March 9, 1926, but it failed to reach agreement. De Valera thereupon resigned from Sinn Fein. On May 16, at a gathering in the Scala Theatre, Dublin, he founded Fianna Fail (Warriors of Fal*). From, or even before, the breach with the IRA, it would appear to have been de Valera's policy to get Sinn Fein back on constitutional lines. Looking at the events from 1925 to 1927, a definite pattern emerges which ends inevitably with the entry of Fianna Fail to the Dail.

Fianna Fail's main plank at the first of the two general elections held the × following year (1927) was abolition of the Oath to the king as head of the Commonwealth. It also proposed to halt emigration by imposing protective tariffs so as to encourage Irish industry and trade, and to withhold the land annuities. Under a financial agreement of February 1923, confirmed by the Ultimate Financial Settlement of March 1926, Ireland had agreed to pay these to Britain in settlement of the sums paid by the latter in compensation to landowners under Land Acts of the past. These land annuities, together with debts contracted for in respect to RIC pensions, entailed on the Irish government obligations amounting to some £5 million a year.

By hiving off from Sinn Fein, Fianna Fail left the latter in the position of adhering grimly to the republic proclaimed by the First Dail in 1919 and of refusing recognition to both Irish parliaments—that in Dublin no less than that in Belfast. When de Valera withdrew from Sinn Fein, the bulk of its members followed him. It became so enfeebled that when Cumann na nGaedheal declared a second election in September 1927, Sinn Fein failed to raise enough gallop to run in the contest. This was ample vindication of de Valera's action in creating Fianna Fail.

The two elections of 1927 came very close together: June and September. The main contenders were Cumann na nGaedheal and Fianna Fail, but they had rivals in the shape of the National League, the Farmers' Party, the Labour Party and Independents of various kinds. The National League was founded in 1926 by Captain William Redmond, a son of John Redmond, leader of the old Nationalist Party at Westminster. The younger Redmond was, in fact, trying to revive this. The National League's main point was that Cosgrave and de Valera, with their parties, should retire from public life and leave the field to parties which had no connection with

* Fal is a poetic name for Ireland, derived from the *Lia Fail*, or Stone of Destiny.

the Civil War. Differing in most things, Cosgrave and de Valera were united in unheeding Captain Redmond's wishes.

The Farmers' Party, sponsored by the Irish Farmers' Union, on the whole represented only the bigger farmers. It was led by D. J. Gorey. For a time it made overtures to the National League (November 1926), but nothing came of the proposed alliance. It then made a pact to join with Cosgrave, but this was rejected by the congress of the Farmers' Union. The result was that Gorey and its secretary, M. P. O'Hanlon, resigned, leaving the party to face the election without any well-known figures. In the Dail it supported Cumann na nGaedheal against Labour but did not accept the government party's whip; moreover it was divided within itself in the controversy of free trade versus protection.

The Labour Party fought the election on a social and economic platform, and on the need for moving away from obsession with the Treaty in order to concentrate on material improvement. It was the official opposition party, led by Thomas Johnson and Cathal O'Shannon. Johnson, who was a courageous and intelligent leader in the Irish Labour movement during the terrible years before and after the Great Lock-out of 1913, was described as an opposition in himself. But he was too moderate a man in parliament to carry the mantle of Larkin and Connolly. He was born in England, and this—coupled with his moderation—made him the object of a good deal of radical Labour–Republican animosity. O'Shannon today, a revered, lively octogenarian, is the union representative on the Labour Court.

The Independents covered a wide field, representing Dublin University (or Trinity as it is generally known in Ireland), businessmen of a rightwing Unionist hue, and individualist Republicans.

The election of June 1927 gave Cumann na nGaedheal forty-seven seats; Fianna Fail forty-four seats; Labour Party twenty-two seats; Farmers' Party eleven; National League eight; Independents sixteen; Sinn Fein five. When the new Dail opened on June 23, Fianna Fail deputies entered parliament to take their seats, but the Clerk of the Dail stayed them, saying he had a 'little formality' for them to comply with first; that is, the Oath as required by Article 17 of the Constitution. When they refused, he had the doors of the chamber locked against them. The ensuing deadlock was resolved by Cosgrave's Electoral Amendment Bill introduced on August 10. Its purpose was to disqualify the election and make vacant the seats of deputies who failed to take the Oath.* This measure brought great pressure to bear on Fianna Fail, involving its members in a crisis of conscience, but

* The murder of Kevin O'Higgins on July 10 had disturbed the country profoundly, and had given a sharper urgency to the need for achieving much greater stability in Irish political life. Hence, the Cosgrave government considered it vital that the major opposition party should assume full parliamentary responsibility.

it enabled de Valera to make his leftwing accept the need for compromise while at the same time preserving a united front. Even before the bill was presented, two of his followers, Daniel Breen, a celebrated gunman, and Patrick Belton, a prominent businessman, had both taken the oath and entered the Dail as Independent Republicans. The bill (it never became an act) had important consequences for Irish democracy in that it compelled the second party in the state to accept a fully responsible role in the parliamentary system and made a change of administration possible in the future: an outcome which the Cosgrave ministry was clearly prepared for when introducing the bill.

On August 10, 1927 de Valera and the Fianna Fail deputies took their seats in the Free State Dail. Speaking in Irish, de Valera declared to the clerk of the chamber: 'I am not prepared to take the oath. I am not going to take an oath. I am prepared to put my name down in this book in order to get permission to go into the Dail, but it has no other significance.' There was a Bible on the table; he put this aside, saying: 'You must remember I am taking no oath'. Later he explained that he had signed the record 'in the same way that I would sign an autograph in a newspaper. If you ask me whether I had an idea of what was there, I say "yes". It was neither read to me nor was I asked to read it.' Thus, a new chapter opened in Irish politics.

It gave promise of being a chapter full of incident, for five days later de Valera almost succeeded in putting Cumann na nGaedheal out of office. A proposal for a coalition of Fianna Fail, Labour and the National League was agreed on by the leaders of the three parties, and a motion of no confidence in the government was moved by Labour. But in the course of the debate a member of the National League, Vincent Rice, KC, revolted against this alliance. His dissent from the coalition proposal transformed the situation, but it was left to the celebrated Alderman John Jinks to decide the matter.

On the morning of the crucial division, Major Bryan Cooper, an Independent from Jinks' home town of Sligo who had an idea that the Alderman was not altogether happy at voting for de Valera, called on Jinks at his hotel, bringing with him another celebrated Sligo man, Bertie Smyllie, editor of the *Irish Times:* a man who thought the heavens would fall if Fianna Fail got into power. They spent the morning and early afternoon talking over the matter—convivially. When Bryan Cooper came into the chamber in time for the voting, it was noted he was wearing a triumphant grin. He and Smyllie had left Jinks sound asleep in the hotel. It had been obvious from the start that Fianna Fail was preparing to dethrone the government, and Cosgrave was so certain he would be ousted that on the evening before the division he had given a farewell party for his staff. The opposition were in high feather; admittedly they could reckon on little more than a majority of one, but a majority is a majority and it seemed certain. But Jinks was still lapped in slumber in his room when the division was called. The result was a tie: seventy-one all. The chairman voted for the government and the Cosgrave administration was kept in power. A racehorse was named after Alderman Jinks—at Cosgrave's suggestion! (It won the Two Thousand Guineas in England in April 1929 and was hot favourite for that year's Derby; but it came nowhere.)

However, the government's position was too precarious in parliament and it called a second election on September 15. The result was a sharp blow to the smaller parties. Cumann na nGaedheal won sixty-two seats, a gain of fifteen; and Fianna Fail won fifty-seven seats, a gain of thirteen. Labour retained only thirteen, losing nine seats—including that of its leader, Tom Johnson. (One of the factors in his defeat was the presence of a communist candidate in the same county, which swung some former Labour voters against him.) The National League was well-nigh extinguished, its representation falling from six to two. The Farmers' Party's strength fell from eleven to six. Twelve Independents were elected and one Independent Labour. The issues were much the same as at the June election. The government stood on its record. Fianna Fail—though moderating its tone somewhat—still pressed for abolition of the Oath, for economies in the public services, for a tougher tariff policy, and for the retention of the Land Annuities. (As we shall see in the next chapter, the Land Annuity question was to be a major factor in Fianna Fail's eventual victory—and a major headache to its leaders when in power.)

Cumann na nGaedheal formed a new administration with the aid of the Farmers' Party, now led by M. R. Heffernan, a former Rugby international. He is today a most charming old gentleman, but in his youth a Welsh paper said of him after a particularly abrasive Irish victory: 'My God, what a coarse Christian that man is!'

The question of the Oath was resolved in the end, not by any radical change in internal Irish politics, but by a change in the character of the British Commonwealth. On December 11, 1931, the Statute of Westminster received the royal assent. The Statute implemented the resolution of the Imperial Conference of 1930 on the question of the co-equal relationship of the Dominions with the United Kingdom. The foundation of this definition of the relationship had been laid down at the Imperial Conference of 1926 and one of its chief architects had been Kevin O'Higgins. At the 1930 conference Ireland was represented by Patrick McGilligan, then minister for External Affairs.

By the Statute of Westminster, Ireland was declared to be a Dominion, and it laid down that 'the Parliament of a Dominion shall have power to repeal or amend any existing or future Act of Parliament of the United Kingdom insofar as the same is part of the law of the Dominion'. Churchill objected in the House of Commons on November 20, 1931 that this would give the Dail the right to repudiate the Treaty and all the articles of the Constitution, thereby making of the Free State 'an inexpressible anomaly'. He proposed an amendment to safeguard the British position, but this was defeated by 360 votes to 50. Accordingly, when de Valera came to power the way was clear for him to remove the obnoxious Oath simply by legislation in the Irish parliament (which he did by means of an act passed on May 3, 1933).

But by the date of the Imperial Conference giving Ireland full legislative sovereignty, the Wall Street crash had occurred and the world was in the grip of the great depression. All the Statutes of Westminster imaginable could make little impression on men faced with wage cuts and unemployment. In response to the economic situation, the extreme Republican wing now began to win recruits and flex its muscles. A new Republican organisation, splitting away from the main body of the movement, was set up to safeguard the purity of the Republican ideal: Comhairle na Poblachta, the Council of the Republic. Parallel with this development a new paper was born: *An Phoblacht* (The Republic). It would have been more fittingly styled *An Polemic*. As might have been expected, persons with their eyes set on wider revolutionary horizons also joined the extremists, and another organisation came into being: Saor Eire (Free Ireland). Saor Eire was one of those organisations which remind one of the advertisement for razors which shows a face smiling or scowling depending on whether it is held this way or that. The Catholic hierarchy declared Saor Eire to be communistic. Some of its founders have assured me that it was simply a radical socialist party within the Republican ethos. All the same, it was suppressed by the Public Safety Act of 1931. It may have been radical, but it was to show itself far from socialist when the health scheme controversy blew up after the second world war.

The wave of unrest gathered force and illegal drilling was carried on throughout the country. Jurors sitting on cases involving IRA men were intimidated to the point of attempted murder, and indeed witnesses in some of such cases were in fact murdered, one of them a police superintendent. *An Phoblacht* condemned the archbishop of Cashel's 'impertinence' in decrying this shooting. The government decided to risk *An Phoblacht's* disapproval and introduced a most drastic Public Safety Bill providing for the establishment of military courts with powers to award the death penalty and for the suppression of diverse Republican and left-wing organisations. On the night it came into force, October 31, 1931, some of the wildest wild geese ever to migrate from Irish shores flitted from the country. The political controversy engendered by these measures was intense and two members of the Labour Party who voted for it—Daniel Morrissey and Richard S. Anthony—were expelled by their colleagues. Hostility to the Public Safety Bill was one of the factors involved in the Cosgrave government's defeat.

With the world depression worsening, the economic situation in Ireland became grimmer. Her agricultural produce piled up with the shrinking of former markets. Between 1928 and 1931 exports of bacon and butter fell by almost half, and egg exports dropped by a third. Between 1924 and 1931 cattle prices fell from £4 7s per cwt to £3 9s. The price of a sheep plunged from £5 13s to £3 14s 6d in the same period, which also saw the closing down of 117 factories: a fearful blow to a nation already suffering from chronic unemployment in the towns. The figures of registered unemployed rose from 21,521 in April 1929 to 31,374 in April 1932. The government strove to deal with the crisis by emergency measures. The fact that these were akin to the desperate solutions being attempted in other countries did not make them more likely to win friends and influence people in Ireland. Measures were taken to reduce police and teachers' pay and to prevent married women from being teachers. The hostility against the government aroused by the economic crisis and the measures taken to deal with it was intensified by the charge of seditious libel against the pro-Fianna Fail *Irish Press* for its publicising complaints against the police. The case was heard by the Military Tribunal, the evidence in which provided powerful anti-government propaganda. Moreover, the Cosgrave administration had been in office for ten years and there was a general feeling, apart from any other motive, that the country was due for a change.

The Dail was legally able to continue until October 1932. But the fifteen-hundredth anniversary of Saint Patrick's coming to Ireland and the Eucharistic Congress were both to be celebrated in June of that year; it was generally agreed that neither Saint Patrick nor the Eucharistic Congress would be suitably honoured if celebrated against a backcloth of ferocious election campaigning. This sensitivity to election atmosphere was not affected, for in the early years of the new state the campaigning really was ferocious. A distinguished Irish journalist, Edward Lawler, calling at the office of J. J. Walsh (Cumann na nGaedheal's director of elections) immediately before an election in the 'twenties, found him by a table heaped with brass knuckledusters, dealing them out to election workers. It was not unusual for men to have a jaw broken or an eye knocked out in the fights that were almost de rigueur at political meetings. The election date was accordingly brought forward to February 16, 1932.

As it turned out, this contest was relatively tranquil.* But the result was a dramatic change. Fianna Fail beat Cumann na nGaedheal by seventy-two seats to fifty-seven, Labour winning seven, Farmers' Party four, Independents eleven, and Independent Labour two. On March 9, 1932, de Valera, with the support of Labour, formed an administration. He was elected president of the Executive Council by a Dail vote of eighty-one to sixty-eight. He took charge of the Department for External Affairs. Sean T. O'Kelly became vice-president of the Executive Council and minister for Local Government. The other ministers were: Frank Aiken (*Defence*); James Geoghegan, KC (*Justice*); Patrick J. Ruttledge (*Lands and Fisheries*); Sean F. Lemass (*Industry and Commerce*); Thomas Derrig (*Education*); and Senator Joseph Connolly (*Posts and Telegraphs*). There was no minister for Home Affairs at this time, most of its functions being exercised by the Department of Justice.

* Ironically it was the Eucharistic Congress rather than the election which gave occasion for violence. Ulster Protestants attacked Catholics returning to their homes in the North after attending the Congress.

4. REIGN OF DE VALERA 1932–48

'The Chief' · The 'Thirties: *Tilting the Crown;*
The Economic War; Fine Gael; IRA, ACA and Blueshirts;
New Constitution of 1937; London Agreements of 1938
The 'Forties: *Neutrality 1939–45; Political Parties 1943–48*

AS Irish politics were extremely complicated during the 'thirties, a few general introductory observations about the atmosphere of the times may help to make the picture clearer. When de Valera took power, both Fianna Fail and the Republican movement felt as though a crucifix had burst into flower. His opponents felt that they were going to be crucified on it.

Substance was added to these fears by incidents like the following. On August 20, 1932 *An Phoblacht* published a resolution passed by the Fianna Fail *cumann* (branch) in Culdaff, County Donegal, which asked if the government, having failed to show any sense of justice by retaining the man's services, would not at least withdraw the police guard on Judge Cahir Davitt (a son of the founder of the Land League). It had been widely believed by Republicans that when Fianna Fail got in, judges who had had the duty, like Davitt, of sentencing them under Cumann na nGaedheal, would be dismissed along with Pro-Treaty civil servants, police and army officers. On November 10, 1932 the IRA leader, Frank Ryan, gave expression in a speech in Dublin to a sentiment which became accepted philosophy for many IRA men. 'No matter what anyone says to the contrary, while we have fists, hands and boots to use, and guns if necessary, we will not allow free speech to traitors.'

On the Fianna Fail side, there were widespread rumours that elements in Cumann na nGaedheal would not allow them to take office. Accordingly, as the Fianna Fail deputies filed into the government benches, almost every man of them carried a revolver in his pocket. But, though they may have hated their erstwhile Civil War enemies, men like Cosgrave and Mulcahy loved democracy.

On the other side, de Valera was widely accused of being a dictator. Yet when the total disarray of his opponents gave him the opportunity, he introduced, not a dictatorship, but a new democratic Constitution. This, however, came later in the decade. Great unease was aroused in his government's early years by its efforts to promote order through recruiting an armed police force and seizing (in July 1933) firearms, even those held under licence by former ministers of the opposition side. Such fears, stimulated by the IRA's policy of breaking up Cumann na nGaedheal election meetings, were largely responsible for the uprise of the Blueshirt movement, described later.

Finally, it should be noted that, though in retrospect Fianna Fail's triumph seems inevitable, it was not at all certain in the first three years. Admittedly, given de Valera's personality and leadership, the homogeneous Fianna Fail was in a strong position in confrontation with the main opposition party, weakened by the deaths of the colourful figures so essential to political success in a new state: Collins, Griffith, Hogan and O'Higgins. But the opening period of de Valera's reign was far from an easy supremacy of power. The deep hostility of Cumann na nGaedheal; the dangerous support of the IRA; the effects of the Economic War with Britain; the slump conditions of the 'thirties—all this made the first year a highly uncertain obstacle race, by no means a smooth path to power.

'THE CHIEF'

De Valera's victory marked the beginning of a new era in Irish politics. His party, Fianna Fail, after its success in 1932 was not defeated until 1948, and by 1951 it was back again in power. Throughout the greater part of the 'thirties and 'forties, and indeed afterwards, de Valera was the dominant figure in Irish life. From the time of the 1916 Rising he had been the greatest single emotive force in the country. From 1932 he became the greatest political force also.

People regarded themselves as supporters of de Valera first and of Fianna Fail second. Without him there could have been no Fianna Fail. Eagle-profiled, appearing at meetings on a white horse, his spare frame dressed in a flowing black cloak, he seemed to his followers to be Emmet, Parnell and Pearse combined in one person. Along with his striking presence there went a masterly political acumen. He was accused of many things by his opponents in Ireland and elsewhere, but never of incompetence in the political art. In particular he never mishandled his main electoral support: the small farmers and rural labourers.

In many ways he resembled Pearse in his piety, his idealised view of Ireland, his devotion to the Gaelic language and culture. In a radio broadcast to the nation on March 17, 1943, he spoke words which give us a key both to his public and private personality.

The Ireland which we have dreamed of would be the home of a people who valued material wealth only as the basis of a right living, of a people who were satisfied with frugal comfort and devoted their leisure to the things of the spirit; a land whose countryside would be bright with cosy homesteads, whose fields and villages would be joyous with the sounds of industry, with the romping of sturdy children, the contests of athletic youths, the laughter of comely maidens; whose firesides would be forums for the wisdom of old age. It would, in a word, be the home of a people living the life that God desires men should live.

Pearse's mother saw him as her son's inheritor, and died with his name on her lips.

But he was a more complex figure than Pearse. He was more like Parnell in being a conservative constitutionalist and at the same time leader of a revolutionary movement. The other great political influence on him was Machiavelli, whom he studied closely. Perhaps the Florentine was responsible for the curious impression de Valera gave of what I can only describe as indecisive intransigence. His approach to a difficult problem was always to weigh up a multitude of possibilities, and this in such a way as to give the appearance of vacillation. But then, once a decision had been arrived at, he pursued his chosen course allowing himself to be deflected by nothing and nobody.

Austere in his devout Catholicism, he always appealed to women, who felt that they could trust a man who led such an exemplary life. When his son Brian was killed in a riding accident in the Phoenix Park in 1936, he made no public display of grief. The furrows around his mouth grew a little deeper, that was all. He has borne with equal fortitude the intermittent blindness afflicting him the last twenty years.

But, if at times he came near to deification, he was vilified more bitterly than any Irish leader since Parnell. His opponents centred all the blame for the Civil War on his head, and the speeches he made against the Treaty were flung back at him with antiphonal regularity during his parliamentary career. As with Parnell, he was always referred to as 'The Chief'. Even today no one would dare to call him 'Dev' or 'Eamon' to his face—except perhaps his wife Sinead, probably the most popular woman in Irish public life, although she has consistently avoided publicity.* Her husband's

---

* Janey Flanagan (Sinead is the Irish for Jane) was one of the most popular girls in the Gaelic League, with her long golden hair, her charm and vivacity. After classes, groups of six or eight escorts were always on hand to see her home. A friend said to one of the young men: 'It must be cold comfort for you to be one of eight seeing Janey home?' The gallant replied: 'I'd rather be one of eight with Janey than alone with anyone else'. (Tragically, if further evidence of the heartbreak of those days be needed, he was one of those whom the Treaty set in conflict against de Valera.)

favourite private relaxations were walking in the mountains (to the torture of his bodyguard) and mathematics. The theatre interested him only slightly; the cinema not at all. But he made a Roosevelt-like use of the radio for political purposes.

Yet he was not a good orator so far as delivery went, and he had a marked tendency to repetition. But the effect of his personality was, and still is, uncanny. Time after time, visiting journalists landed in Dublin resigned to (or professionally relishing) the prospect of scarifying interviews, only to come away starry-eyed, telling the local inhabitants what a wonderful person they had got for leader of Ireland. Today, removed from the bitterness of the past, young people are free to admire his integrity and regard him as the great old warrior who can talk for twenty-five minutes without notes to a joint session of Congress, or leave a nursing home (as in March 1965) to deliver a long, strong-voiced oration standing bare-headed on a sleety day by the grave of his friend and fellow patriot, Roger Casement.

Eamon de Valera was born in New York in 1882, the son of Vivion de Valera, a Spanish musician whose father was a prosperous sugar planter in Cuba, and of Catharine, née Coll, of Bruree in County Limerick. His father died when he was a child of two. At about the same time, his maternal uncle, Edmund Coll, got malaria. Ordered home to Bruree to convalesce, Edmund took his infant nephew with him. A few days after the boat sailed, his paternal grandfather arrived to take him to Cuba. The mind boggles at the thought of what the history of that troubled isle would have been had old de Valera arrived in New York earlier. It is extremely improbable that de Valera, with or without beard, would have allowed Khrushchev to put his rockets there; but it is morally certain that if he had so agreed, not Kennedy himself would have got them out again. It is awesome to think of two men of the calibre of Kennedy and de Valera confronting one another across the Tropic of Cancer.

Bruree was notable for being one of the few places in Ireland (or in Western Europe for that matter) in which a Soviet was formed during the troubles.* The young de Valera was reared by Patrick Coll, Edmund's

---

* In May 1920 workers at Knocklong in County Limerick settled a strike by setting up a Soviet! For a few weeks, the local Trades Council ran the town, issuing ration cards to the people and commandeering the means of production. Their example was followed at Bruree where the workers declared: 'We make bread, not profits'. However, with Connolly dead and Larkin in America, the moderates in the trade union leadership, who eventually became controllers of the movement, praised these socialistic experiments with faint damns, and they came to nothing. When in the following year dockers at Cork went on strike for a minimum wage and improved the shining hour by proclaiming a Soviet, the Dail intervened. The dispute was settled largely through the mediations of Countess Markievicz.

brother: a nationalist who, prior to 1916, supported Labour. De Valera accordingly grew up in an atmosphere of politics. He steadily made his way by scholarships from Bruree National School to Blackrock College, the school of the Holy Ghost Fathers in County Dublin. Here he later taught mathematics after graduating from the old Royal University and spending a year at Trinity. At school he was always somewhat apart from his fellows. Hurling, yes; pitch and toss, no. He and a friend developed a curious pastime of digging for springs in the summer evenings.

He joined the Gaelic League and became involved, first in the Volunteers and then in the IRB. In the Rising he commanded the key point of Boland's Mill—whence, as the last commandant to surrender, he stepped out on to the stage of history.

THE 'THIRTIES

Tilting the Crown

Once in power, Fianna Fail immediately set about implementing its election pledges. These were, principally, to abolish the Oath of Allegiance to the British Crown; to retain in Ireland the sums due to the British government in respect to settlement of the land annuities embodied in the Treaty; to release the IRA prisoners; and to establish new industries. This programme was interrupted by a fresh general election ten months after Fianna Fail came to power, but the bill to abolish the Oath was introduced on April 20, 1932. It got through the Dail but was ravaged by the Senate, becoming law only after much travail in May 1933. With its passing, a cause —though not an effect—of the Civil War disappeared.

Along with abolishing the Oath, de Valera set about demeaning the office of governor-general. After a number of official insults were offered to the office—though not the man, James McNeill, a well-liked former British civil servant—the governor-general was dismissed on October 3, 1932. The dismissal followed an exchange of letters between the governor-general and de Valera, who, as president of the Executive Council, had given a state reception for guests at the Eucharistic Congress without inviting the Crown's representative. The letters were subsequently published by McNeill, despite attempts by the government to suppress them. Referring to the reception insult and other incidents, McNeill protested at the 'calculated discourtesy to the Governor-General from whom you received your appointments'.

The official government announcement of the dismissal said: 'In accordance with the advice tendered to His Majesty by the President of the Executive Council, the King has approved of Mr James McNeill relinquishing the office of Governor-General of the Irish Free State'. The announcement of his replacement came from the High Commissioner's office in London on November 26. 'His Majesty the King, on the advice of the Executive Council of the Irish Free State, has appointed Domhnall Ua Buachalla, Esq. to the Office of Governor-General of the Irish Free State.' Buachalla, a veteran of 1916, had been a defeated Fianna Fail candidate in 1927 and 1932. He performed only rubber-stamp functions and lived in a private house, the Vice-Regal Lodge being left vacant. (It subsequently became the residence of de Valera himself as president of the Republic.) The whole style of the new administration was away from Edwardian formalism. De Valera and his ministers appeared at state functions in lounge suits and eschewed top hats. This gave the party something of a 'cloth cap' image which it was careful to discourage in the later 'fifties and the 'sixties. De Valera's personal style has always been as formal and remote as de Gaulle's, if not more so.

The main social and economic measures introduced were tariff encouragement for farmers to grow wheat (until then a crop little cultivated in Ireland); widows' and orphans' pensions (introduced in 1935); unemployment assistance (1933); and the initiation of a house-building campaign which saw the creation of 132,220 houses between 1932 and 1942. Far more so than its predecessor, the de Valera administration was protectionist, seeking to build up industries in the shelter of tariff walls and discouraging foreign investment. New factories were located mainly in rural areas so as to avoid concentration of industries in a few centres and to provide new employment opportunities in the countryside.

On the political front, de Valera (as we shall see) introduced a new Constitution which eliminated the monarchy from the superstructure of the Irish state; fought an economic war against Britain; extinguished the Blueshirts, a militant rightwing movement; and pursued a shadowy—but, all things considered, an effective—policy towards the IRA. Apart from a spurt of ameliorative legislation in the early 'thirties, social reform did not become one of Fianna Fail's priorities until the election of 1965. This saddened a good many of the party's supporters, but perhaps the thing which gave some of its adherents the most heartache was the lack of success in reviving the Irish language: an explosive subject which is dealt with separately in chapter 9.

The Economic War

The 'Economic War' arose out of the question of the land annuities which became a matter of acute dissension between Ireland and Britain following the victory of Fianna Fail in 1932. De Valera, with memories of the Boundary Commission, refused to accept arbitration from a tribunal composed of representatives of other states in the British Commonwealth; while the British for their part refused to be bound by an international body composed of other than Commonwealth citizens. The Economic War began in July 1932, with the Irish defaulting on the annuity payments due on July 1. The British retaliated with a bill, enacted on July 11, whereby the government of the United Kingdom was empowered to recoup the moneys due to it under the Treaty by imposing extra duties on imports from Ireland. The Irish responded with a similar bill, passed on July 23. Battle was now joined. Many were the glad hearts among staunch Republicans at the prospect of having 'another go at England'—even if it meant Ireland's getting some hard knocks in the process.

The land annuity problem stemmed from the settlement of the land question by the Land Acts of 1891 to 1909. Landowners were bought out by the state, government loans for the purpose being raised, and their former property distributed among the peasantry. The government stock given the landowners in exchange for the land bore three per cent interest. The rent paid by the new owners was termed 'land annuity' and was collected by the government as a defrayal of the interest charge. More and more land gradually came into the hands of the peasantry up to 1914, but the post-war economic situation, and particularly the fall in gilt-edged stock, deterred landowners from making available more land in return for government stock. As a result, the process of land subdivision ceased and the First Dail found its prosecution of the struggle against Britain impaired by agrarian unrest. Robert Barton, minister for Agriculture, suggested that a loan be floated and a Land Bank set up. Collins as minister for Finance supported him and the National Land Bank was founded in August 1919.

Its first purchase was that of the Lewen estate in County Meath in 1920, at a cost of £10,000. This managed to alleviate the worst of the land hunger in that area. In Waterford, however, the delay in land distribution, coupled with the strike over agricultural wages, gave rise (as we saw in chapter 3) to a land war: shootings, cattle drives and so forth. The Land Act of 1923 abolished the Land Bank and set up in its stead the Land Commission, which put the question of land distribution on a formal state-sponsored basis. The commission acquired land and subdivided it, while the Irish government was responsible to England for payment of the land annuities. Under the Free State, and until de Valera took office, the annuities were paid to the British National Debt commissioners under the terms of the British and Irish Financial Agreement of February 1923 and of the Ultimate (ill-chosen word!) Financial Settlement of March 1926. The second was published eight months after it had been signed; the first not until Fianna Fail came to power. Neither was ever submitted to the Free State parliament. Other payments became involved in the dispute: the annual contribution of Ireland to the British Local Loans Fund and the defraying of 75 per cent of the cost of RIC pensions. Both these payments, involving some £2 million annually, had been agreed to by Cosgrave in the financial agreements of 1923 and 1926.

By 1938, the Economic War had cost Ireland some £48 million. In the first year of the conflict alone, imports fell from £42·5 to £35·75 million, while exports went down from £27 to £19·5 million. A loan of £1 million at $3\frac{1}{2}$ per cent, floated by the government, flopped. In 1933 legislation was passed cutting the pay of public officials. Emigration to Britain fell off as the hungry 'thirties there became hungrier, and in Ireland unemployment reached in 1935 the peak figure of 138,000 per annum. The figure in 1931 had been 28,934; by 1933 it had risen to 95,577, but since it was in this year that the Unemployed Assistance Act enabled small farmers to sign on for the 'dole', the figures both for it and subsequent years are probably in part artificial. The figure for 1935, however, seems 'solid' enough. The wage of the agricultural labourer sometimes dropped as low as from 12s 6d to 8s a week for a seven-day week, and work in summer time often began before 5 a.m. Although the national average wage was higher than this, at almost all levels wages dropped sharply.

De Valera countered the effects of the Economic War on the poorer classes by distributing free meat. Cattle prices fell away to practically nothing, but some help was given by a subsidy scheme launched in 1934 which gave a bonus of 10s on each head of slaughtered cattle. Even so—and making due allowance for the fall in money values since then—an official of the National Farmers' Association calculated for me that a calf which today would fetch about £25 would then fetch only 12s 6d.

Fine Gael

While the Economic War was the major external development of the 'thirties for Ireland, some major developments took place within the country also—constitutionally and unconstitutionally.

The constitutional events began in October 1932 when a new party, the Irish Centre Party, was formed under the joint leadership of James Dillon and Frank MacDermot, which to all intents and purposes subsumed the old Farmers' Party. Dillon, a businessman and, from 1959 to 1965, leader of the main opposition to Fianna Fail, is the son of John Dillon who succeeded John Redmond as leader of the old Irish Parliamentary Party. MacDermot, now retired from politics, comes of a 'county' family and was educated in England. He served as an officer in the British army during the first world war and is a former New York banker. The Centre Party represented the interests of big farmers. Its objectives included the ending of Partition by a policy of goodwill to the North and the removal of Civil

War rancour. It made an immediate appeal to the middle-of-the-road voter.

This development was in part a reflection of a general uncoördinated feeling in many quarters that all the opposition parties should form one group, with a policy based on better relations with Britain. With the Centre Party making a serious bid for political influence, this feeling gained strength and took tangible shape. A meeting called by the lord mayor of Dublin on December 29, 1932, and attended by prominent citizens, passed a resolution urging that such a coalition of forces be formed. De Valera viewed these proceedings with something less than joy and four days later the Dail was dissolved. At the ensuing election (January 24, 1933) Fianna Fail won seventy-seven seats, and de Valera formed a new administration with the support of Labour, which had won eight seats. (A curious feature of this election was that, although Labour dropped nearly 19,000 first preferences, under PR it gained a seat.) Cumann na nGaedheal had only forty-eight candidates returned. The Centre Party and the Farmers' Party, now in alliance, won seven and four seats respectively. There were nine Independents elected.

Balancing the Fianna Fail–Labour link-up, on September 8, 1933 Cumann na nGaedheal and the Centre Party completed the merger interrupted by the election. The new party was known as the United Ireland Party; its name in Irish, Fine Gael, means Tribe of Gaels. It eventually became generally known as Fine Gael. Cosgrave was its parliamentary leader, assisted by Dillon and MacDermot. But its overall national leadership was entrusted to a man who had no parliamentary seat and never won one: General Eoin O'Duffy, whom Fianna Fail had dismissed the previous February from his post as commissioner of police.

O'Duffy seemed an ideal choice to the architects of the new party. Centre Party supporters had earlier shown little enthusiasm for uniting under Cosgrave, who had been twice defeated in elections. O'Duffy, on the other hand, though having no experience of politics whatever, was well known throughout the country as a military figure, a police officer and a celebrated sports organiser, particularly of cycling. Moreover it was thought that, having been fired by de Valera, O'Duffy would give a tinge of martyrdom to the new party, which it was hoped would present an electoral shading attractive to all elements opposed to Fianna Fail. However, the shade which came to be associated with the mercurial general literally made his leadership a blue look-out for the plodding but democratic constitutionalists of Fine Gael.

The party's policy was declared to be: 'The voluntary reunion of all Ireland in a single independent State, as a member, without abatement of Irish sovereignty, of the British Commonwealth of Nations in free and equal partnership'. It also planned to abolish PR and to set up agricultural and industrial corporations.

So much for orthodox political developments. Outside the party arena much that was far from orthodox was to take place.

IRA, ACA and Blueshirts

On coming into office in 1932, Fianna Fail had immediately made good its promise to 'release the prisoners'. The IRA prisoners at Arbor Hill barracks were set free, and the drastic public safety measure of the Cosgrave administration was revoked. By removing the Oath, by introducing in 1934 a volunteer force ancillary to the regular army in order to give young men an outlet for military ardour, and by granting in the same year pensions to those who had fought on the Anti-Treaty side, de Valera hoped that the IRA's fangs would be drawn—and in a manner which would not offend its supporters within his own party. When IRA activities became too extreme, the culprits were punished; but unless the misdemeanours were flagrant, the authorities avoided taking action which would have made martyrs of them. These moves were eventually successful. Given enough rope, the IRA finally hanged itself.

But for a time it was a serious threat. A hard core still sought the abolition of Partition by force of arms. This hard core maintained towards Fianna Fail an attitude which was interpreted by Cumann na nGaedheal as outright collusion. The IRA's leaders saw in it nothing more than a toleration of the government's policies so long as it took good care not to interfere with the IRA. Many IRA men at election time would vote for Fianna Fail and some would go so far as to campaign for its candidates. Towards Cumann na nGaedheal, which had executed friends and relations both of IRA and Fianna Fail supporters, the attitude of the hard core in the IRA was one of unrelenting hostility. Under the slogan of 'No Free Speech for Traitors', the IRA organisation pursued a policy of breaking up Cumann na nGaedheal's election meetings, particularly those of Cosgrave and Mulcahy. There was at this time a strong element in Fianna Fail which favoured these tactics, having been chagrined at de Valera's laudable refusal to initiate a purge of 'Staters' from the army, police and civil service when he took power. The police, unarmed and too few in number, were unable to prevent or control these violent disturbances of the peace. The IRA vendetta against the Treatyites provoked a reaction in kind: the Army Comrades Association, which in turn developed into the Blueshirt movement.

The Army Comrades Association, founded in August 1932 by Thomas O'Higgins, a brother of Kevin O'Higgins, was another 'smiling-scowling advertisement' organisation. To the IRA, it was a fascist body organised prior to Fianna Fail's victory in 1932 to prevent the transference of power from Cumann na nGaedheal to de Valera's party. To Cumann na nGaedheal, the ACA was a body of upright defenders of free speech, men who donned blue shirts only in order to recognise each other and prevent embarrassing mistakes in the flourishing of knuckledusters at election meetings. There is a certain basis of truth in both viewpoints. Before the 1932 election, a series of meetings was indeed held at which certain senior civil servants, army and police officers discussed plans to disregard the election result should it be unfavourable and set up a military dictatorship under General O'Duffy, the commissioner of police. But ACA links (if any) with these meetings are hard to establish, and its leaders held that the movement was nothing other than a benevolent association of ex-servicemen formed from former Free State soldiers.

The ACA and the IRA soon came into conflict. Some IRA members decided to add their support to the Economic War and a boycott committee was set up. The products of Bass, the English brewing firm, were singled out for attack after a senior executive of the firm had been reported as making hostile comments on Ireland and the Irish. Following the example of somewhat similar proceedings at Boston, Massachusetts, some years previously, a Dublin Ale Party took place on December 14, 1932. A lorry-load of Bass was poured away and the barrels burned. On the face of it this was a catastrophic error of judgement by a movement which hoped to win the public sympathy of Ireland. Wasting drink! The Dublin vintners who had imported the ale appealed to the ACA for protection, and subsequent movements of Bass's cherished liquid were guarded by men of the ACA to the frustration of those colloquially known as the Basstards. By this time the ACA had a membership of about 30,000.

General O'Duffy was dismissed from his post as commissioner of police, reputedly for incompetence, on February 22, 1933. The fears which this aroused among supporters of Cumann na nGaedheal (which, as we saw, became Fine Gael later in the year) have to be seen in the light of the fact that the side which the Cosgravites were now uncomfortably aware of having defeated in war had become the rulers of the country. The police force had been unable to prevent their election meetings from being broken up even with O'Duffy as commissioner. What would things be like now he was sacked from the police force? It was decided to reorganise the ACA and appoint O'Duffy as its leader. The transformation took place in April 1933. Comforting as this was to minds in Cumann na nGaedheal, it was viewed with displeasure, to put it mildly, by both Fianna Fail and the IRA.

The stage was thus set for a tense period of struggle between the ACA and the IRA, and of efforts by the government to contain both of them. One outcome of the government's policy was a bewildering series of name-changes by the ACA. On O'Duffy's acceptance of the leadership, it became known as the National Guard. At the suggestion of Commandant Ned Cronin (who had married Kitty Kiernan, the ex-fiancée of Michael Collins), the National Guard adopted the blue shirt as its official uniform. Its object was to safeguard 'national interests and national culture'. It would wear the blue shirt but keep within the law. 'Illegalities will not be tolerated. Physical drill will be practised only as a means of promoting good health, character and discipline.'

As his first show of strength, General O'Duffy announced that on August 13, 1934 he would hold a march of the National Guard to Government Buildings to revive the ceremony of wreath-laying at a cross in memory of Griffith, Collins and O'Higgins. Uneasily aware of how Mussolini had become Il Duce, the government suspected O'Duffy might feel disposed to linger when he got as far as Government Buildings. Accordingly, it revived the Public Safety Act of 1931 which had contributed so much to Cosgrave's defeat. The s-division was set up,* the Military Tribunal revived, and the parade banned. Had it been held in defiance of the ban, there might well have been a bloodbath for, apart from the s-division, the IRA had threatened to make an armed attack on the marchers. The Blueshirts, nominally at least, were an unarmed force, whereas the IRA was known to have large stocks of weapons and ammunition. By the end of the struggle, however, the Blueshirts certainly had some guns, and neither side was short of coshes and knuckledusters.

Banned after the abortive parade, the National Guard changed its name to Young Ireland, still retaining the blue shirts. The Young Ireland movement was banned in its turn after clashes between it and the IRA. It then became known as the League of Youth. The administration tried various legal moves to have O'Duffy restrained, but without success; when it put him in gaol, the Fine Gael lawyers immediately got him out. It had earlier introduced a bill prohibiting the wearing of uniforms, but this the Senate had rejected on March 24, 1934, on the grounds that it hindered the free expression of opinion. However, by the time its statutory suspension period had elapsed the following year, there was no need to proceed with the bill because by then both the Blueshirts and the IRA had been crippled by internal schisms.

O'Duffy was a first-class military organiser but an inexpert politician. As a friend said to him: 'When you stick to your notes you're the greatest speaker going, but let someone in the crowd shout "Up Dev", and you lose

* The s-division was an armed branch of the police force recruited from former Anti-Treaty members of the IRA. It was colloquially known as the 'Broy Harriers', after Colonel Eamonn Broy, Collins' informant in the old G-division of the British administration. Broy succeeded O'Duffy as commissioner of police.

your head entirely'. The Blueshirt movement began to break up when the League of Youth's first annual congress passed a resolution calling on farmers to withhold the land annuities. Fianna Fail, of course, had a mandate from the electorate for withholding the annuities from the British government, but the League resolution proposed withholding them from the Irish government as well. This served to bring to a head the dissatisfaction with O'Duffy's leadership. After a series of rows and resignations, he was ousted in September 1934 from the leadership both of Fine Gael and the League of Youth. He was succeeded as leader of the League by Commandant Cronin, whereupon the organisation split, some following O'Duffy, some Cronin. O'Duffy's section changed its name in 1935 to the National Corporate Party and adopted a programme which, abandoning the Commonwealth idea, called for a Republic. The following year O'Duffy formed an Irish Brigade which fought for Franco in the Spanish Civil War. The Blueshirt movement vanished from Irish politics in October 1935 when Cronin failed in his efforts to keep the League of Youth alive as a separate organisation from both Fine Gael and O'Duffy.

O'Duffy had some curious traits. He was terrified of women, but his bluff, friendly personality made him a figure in the land rivalling de Valera for a short time. As well as being welcomed for a period by the main opposition parties whose desire to oust de Valera made them willing to accept O'Duffy's leadership, he also attracted the support of a number of intellectuals. Yeats—at heart a man of the right—was so greatly taken with him that he wrote a marching song for the Blueshirts. The movement's eponymous organ—a paper of thunderous boredom—attracted a wide circulation for a time. The idea of the corporate state was publicised (in the organ of the constitutional wing of the movement, *United Ireland*) by reputable scholars, like James Hogan, professor of history at University College, Cork (and a brother of the minister for Agriculture in Cosgrave's government) and Professor Michael Tierney, who afterwards became president of University College, Dublin. The support of these Mosca-like figures crumbled before the onrush of the general's megalomania, vanishing altogether at the implications of the land annuities resolution. Both of them had inclined more towards Fine Gael and the parliamentary side of the movement than towards Blueshirtism, although their writings did convey an impression of fascism to the leftwing IRA men.

'The Corporate State must come in the end to Ireland as elsewhere', wrote Tierney on December 13, 1933. Hogan wrote the most celebrated articles, which were later published in a booklet, *Could Ireland Go Communist?* The answer was that it could if the IRA and Fianna Fail were not replaced by Fine Gael. But, like a number of committed Catholic intellectuals of the period, both Hogan and Tierney were more influenced by the teachings of Pius XI in the encyclical, *Quadragesimo Anno*, than by Mussolini. Writing in *United Ireland* on March 24, 1934, Tierney said it was 'not in the least necessary to share Mussolini's rather drastic and in some ways excessive views on the exclusive rights of the State'.

However, confronted by the sight of many serious figures in Fine Gael wearing blue shirts, the IRA was in no mood to speculate as to whether a Blueshirt-run state would be dominated by the thinking of *Quadragesimo Anno* or of *Mein Kampf*. Many of its members were imbued with the principles of Connolly and Mellows, and their dream was not only of a Thirty-Two Counties Republic, but also of a socialist state. Voicing the opinions of this wing, *An Phoblacht* in issue after issue demanded that the banks be taken over and the big farms broken up. The struggle for the abolition of the Oath and of Partition was of a piece with the struggle for the abolition of imperialism and capitalism.

These conflicting ideologies gave the Blueshirt upheavals not simply the aspect of an extension of Civil War animosities—which they certainly were—but also of a reflection of the European struggles of corporativists, socialists, fascists, imperialists, capitalists and all the hydra-headed manifestations of the ills of the 'thirties. Somewhat paradoxically, the Blueshirts saw themselves as standing for the rights of free speech and, according to *United Ireland* in October 1933, 'the end of *laissez-faire* and all the shibboleths of liberalism'.

The IRA supported the retention of the land annuities, and the Blueshirts intervened at sales to prevent the selling of cattle seized at the government's behest from farmers who defaulted on their payments of rates or land annuities: these latter being still collected albeit withheld from Britain. They organised a campaign for the non-payment of rates in which furniture and other property was hidden away from the bailiff. This campaign was strongest in Waterford. These incidents, conflict with the law, conflict between the IRA and the Blueshirts, together with parades and drillings by the rival groups, made the Irish countryside a lively, if not a prosperous, place to live in.* The felling of trees and telegraph poles was widespread. When the opening day arrived for one of the new factories which Sean Lemass, as minister for Industry, was diligently working to establish, it was remarked as something quite in the ordinary run of things that visiting dignitaries had to make long detours to avoid roads blocked by felled trees.

* The Republican Congress newspaper in July 1934 gave an account of the working day of a servant girl, taken on at a hiring fair in Donegal. Her day began at 4.30 with a breakfast of stewed tea, bread and margarine. Her duties included lighting the fires, washing potatoes, milking cows, churning, feeding cattle, baking bread, washing clothes, scrubbing floors and picking turnips. Her pay was on a sliding scale, which didn't slide very far, ranging from £12 to £18 a year. The report said nothing about time off.

As the Economic War continued, the class factor in the struggle created a cleavage in the life of the country which has persisted until today. The labourers and small farmers sided with de Valera and the IRA. Not being directly affected by the Economic War, they regarded it as the struggle with England all over again. The bigger farmers tended now to take their social attitudes from the 'gentry' with whom they became allied under the pressure of the Economic War, which most affected the bigger farmers and the landowners. The resulting cleavage went far to destroy the old ease and familiarity of rural relationships. In Tipperary, for instance, the 'platform' dances vanished. (The 'platforms' were timber dance-floors, usually sited at cross-roads during the summer. The hat was passed round for the musician, either a fiddler or an accordionist.) The daughters of 'strong' farmers began to stay away from them, favouring more sophisticated forms of amusement. This trend was accentuated by the fact that many of the platforms were burned down in the post-war conflicts, and the rural clergy were opposed to such dances anyhow.

But this cleavage between the classes was not solely due to the indirect reflection of political differences in the shape of changed social attitudes. There were direct consequences of political dissension in the shape of threats to life and limb. Some terrible acts of violence occurred. On August 13, 1934, at a sale of cattle in Cork, an unarmed youth was shot dead when the s-division attempted to forestall a Blueshirt plan to break it up. In the following year, on February 11, a bomb was exploded against a Blueshirt house in Dundalk which killed an old woman of seventy and injured two small boys. Shootings occurred, and floggings and beatings-up were commonplace.

The Blueshirt organisation, as we have seen, began to disintegrate. The IRA now began to break up also. This is described more fully in chapter 11. Here we need only mention that in 1934 it split into two groups: one adhering to the old IRA policy of fidelity to the First Dail; the other, and smaller group, turning itself into the Republican Congress Party with the intention of setting up a Workers' Republic. But the splitters themselves split at a meeting on October 1, 1934 over the issue of the Workers' Republic.

All de Valera's opponents were now dropping by the wayside. On the constitutional front, the United Ireland Party (i.e. Fine Gael) became further disunited with the resignation on October 10, 1935 of Frank MacDermot, who objected to his party's critical attitude to de Valera's line at the League of Nations, which was one of courageous opposition to Italy's actions in Abyssinia. There had been other disagreements before this between rightwing and liberal elements in the new party. Geneva was the stated issue which brought matters to a head.

The New Constitution of 1937

The turbulence of the Blueshirt episode contributed to the next and most important phase of de Valera's reign: constitutional development. The Senate was regarded by Fianna Fail and its supporters as being Unionist in tone, representative of a minority belonging to another era and not in harmony with the Republican electorate which had returned Fianna Fail to power. Furthermore, it had baulked de Valera on occasion by rejecting some of his most cherished legislation, notably the Abolition of the Oath Bill and the Prohibition of Uniforms Bill. Accordingly, under the Abolition of the Senate Bill, that body duly vanished on May 29, 1936. The Senate had done some good work in its day, and the bill abolishing it was a highly controversial piece of legislation. But the opposition was so disorganised that de Valera did not have to submit the issue to a referendum. However, the removal of the Senate from the scene facilitated the enactment of two important measures which did go to referendum the following year.

On December 11, 1936 Edward VIII abdicated. The Dail was then in recess but was summoned to meet the following day. It was presented with two government bills—the Constitution (Amendment No. 27) Bill, and the Executive Authority Bill—both of which under a guillotine motion were passed within the next two days. The effect of the first was to remove the king from the Irish Constitution and with him the Crown's representative, the governor-general. The second measure devised a formula for external relations whereby the king was to be regarded as in a position of 'external association' whenever Ireland acted in conjunction with other members of the Commonwealth. This was an ingenious device. The link with the Commonwealth was preserved, with a view to facilitating the eventual unity of the country. At the same time, it went some way to meet the separatists' desire for a Republic. Although it was the end of the Free State, Britain and the Dominions still regarded Ireland as belonging to the Commonwealth, and still considered Ireland as entitled to imperial preference.

These changes in the superstructure of the state, coupled with the earlier abolition of the Oath, made a new Constitution necessary. The draft for this was introduced into the Dail on March 10, 1937. Grudgingly approved by the Dail on June 14, it was narrowly endorsed by the electorate in a plebiscite held concurrently with a general election on July 1. The percentages were: *For* 39 per cent; *Against* 30 per cent; *Abstentions* 31 per cent. The election (for a Dail with a reduced number of seats and with an increase in the number of three-member constituencies) cut the number of Independents to eight and gave Fine Gael the same number of seats (forty-eight) which the United Ireland Party had held in the old

House. Labour held the balance of power with thirteen seats. Fianna Fail, its strength having fallen to sixty-nine, continued in government with the support of Labour. Frank MacDermot did not stand. His was an honourable but rather dilettante intervention on the political scene, and his career served to underline the fact that in Ireland a party without roots in the national struggle had little chance of survival—unless of course it presented a radically new programme and quickly built up a good election machine.

The new Constitution, one of de Valera's most enduring achievements, owed much to *The Social Code*: a compendium of Catholic social principles compiled by the Malines International Union of Social Studies set up by Cardinal Mercier in 1920 to study social problems from a Catholic standpoint. The Union's findings were reflected in the papal encyclical of May 1931, *Quadragesimo Anno*. Other papal encyclicals which found an echo in the new Irish Constitution were *The Christian Education of Youth*, December 1929, and *Christian Marriage*, December 1930—all promulgated by Pope Pius XI. This Constitution was to form a model for those of India, Pakistan and Burma—the latter country in particular largely adopting the form of the Irish provisions on religion.

The Constitution provided for a president; reintroduced a second chamber, now called the Seanad; ordained that the head of government be known as An Taoiseach (prime minister); stipulated that the name of the state be Eire in the Irish tongue and Ireland in the English; and ended the Irish Free State. The Seanad was to have sixty senators: forty-three elected members, six university representatives and eleven nominees of the Taoiseach. The Oireachtas (parliament) was to consist of the president, the Dail and the Seanad. The Constitution applied in theory to the whole of Ireland, but 'pending the reintegration of the national territories' its jurisdiction was limited to the area of government of the Free State. An attempt was made to give the new Seanad a 'vocational' character, but this failed. It is now to all intents and purposes a party assembly. Since it had, and has, the power only to delay a bill for ninety days, not to reject it, the second chamber became in reality simply a reviewing body. The first president was a Protestant: Dr Douglas Hyde, elected unopposed on May 4, 1938.

The previous Constitution had had a contradiction in it. Though stating that the people were the source of all power, the Crown was acknowledged as the fountain-head of power. De Valera's Constitution resolved this contradiction, recognising God alone as the source of all power and safeguarding the people's rights by free elections and the referendum.

The London Agreements of 1938

Concurrent with the establishment of the new Irish state system, steps were taken to end the Economic War with Britain. These reached fruition in three major agreements signed in London on April 25, 1938. The British discriminatory measures against Ireland were abolished and a reciprocal trade pact was agreed whereby certain British and Irish goods were given duty-free access to the respective national markets. The ports retained by Britain under the Treaty of 1921 were handed back to Ireland. For her part, Ireland paid £10 million in 'final settlement' of the land annuities question and other secondary points at issue.

Apart from the obvious advantages of the economic relaxation, the agreement concerning the 'treaty ports' was to be of crucial importance in making possible Ireland's neutrality in the second world war. The signing of the London Agreements of 1938 was, of course, greatly expedited by the darkening threat on the continent. A hostile Ireland on her backdoor would have been a terrible handicap to Britain. Curiously, in view of the exacerbation of Irish–British relations during the war by the closing of Irish harbours to British ships, the Admiralty made no protest at the hand-over of the ports in 1938. It was possibly the only successful application of Chamberlain's appeasement policy. It reflected credit both on his magnanimity and on de Valera's skill as a negotiator.

In the glow of popularity engendered by the London Agreements, Fianna Fail improved its political position when de Valera went to the country again on June 17, 1938. He had been defeated in the Dail on a motion concerning the setting up of an independent arbitration board on pay, conditions and promotion for civil servants. He cut the representation of all parties, and Fianna Fail returned with seventy-seven seats: a clear majority of sixteen which ensured its independence of Labour.

Although by the end of the 'thirties the economic situation was improving, there was still a great deal of poverty in Ireland. During the budget debates in May 1931, the Dail was told that in Cork a survey taken of 779 municipal tenants had shown that 331 families, averaging six persons each, were living on an income of between twenty and thirty shillings a week. The administration made an effort to deal with the social problem, but unrest within the country and the tense situation in Europe made impossible a single-minded concentration on national development.

In January 1939, the IRA began its bombing campaign in England. (See chapter 11.) This was met by new edicts of the Irish government: the Treason Bill, and the Offences against the State Bill. As Britain prepared for war, the question of enforcing conscription in the North disturbed the relative harmony which had followed the London Agreements. But the British government did not pursue the conscription proposal, which would have rendered a third of the North's population liable to be enlisted into the army of the United Kingdom: the power which Nationalists held to be unjustly perpetuating Partition. On May 4, 1939 Chamberlain told the House of Commons that the Military Training Bill would not be applied to Northern Ireland.

THE 'FORTIES

Neutrality 1939-45

The day after Germany invaded Poland, the Dail without a division passed legislation asserting Ireland's neutrality for the duration of the conflict. Speaking on this occasion, de Valera said:

> We have known what invasion and partition mean. We are not forgetful of our own history, and as long as our own country, or any part of it, is subject to force, the application of force by a stronger nation, it is only natural that our people, whatever sympathies they might have in a conflict like the present one, should look at their own country first and should, accordingly, in looking at their own country, consider what its interests should be and what its interests are.

There was a good deal of hostile comment in British newspapers following Churchill's statement during the U-boat campaign that the loss of the ports was a 'most heavy and grievous burden'. But, despite this, during the course of the war—a period always referred to in Ireland as 'the Emergency' —there was a great deal of unofficial co-operation between Ireland and Britain. But official neutrality remained unimpugned.* The British, though sorely tempted, refrained from introducing conscription into the North.

When the war started, Ireland had a regular army of under 12,000 men. By 1945, auxiliary and regular forces, enlisted by voluntary recruitment, totalled a quarter of a million men. But, save for some members of the IRA who died on hunger-strike, people endured discomfort for Ireland rather than dying for her. Lemass set the tone for the whole period when on October 12, 1943 he said: 'Our main task now is to stay alive in a world where we have few friends'.

To the normal censorship there was added the stricter wartime variety. Cattle producers benefited from the war and emigration to England rose steeply, encouraged by the labour demand in the war-production factories there. But for most people, tightening the belt became a daily exercise so far as imported commodities were concerned. Although shortages never reached the grim depths experienced in Britain, many commodities were rationed. Private motoring ceased in 1943 due to the petrol shortage. At one stage, the weekly allowance for each person was down to half an ounce of tea, half a pound of sugar and six ounces of butter. Clothing was also

---

* Ireland's relations with the belligerents are described in chapter 6 below.

rationed severely. Bread went on the ration in 1942, and gas and electricity could be used only at certain hours. The fuel shortage was perhaps the greatest single problem. Vigorous efforts were made to replace the almost diamond-rare coal by more intensive exploitation of the country's turf resources. The quality of much of this turf may be judged by the everyday sight of strands and colpoons of it hanging from clothes-lines to dry. Wheat cultivation was enormously increased, from 200,000 acres in 1937 to 662,498 acres in 1945. The total area under crops increased from 867,943 acres in 1939 to 1,680,327 acres by the end of the war. But the production rate per acre fell because of lack of fertilisers and because much of the soil brought under the plough was unsuitable for crops. When British ships ceased carrying cargoes to Irish ports, in 1942, the government sought to ensure at least a minimum flow of essential materials by setting up a state shipping service.

Although here and there there were a few armchair Nazis, and the IRA (as we shall see in chapter 11) had contacts with the Germans, the country as a whole was pro-British—though curiously glad at seeing England take a knock. Popular attitudes were simplified, however, when the Germans started bombing Belfast. Pro-British feeling certainly was not diminished when, on two occasions in May 1942, German bombs fell on Dublin by mistake (though some wags said that at least the Germans had the decency to consider Ireland as a united, not a partitioned, country for the purposes of external contacts!). Irishmen volunteered in their thousands for the British army, even deserting from the Irish forces—particularly after Dunkirk. It is estimated that by the end of the war there were some 50,000 Southern Irishmen serving in the British forces. In the persons of these volunteers, and of the great numbers of Irish men and women at work in war factories in Britain, Ireland made an important if vicarious contribution to the defeat of Hitlerism. Of the VC awards in the second world war, Southern Ireland's seven is higher in proportion to population than the 'medal ratio' of any other country in the Commonwealth. (In the North-East, they only got three! Incidentally, as the Royal Ulster Rifles unit marched on to its D-day landing craft, they sang the *Soldier's Song*, the national anthem of the Republic: 40 per cent of the unit were men of the South.) The best of Britain's commanders were either from the North or the South of Ireland: Montgomery, Dill, Alexander, Brooke, O'Connor, the two Admiral Cunninghams and so on. At some of the Big Three meetings, half of Churchill's staff was Irish.*

* There are many stories, cherished by English and Irish alike, deriving from the 'aggressive neutrality' of many Irishmen during the war. The navigator of a wholly Irish bombing crew in a plane buffeted by the flak over Berlin is said to have muttered under his breath over the intercom as something nasty came through the fuselage: 'Thank God de Valera's kept us out of this!'

The only Irish politician of note to disagree with the neutrality policy was James Dillon, who resigned from Fine Gael on this issue in 1942, sitting as an Independent until 1952 when he rejoined his old party. His stand was expressive of the old Redmondite feeling, but the general tone of Irish policy was determined by the stronger feelings of the old Sinn Fein elements and also of Labour on this question.

Ireland had traditionally tended to be cut off from the rest of the world (*Mora Insula* has often meant plain insulation), but the war heightened this. At the end of it, many young Irish folk had never seen a coloured person or even a continental European. It was practically *huis clos* on a national scale.

Political Parties 1943–48

The war period saw some new political developments. When a general election became due in 1943, it was contested by a new farmers' party, Clann na Talmhan (the Party of the Soil), led by Joseph Blowick and Michael Donnellan—both big farmers in the West. Like the earlier Farmers' Party, Clann na Talmhan was mainly representative of the interests of the larger farmers. It advocated extensive land-drainage and afforestation schemes. The reaction against wartime conditions, combined with dissatisfaction with Fianna Fail's farm policy, brought support to this party and to Labour at the expense of both Fianna Fail and Fine Gael. The government party's strength fell to sixty-seven seats and Fine Gael's to thirty-two.

But just when it seemed that the good ship Labour was about to reach port at last, it fell into the doldrums. A split developed arising out of personal differences between William O'Brien, secretary of the Irish Transport and General Workers' Union, and James Larkin. These dated back to the great clashes of the 'twenties and to Larkin's breaking with the ITGWU to take over the Workers' Union of Ireland. The breach between them began to affect Labour's parliamentary position when O'Brien took umbrage at the defeat of a motion he put to a meeting on July 10, 1940. This would have placed power to act in an emergency into the hands of a small group of party officials. The motion was interpreted as a move to enable O'Brien and his supporters to oust Larkin. In May 1943 there was a further rumpus, this time over Larkin's parliamentary candidature. Following his election to the Dail, it came to a head on December 23, 1943 when the ITGWU moved to exclude Larkin and his son (also called James) from the Labour Party. Defeated on this, the union disaffiliated from the party on January 7, 1944: a severe loss to Labour for the ITGWU was, and is, the biggest in Ireland. Four pro-ITGWU deputies resigned from the parliamentary party and sat in the Dail as National Labour, taking the whip as it were from the union which sponsored them. Labour proper continued with eight deputies, but the dispute cost the Labour movement as a whole five seats when de Valera called a snap election in 1944. Throughout the controversy, the protagonists of the ITGWU anticipated the tactics of the late Senator Joseph McCarthy, making vociferous references to the communist associations of the elder and the younger Larkin, both of whom had stood as communists in the 1927 election. The split in the parliamentary party was paralleled by the division of the Trade Union Congress into two factions. (Although the parliamentary breach was healed in 1951, the factions in the Irish TUC did not unite until 1959.)

Another cause of Labour's weakness arose from the row over the Trade Union Act of 1941. This sought to set up a tribunal with power to license those unions which had the greatest number of members in a given industry as the sole negotiators for workers in that industry. The aim was to promote the reorganisation of Irish trade unions on 'industrial union' lines, and to help strengthen them against the pressure from English-based unions. But it was seen by the Larkinite section as an attempt to strengthen the ITGWU at the expense of the Workers' Union, with the ulterior motive of benefiting Fianna Fail by a split in the Labour movement. The tribunal was set up in 1943 and proved a source of constant inter-union rancour.*

In addition to the weakening effects of these inter-union divisions, the communist scare frightened away from Labour a good deal of actual and potential support. It was regarded as neither safe nor respectable to belong to the Labour Party. The attraction of Oxbridge intellectuals to the Labour movement in Britain found no parallel in Ireland until the 'sixties.

Watching the Kilkenny catfights of the Labour Party from his parliamentary position of a mere sixty-seven seats, de Valera—who was noted for his fondness for electioneering ('Dev would have a general election at the drop of a hat')—calculated that Labour Party minus National Labour Party equalled General Election. The formula proved correct when applied in 1944. Fianna Fail gained nine seats. At the previous election, in 1943, aided by the wage-frozen dreariness of the wartime economy, the Labour Party had recorded the highest number of votes in its history: 208,812. But in the election of the following year the combined Labour and National Labour poll amounted to only 138,348 votes. This was a disastrous setback. Instead of being in a position to make a strong thrust for power when the ending of the war cut the strings of the straitjacket on Irish life and

---

* In 1947 the National Union of Railwaymen applied to the Supreme Court for an injunction against the tribunal to prevent it from putting the NUR under review. It was feared, though not stated, that this might result in refusing the negotiating licence to the NUR and in the ITGWU gaining its members. The Supreme Court upheld the NUR, and declared that Part III of the Trade Union Act was repugnant to the Constitution, section 40 of which guarantees the right of citizens to form associations and unions.

politics, the Labour movement saw a new party—but one with an old theme, Republicanism—make the running at the 1948 election. And it was this new party, Clann na Poblachta, and not Labour, which dethroned Fianna Fail after sixteen years in office.

The new party's leader was Sean MacBride, son of Major John MacBride, one of the Republican leaders executed in 1916, and of Maud Gonne, the woman Yeats once loved. Personally charming and speaking English with a strong French accent (he had been educated in Paris), MacBride right from his teens was a prominent and romantic figure in the Republican movement. On the night of December 8, 1922, when the Free State soldiers came to Mountjoy prison to execute Rory O'Connor and his three associates in reprisal for the assassination of Hales, young MacBride (then a lad of eighteen) was sharing O'Connor's cell. He became one of the best-known counsels at the Irish Bar, and his spectacularly successful defence of men charged with ·45 politics in the Republican interest led to his becoming the leader of the new party which was beginning to take shape after 1945.

Clann na Poblachta (the Republican Family) was a product of the 'Republican University': i.e. gaol. Many of its principal workers had been interned during the war for IRA activities. Its nucleus was the hard core of advanced Republicans who had hung together since the Saor Eire days, though support also came from an organisation known as Coras na Poblachta (a group of old Republicans who had left Fianna Fail; its principal leaders were Simon Donnelly and Sean Dowling). On a ticket of radical Republicanism and social reform, combined with novel ideas for ending Partition (which included an invitation to the members of Stormont to come and sit in the Dail), the new party began to find for itself a surprising amount of support at meetings and discussion groups throughout the country. MacBride himself proved a strong draw, with his austere presence and man-of-destiny aura. However, although for a time Clann na Poblachta became quite a sizeable family, events were to prove that its development was not a high road to progress and social reform but a pusillanimous cul de sac of sterile controversy. The party's exposition of the need for reform was in the event not matched by its deeds.

By the time MacBride's movement got under way, Fianna Fail had been in power for fifteen years and was beginning to fray at the edges. Allegations of a profitable leak of the government's intentions of taking over the Great Southern Railway were so serious that an official inquiry was necessary. An involved scandal over the sale of bacon to the army led to the resignation of a minister. This, and an outcry over the affair of Locke's Distillery (a case of fraudulent practice in the selling of whiskey) naturally obscured for a time all lighter considerations, such as unemployment, emigration and the cost of living.

But these considerations bit sharply into the public awareness when, on October 16, 1947, a supplementary budget introduced new taxes. Prices became an issue. A militant housewives' association—led by women trade unionists like Helena Maloney, Helen Chevenix and Louie Bennett—held big protest meetings. As the wartime wage-freeze thawed and unions began submitting claims aimed at restoring the pre-war wage climb, long and bitter strikes developed. These were particularly long and hard-fought by teachers and by employees in the transport and banking trades. From them came a rhythm of regular rounds of increase; pre-war demands for 5s more a week were converted into pounds. There is an old saying in Ireland that when England catches cold Ireland gets pneumonia. In 1947, the England of controls and a raging dollar-payments crisis was running a high temperature; this provoked a fever in Ireland which was already suffering severely from the twin maladies of emigration and unemployment.

The political barometer of the country was set for change. Superficially it seemed that the change was made at the election of February 4, 1948. Although Fianna Fail's poll slipped by only 41,564 votes from its 1944 total, under the system of proportional representation it managed to retain only sixty-eight seats. The Election Act of 1947 had increased the number of constituencies from thirty-four to forty. This change, brought about by population shifts, raised the number of Dail deputies from 138 to 147. The total electorate rose from 1,210,763 in 1944 to 1,322,878. Most of this 'new' vote went to Clann na Poblachta, which polled 173,166 votes and won ten seats.

Fianna Fail could not retain control of government without allies. The other parties, interpreting the election result as a vote of no confidence in Fianna Fail and not unmindful of the private as well as the national advantages of bringing in 'new men', resisted the temptation to come to de Valera's rescue. Instead there arose a heterogeneous coalition of Fine Gael, Labour, National Labour, Clann na Poblachta, Clann na Talmhan and Independents: an unlikely alliance, the inherently fissiparous nature of which was to be demonstrated without much delay. After sixteen years of rule by the inheritors of 'constitutional' Sinn Fein radicalism, Ireland now experimented with a governmental amalgam of almost every conceivable political element in the country: a compound of right, left and centre, with sufficient encrustations of left and right extremism to make it one of the great marvels of political morphology.

5. SYNCLINE AND WATERSHED
1949–57

The Coalition 1949–51: *Ireland a Republic; Mother and Child Scheme; Seesaw Politics*
The Watershed: *Development Programme; Lemass and the New Men; Politics in the 'Sixties*

TO the young people who had voted in the hope of seeing new faces and policies; to occupational groups like the teachers with memories of the 1947 strikes; to the older Republicans who resented Fianna Fail's 'betrayal' of the IRA and still saw Fine Gael as the hated upholders of the hated Treaty—to these and to many other Irishmen, Clann na Poblachta seemed to offer a 'nouvelle vague'. But the Clann had scooped up its candidates and policies too suddenly. One deputy, Captain Peadar Cowan, had sat in the Dail for only five months before he broke with the party and became an Independent. There was for a time a division of opinion about admitting ex-Blueshirts, but the argument 'It doesn't matter what colour shirt you wore in 1932' prevailed.

The fundamental political position was unchanged by the 1948 election. Since April 1918, when the Irish Nationalist Party withdrew from Westminster over the conscription issue—thus breaking with a hundred years of tradition—the Irish political mainstream had flowed along a totally new course. Power from then on lay in the hands of Irishmen in Ireland. But socially and economically, the struggle against Britain had been a revolt of conservatives against conservatives. If the course of the mainstream was new, its waters were sluggish. Into them had crashed the boulder of the Civil War, sending up bubbles of dissension which have not yet all died away. As the current flowed over the boulder, two main eddies had emerged: Fianna Fail and Fine Gael, both of them parties with electoral machines and with personalities hallowed and envenomed with the blood of martyrs. However, so far as the political parties and their leadership were concerned, the Civil War had essentially been a split between men of the right and men of the further right. By the mid-'forties, new eddies were disturbing the mainstream, but as yet—with the exception of the introduction of Children's Allowances—no big social policies had floated to the surface since Fianna Fail's first burst of legislation on first taking office in the 'thirties.

Perhaps one revolution is enough for the lifetime of any generation, but that generation was now in its sixties. In the frozen political climate of the war years, the growth of its replacement had been atrophied.* Thanks to de Valera, from whose mind and personality had evolved almost every major political development for nearly three decades, and to Sean Lemass, whose pragmatism had translated his chief's mystique into bread and butter politics, Fianna Fail had achieved such seemingly unalterable permanence in government that the principal issue in Irish political life seemed simply whether it would govern for ever and a day, or just for ever. How to end its reign: this was the Coalition's only raison d'être.

THE COALITION 1949–51

On the Fine Gael side, W. T. Cosgrave had retired in 1944, to be succeeded as leader by General Mulcahy. But when the horse-trading for ministries began, Mulcahy was found unacceptable as head of the Coalition government. Considering he had been in charge of the Free State's military operations against the Republicans' war campaign opposing the Treaty—a campaign organised and supported by men who were now to be his political bedfellows—this is hardly surprising. But it does serve to underline the incongruity of the Coalition. John A. Costello, a former attorney general for Cumann na nGaedheal, was chosen in his stead.

When the new Dail met on February 18, 1949, the following administration was approved: *Taoiseach*, J. A. Costello (Fine Gael); *Tanaiste* and *Social Welfare*, William Norton (Labour); *External Affairs*, Sean MacBride (Clann na Poblachta); *Finance*, P. McGilligan (F.G.); *Justice*, General Sean MacEoin (F.G.); *Defence*, Dr T. F. O'Higgins (F.G.); *Agriculture*, J. M. Dillon (Independent); *Lands and Fisheries*, Joseph Blowick (C. na Talmhan); *Industry and Commerce*, D. Morrissey (F.G.); *Education*, General Mulcahy (F.G.); *Local Government*, T. J. Murphy (Lab.); *Health*, Dr Noel Browne (C. na P.); *Posts and Telegraphs*, J. Everett (National Lab.).

The Coalition administration was not to be the quietest period in politics since Independence. Fianna Fail was prowling round seeking whom it

---

* And yet, as one of a younger generation who has met many of them, I cannot disguise my admiration—for all that I disagree with much that they say and do—of the men who made and kept Ireland free and independent. A life on the run, of prison hardship and complete self-sacrifice for their country seems to have given the survivors of the grim struggle a vibrant longevity. 'Were there no weaklings?' I asked one of them. 'There were, but you don't see those men any more. *We* were hammered on the anvil.' They were!

might devour on the government benches; and the administration, in a seemingly neurotic hesitancy between boldness and timidity, initiated two measures which set the country by the ears.

Ireland a Republic

In the autumn of 1948, legislation was laid before the Dail to repeal the External Affairs Act of 1936 which had confirmed Ireland's membership of the Commonwealth despite the abolition of the Crown as head of the Irish state. For most of 1949, instead of getting to grips with post-war social and economic problems, the country was engulfed in the politics of retrospection. A campaign against Partition was launched at an all-party meeting at the Mansion House on January 27. On the following Sunday £50,000 was raised for the campaign at church-door collections throughout the country. Some of this money went to support anti-Partition candidates in the North. In the wave of Republican feeling thus aroused, the government went forward with the Republic of Ireland Act. This took Ireland out of the Commonwealth and made the Free State a Republic.

What advanced Republicans in Fianna Fail had long but vainly cherished was achieved by a government dominated by Fine Gael, whose elder members had spent the best part of their lives in attacking the 'dangerous extremism' of Fianna Fail. It was an extraordinary volte-face by men of the old Cosgrave tradition. As if this were not wonder enough, there was the spectacle of Fianna Fail, the Republican party, opposing the measure to make Ireland a Republic. Its leaders argued that, by breaking the link with the Commonwealth, the Republic of Ireland Act would make the ending of Partition much more difficult. De Valera indicated his displeasure by staying away from the ceremony at the GPO where the flag was hoisted to inaugurate the Republic. The Republic which he and his comrades had fought for in 1916, he said, had been an All-Ireland, not a Partitioned, Republic. However, when it came to the vote, Fianna Fail had no choice, in view of its record, but to support the government.

The Ireland Act, which the Unionists forced out of the Labour government in retaliation, sought to regularise, from the point of view of the United Kingdom and the Commonwealth, the situation created by the inauguration of the Irish Republic at Easter 1949. It declared that 'the part of Ireland heretofore known as Ireland ceased as from the eighteenth day of April 1949 to be part of His Majesty's Dominions', stated that Northern Ireland remained within the United Kingdom, and affirmed that 'in no event' would the North cease to be part of the United Kingdom 'without the consent of the Parliament of Northern Ireland'. In the debate on the bill in the Lords, Viscount Samuel, leader of the Liberals there, commented:

It would seem that the purpose of Eire in deciding to become an independent Republic was to secure the reunion of Ireland, but if they regarded that as a matter of the highest importance, they had now taken the one step most calculated to defeat that purpose.

This view was also taken by a great many people in Ireland. But Britain's Ireland Act raised a storm of protest throughout the country because of its specific guarantees of the North's right to maintain Partition. For a month or so the country rang with cries that the Labour government should end 'British occupation' in the North. When the public posturing was over, considerable relief was privately felt at the fact that imperial Britain still regarded republican Ireland as 'non-foreign'. Irish citizens to all intents and purposes continued to have the same rights in Britain as citizens of the United Kingdom, so there was no necessity for anyone to worry himself unduly about providing republican jobs for would-be emigrants.

Although there had been strange rumours in Dublin for some time, it was not until September 1, 1948 that the campaign within the Coalition to sever Ireland completely from Britain came to the light of day. Speaking at a meeting of the Canadian Bar Association, Costello referred to the External Relations Act of 1936 as being 'full of inaccuracies and infirmities'. Theories as to Costello's motives in making the statement have ranged from a suggestion that Mrs Costello (a lady of great charm and amiability) had been insulted at a state occasion in Ottawa to the assertion that MacBride was going to do it anyway and that Costello was merely forestalling him. The most likely explanation, however, is that Costello—who, as a lawyer, had been involved in a number of IRA trials—was appalled at the suffering caused by this sterile republicanism, and sought to take the gun out of Irish politics once and for all by giving the republicans their Republic. But he could not give them their equal desire: the end of Partition. The IRA was not appeased, as its 1957 campaign was to prove only too clearly.

Mother and Child Scheme

More controversial even than the Republic of Ireland Act was the Mother and Child Health Scheme, and the Coalition was to break up over it. The scheme was intended to provide mothers with free maternity treatment and their children with free medical attention up to the age of sixteen. It involved the government in conflict with the medical profession, with the Catholic hierarchy over the question of a means-test, and it provoked dissension in the cabinet itself. The minister for Health, Dr Noel Browne (a member of Clann na Poblachta), remained adamant throughout on the necessity of not having a means-test. In the end MacBride, as leader of Clann na Poblachta, asked him to resign, which he did on April 12, 1951. But Browne refused to die in silence, and on resigning he released the correspondence in the affair to the *Irish Times*, so that the public got an unprecedented insight into the workings of Church-State relations.

In a letter dated October 10, 1950, the secretary to the hierarchy outlined the grounds for the Catholic bishops' opposition.

> [In their opinion] the powers taken by the State in the proposed Mother and Child Health Service are in direct opposition to the rights of the family and of the individual and are liable to very great abuse. Their character is such that no assurance that they would be used in moderation could justify their enactment. If adopted in law they would constitute a ready-made instrument for future totalitarian aggression. The right to provide for health of children belongs to parents, not to the State.
>
> The State has the right to intervene only in a subsidiary capacity, to supplement, not to supplant. It may help indigent or neglectful parents, it may not deprive 90 per cent of parents of their rights because of 10 per cent necessitous or negligent parents.
>
> It is not sound social policy to impose a state medical service on the whole community on the pretext of relieving the necessitous 10 per cent from the so-called indignity of the means-test. . . .

Sex teaching aroused dire forebodings:

> . . . We regard with the greatest apprehension the proposal to give to local medical officers the right to give instruction to Catholic girls and women in regard to this sphere of conduct. . . . Gynæcological care may be and in some countries is interpreted to include provision for birth limitation and abortion. We have no guarantee that State officials will respect Catholic principles in regard to these matters.

In a word, the objections of the hierarchy could be summarised by saying that they opposed Part III of the Act which empowered a public authority to provide for the health of all children, to treat their ailments, educate them in regard to health, educate women in regard to motherhood and provide all women with gynæcological care. All this, it was said, ran contrary to Catholic teaching on the rights of the family, of the Church in education, of the medical profession and of voluntary institutions.

The Irish Medical Association's objections ran on the customary line of opposition by doctors to 'socialised medicine', and it opposed the scheme tooth and nail. Browne had had difficulties with the IMA before the Mother and Child controversy over a ministerial order telling local authorities to report to him personally within twenty-four hours any complaint made against a medical officer. He had also refused to sanction the appointment of a nun as matron to a hospital, holding that the appointment of nuns to high posts formerly held by lay staff would discourage girls from becoming nurses. An unpleasant aspect of the affair is the fact that, although the clergy—particularly the younger priests—now generally show a more lenient attitude to Browne (at least, in conversation), he has not been forgiven by his fellow doctors. Though he has applied often, he has failed to secure any significant medical post.

Some provisions of the Mother and Child Scheme have since passed into law in one form or another by legislative manipulations more adroit than Dr Browne's; but the means-test remains. The Health Act, in fact, was introduced by Fianna Fail in 1947 with a view to enabling the Department of Health to promote various public health schemes. Certain of its provisions were found to be unconstitutional by the Supreme Court. These need not concern us. What is significant is that Noel Browne was attempting to put some of the surviving provisions into effect. At the outset of his attempt, neither Browne nor the rest of the cabinet was aware that the hierarchy before the change of government had already notified de Valera of its disapproval of parts of the 1947 Act.

A feature of the controversy—which at times reached heights of emotion unequalled since the Parnellite split—was the conflict between statements of some of the principal actors in the drama as to what happened and why. Browne averred that he had satisfied the hierarchy's objections at a meeting with its representatives, Archbishop McQuaid and bishops Browne and Staunton. In a letter of March 19, 1951 to Costello, he recalled that he had seen him after the meeting and given him to understand that all was well, and that the prime minister was 'in a position to corroborate His Grace's and their Lordships' satisfaction with the explanation which I [Browne] gave in relation to their misapprehensions concerning the Scheme'. He claimed that a memorandum of his setting out his full position on the scheme made clear his intention to introduce nothing contrary to Catholic teaching. This he had given Costello in mid-November 1950 as an answer to the objections in the hierarchy's letter which Costello had shown him on November 9. This communication was dated October 10: the day before Browne met the three ecclesiastics. 'I learned to my amazement and distress', Browne told the Dail on April 11, 1951, 'that the reply which I had prepared and sent to the Taoiseach had in fact never been sent by him' to the hierarchy. Replying the next day, Costello said he had understood that the envelope given him by the Health minister simply returned the hierarchy's letter, Browne having made no indication that the envelope contained anything else. Costello contended that the archbishop's version of the meeting differed from Browne's—Dr McQuaid informing him that it was 'an incredible interview' in which the Health minister had 'brushed aside' the questions of the means-test and the free-for-all scheme and 'would consider nothing but the question of education'. Browne was said to have terminated the interview himself by walking out.*

The inheritors of Saor Eire—by now fat, balding and enamoured of the fleshpots—ran from the brandished croziers with disgraceful speed. Extreme Republicanism had withstood clerical censor of zealots who had not only taken life in defiance of every known Church canon, but had also encouraged young men to do the same. For a party which stemmed from a militant organisation once proscribed by the Church, Clann na Poblachta's tergiversation was astounding. Had they stood by Browne in the crisis, they might well have been denounced. But the Irish recognise a good cause when they see it, and MacBride and his supporters would have been treated with respect at the polls. As it is, their subsequent history (two seats in 1951, three in 1954 and only one in the three subsequent elections) makes one inclined to paraphrase Burke: loyalty in politics is not seldom the greatest wisdom.

The 'health question' was one which had exercised the minds of humane, thoughtful Irishmen for some time. Tuberculosis in Ireland was at that time a shameful affliction in the eyes of all but the most enlightened. If TB struck a country family, it was described to the neighbours (if mentioned at all) as a 'weakness' or a 'delicacy'. Sufferers usually slept in the same room as other members of the family, spreading the infection further, and the disease was sometimes not notified to the doctors until too advanced to be cured. It often took up to a year to get into a sanatorium. Browne rectified this situation and improved that in the County Homes, all of which he visited personally. Some of these had open sewers running through their yards; roofs leaked, cooking was often done in large open pots, knives and forks were in short supply. In one case, the only washing facilities for a home full of old women was a galvanised bath with a cold tap. (Despite Browne, many of these homes are still in a deplorable state.)

To deal with the TB problem, Browne liquidated the Health Department's assets (which stood at around £20 million in investments), got a mortgage on the next £10 million which could be expected from the Hospitals Sweepstake, and embarked on a gigantic scheme for rebuilding sanatoria. For this he was afterwards referred to in the slums of Dublin as 'the man who gave us free TB'. How much credit was due to Noel Browne

---

* When interviewing Dr Browne I made a discovery which, simple as it might appear, could possibly explain, in view of the excitement of the time, the different accounts of the meeting. Browne is completely deaf in one ear, and I understand that the archbishop is rather hard of hearing also. Lesser factors than these have influenced politics before now.

and how much to BCG will always be a subject of debate. It is a fact that TB claimed 3,103 lives in 1948, 581 in 1958 and 432 in 1961. Whomever it is most due to, in the light of this decrease the credit is certainly there.

Browne served no apprenticeship in politics and had no 'national' background. The day he entered the Dail he became a minister. After his brushes with the hierarchy, it is not surprising that he can hardly be called an orthodox Catholic; but he is not a communist. He successfully twice sued people who said he was; and gave the damages to convents. 'I'm a socialist', he told me, 'but I think Christ said everything there was to be said'.

His father was a RIC man who resigned during the Tan War. For a spell he worked in the shirt mills of Derry. Browne's boyhood memories are of his mother working late at night on piecework brought home by his father. Later the family moved round the country in the father's search for work; he contracted TB and died in Athlone, leaving his widow to cope with a family of six or seven.*

His mother, who believed that all the family's troubles were the will of God, took the family to Ballinasloe where her people came from, thinking things would be better for them there. They weren't. They then moved to London where she died in great agony of tuberculosis and nephritis, and was buried in a pauper's grave. One of his sisters reared the children and got a job at Saint Anthony's, a private school in Eastbourne. While she was working there another brother, a hunchback, died in the workhouse, and finally she caught TB herself. But before she died she succeeded in getting young Noel into the school where she had worked. This was to transform his life. The Jesuits took him without fees into Beaumont, one of the most exclusive schools in Britain. He told me that, on a holiday to Ireland, a wealthy Dublin family, the Chances, met him, took an interest in him and sent him to Trinity where he qualified as a doctor. He was an excellent athlete: a member of the Rugby First XV and of the boxing club, and founder-captain of the squash team. Ironically, and typical of his tendency to give the wrong impression, he is remembered at Trinity for having more money than the average undergraduate, owning a red sports car—the only one in the university. After qualifying as a doctor, he returned to England where his then militant Catholicism cost him a medical post in Cheshire, and where he first contracted the TB which has recurred since at intervals.

He went back to Ireland in 1944 and got a medical post in Newcastle Sanatorium, County Wicklow. Here he began trying to raise money for a

---

* Browne is not sure how many there were. He is also hazy about dates. 'Where was the workhouse, doctor? What year did your father die?' 'Ah, I don't know. He just died, that's all. My sister died too. As I was saying . . .'

plan he had devised for fighting tuberculosis. It required £250,000. For an unknown doctor in wartime Ireland to attempt this was a venture from which Quixote would have shrunk. However, in 1947 a journalist called Harry Kennedy, who had been a patient in the Newcastle Sanatorium, introduced Browne to Sean MacBride, Noel Hartnett and Jack McQuillan who were then formulating policy for Clann na Poblachta. It was decided that TB would be a good plank. Browne was selected as a candidate for the party. Despite the fact that in the course of his campaign he made a speech at Rathdrum, County Wicklow, saying that the country was 'sick of 1916', he was elected. During the Mother and Child crisis, he was advised by an eminent theologian. For the alarm he aroused when trying to explain to cabinet meetings the difference in terms of sanctions on believers between the Church's social teaching (directional) and its moral teaching (binding), he might well have been advised by Stalin!

After the crisis Browne dallied for a brief interlude with Fianna Fail (from 1953 to 1957), and then in 1958 founded his own party, the National Progressive Democratic Party. When the years proved that this had no great hopes of becoming either national or progressive, he and Jack Mc-Quillan, the other Dail member of the party (who had also resigned from Clann na Poblachta), joined Labour in 1964. Ironically, he was defeated the following year, mainly as a result of the hard campaigning of Conor Cruise O'Brien's father-in-law, Sean MacEntee—the old guard Health minister who had been in power when the Mother and Child scheme was first introduced under Fianna Fail.

Although in a sense Browne had his finger on the national pulse in pursuing the Health scheme, neither he nor the country was then ready for it. There was a yearning for improvement but he was too inexperienced to canalise it, too prone to mount the barricades rather than seek compromise: a tendency which sadly, but perhaps inevitably in view of that traumatic controversy, has grown with the years.

The defections from Clann na Poblachta's parliamentary group following Browne's resignation altered the balance of forces in the Dail. The government had planned to reduce agricultural subsidies, but could not hope now to carry out this programme, and so the Dail was dissolved on May 7, 1951. The election gave no party an overall majority. When the Dail reassembled on June 13, Browne with the Independents voted with Fianna Fail, thereby putting out the Coalition. He told me that, looking back, he was sorry he had done this. 'It was wrong of me.'

Seesaw Politics

Fianna Fail, back in office in 1951, went out again following the 1954 election when Fine Gael and Labour both increased their votes, and returned to government in 1957 when Fine Gael and Labour dropped votes. It seemed a seesaw situation in more things than the balance of parties. Everything was still the same, only different! Unemployment remained consistently in the high eighty thousands. There was even an 'unemployed candidate': John Murphy, a Dublin carpenter whose sincerity was unmatched by his parliamentary skill. He left politics in 1961, deciding that since he wasn't able to influence the course of events, he ought not to sit in the Dail.

There was a slight increase in the national output between 1952 and 1955, but this vanished in the post-Suez vortex of levies, credit restriction, suspension of public works and undersubscribed national loans. In the financial year 1953–54, revenue increased from £98 to £103 million, but expenditure went up from £107 to £121 million. The opposition made political capital out of the fact that public spending had increased but taxation had reached its highest possible limit. Coupled with the prevailing discontent, this ammunition shot down two Fianna Fail candidates at by-elections in Cork and Louth on March 3, 1955. A general election became inevitable and Fianna Fail were defeated on May 13.

The New Dail met on June 2. Costello was again head of the administration. His Cabinet was: *Tanaiste* and *Industry and Commerce*, William Norton (Labour); *External Affairs*, Liam Cosgrave (Fine Gael); *Finance*, Gerald Sweetman (F.G.); *Justice*, J. Everett (National Labour); *Defence*, General Sean MacEoin (F.G.); *Agriculture*, James Dillon (F.G.); *Lands and Fisheries*, Joseph Blowick (Clann na Talmhan); *Education*, General Mulcahy (F.G.); *Local Government*, P. O'Donnell (F.G.); *Health*, Dr T. F. O'Higgins (F.G.); *Social Welfare*, R. Corish (Lab.); *Posts and Telegraphs*, M. J. Keyes (Lab.).

MacBride refused to join the government but promised his support to the Coalition. However, on January 28, 1957 he unexpectedly withdrew Clann na Poblachta's support, and tabled a motion of No Confidence in the government's handling both of the economic situation and of the Partition question. The motion condemned the failure 'to formulate and to pursue any positive policy to bring about the reunification of Ireland'. The election of March 5 which this manoeuvre brought about showed very little confidence on the part of the electorate in Clann na Poblachta's ability to achieve unification. The party's vote declined from 51,000 to 22,000. Fine Gael's vote also fell: from 427,000 to 327,000. Faced with the third election in less than six years, the electorate was apathetic and the total poll was only 1,223,000 (as compared with 1,337,000 in 1954). But the slight increase in Fianna Fail's vote—from 580,000 to 592,000—was enough to give it seventy-eight seats as compared with sixty-five in the previous Dail. Labour lost seven seats, its representation falling from nineteen to twelve.

The controls imposed by the Coalition were undoubtedly effective economically. The deficit for the balance of payments was cut from £35 million in 1955 to £14 million in 1956; and a far-reaching set of import levies, even on such things as oranges, reduced imports from £204 to £181 million in the same period. But, introduced in the gloomy crisis-laden atmosphere of the time, they were disastrous politically.

Had it not been for the safety-valve of emigration (400,000 in round figures for the decade 1950–60), the frustration and desperation of these years must have led to mass riots. As it was, the gun re-entered Irish politics with the IRA onslaught of 1957. In the general election held that year, Sinn Fein—the 'constitutional' wing of the IRA—made its first electoral appearance since 1927, winning 65,640 votes and four seats. But, true to the old tradition, the four Sinn Fein deputies did not enter the Dail. Most of the party's re-awakened support reflected the feeling that anything which offered some prospect of economic or social betterment was worth trying. The reunification of the country, albeit by force as Sinn Fein urged, did for the moment seem to offer such a prospect. But this support fell away as the Border Campaign became bloodier and more ineffective.

Before going out of office, the then minister for Finance, Gerald Sweetman, had taken one of the most fortunate decisions of Irish politics, appointing in 1956 T. K. Whitaker as secretary of the Finance Department. It was Whitaker's development programme (described later) which was to achieve the peaceful revolutionising of Ireland. Under Whitaker's initiative, 'planning' and 'growth-rates' were to replace 'civil war', 'oath', 'partition' in the national vocabulary.

One must in fairness ascribe more than Whitaker to the Coalition's credit. Apart from the valuable democratic service of providing the country with an alternative government, there was the setting up of the Industrial Development Authority under the Industrial Development Act of 1951 from which much of the subsequent industrialisation flowed. Under Liam Cosgrave, a son of W. T. Cosgrave and Sean MacBride's successor as minister for External Affairs, there came the horizon-widening experience of joining the United Nations in 1955. Nor should an innovation like the establishment of the Voluntary Health Insurance Board be overlooked. This was a tremendous benefit to people, particularly those with dependants, whose incomes cleared the level of £800—beyond which the state benefits did not apply. Yet these advances, valuable as they were, cannot be taken as marking the onset of that fundamental change to which the country was groping. It is to the election of 1957, which showed that in their desperation for change people were even prepared to vote for violence, and to the adoption in 1958 of Whitaker's programme, that one must look for the Watershed in modern Irish life.

De Valera's new cabinet made few changes from other administrations. One unusual feature of it, however, was the fact that Sean Moylan—one of the great old guard—though defeated for the Dail, was made minister for Agriculture, having been nominated to the Seanad on the prime minister's panel. In March 1959, the Seanad for the first time since its establishment in 1937, rejected a bill: the government's proposal to hold a referendum on the abolition of Proportional Representation. The voting was close: twenty-nine to twenty-eight. After the ninety-day suspension period had elapsed, the bill became law and the referendum was fixed for June 17—which was also the day of the presidential election. Sean Lemass succeeded de Valera as Taoiseach on June 23, approved by seventy-five votes to fifty-one on the Dail. Two days later, de Valera was installed as president of the Republic, having defeated General Sean MacEoin by 538,000 votes to 417,536. But 'Dev' had failed to win his last great campaign. With a nice discrimination, the majority of his countrymen on June 17 had put him in the president's chair and his abolition bill in the dustbin.* General Mulcahy retired from politics in October 1959, and James Dillon took his place as leader of Fine Gael.

The day de Valera took over power, most of his followers carried revolvers in their pockets as they took their seats with him. He left it thirty years later, probably to go down to history as an even greater figure than Parnell. He had used every possible political manoeuvre during his career on the national stage: a career longer than Franco's, Salazar's, or Stalin's—and, unlike theirs, devoted to democracy. Few statesmen of this century could claim to have pursued their aims with more tenacity, skill and simplicity. After his withdrawal from parliamentary politics, and despite the fact that the country was now visibly beginning to lift itself from the long stagnation, Fianna Fail's majority fell by eight at the election of 1961, and both after it and at the election of 1965 the government required to be supported in time of need by Independents.

THE WATERSHED

In the last few years an enormous psychological change has occurred in Ireland. The conviction that things could be improved has dawned on a people conditioned to believe that they could only get worse. For most of the 1950s Ireland as a nation seemed unaware that the clash of arms and the blare of trumpets had ceased on the constitutional front. A new battle

---

* The Freemasons instructed their members to vote for the continuation of PR: a fact which, had it been generally known at the time, would have abolished PR three times over!

was calling to be fought on the economic and social sectors, but—despite four changes of government in ten years—Cathleen ni Houlihan remained weeping over her dead on an old battleground. The man who dried her tears was a civil servant.

The Development Programme

Thomas Kenneth Whitaker was born (appositely enough in 1916) at Rostrevor in County Down. It was his report on the economic measures needed to lift Ireland out of the slough of despond which initiated the country's present prosperity. But he is responsible for something else: it was he who made possible the meeting between Sean Lemass, prime minister of Eire, and Terence O'Neill, prime minister of Northern Ireland.

Tall and with aquiline features, Whitaker is inclined to be self-deprecating in conversation. He told me how much he disliked his early job in the civil service, pasting things into ledgers; but did not mention that he had taken first place in his entrance examination, gaining marks which have yet to be surpassed. Even a few minutes' talk with him explains the apparent paradox of a senior Treasury official's initiating adventurous financial policies. He is an accomplished diplomatist. As a colleague of his puts it: 'Ken plays human chess all the time, moving this man here, that man there; and if one move doesn't come off, he always has others to fall back on'. Perhaps so; my own impression of him is of a very personable man who is also a very brilliant one. Very approachable, he nevertheless keeps a careful bridgework of safe ideas between an interviewer and his sensitive, original mind until a rapport is established. Then he talks with great ease and sincerity about things like the kind of society Irishmen should be working for; about social and cultural questions; and even about his schooldays.

He was educated by the Christian Brothers at Drogheda, and took a postal degree in economics through the London School of Economics and Political Science. In 1956 Gerald Sweetman, minister for Finance in the Coalition government—an able man himself with a talent for discerning ability in others—leapfrogged Whitaker up the ladder of promotion and appointed him, out of turn, as secretary of the Finance Department. He took this post at the unprecedentedly early age of forty. For a time Sweetman's colleagues may have wondered if he had done the right thing because, ironically, it was Whitaker's department which recommended the unpopular levies and controls that brought down the government in 1957.

The genesis of his policy statement, *Economic Development*, published in 1958, is reminiscent of that of the law of gravity. Newton's intellect was aroused by the fall of an apple in a Lincolnshire orchard; Whitaker's by a cover cartoon in a humorous magazine. In September 1957, *Dublin Opinion* depicted Cathleen ni Houlihan, no longer young but still beautiful, anxiously saying to a fortune-teller: 'Get to work! They're saying I've no future.' 'No future' was all a great number of people could see for Ireland that year. Speaking for myself, I remember only too vividly the depressing experience of saying goodbye seemingly every week to yet another bank clerk, lawyer, student, carpenter or whatever—all of them emigrating. 'This bloody country is finished' was a phrase heard with dirgelike regularity. Whitaker expressed the prevailing dejection, though rather more circumspectly, when he wrote in *Economic Development*: 'The growing comment on the absence of a comprehensive and integrated programme is tending to deepen the all-prevalent mood of despondency about the country's future'. He says he brooded over the cartoon. Taking its implications into consideration with the national crisis of confidence produced by the deflationary measures of the previous year, he decided to try something new. Working at first on his own, and then gradually gathering around him a team of civil servants, he began to draw up a development programme.

On December 12, 1957 he indicated to the minister for Finance, Dr James Ryan, the lines he was working on. Five days later (December 17) he got his chief's official blessing. The speed with which a departmental decision of such magnitude was made reflects the urgency of the situation and—hearteningly—a new constructive temper in government. Thus was prepared the Irish 'great leap forward'—not to be compared perhaps with the post-war recoveries of, say, Germany or Japan, but certainly a brisk step in the right direction. Following the publication in May 1958 of *Economic Development* (a government white paper outlining the proposals of Whitaker and the civil service), the government in November adopted the first long-term plan: the Programme for Economic Expansion. This was followed in August 1963 by the Second Programme, covering the period up to 1970.*

What Whitaker did in economic terms was to change governmental policy from a rigid reliance on the gold-standard mechanisms whereby the commercial banks, which held most of the country's external assets in short-term sterling investments, inflated and deflated the Irish economy in response to the frequent variations in the balance of payments. Helped by the fact that the Irish currency is one of the most solid in the world, Whitaker managed to change the emphasis to productive investments in exports, to establishing new industries, and to supporting private enterprise by governmental encouragement of new initiatives. It stands highly to the credit of Ryan and de Valera that they sponsored Whitaker's initiative so promptly and wholeheartedly. Had certain other members of the Fianna Fail cabinet been in Ryan's shoes, the proposals would have

* The implications of Whitaker's proposals are discussed in chapter 7.

been rejected out of hand. It was not the least of de Valera's achievements in the evening of his parliamentary career that he, ever dedicated to the principle that authority comes from the polls, should have thrown all his great influence behind the electorally unsanctioned plans of a civil servant. But the main responsibility for activating the economic leap forward must be attributed to Sean Francis Lemass.

Lemass and the New Men

This pipe-smoking pragmatist is one of the most remarkable politicians in Europe. I once heard an Aran Island fisherman describe him as 'a good man, but my God, he's got the face of a shark on him!' This is a fair illustration of his pre-Taoiseach image. Lemass has always been popular in the towns because of his success in building up industries. But in the emigration-bled countryside he has tended to be regarded as a 'smooth man' and little interested in rural problems. Part of the criticism he arouses is caused by his flexibility. He is strong-minded enough to pull down in an hour what it has taken him a lifetime to build if he thinks he can get better results that way. The conservative element in Fianna Fail would have preferred to see Frank Aiken succeed de Valera. At the crucial party meeting it is said that one vote—that of Dr James Ryan—decided the issue. Significantly, in the 1965 election Lemass's personal vote broke all records, whereas Aiken's fell appreciably.

Lemass's political career began in the besieged GPO when, as a boy of sixteen and under the influence of his brother Noel, he took part in the 1916 Rising. He escaped imprisonment because of his youth and went on to fight in the War of Independence and the subsequent Civil War.* (He was one of the insurgents in the Four Courts.) He broke with the IRA to join de Valera in the formation of Fianna Fail, and in 1932 he became, at the age of thirty-two, the youngest minister in Europe. He has evolved politically from the days when he described Fianna Fail as a 'slightly constitutional party', maturing through the lounge-suit era and the Blueshirt upheaval to the coming of the men in the mohair suits. During the war, as minister of Supplies, the country was almost completely in his control. With more reasons than most for bitterness, he has been much less concerned with harping on the grievances of the past than many of his fellow politicians on both sides of the chamber. Lemass's speeches— delivered in a rather pleasant, husky voice of indeterminate accent—have

---

* His early life tended to be so interlarded with prison sentences that when he paid court to the pretty daughter of a Dublin carpenter, Miss Kathleen Hughes, the marriage was opposed on the grounds that he would never be able to make a home for her. The marriage was and is one of the great stabilising influences of his life. They have four children—three girls and a boy, Noel, who is a Fianna Fail deputy, called after Lemass's brother who was brutally murdered after the Civil War had ended.

dealt with constructive policies and the future rather than with recriminations and the past.

Lemass is sixty-six but, as Captain O'Neill, prime minister of Northern Ireland, said to me, 'He doesn't talk sixty-six'—a tribute which, in Irish circumstances, is a mark of what has been achieved by this small, vigorous man with the clipped moustache and the managing-director presence. The younger element in Fianna Fail worship him. Great leaders seem to evoke distinctive labels. With Kennedy it was 'Style', with de Gaulle, 'la Gloire' (or 'Magloire'!), with de Valera 'Principle'. With Lemass it is 'Dynamism'. He has changed the concept of Ireland from that of an ageing Cathleen ni Houlihan to that of Ireland Inc.

With Lemass in charge, new faces began to peep out of the Fianna Fail firmament. The rightwing, however, continued to be suspicious. In 1964, faced with a rising cost of living, militant trade unionism and an unpopular new purchase tax, the right washed its hands of him when two by-elections fell due in Cork and Kildare, defeat in which could have destroyed the government. The thinking was that it would be better to let in the opposition, for Fine Gael and Labour were both showing signs of renewed strength, and leave them to deal with the apparently insoluble problems. But the younger men in Fianna Fail, with a Kennedy-inspired panache, manned the electoral machine which fought and won both by-elections.

It was not until November 1964 when Patrick Smith, the minister for Agriculture, resigned that the extent of the right–left rift in Fianna Fail became public. Smith hitherto had been somewhat of an agrarian Melba in so far as word-of-farewell appearances were concerned, but these had been kept within the party. When he finally decided that the government was making undue concessions to trade unions—which, in his phrase, were being led by people 'who could not lead their own grandmother'—Smith informed the press and Lemass simultaneously of his decision. It was the first time in forty years, since McGrath had resigned in 1924 over the Army Mutiny, that a minister had voluntarily relinquished his office. To Smith, who is an attractive man socially, the post-Watershed talk of 'selling Ireland' and 'the new image of Ireland' was all nonsense. To him and to many like him in political circles, the small farms of his native Cavan and their small horizons were all-important. But after the 1965 elections there were few Paddy Smiths left in the seats of power. By then his avenue to success—the independence struggle and prison (only the Truce prevented Smith's execution)—was closed off. With or without his earlier idealism, younger men swept into the ministries. Nothing so forcibly underlines the new situation as the choice of his successor at the Department of Agriculture: Charles Haughey.

Haughey is Lemass's son-in-law, Fianna Fail's director of elections and the epitome of the men in the mohair suits. He is one of the strongly tipped favourites to succeed Lemass. A short, Napoleonic figure whose rather heavy features are relieved by his use of a particularly charming smile, Haughey had a brilliant professional career—taking degrees in law and accountancy and becoming a rich man—before his appointment as minister for Justice at the age of thirty-five. With the possible exception of Gerald Boland, he was probably the best to hold this office since Kevin O'Higgins—and not only because he made it legal again to drink on Saint Patrick's Day! Haughey is a strange blend of confidence and uncertainty, concerned for his image and sensitive to newspaper comment. He hunts, is a bon viveur and a generous host. (His favourite brand of port, which he buys by the case, costs thirty-four shillings a bottle.) He drives his civil servants hard and can be Tammany-tough in a crisis: witness his handling of the opposition which, after a colleague of his had been fined for drunken driving, was unsporting enough to enquire into the strange happenings that befell the policeman who made the arrest. He routed them all by alluding to files in his office at the Department of Justice. These were generally understood to contain embarrassing information about senior members of Fine Gael. Haughey has a fundamentalist approach. 'There has to be a commercial' is a phrase he uses often. One of the most important things about him is the fact that his father was an officer in the Free State Army during the Civil War. That a man with such a background can marry into the family of a Fianna Fail prime minister and become a leading member of his cabinet and the party's director of elections—this is one of the best examples of the change which has come over Irish public life in recent years.

Along with Haughey, the present government contains some men of outstanding ability: politicians of the younger school who were drawn into public life partly through family background but also through an interest in political action rather than through involvement in a revolution half a century before. The most outstanding are Dr Michael Hillery, minister for Industry and Commerce; Donough O'Malley, minister for Health; Brian Lenihan, minister for Justice; George Colley, minister for Education and Jack Lynch, minister for Finance. The outlook of such men and their group probably differs more radically from that of their predecessors in Fianna Fail than from that of their present opponents in Fine Gael.

Irish Politics in the 'Sixties

Characteristically, Fine Gael did not come to its own Watershed until 1965. During the year before the election, its more progressive elements tried to get a new policy document, *The Just Society*, accepted. But they did not succeed in getting it adopted as official policy until just three weeks before the election. The new policy was the brainchild of Declan Costello, a son of the Coalition leader and, like his father, a lawyer. Slightly built, this grave-faced young man with the high forehead is one of the most attractive figures in Irish politics. *The Just Society* intended to make Ireland precisely that; it placed heavy emphasis on social welfare, planning and education.

As an indication of how the country has moved from the days of controversy over the Mother and Child scheme, it should be noted that Costello's 'just society' is to be one in which the provision of public medical care would carry no means-test. Everyone in 1965 accepted this feature of Fine Gael's policy as being something normal in political discussion. Shortly before the new policy was published, I put it to Costello that he would have great difficulty in getting his plan accepted by his extremely conservative party. We were sitting in his old-fashioned home in the comfortable suburb of Clonskeagh—cut glass, mahogany and idealism gleaming around us. He replied: 'Ah yes, but the fact that a thing will be opposed is no reason for not doing it'. A couple of months later, Fine Gael lost an election but gained a new policy and a new leader.

James Dillon, who had been leader of the opposition since 1958, abdicated dramatically and unexpectedly on the day the Dail reassembled. In the election much of the conservatism of Fine Gael had proved unwelcome to the electorate. Among those who lost their seats was Patrick McGilligan, now in his seventies. There was a poignant irony to this for, with the same enthusiasm with which he had sponsored the Shannon Scheme, McGilligan had been one of *The Just Society*'s chief supporters within the party. The succession passed to Liam Cosgrave, a son of W. T. Cosgrave: a friendly, unobtrusive little man, very much of the same quietly effective stamp as his father.

Dillon is a son of John Dillon who succeeded John Redmond as leader of the Irish Parliamentary Party. He had two energetic interludes as minister for Agriculture in the Coalition governments. He held that farmers should be helped by the state but should resist state supervision. Among its provisions *The Just Society* had envisaged increased state supervision of farmers. As we have seen, Dillon was the only politician to oppose Ireland's neutrality during the war. An honourable, almost nineteenth-century figure and probably the best orator in the Dail, his career has been almost a carbon copy of his father's: years of hard work suddenly carried away by a tide of history whose significance he did not appreciate.

The Labour Party has made considerable gains under Brendan Corish, a local government official from County Wexford with the distinction of being the best-looking man in the Dail. He succeeded William Norton in the Labour leadership in 1963. By virtue of the fact that the country's

policies are veering slightly to the left anyhow, and that changes in the
trade union set-up may be in train, the Labour Party would appear to
be in a position from which it could grow stronger. The biggest trade
union, the Irish Transport and General Workers' Union, is still not affiliated
to the Labour Party. But efforts to heal the breach between the ITGWU and
the Workers' Union of Ireland were for the first time publicly hinted at by
John Conroy, president of the ITGWU, at the opening of the new Liberty
Hall on May Day 1965.* If this comes about, the way would be clear for
the ITGWU to affiliate to the party, in which event Labour politics in Ireland
will acquire a new unity and a powerful new strength.

By 1970, and barring any exceptional developments, Fianna Fail will
have been in power for thirteen consecutive years. It is understood that
Lemass will not seek the leadership of the party at the end of this period.
A new-look coalition of Fine Gael and Labour seems a not unlikely
governmental prospect.

The 1961 election was of particular interest in that it was the first to be
fought in the history of the state on an international issue: joining the
Common Market. The military gentleman in the Elysée not having made
his views known at this stage, Lemass went to the country on October 4
to test the strength of popular support for Ireland's application to join the
EEC. Though Fianna Fail won only seventy seats, he was able to form a
government with the aid of two Independents, the total strength of the
opposition parties being sixty-eight. The new Dail was smaller than the old.
An electoral law, coming into operation on July 16 after having been declared
not repugnant to the Constitution following an application to the Supreme
Court by Fine Gael, had reduced the number of seats from 147 to 140.
The reduction was caused by population shifts to urban areas and by
emigration. The 1961 census showed the population to be 2,814,703: the
lowest figure ever recorded.

But if 1961 was interesting, 1965 was gripping. Labour made a surprisingly good showing, increasing its strength from sixteen to twenty-two seats.
It was a Labour gain in a by-election, in fact, which caused the election. In

---

* Though one can already see that it has given the trade union movement a great
psychological fillip, the significance for the future of the opening of the new Liberty Hall
cannot yet be gauged. Seventeen stories high and the tallest building in Ireland, Liberty
Hall stands on the site of the Labour headquarters of the same name from which Larkin
fought the strike battles of 1913 and from which Connolly led out his Citizen Army to
start the Rising in 1916. What with its historical associations and the fact of its construction's being halted by a strike of the builders over a demand for a forty-hour week, it is a
true symbol of modern Ireland. I ought to be able to recall stirring speeches, but the
only memorable thing I can remember of the opening was an argument between a Labour
deputy and a trade unionist as to whether it would be possible to picket any of the employers who were leasing office space in the building. The answer was, Yes.

Mid-Cork on March 11, Mrs Eileen Desmond retained her late husband's seat. (All the women members of the Dail, it is worth noting in passing, are holders of 'family' seats.) Faced with an undercurrent of economic disquiet, Lemass took this as the occasion for dissolving the Dail, going to the country before the 'base contagious clouds' of the economic situation (which later became plain for all to see) could have a chance of overcasting his beauty from the sun of the historic meeting with Captain O'Neill of the North. (See chapter 12.) He was proved right in his judgement, despite a widespread view that he should have waited until 1966 when the sunburst of the anniversary of the Rising could be expected to give him a large majority. But Lemass—with one eye on the new Labour government in Britain, starting to credit-squeeze Cathleen ni Houlihan where it hurts: in her exports; and with the other on threatened wage claims and the trade figures—knew what he was doing. It is unlikely that he would have been confirmed in office if the election had occurred after the summer recession of 1965 when the full effects became felt in Ireland of Britain's fight to save sterling. Certainly it would not have left him secure, as he now apparently is, for some years to come.

Lemass's new cabinet was: *Tanaiste* and *External Affairs*, Frank Aiken; *Finance*, Jack Lynch; *Justice*, Brian Lenihan; *Defence*, M. Hilliard; *Agriculture*, C. Haughey; *Lands and Gaeltacht*, M. O Morain; *Industry and Commerce*, Dr Hillery; *Education*, George Colley; *Local Government*, Niall Blaney; *Health*, Donough O'Malley; *Social Welfare*, Kevin Boland; *Transport and Power*, Erskine Childers; *Posts and Telegraphs*, J. Brennan. Parliamentary secretaries were: M. Carty (secretary to the Taoiseach and to the minister for Defence); J. M. Gibbons (Finance); P. J. Lalor (Agriculture); Sean Flanagan (Industry and Commerce); Padraig Faulkner (Gaeltacht); P. Brennan (Local Government).

This election, held on April 7, was noteworthy for two extraordinarily protracted counts and recounts in Dublin and Mullingar. Days after the poll, a Labour and a Fianna Fail deputy were eventually declared elected, each by single-figure margins. But, more important, it marked the end of the parliamentary careers of men who had been household names ever since the inception of the state. On the Fine Gael side, General Sean MacEoin was defeated in the marathon contest at Mullingar, and Patrick McGilligan, the promoter of the Shannon Scheme of the 'twenties, was defeated in Dublin. On the Fianna Fail side, Dr James Ryan retired, as did Gerald Bartley, who had been minister for Defence in the previous cabinet. Sean MacEntee stood as an ordinary deputy, and Dan Breen, in many ways the most colourful figure in the Dail, retired.

Breen had been one of the great berserkers of the War of Independence, the man who fired the shots at Soloheadbeg while the First Dail was sitting.

In the subsequent fighting he displayed enough courage for ten men. He and Collins each had £10,000 set on their head by the British. Breen came back from America to take the Anti-Treaty side in the Civil War. On the day he left the Dail, he paid tribute to all his former comrades, including Collins, and welcomed the North–South talks. In an interview he said: 'My definition of an Irishman is Tone's definition. I don't care what altar he adores at, or if he ever goes to an altar at all.' He had no hate for either Orangemen or Englishmen. 'I fought to get control of our thirty-two counties so that we could manage them ourselves.' Speaking of the contemporary situation he said something which I feel should be hoisted in the skies above Dublin and Belfast in letters of fire:

> If they would only stop squabbling and get down to work, they would make a great country out of it.

6. IRELAND IN WORLD AFFAIRS

League of Nations · Neutrality 1939–45

Post-War Problems: *Cold War and Disarmament; Congo;*

Ireland and the Third World; New Commitments

IN the sphere of external relations, Ireland has generally played a constructive, honourable role. The country has certainly taken a more prominent part in the world's business than might have been expected in view of its size.

LEAGUE OF NATIONS

The Free State's first steps into the world at large were taken in 1923 when, with the Civil War still vibrating round his head, W. T. Cosgrave led her into both the Assembly of the League of Nations and the International Labour Organisation. In 1924 Ireland became the first country within the British Commonwealth to appoint its own minister to Washington, an initiative soon followed by similar appointments to the Holy See, Berlin and Paris. Two years later, Desmond Fitzgerald, then minister for External Affairs, proposed his country for membership of the Council of the League of Nations. Ireland was seeking election to the League of Nations Council rather than admittance as a right. A commission had proposed a reorganisation of the Council (the Cecil–Fromagest plan) which, the Free State believed, threatened to establish an oligarchy within the Council. As a protest against this scheme Ireland contested a seat on the Council. This attempt was unsuccessful, but Sir George Foster, the Canadian delegate, took the opportunity offered by Ireland's application to make the point that the Dominions had equality with Britain and the other members of the League. The Balfour Report on Inter-Imperial Relations of the same year (1926) took this principle a stage further. It stated that the Commonwealth countries were 'autonomous communities within the British Empire, equal in status, in no way subordinate to one another in any aspect of their domestic or external affairs, though united by a common allegiance to the Crown, and freely associated as members of the British Commonwealth of Nations'. It was agreed at the time that O'Higgins and Fitzgerald had played a leading part in formulating this principle at the Imperial Conference.

In 1929, Patrick McGilligan, as minister for External Affairs, steered through the Dail a small but significant measure towards an independent posture vis-á-vis the United Kingdom. This was Ireland's signing, without reservation, Article 36 of the Statute of the Permanent Court of International Justice by which contracting states agreed to accept the compulsory jurisdiction of the Court in matters of legal dispute between them. Britain and other Commonwealth countries, however, reserved the right to settle Commonwealth disputes among themselves. 'Our decision', said McGilligan, 'is always come to in circumstances that are peculiar and appropriate to this State. . . . We will take, as we have always taken, quite an independent point of view.' Ireland's acceptance of the High Court's jurisdiction was dictated largely by domestic politics. It was intended to emphasise the freedom of her government from British influence in order to counter the Fianna Fail opposition in the Dail.

An even more significant development occurred on December 11, 1931 when the Statute of Westminster received the royal assent. It was this new definition of the sovereign rights of Dominions which (as we saw in chapter 4) made it possible for de Valera in 1933 to unshackle Ireland from the Oath of Allegiance to the British Crown. Two years later, in 1935, the 'free' character of the Free State was emphasised by the passing on April 15 of the Irish Nationality and Citizenship Act. By this measure, citizens of Ireland ceased in Irish eyes to be British subjects, although by British law they remained British. But in fact the Nationality and Citizenship Act made little practical difference to the existing situation. Then (as now) British subjects in Ireland enjoyed rights similar to those enjoyed by citizens of the Republic in Britain. Although during the second world war Irish citizens in Britain became liable to national service, the arrangement on the whole has benefited Ireland. For one thing, all Irish technical and professional qualifications are recognised in Britain. To advance in the subject a little further, it should be noted that the British parliament's Ireland Act of 1949 specified that the Republic of Ireland was not to be regarded as a foreign country or its citizens in Britain as aliens. The only important restriction on them is that they cannot vote in British elections.

Ireland's relationship with the Commonwealth is somewhat ambiguous. As the *Annual Register* for 1949 noted, the Republic has 'an intermediate status between membership and "foreignness" '. The Department of External Affairs has so far dealt with the Commonwealth Relations Office, not the Foreign Office.

In 1930 Ireland was at last elected to the Council of the League, and her status in world affairs was further enhanced when de Valera was elected president of the Council in 1932. He immediately made his presence felt! Instead of reading from the script prepared for him by the League secretariat, he criticised the League for allowing a 'suspicion' to get abroad that 'little more than lip-service is being paid to the fundamental principle on which the League is founded'. He made world headlines the next day, the *New York Times* saying that the speech had made him 'the personality of the Assembly'. De Valera set the dovecotes fluttering again when, in 1934, he joined with France and Britain in advocating the admission of Russia to the League. There was strong hostility in Ireland to atheistic communism, but de Valera took an objective view. 'The question should be openly and frankly faced', he said.

> It is obvious that anyone who has the interests of the League at heart must desire to see in it a nation of such importance as Russia. I represent a country which, if you consider its political and religious ideals, is as far apart as the poles from Soviet Russia. But I would be willing to take the responsibility of saying openly and frankly that I would support and vote for the entry of Russia into the League on account of the reasons I have mentioned.

The Irish proposal to discuss the admission of Communist China to the UN, discussed on pages 124-7 below, was consistent with the line taken by de Valera in regard to Russia.

De Valera became president of the Assembly in 1938, and another Irishman, Sean Lester, was secretary-general of the League from 1940 to its dissolution in 1947. Ireland's increasing prominence in the League unhappily coincided with the increasing weakness of that body as an instrument for maintaining peace and settling international disputes. In many ways its representatives were also representatives of the liberal conscience of the world and, like other upholders of that conscience, Ireland had the bitter duty of seeking peace without being able to ensue it. Speaking on the Italian aggression against Ethiopia, de Valera said:

> If the Great Powers of Europe would only meet now in that peace conference which will have to be held after Europe has once again been drenched in blood; if they would be prepared to make now in advance only a tithe of the sacrifices each of them will have to make should war begin, the terrible menace that threatens us all today could be warded off.

His words re-echo uncomfortably down the years to us today, locked in the frightening tedium of endless, unproductive disarmament conferences.

Ireland voted against Italy on the sanctions issue in 1935, supported non-intervention in Spain and refused to recognise Franco: all of which took a high degree of moral courage on the part of the Irish government in view of the character of Irish Catholicism.

Ireland's attitude to Hitler has never been objectively assessed. Newspapers were generally cool to him. The Anschluss met with some public approval: it was the end of a partition of sorts and this had an emotional impact in Ireland. Munich aroused no strong feelings and the country looked on it as something happening outside its immediate interest. On the day Chamberlain flew to Germany, the *Irish Independent's* leading article was about National Monuments. This is indicative of the Irish attitude. The *Irish Times* took a pro-British line rather than condemning Germany on idealistic grounds. The *Irish Press* on September 22, 1938 spoke with mild regret of the methods used to dismember Czechoslovakia, but here also overtones of Partition were not without influence. Nor with the approach of war and the certainty of Irish neutrality did newspapers adopt more positive attitudes. On September 4, 1939 the lead sentence of the *Irish Times* was 'The British Empire is at war'. It went on to say that this appalling fact overwhelmed every other consideration. Poland, the threat to Europe, the brutality of Nazism—none of these apparently counted against the fact that the British Empire was at war. The *Irish Press* on September 1 had a leader which sympathised with Poland without condemning Germany. Strict neutrality and censorship ended all comment on the war issues for the duration of the conflict, and even reports of a bishop's encyclical later in the war mildly condemning Nazi crimes were cut by the censor. Not until the *Irish Times* set out photographs in a triumphant 'v' on V-E Day was the censor's hand evaded. All newspapers throughout the war referred to Hitler respectfully as 'Herr Hitler'.

NEUTRALITY 1939–45

With great diplomatic finesse, de Valera had long prepared for neutrality. On February 19, 1939 he stated in a broadcast: 'The aim of the Government's policy is to maintain and preserve our neutrality in the event of war'. Later, on May 29, he spoke of how 'our territory will never be used as a base for attack against Britain'. No assurance of this kind was given to Germany, however. Thus, when war broke out he did not have to make any sudden formal declaration of neutrality, but simply made, on September 2, a passing reference to his speech in February. The only Irish politician to disagree with this policy, supported by the overwhelming majority of the people, was James Dillon.

The policy inevitably subjected Ireland to tremendous pressure from the

Allies to get the use of Irish ports. The British had secured a clause in the Treaty specifically allowing them the use of these, but this right had been formally relinquished in the 1938 Agreement. It was this which made the policy of neutrality possible. Although by 1938 war-clouds were thickly looming, the Admiralty made no protest over the abrogation of the ports clause in the Treaty. But when war broke out, and up to the development of radar, the British exerted strong pressure to regain use of the ports. This pressure was renewed when the United States entered the war. Ireland's relations with both countries were complicated by personal factors, notably the antipathy between Churchill and de Valera, and the anti-Irish attitude of the American ambassador, David Gray. The latter had no hesitation, for example, in proposing to Admiral Leahy on June 3, 1943 the seizing of bases in Ireland by force. In effect, if not formally, Gray was *persona non grata* with the Irish government during the last year of the war.

Germany never seriously entertained thoughts of invading Ireland.* The attitude of the German ambassador, Dr Hempel—a career diplomatist, in contrast to Gray who was a friend of Roosevelt—was on the whole understanding. For a neutral country, Ireland's relationship with Britain did call for a fair amount of 'understanding' from a German envoy. Facilities were given for the return to Britain of its airmen landing in the Republic, and there was, of course, the great contribution made by Ireland to Britain's war manpower which has been described in the previous chapter. There were difficulties arising from the presence of a radio transmitter in the German embassy, and from the Irish distinction between 'operational' and 'non-operational' flights over Donegal, which favoured Britain. The transmitter occasioned the delivery in February 1944 of two Notes from Britain and the United States, protesting against the presence of German spies in Ireland. Preparations were being made at this time for the Normandy landings of June 1944, and the Allies' concern for secrecy was understandable. But in fact, as the British were aware, the transmitter had been handed over by the Germans before the Notes were delivered. The only effect of this diplomatic pressure was to create an atmosphere favourable to Fianna Fail. One of its winning slogans in the 1944 elections was: 'Vote for Fianna Fail or the bombs will fall'.

It is not generally known that, shortly before the war, the British representative in Ireland, Sir John Maffey (later Lord Rugby) had a confidential meeting with the editor of the *Irish Times*, Bertie Smyllie. He

---

* Although, of course, had the Battle of Britain been won by the Germans, Operation Sealion—the German plan for invading Britain—would have been put into effect and Ireland would have been automatically included in German plans for conquering and controlling the United Kingdom.

told Smyllie that his mission was to discover what the likely reaction would be to the landing of British troops in the Free State. Smyllie assured him it would be instant and violent. He was left with the impression, however, that an invasion of Ireland by the British was a distinct possibility.*

The only overt acts of pressure were the 'economic sanctions' of December 13, 1941. Up to this date Britain had brought 400,000 tons of food supplies to neutral Ireland at the risk of lives and ships. But from this date onwards her vessels ceased to carry supplies to Ireland, and trade between the Free State and other countries—except Britain—was made subject to the 'Navicert' system. (A 'Navicert' was a document issued by British consuls in neutral ports attesting that a cargo did not contain contraband and so could pass through the blockade.) Moreover, Irish ships were refused bunkering facilities in ports under British control. These measures resulted in the imposition of rationing (as described in chapter 4) which lasted from 1941 to the end of the war. In 1941 the Americans leased two ships to the Irish government but refused to replace them when these were sunk.

In January 1944, 40,000 American troops landed in Northern Ireland. In the South the atmosphere was electric in the expectation of an invasion. The tension slackened after a time, but Irish public opinion continued on tenterhooks. In March 1944, when the preparations for the Normandy landings were under way, the movement of Irish ships to and from the continent was stopped as a precaution against intelligence leakages. In a memorandum of March 19, Churchill wrote to Roosevelt that he had no intention of employing further economic sanctions, but 'we should let fear work its healthy process'. By this time Roosevelt and Cordell Hull, the US secretary of state, were in favour of increasing the pressure on the Irish government; but, recognising Ireland as a British 'sphere of influence', they left the last word in the matter to Churchill and his colleagues. London by now had come round to the realistic view that, since Ireland was no longer essential to the Allied war effort, there was no point in going further in suborning her. Not all British leaders were unfriendly to Ireland: Eden and de Valera, for instance, got on well.

As has been described in the previous chapter, to meet the difficult situation created by the war the Irish made impressive efforts to become as independent as possible of outside supplies, and, by urging volunteers to enlist, to strengthen the Free State's defences against an attack which many in the country thought might come at any time. With so many of her

---

* Senior members of the staff of the *Irish Times* were summoned, some of them from their beds, by the editor immediately after Maffey left him. Smyllie did not publicise the visit, but committed the conversation to a long memorandum which I was allowed to see by the paper's present editor.

citizens serving in the British forces, and with 250,000 enrolled in her own national emergency services, neutral Ireland had almost as much of a 'war atmosphere' in public and private life as if she had been one of the belligerents. There was a considerable body of anti-British—but not pro-Nazi—feeling in the country, on which the IRA as a whole and in particular those of its members in contact with the Germans tried to capitalise. But, as will be seen in chapter 11, the IRA, though a serious problem, was not a grave threat during the war, thanks to the government's measures against it and to the pro-Allies spirit of the bulk of the people.

POST-WAR PROBLEMS

With the end of the war, many in Ireland looked to see their country play a constructive role in international and particularly in European affairs. This expectation has in many ways been amply justified. Yet there was an aspect of Ireland's contribution to international relations in the immediate post-war period of which Irishmen can have little reason to be proud: namely, the tendency to use the Council of Europe as a platform for domestic grievances. Ireland was a founder-member of the Strasbourg Assembly in 1949, but from the line her delegates took it would seem that she arrived there hot-eyed and bristling with a sense of grievance over Partition which the cloistered wartime years had allowed to fester. Her first years at Strasbourg were devoted to what came to be known in Dublin as 'the sore thumb policy'. Sean MacBride and his Clann na Poblachta advocated raising Partition abroad at every possible opportunity. The vibrant speeches of her representatives exacerbated the Northern Unionists, bored other delegates into weary unconcern, and diverted Ireland's energies from more fruitful courses in international affairs.

Even so, there were encouraging signs that Ireland was capable of playing a distinguished part on the new international scene, and after a time her European colleagues became aware that there was a deep, constructive current in Irish attitudes to world problems. Ireland was the first country to agree to accept the jurisdiction of the European Court of Human Rights, continuing thus the position taken by Patrick McGilligan in 1929 in regard to the International Court of Justice. Today, Irish citizens are able in Irish law to institute proceedings before the Court of Human Rights against the Irish state. Sean MacBride, the minister for External Affairs when Ireland took this decision, was also counsel for the defence of Gerard Lawless. Detained as an IRA suspect during the 1956 campaign, Lawless became the first Irish citizen to avail himself of this provision. This particular guarantee of the individual's rights, entailing as it does a restriction on national sovereignty, was one which Britain was then, and still is, unwilling to accept. Ireland was also one of the first countries to ratify the Council's Social Charter which guarantees basic rights for workers. After her rather indifferent start, Ireland soon put a discreet finger-stall on the 'sore thumb', and now sends some of her ablest politicians as representatives to play an altogether more dignified and constructive role.

Ireland applied for membership of the United Nations in 1946, but the Soviet Union used the veto to keep her out until 1955. In the end her admittance was part of a deal between East and West, balancing new members from one 'bloc' with those from the other. The Irish representatives took their seats in the Assembly for the first time in the session of 1956. Then began a period in which Ireland played a role in the UN out of all proportion to her size—until the growing number of Afro-Asian countries and the financial sclerosis induced by Russian and French attitudes to the UN debt inhibited Ireland's initiatives. However, the 1965 compromise over the debt may yet be the green light for another period of Irish initiative. The speeches of Liam Cosgrave, minister for External Affairs at the time of Ireland's entry, made a good impression both at home and on the General Assembly. One can claim without chauvinism that Irishmen have shown at international gatherings an extra dimension of responsibility. Ireland in 1956 voted to condemn both the Russian intervention in Hungary and the Anglo-French foray in Egypt. Her votes on both these issues were in line with the current American policy and Irish public opinion. They did not of themselves indicate any new trend in Irish foreign policy.

A new trend can be identified as beginning with the assumption by Frank Aiken of the leadership of the Irish UN delegation. In view of the fact that he is one of de Valera's closest friends and admirers, and has been a member of every Fianna Fail cabinet since 1932, it might have been expected that he would follow de Valera's 'independent line' of the 'thirties. However, so firmly was he identified as a member of the conservative old guard that the initiatives he took at the UN came as a complete surprise to the Irish public.

Aiken was born on February 13, 1889 on a farm near Camlough in Armagh. He commanded the 1st Northern Battalion in the War of Independence. When the clouds of Civil War began to darken the country, he tried to make peace between the dissident factions, but after the attack on the Four Courts he decided to fight on the anti-Treaty side. Having made this decision, he was one of the last to lay down his arms. He was with Liam Lynch when the latter was shot, and became chief of staff in his stead, issuing the cease-fire which brought the fighting to an end. As with many another good man in Irish public life, the Civil War left Aiken with bitter memories which occasionally lead him into byways not reflective of his general conduct. As late as 1964, a guidebook produced by his Department of External Affairs aroused sharp controversy in the Dail when it was discovered that in the section giving a potted history of the Irish state, all mention of Griffith, Collins, James Larkin and of Cumann na nGaedheal had been omitted. During the 1939–45 war, the *Irish Times* sometimes exchanged headlines on the war between the Allies and the Axis for those relating to the war between Aiken and the newspaper over his activities as censor.

It was fitting that, being so closely associated with Ireland's separation from the world during the war, he should have been the main agent for bringing Ireland to the fore in world affairs after the war.

Under Aiken, the Irish delegation at the UN was one of the most remarkable to represent any small country. Dr Conor Cruise O'Brien, who was later to attract no small notice when he smote the Katanga Lobby over the head with the white man's burden, was Aiken's principal adviser in his capacity as head of the United Nations section of the Department for External Affairs. Dr Frederick Boland—who became president of the General Assembly on September 21, 1960: the famous session attended by Eisenhower, Khrushchev, Macmillan, Nasser and Castro—was Ireland's permanent representative to the UN.*

The delegation also included Maire MacEntee, one of the best of the school of younger Irish poets. She is the daughter of Sean MacEntee, who was at the time minister for Health, and a niece of Cardinal Browne: one of the most conservative members of the Roman Curia. Another outstanding personality was Eamonn Kennedy, the delegation's African expert who is now Irish ambassador to Bonn. Served by such a delegation, Ireland made an outstanding contribution to the cause of world peace. Aiken's resistance to the pull to the right exerted from Dublin and the tug to the left exerted at his elbow by Dr Cruise O'Brien constitutes one of the most remarkable balancing acts in contemporary politics.

Scrupulously honest in his private and public dealings, Aiken's attitude to complex international problems is generally governed more by his conception of right and wrong than by material interests. He is also motivated by the conviction, shared by the old guard, that in some way this sort of policy can outweigh the effects of the past. When, in the course of an interview, I said that he had done remarkably well in guiding his country's foreign policy, he replied: 'Oh well, there are the effects of seven hundred years of propaganda to overcome'. This attitude of strong principle caused

* An outstandingly charming man in a nation of charmers, directorships fell on Boland like indulgences on a pilgrim to Lourdes when he retired from the Irish diplomatic service in 1964. (He was also the first Catholic to be made chancellor of Trinity College, Dublin.)

those of his colleagues who were favourable to the European Economic Community to disagree with him when it came to such matters as voting for the Algerian independence movement and against France. But by a combination of elementary shrewdness and sheer hard work, he built his Department into a position of near-autonomy as far as the rest of the cabinet was concerned.*

Cold War and Disarmament

It might have been de Valera speaking when Aiken, in 1958, told the General Assembly: 'My country is unalterably opposed to doctrines which involve the suppression of religious freedom, and to methods which have caused death and suffering on a great scale inside China'. But he added later: Can the cause of freedom really be served by shirking discussion ? In 1959, Ireland jointly tabled with Malaya a resolution condemning Chinese aggression in Tibet (adopted October 21). Under Aiken there was never any doubt about the liberal values animating Irish foreign policy. Equally, he left no one in Ireland or elsewhere in doubt about his attitude to the admission of Communist China to the United Nations. This was given its first major expression in a three-paragraph speech he made to the General Assembly on September 23, 1957, in support of an Indian amendment asking that the report of the General Committee should include an item entitled 'The Representation of China in the United Nations'.

> . . . We have no sympathy whatever with the ideology of the Peking Government. We condemn its aggressive policies in China itself, and particularly its conduct in North Korea. No country has a greater horror of despotism, aggression and religious persecution than Ireland has. On all these grounds we reprobate the record of the Peking regime.
>
> If merely by refusing to discuss the question of the representation of China in the United Nations, we could do anything to improve the situation in Korea, we would vote without hesitation in favour of that course. We are not, however, convinced that refusal to discuss the question can now serve such a purpose.
>
> Our aims should be to win acceptance for the principles of the Charter in China, and to secure self-determination for the people of Korea. The belief of my delegation is that in the present circum-

---

* During the 1965 election, he worked in the Department every morning, postponing his constituency canvassing and speaking to the afternoon and evening. His vote slipped appreciably but—for the sake of party unity, one imagines—Lemass made him Tanaiste (deputy prime minister) in succession to Sean MacEntee: a position which, at the time of writing, he holds in conjunction with the External Affairs Department.

stances progress can best be made to these ends by having full and open discussion of the question of the representation of China in this Assembly. We are voting, therefore, in favour of the amendment proposed by the delegation of India.

The 1957 amendment was defeated by forty-three to twenty-nine with nine abstentions. With grim irony India was soon to learn at first hand what Chinese 'aggressive policies' could mean.

Aiken's China policy aroused lively reactions, and not only in Ireland. The *Irish Press* and the *Irish Times* reported Ireland's vote the day after it was made, receiving it with approval. But the *Independent* did not do so until October 8, and then only at Aiken's urging. Between the day of the vote (September 23, 1957) and October 8, the paper had carried reports of reactions to the speech, most of which took their tone from rightwing American comment in publications like the *New York Post*, the Jesuit periodical *America*, and the *Catholic News*, the organ of the Catholic diocese of New York. The transatlantic shock-waves took some time to stir opposition circles, mainly because Fine Gael under Liam Cosgrave had become committed to the view that China's membership would have to be discussed. But eventually Fine Gael put down a motion of No Confidence over Aiken's handling of the issue. This was rejected by seventy-eight to thirty-eight votes on November 28. Fine Gael's case took the form of a general attack on mentioning or discussing such a matter. Having done as much in this way as it felt called on to do, Fine Gael ignored the issue when Aiken again voted to discuss the China issue in September 1958. The *Independent* contented itself with publishing comments from America which had been made about the 1957 vote.

However, the question blew up in a more serious form when it was made an issue in the presidential election of 1959. Though it failed to have an adverse effect on de Valera's candidature, Lemass regarded it as sufficiently serious as to require a statement from him in the Dail supporting Aiken up to the hilt. Speaking on the same occasion (July 7), Aiken replied directly to his critics, notable among whom were the Fine Gael deputies Oliver Flanagan and Patrick McGilligan. During the presidential campaign it had been suggested that the Irish delegation to the United Nations had been emulating Burgess and Maclean; was indifferent to the spiritual and moral values of the country; was going communist; and was showing unmistakable signs of conveying the Island of Saints and Scholars into the Atheist Bloc by inviting a Russian group to a reception in New York. McGilligan made a remark in debate to the effect that Ireland's foreign minister should have gone to Rome for the obsequies of Pius XII instead of 'hopping and hovering around the United

Nations'. Aiken retorted: 'If Deputy McGilligan had to climb on to the bodies of his grandmothers and grandfathers for several generations to get a crack at Fianna Fail, he would do it. He is a low type who would climb on the body of a dead Pope to have a crack at Fianna Fail.' After dealing with the criticism in the *Brooklyn Tablet* that five hundred young Irish people had come back indoctrinated from a music festival in Moscow (not a single Irish passport had, in fact, been issued for the festival), Aiken demolished a hysterical attack on his China policy in the *American Mercury*. 'On the basis that you cannot have any contact and that it is betraying civilisation and spiritual values if contact takes place with people of whom you do not approve, Saint Patrick would have kept out of Ireland.'

The China Sea, however, became temporarily unnavigable for Aiken's coracle when, at the 16th Session of the General Assembly in 1961, the United States modified its course. Hitherto the question had been one of discussion, not recognition. But after the United States faced Peking with the question as to whether it accepted previous decisions of the UN and recognised the Charter, Communist China was forced to react negatively since the UN had already branded her as an aggressor. If China would not accept the Charter and previous UN decisions as binding, what was her membership of the UN worth? Such was the problem Aiken and others like him had to face.

Speaking to the General Assembly on the new situation on December 11, 1961 (when we may justifiably assume that he was also under some pressure in consequence of Cruise O'Brien's resignation earlier that month), Aiken said: 'We were glad when the Assembly decided . . . to inscribe the question of the representation of China on the Agenda and to debate that question. . . . With that decision the whole matter enters a new phase. . . . How and by whom should China be represented in this world organisation?' He went on to say that, under Article 1 of the Charter, the Irish government felt in duty bound not to take any action which would admit China to the UN until Peking made guarantees of non-aggression against its neighbours (particularly Taiwan), accepted internationally supervised elections in Korea, and respected the personal rights and liberties of the Chinese people. The important point about this speech is not its content, which followed the same line as Aiken had taken since 1957, but the vote which followed it. He had always stipulated that Ireland's insistence on discussion of the China question was subject to the above conditions being observed. But since even 'discussion' ran counter to American policy, the ensuing Irish votes in favour of it were always in the opposite lobby from America's. On this occasion, however, Aiken voted with the American delegates, being prompted thereto by China's refusal to give the desired guarantees. Since fundamentally the object of 'discussion' was to determine the *seating* of China, Aiken's 1961 vote was, equally fundamentally, a vote against representation of Peking at the UN.

But this was tacking, perhaps, rather than a wholly new course. He took another bearing in the China Sea when he suggested to the General Assembly on December 8, 1964 that the secretary-general and the four nuclear powers on the Security Council should negotiate between Taiwan and Peking on the basis that 'Taiwan would take a seat in the Assembly and that Peking would assume the position of a permanent member in the Security Council, accepting to be bound by the purposes and principles of the Charter'. This proposal was to prove highly useful the following year when, on September 30, 1965, Aiken was able to quote it to refute a Russian allegation that the Irish plan for financing peace-keeping was part of a plot to undermine the position of the five founder-members of the United Nations (of which China is one).

The Irish resolution of 1965 for new peace-keeping machinery advocated that the authorisation should be changed, proposing that a two-thirds majority in favour of a given operation be drawn from a quorum consisting of three-quarters of the voting members of the General Assembly. Before the Assembly votes, it must be informed how the members of the Security Council have voted on the issue. Supporters of the Irish plan argue that, necessary as it is for the Assembly to know how the bigger powers view a particular operation, it is also necessary that members of the Security Council be prevented from imposing a *de facto* veto in terms of finance in addition to the *de jure* veto they can exercise once a peace-keeping decision is taken. On the financial mechanism, the Irish resolution proposed that the permanent members of the Security Council pay 70 per cent of the net cost of financing each peace-keeping operation, with the proviso that only those who vote in favour of it need pay up. As a corollary of this, the Irish plan envisaged that if only one member of the Security Council supports a given operation, that member becomes responsible for the entire 70 per cent share of the total cost ascribed to the Council. The remaining 30 per cent is to be provided by states in the General Assembly other than the Security Council powers: 25 per cent from the economically developed members, and 5 per cent from the poorer countries.

Ireland has perhaps been more genuine in her claim to be attempting to follow a policy of 'non-commitment' than most other countries who make this claim. Her international policy has been more concerned with finding rational solutions to specific problems than with taking up hard-and-fast positions. Though psychologically sympathetic to the Western alliance, Ireland has not been tied to the specific policies pursued by the states which are commonly regarded as belonging to 'the West'. Ireland opposed Britain

over Suez, took a line over China which was seen as anti-American in
some quarters, and has all along opposed the apartheid policies of South
Africa. A good example of Ireland's general stance is Aiken's speech on the
Cuban missile crisis in October 1962. It was a reasoned speech which
sought to condemn neither side and expressed understanding for 'the
concern which the Revolutionary Government of Cuba feel for their
national security . . . in view of the attempt made by Cuban refugee
elements to invade their territory in April last year'. At the same time,
while not endorsing the State Department's line, he appreciated the
American anxiety over the installation of Soviet missiles in Cuba.

In 1958 Aiken made a major venture in the field of disarmament policy,
tabling a proposal to the Political Committee of the General Assembly to
the effect that the 'nuclear club' should be limited to those nations which
already possessed the Bomb, and urging them not to share their nuclear
weapons with other countries. He asked for a total of fourteen other
nations to join Ireland in sponsoring this plan. Though he failed to get the
support needed and his motion was withdrawn, Aiken's initiative bore
fruit a year later when, on November 20, 1959, the Irish resolution on the
prevention of the wider dissemination of nuclear weapons was, with no
votes against and twelve states abstaining, adopted for reference to the
ten-nation disarmament committee. The British Labour Party's nuclear
policy owed much to the situation created at the UN by the Irish initiative
on this issue. The subsequent disarmament conferences at Geneva have
had the Irish resolution before them as a major blueprint for world peace.

Aiken's plan urges a 'non-dissemination' agreement to prevent the spread
of nuclear weapons—in particular, by getting the nuclear powers to
guarantee that they will not provide other countries with these weapons or
give them the assistance necessary for making them. Crucial to his plan is
the insistence that non-nuclear powers shall open up their territories to
international inspection. He enlarged on this in a speech to the General
Assembly on October 3, 1963, suggesting that, in the event of conflict, a
UN conciliation force, drawn from a permanent corps, should be sent to
the war area immediately with the aim of 'freezing' the situation while the
UN worked to bring the combatants to the conference table.

Another of Aiken's proposals—the one which, he told me, he regards as
potentially the most valuable of all his country's initiatives—is the 'areas
of law' concept. As defined by him in a speech to the General Assembly on
September 30, 1965, an area of law 'is an area in which a group of states
will agree not to attack each other, to settle their differences peacefully and
to restrict their armaments to police level, on the condition that the United
Nations, backed by the nuclear powers, guarantees them against aggression
from outside or inside the area'.

Ireland's role in this and other matters has not received universal approval. When first made, Aiken's proposal on nuclear limitation and disarmament was condemned by America as communistic, by the Russians as a capitalist plot, and—unkindest cut of all—by Franco's Spain as undemocratic! In 1959 Aiken was lampooned in *Krokodil*; South Africa denounced Ireland as an 'unfriendly government'; while Peking—blowing a raspberry at the small nation which had risked strong American displeasure in opposing the 'ban China' policy—informed the world that the Irish delegation were 'lackeys of American imperialists'. In Dublin, during the Dail debate on his Department's estimates (July 7, 1959), Aiken was accused of 'betraying the moral and spiritual values of the country'. It did for a time seem possible to displease all the people all of the time. When I asked him how he felt about all the pressures, he said: 'Ah, sure you have got to put up with that sort of thing if you're going to get anything done'.

In response to the widespread distortion in Ireland of Aiken's support for discussion of China's admission to the UN, the Irish United Nations Association was set up to educate public opinion. Generally speaking, however, public opinion in Ireland plays no obvious part in forming the Irish delegation's attitude. During a UN debate on a given question, greater influence is usually exerted by the embassies in Dublin—as was the case, for example, with French representations over the Algerian question. But, China apart, Irish opinion has on most questions been strongly behind the line taken by its minister for External Affairs and its delegation at the United Nations.

The Congo

So far, we have discussed Ireland's contribution to world problems in terms of speeches and resolutions. But the country has also made its mark by direct involvement in the physical task of helping to keep the peace. In June 1959 the first of its UN contingents took service as observers in the Lebanon. Irish observer forces have since been sent to other parts of the world as required, most notably to the Indo-Pakistani war front in Kashmir in September 1965. But it was on November 22, 1960 that the full implications of actively supporting the United Nations was brought home to Ireland. On that day the country virtually closed down for the funeral of ten Irish soldiers, killed in an ambush by Baluba tribesmen.

In response to the UN request of July 18, the first contingent of Irish troops left for the Congo on July 27. It was the first time in the history of the state that members of its regular forces had gone abroad—and they were serving in the cause of peace. (At a moment of such permissible national pride, no one thought it proper to say anything about the intervention of the IRA and O'Duffy's forces in Spain.) The sight of the coffins going along O'Connell Street made people realise that in today's world all nations are in the struggle for peace together.* The Congo operation left a deep mark on the Irish collective mind. Even today, police sergeants giving evidence in county courts involving drunken and riotous behaviour are apt to tell the judge that 'the Balubas wouldn't do as bad'. Mr Tshombe's subsequent elevation was to give many Irish people occasion for long, long thoughts about those coffins. But not in the early days of 1961. Then it was a case of Irish soldiers doing their duty, and dying, in a clear and unambiguous cause. The feeling was widespread, encouraged also by the moves being made at the same time towards association with the Common Market, that Ireland was emerging fully into the world out of the shadows of the post-war years.

Dr Conor Cruise O'Brien had been appointed UN representative in Katanga. Another Irishman, Lieutenant-General Sean MacEoin, had been appointed commander-in-chief of the UN forces in the Congo. This, with Lemass's announcement at the beginning of August that his government was seeking membership of the EEC, did indeed make it seem that Ireland had an increasingly useful and satisfying role to play in the world. But though the Congo operation was certainly useful, it was far from satisfying. It claimed the life of Hammarskjöld—a world-depleting loss. For Ireland, the Baluba ambush at Niemba was to be only the first item on the Irish casualty list. There were several accidents to soldiers in the course of duty, the most prominent being the car crash on October 27, 1960 in which Lieutenant Colonel Justin MacCarthy, deputy chief of staff of the UN forces, lost his life.

On September 14, 1961, a news agency report reached Dublin of an action at Jadotville in which there had been tremendous Irish casualties. A general election was due on October 4, and it seemed that in its small way Ireland might suddenly go isolationist. Aiken flew to Elisabethville where, happily, he found that the story was untrue. Hammarskjöld denied that Cruise O'Brien had begun hostilities against Katanga without authority. A cease-fire between Katangese and UN troops was arranged. On Aiken's return, both Fine Gael and Labour gave tacit but unmistakable endorsement to the Irish presence in the Congo by making no mention of foreign policy during the campaign.

In the heady days of the Congo operation, when M. Spaak was calling Cruise O'Brien 'l'inqualifiable M. O'Brien', the UN representative's statement of September 14 ('The secession of Katanga is ended. Katanga is

---

* Although let it be said that, with the Irish gift for enhancing any emotional or solemn occasion, hawkers under the portico of the GPO did a roaring trade selling tricolour ribbons with black edging. 'Get your mourning badges', they cried. 'Souvenir of the hysteric occasion.'

now a Congolese province run by the Central Government in Leopold-ville') was understandable. He had written a week or so previously (August 29): 'We're very happy here and probably dangerously cocky and euphoric about our coup'. Hammarskjöld had just sent him a telegram expressing 'congratulations, gratification and sincere respect for an exceedingly sensitive operation carried out with skill and courage'. But subsequent events raise the permissible query as to whether the UN representation in the Congo had appreciated, in the military sense, the strength of the Katangese resistance. The fact that the UN mission was to all appearances sabotaged by the action of pro-Katanga interests in holding up aircraft and other military supplies, does not absolve those responsible for launching the attack from the suspicion that something larger was chewed at than was chewable. On the other hand, if the political decision had not earlier been taken to pull back after the capture of Elisabethville, the UN would have remained in control and the Katangese would not have regrouped.

Cruise O'Brien's resignation from his UN post on December 1, 1961 sent violent shock-waves through Irish society. Three deputies were suspended from the Dail and there was uproar as Fianna Fail was accused of his 'diplomatic assassination'. The Dail was reflecting the general feeling that a good and courageous man had been 'got at'. Public reaction was emotional and Cruise O'Brien was widely supported. The government, in possession of all the facts, was non-committal, taking the view that he was an international civil servant and that Dublin had no function or obligation in the matter. Fine Gael endorsed the government's attitude by a strict silence on the subject of the former UN representative. A newspaper correspondent attacked Cruise O'Brien in the letter page of the *Evening Press* in December 1962, contending that his resignation had not been voluntary and that he had, in fact, been dismissed on the sufficient grounds that he had been indiscreet and incompetent in Katanga. In a long reply, Cruise O'Brien demolished these accusations, but made the significant remark that the correspondent's views coincided with those of Aiken. So we may reasonably conclude that the minister was not altogether pro-O'Brien.

Lemass held firm both against the vociferous critics of O'Brien's resignation and against certain influential voices which were raised on behalf of Katanga. Notable among these was that of Dr Michael Browne, bishop of Galway, who expressed the feelings of a substantial body of conservative opinion in Ireland when laying stress on the great improvements brought to the Congo by Belgian administrators and Catholic missionaries. He pointed out that Katanga was very rich and a tempting prize to Russian and Chinese elements which were beginning to make their presence felt in Central Africa. Against such arguments Lemass reiterated Ireland's

support for the UN's operation in the Congo. In so doing he spoke for the
larger section of Irish opinion. Though they may have known little about
the Congo, most Irishmen felt that the Belgians' precipitate withdrawal
after years of unbudging authoritarian rule had thrown the entire social
order into such chaos that the UN presence there was essential.

Ireland and the Third World

To the casual observer, it may have seemed almost weirdly strange that
Ireland should have got herself so deeply and dramatically involved in the
Congo. Yet, questions of foreign policy apart, the association of Ireland
with an African problem is far from being a *lusus naturae*. Africa is an area
in which Ireland has created a surprisingly large presence, mainly through
historical and religious circumstances. Irish missionaries of both denominations have been active there for over a hundred years, while many of the
personnel in the British colonial service were Irish. The missionaries have
tended, by association, to make some leftwing or predominantly Muslim
circles in Africa suspicious of Ireland. Nevertheless, there is a strong
feeling of friendship for Ireland in countries like Nigeria, Sierra Leone
and, in particular, Zambia. A high proportion of Africa's present rulers
was educated in Ireland. At present, some 10 per cent of all students in
Irish universities are foreign. (Irish universities are easier to enroll in than
British.) Some Africans, mainly Zambians, have been trained in administrative methods by the Irish Institute of Public Administration. The
present attorney general of Zambia, James Skinner, is an Irishman: the
only European in Kaunda's cabinet.

Both as a UN police-force nation and as a country with close personal
links in Africa, Ireland has an interest in the stability of the newly independent states there. The Second Programme provides a further imperative,
for in it the government specifically recognises the country's duty to help
underdeveloped societies. The minister for External Affairs is typical of
many Irishmen, for he has a daughter who is a lay missionary in Zambia,
while one of his two sons, an engineer, devoted a year to building a
cathedral at Oweri in Nigeria. Aiken says that Africans should be helped
in Africa 'to avoid being de-Africanised'.

This sounds reasonable enough, but the tricky problem in this association is that the colour question sometimes leads to fights, even in Dublin.
There are practical reasons for helping Africa towards rapid self-develop-
ment, not only to safeguard Irish lives in Africa, but also Irish lives in
Ireland! Since the Africans involved in shindies are usually the sons of
important people, such incidents get headline treatment in Africa, though
they may pass unnoticed in Dublin. Adverse publicity of this kind affects
the work of the missionaries and also certain commercial ventures, like

the Guinness brewery in Nigeria. The fact that the students are normally away from their home countries for four or five years at a stretch leads to other complications. Some colleens find themselves having a closer concern with black babies than ever they envisaged as they trotted to school clutching their pennies for the mission box.

Personal factors such as these play a not unimportant part in Ireland's relations with the 'third world'. On the level of formal relations, her government reached what is likely to prove the high point of its good standing with that world during the Congo crisis. But from the China vote in late 1961 and the moves made towards closer association with Europe, Ireland's standing as an 'uncommitted nation'—a sort of white cousin of the Afro-Asian family at the UN—has been somewhat reduced in those quarters where 'non-commitment' tends to mean commitment to their 'love-me-love-only-my-dog' view of things.

New Commitments

At the Fianna Fail Ard Fheis (annual conference) in November 1962, Lemass made it apparent that Ireland henceforward would no longer be neutral or unaligned. (In fact, Irish 'neutralism' has been more of a 'moderate' Western position than a strictly unaligned stance.) Having declared the new line in his country's foreign policy, Lemass went into chilling details to make it clear what this could mean in the event of a nuclear war. Nevertheless, his speech was cheered to the echo, particularly when he asserted that the United States was the bulwark of the Free World, underlining this point by a strong attack on the Communist bloc.

This noted, it must be added that Lemass did not there and then spring into the breach with the Western powers, breathing fire and fury on their behalf. When analysed, what his speech amounted to was an indication that Ireland would no longer maintain the position she had taken hitherto: namely, refusing any direct association with NATO so long as Partition continued. The new line of policy demonstrated readiness to co-operate in whatever form of defence-union was entailed in membership of the European Economic Community. Official circles at the time were hoping that Ireland could somehow have one of these 'special relationships' international statesmen talk about: one which would allow her to act as a sort of listening post between the NATO and the Warsaw Pact countries.

From the signing of the new trade agreement with Britain on April 13, 1960—which tied sheep and cattle prices in Ireland closer to the British guaranteed-price system—support had grown for an approach to the Common Market. On June 17, Lemass declared that Ireland would have to join the European movement towards freer trade. Formal announcement of Ireland's application to join the EEC was made by him on August 1,

1961. France's slamming of the door in Britain's face also thrust Ireland's foot from the threshold. It put a grim question mark over the country's future. Not only had the objective disappeared—at least, as a current possibility—for which the radical change in foreign policy had been made; with it there also disappeared the target at which the entire Second Programme was aimed. However, though now a misty blur on the far horizon, the urge to keep the sights on it remained. (And it is possible to argue that Irish industry may have benefited from the enforced breathing space.) The government, albeit not yet a member of GATT, pressed on with support for the 'Kennedy round' of tariff cuts by observing the 10 per cent reduction this prescribed.

It was economic considerations which had induced the change of line in foreign policy in 1962. The emphasis on the economic factor continued, and 1963 saw the opening of Czech and Polish trade missions in Dublin: the first permanent missions from Communist countries to be established in Ireland. The Communist states with which Ireland trades most (Czechoslovakia, Russia, Poland and East Germany) sold to the Irish four times as much in 1964 as they did in 1963. The unbalance in Irish–Eastern bloc trade has been attacked by the country's exporters, and a development of this trade on lines more favourable to Ireland is the aim of her industrialists and trade organisations.*

Another manifestation of the new concern for trade is the change of emphasis in recruiting to the Department of External Affairs. Entrants with economics degrees now predominate over Arts graduates. This follows criticism in recent years that the Department was not doing enough to encourage Irish trade. The criticism, it should be noted, was of the lack of specialists in economics in the Irish foreign service, not of the calibre of the men representing Ireland abroad. Indeed, there is an undertow of complaint in Dublin that Ireland puts itself to perhaps too much trouble and expense in maintaining the kind of ambassadorial representation which is really proper only to a bigger and more 'important' country. Some resentment is felt at the fact that a good many other countries, particularly the United States, send to Dublin ambassadors who are not far from rating as hacks.

It would be completely wrong to deduce from Irish aspirations to join the EEC that the country has become a sort of British Guatemala: politically as well as economically dependent on the big neighbour. Although her

---

* For the year ending 1964, the figures were:

Imports: USSR £826,854; E. Germany £1,379,411; Czechoslovakia £440,137; Poland £1,728,000 (approx).

Exports: USSR £28,693; E. Germany £337,524; Czechoslovakia £228,989; Poland £293,000 (approx).

government docilely supported Britain over Rhodesia at the UN,* the 'independent point of view' enunciated by McGilligan in 1929 has been exemplified both in votes at the UN expressing disapproval of British policies and—as we have seen—in purely Irish initiatives in UN affairs. The Irish government, for example, at first refused to accept the normal UN payment of an allowance towards the cost of its troops in Cyprus (sent there in March 1964, with the loss of four men) in order to signify its disapproval of the 'voluntary fund' method whereby peace-keeping costs are maintained solely at the behest of a few states. Ireland has supplied more troops to peace-keeping missions, in proportion to size of country, than any other nation in the world.

Yet the realities of her situation forbid 'splendid isolation' from the nation across the Irish Sea. Geographically, historically and economically, Ireland's face is turned towards Britain, with whom she does the great bulk of her trade. Whatever happens within and to the United Kingdom is of immediate concern for Ireland. The British economic crisis of 1965 became an Irish crisis, slowing down the development programme and eventually forcing the country to ask, like Britain, for international financial assistance. The Free Trade Agreement signed with Britain in late 1965 (discussed in chapter 7) is a formal acknowledgement, in economic terms, that Saint George's Channel is but a small stretch of water.

Ireland is a country with a standing army of 8,373 men, a handful of obsolete Vampire jets, and a navy of three corvettes—one with crew. Her role in international affairs must be seen in this light. It is something of an achievement that so small and modestly accoutred a country has accomplished so much in its external relations.

*At the declaration of UDI by the Smith regime, Ireland realised uneasily that there were 6,000 Irish citizens in Rhodesia.

7. STATE AND ECONOMY

Structure of the State: *Local Government; Legal System;*
Armed Forces; Central Financing; Social Services
The Economy: *Agriculture; Industry and Commerce; Setting and*
Co-ordinating Targets; Trade Unions; Free Trade Agreement of 1965

STRUCTURE OF THE STATE

THE Irish state is formally embodied in the Oireachtas (parliament) and the president. Parliament has two houses: the Dail and the Seanad. In de Valera's words in a Dail debate on May 11, 1937: '. . . The people are the masters. They are the masters at the time of an election, and their mastery is maintained during the period from election to election through the president.'

Although the presidency does not carry with it the type of control which a head of state like Lyndon Johnson or de Gaulle, for example, can exercise, the holder of the office is more than a ceremonial figurehead. No bill may become law without his signature. He summons and dissolves the Dail on the advice of the Taoiseach (prime minister), whom he formally appoints after the Dail has nominated a head of government. Subject to the prior approval of the Dail and on the nomination of the prime minister, the president appoints the members of the government; he accepts their resignations and terminates their appointments should need arise, again advised by the Taoiseach. Among his discretionary powers is the right to refuse a dissolution of the Dail in cases of political crisis where the prime minister has lost his parliamentary majority. There is as yet no precedent for what constitutes a reason for the president's refusing a dissolution.

The president may summon on his own initiative a meeting of both houses, after consultation with the Council of State* set up under Article 31 of the Constitution to 'aid and counsel' the president. If petitioned by a majority of the Seanad and by not less than a third of the Dail, the president

---

* The Council of State's *ex officio* members are: the Taoiseach, the Tanaiste (deputy prime minister), the chief justice, the president of the High Court, the chairmen of the Dail and the Seanad, and the attorney-general. Former holders of the presidency, the premiership and headship of the judiciary may also belong to it if 'able and willing to act'. The president is empowered to nominate to the Council up to seven persons of his own choosing.

is empowered under Article 27, after consultation with the Council, to withhold his consent to a given bill and to refer it to the people for acceptance or rejection by way of referendum. The Referendum Act of 1942 defined the procedure to be followed. After the president has announced his decision to hold a referendum, the minister for Local Government must make an order within a week of the decision specifying the date of polling, which must not be less than thirty or more than ninety days after announcement of the decision. The order is published in the *Iris Oifigiul* (the official gazette). Two types of referendum are provided for: constitutional amendments, and any legislative proposal passed by parliament. In the case of constitutional amendments, the short title of the bill containing the disputed proposal must be given on the ballot paper; in the case of general bills, the section of the bill embodying the proposal must be stated on the ballot paper. These two provisions were added by the Electoral Law Act of 1963. The returning officer for the referendum prepares a provisional certificate giving the results for and against, nationally and in each constituency. If no petitions are made against the results, the certificate becomes final and enshrines the decision of the people. The president also has the power to submit bills to the judges of the Supreme Court to determine whether or not they are 'repugnant to the Constitution'.

In the event of the president's death or incapacity, his functions are exercised by a commission consisting of the chief justice and the chairmen of the Dail and the Seanad.

The Taoiseach is the head of government, members of which are collectively responsible to the cabinet and individually responsible to the Dail for their own and their departments' activities. The prime minister chooses the members of the cabinet and the parliamentary secretaries; and through his own parliamentary secretary in the Department of the Taoiseach, he co-ordinates ministers' departmental and parliamentary work. In general, pronouncements on important aspects of government policy are made by him. Sometimes he will also act directly in international affairs. For example, Sean Lemass made personal representations to Harold Wilson when Britain imposed the 15 per cent surcharge in late 1964; and later he conducted the Irish side in the talks on the proposed Irish-British free trade area.

It is for the Taoiseach to decide whether to call an election before the expiration of a parliament's constitutional term, to ask for a minister's resignation, and to determine finally, at cabinet meetings which are usually held twice a week, what action the government will take in day-to-day and long-term questions. In fact, therefore, although the president has great powers, the prime minister has always been, since the Constitution of 1937, the most important figure on the Irish political scene. The president is the ultimate guarantor of the rights of the people in times of crisis, but Irish political life has hitherto been so stable that holders of the highest office in the state have not had occasion to exercise their full powers to check the executive.

The main institutions of the Irish state have two things in common: derivation from British institutional forms; and the need of most of them for overhaul. The similarities between the Irish and the British parliamentary systems are paralleled in the central and local administration, the civil service, and the legal system. In 1920 Ireland, in a popular phrase, 'had as many boards as would make her coffin', answering to control in three different directions. Some were responsible to the chief secretary for Ireland, who was always a member of the British cabinet; some to more or less autonomous authorities; and some directly to Whitehall. The Ministers and Secretaries Act of 1924 divided these different agencies of administration into eleven departments, each under specific ministerial control. This measure also provided for the inter-relationships of ministers and departments, for an attorney-general and for parliamentary secretaries (junior ministers). It is today the statutory basis for the central administration.

The Irish Constitution differs from most in specifying the upper and lower limits of the ministerial body. Article 28 states that it must be 'not less than seven and not more than fifteen members'. This provision could prove an obstacle to cabinet-making. Since the 1965 elections the difficulty has been overcome by copious recourse to the device of parliamentary secretaries, who are in effect junior ministers. In some cases, a parliamentary secretary will handle specific matters within a minister's Department. For example, at the Department for Finance, a parliamentary secretary (the most important of his order) controls the Board of Works which deals with public buildings (in association with the Department for Education), harbour installations, bridges, etc. The parliamentary secretary to the Taoiseach serves as a liaison officer between ministers and also as 'chief whip'. Other parliamentary secretaries do not have such clearly defined functions, but serve as general assistants to their ministers in the Dail and in administration. The strength of the present, Lemass administration is fourteen ministers, including the Taoiseach, and six parliamentary secretaries.

This device of parliamentary secretaryships—responsible to the Dail but not part of the cabinet—seems to have proved itself a successful experiment. Not so another constitutional experiment: the 'Extern system'. This was an attempt, inspired by Swiss experience, to break away from British usage by appointing to the Executive Council (cabinet) men who were intended to be administrative experts rather than politicians. The externs were to owe allegiance to the Dail rather than to the cabinet. In all, seven were appointed. Begun at the start of the Free State, the system was ended by a constitutional amendment in 1927 after one of the externs, J. J. Walsh, a protectionist, had repeatedly used his position to dissent publicly from cabinet economic policy and particularly from the free trade views of Hogan, minister for Agriculture.

The Irish financial system places great power in the Department of Finance. The system of budgetary control gives the Department the same relationship with the government as the Treasury has with the government in Britain. The Department of Finance collects the estimates for the coming year's expenditure from the other departments and then, having tried with varying degrees of success to prune them down, it presents the result to the minister who in turn bases his budget on these figures. With the growth of state planning, the Department of Finance is now cutting across the provinces of such departments as Agriculture, and Industry and Commerce. Something on the lines of the French 'Commission du Plan' is emerging.

The Dail, Seanad and local government bodies are all elected by proportional representation in the form of the single transferable vote. The system provides for multimember constituencies. It was adopted in 1922 largely because of Arthur Griffith, a founder member of the Irish Proportional Representation Society, and because Protestants and the people still favouring maintenance of the Union with Britain saw in it a valuable safeguard for minority rights. In 1959 Fianna Fail put the question of abolishing PR to the people by a referendum. The abolitionist case was defeated by 486,989 votes to 453,332. But, following a number of recounts in the 1965 election—in two cases deputies were elected by single-figure margins—Fine Gael has also come round to the view that some future modification of the system would be advisable. The two cases mentioned arose more from local difficulties in administering the system than from any inherent defect in this democratic procedure. But, from the politicians' point of view, there is the weighty fact that power changed hands four times in the five elections held between 1948 and 1961. The Fianna Fail vote never fell more than 8 per cent or rose more than 11 per cent above its average national vote of 571,000 in that time. The combined total votes of the candidates of other parties never went up by more than 9 per cent or down by more than 10 per cent during the same period, when the average total of non-Fianna Fail votes was 706,000. What exactly the floating 10 per cent were thinking must necessarily be a matter for conjecture. But as Civil War loyalties weaken their grip, it is obvious that PR is making it hard for either of the two major parties to get a strong overall majority and is thus making coalition government a regular feature of Irish political life.

If PR goes, so do the Independents. It is difficult to judge accurately what its abolition would mean to the three major parties: Fianna Fail, Fine Gael and Labour. Certainly Fianna Fail would not be a sufferer. It is the most efficient of the parties, and has never got less than 45 per cent of the total vote cast since 1932, although judging by its card-carrying membership, only 3 per cent of those who vote for it actually join it. Fianna Fail has a tradition of tight discipline. Even in opposition the party's shadow cabinet met twice a week, and 'Dev' expected each of his potential ministers to have something to say for himself. It has committees on such matters as foreign affairs and television, and has a pretty shrewd understanding of what goes into an electoral machine. Fianna Fail's support covers a wide spectrum, ranging from industrialists to farm labourers.

A matter of strong concern in recent years has been the question of the quality of the membership of Dail and Seanad. The latter tends to be a place wherein, to parody the catechism definition of purgatory, some souls suffer for a time before they are translated to the Dail; or, alternatively, if they have lost their seats in the Dail, a place wherein they suffer until restored to electoral felicity. In effect, the Seanad's main function is to fill the gap caused by the absence in the Irish Republic of an honours' list. But perhaps this is a trifle too sweeping as a generalisation. The Seanad to some extent also provides a platform for the kind of thinking which does not conform with the more rigid discipline of the party system in the Dail. The 1965 elections, for example, returned to the Seanad two outstanding representatives of this category of politician: Garret FitzGerald (Fine Gael) and Sheehy Skeffington (Independent representing Trinity). FitzGerald is an economic journalist of Griffith-like stature; Sheehy Skeffington does as a one-man show for Ireland what the BBC television programme, 'That Was The Week, That Was', sought to do for England.

The local constituency organisations have a stern grip on the selection of candidates. In one constituency at the 1965 election, Fianna Fail's national executive tried to secure the retirement of one of the sitting deputies. A veteran of 1916, he had been in the Dail since 1927, and over the years the decent man hadn't disturbed the peace of the place by speaking very much. The national executive failed; he stood again. For the first time in his political career, he experienced defeat—at the hands of a man of twenty-eight. But the local organisation had shown itself strong enough to resist the pressure from headquarters, even if it lacked the power to retain its favourite son in the seat.

Although this particular election may be taken as a precedent for the future, it was unusual. Between 1944 and 1961, out of the thirty-seven by-elections, ten were fought by near relatives of the previous member; and out of the six fought between 1961 and 1964, *all* were successfully contested by widows, brothers or sons of the deceased deputies on behalf of whatever party had suffered the loss. It began to look as if deputies had not only a constitutional but also a testamentary right to their seats! Yet so many of the old guard were swept away in the 1965 elections (out of a total of 144 deputies only twenty-four were members of the Dail at the end of the 1939–1945 war) that it is possible this trend may be on its way out.

The parliamentary machine requires restructuring. There are only two permanent committees keeping a parliamentary eye on public business. These are the Seanad's Committee on Statutory Instruments (set up in 1948) and the Dail's Public Accounts Committee which reviews the government's financial proposals. But neither body possesses the secretarial and research facilities necessary to put teeth into their investigations. New deputies find it difficult to find out exactly how the country is run. If a controversial piece of legislation is tabled, the matter is usually dealt with by a few party spokesmen, and it passes over the heads of the bulk of those present at the debate.

Three bills in particular have shown up the deficiencies of the present system, or rather lack of system. One of them, a Finance Bill, caused great controversy throughout the early part of 1965 and made the government highly unpopular in business circles. The rumpus was over a clause which proposed to aggregate pensions and insurances with the rest of a person's estate for the purposes of death duties. The two other legislative measures —a Land Bill and a Succession Bill—were felt to interfere too greatly in the rights of property. The first was held by the opposition to give the minister for Lands too great a power in the acquisition of land. The second, which set out to safeguard the rights of widows and children to a share in a father's estate, provided for a portion of one third of the estate for widows without children and one half for those with. This was held to be an interference with a man's right to leave his property to his family as he wished. The three bills were all amended, since the contentious clauses were spotted by alert newspapers. It was widely felt to be a very bad system which allowed parliamentary draughtsmen so much latitude that they were able to get their notions to within an ace of becoming law without deputies being aware of it. These experiences may yet result in the setting up of a proper committee system. (Fianna Fail set up its own Party Committee in the autumn of 1965.)

What has been all too evident is the effect of the present system, which is to reduce the average deputy's role in decision-making to the point where he becomes little more than a letter-writer on behalf of his constituents in their relations with the civil service. Such men know the score, perhaps, but they contribute little to its total. Up to the time of writing, the life of the majority of rural deputies when the Dail is in session tended to be a round of lonely hotel bedrooms and an uncomprehending participation in divisions. Nor do they lead a social life which would enable them to find out what people are thinking. How some deputies spend their time is one of the mysteries of modern Ireland. A Dublin branch of Fine Gael was thrown into convulsions one evening when a friend of mine proposed a vote of sympathy for the relatives of the member for the constituency. Ashamed at its unawareness of the poor man's demise, the branch was passing the resolution at guilty speed when someone thought to enquire when he had died. My friend replied: 'I don't know, but since no one has seen him in the constituency since he was elected, he must either be dead or taking money under false pretences'. Still, it is perhaps some comfort to us in the South that the calibre of Dail deputies is far from being outshone by the average members of Stormont!

Local Government

For local government purposes, the Republic is divided into thirty-one main administrative areas which, with subsidiary bodies, entails 115 administrative units all told: county councils (twenty-seven), county boroughs (four), boroughs (seven), town commissions (twenty-eight) and urban district councils (forty-nine). The system grew up much as it did in England during the nineteenth century, with the creation first of specialised authorities and then the gradual grouping together of functions with the county as the principal unit. The only marked difference from the English experience is that in Ireland the parish never became a unit of local government.

County councils have from twenty to forty-six members, county borough councils from fifteen to forty-five, borough councils twelve, urban district councils and town commissions nine each. Election to these bodies takes place annually and all citizens over twenty-one resident in the area concerned may vote, by proportional representation, for local government candidates. These generally represent either the main political parties or sectional groupings such as Ratepayers, although a good many Independents are to be found on councils. Local councils often provide a useful springboard for a parliamentary career, though the general calibre of their membership fills one less with awe than compassion.

The duties of these bodies may be broadly summarised as: health, mental health, public assistance, sanitary services, housing, roads and general purposes. The last may range from the fire brigade service to providing scholarships. There are differences in the scope and responsibility of the various levels of local government. For instance, road building and repair is divided into three categories: main, county and urban. Responsibility for main and county roads falls on the county councils through whose areas they pass. Urban roads and public roads, other than main roads, are in the charge of the urban district councils. Local government in Ireland may be thought of principally as county government. Except in the case of the four county boroughs of Dublin, Cork, Limerick and Waterford—which are wholly autonomous—all smaller units of local government are to a greater or lesser degree ultimately subordinate to the county councils. Town commissions have died out in England but in Ireland they still survive with limited powers for housing, fairs and markets.

As in Britain, local government has a mixed system of finance. Money for running it comes partly from state grants and partly from the rates: a form of local tax calculated on the value of a property. (For example, premises with a rate-valuation of £2 would pay £6 a year in rates if the local authority rate was sixty shillings—£3—in the pound.) The rating system has been increasingly criticised in recent years on two main grounds. In the first place, the existing system makes the local rate carry a sizeable burden of the nation's health services. In 1965 the rates contributed £14·4 million of the total amount of £30·2 million alloted to health expenditure. Secondly, the system operates as a disincentive to the improvement of property, since alterations to, say, a house generally result in an increase in its valuation and hence in the rate levied on it, irrespective of the income of the occupants. State grants to local authorities for health and housing in 1965-66 are estimated to be £47,477,000. Rates collected in the same year are estimated at £29,114,000.

Nevertheless, local government in Ireland has shown a high degree of efficiency. A good deal of this can be attributed to the 'manager system', which represents a marked departure from the inherited traditions of English local government. In a sense it is the equivalent on the local level of the Extern system attempted in central government in the 1920s. Influenced by the American example of 'city managers', Cork initiated the Irish development in 1929 in its attempt to replace amateur committees by professional experts. At that time the experiment aroused a good deal of controversy, but it has proved its worth and is now operative in all local authorities. The manager prepares the budget for the council to vote on, and usually he initiates major schemes on the authority of the council, to which he is responsible for their administration. Such managers are generally men of outstanding ability selected from within the local government complex.

The most eminent among them often take on important responsibilities in national life. M. N. Conlon, who became county manager of Cork at the age of thirty-three, has now been appointed, seven years later, by the government to reorganise the Pigs and Bacon Commission. P. J. Meghen, an engineering inspector before 1921 in the department of Local Government and Public Health, rose through various local government posts to become manager for County Limerick. Since his retirement in 1961 he has been a director of studies in the Institute of Public Administration.* Michael Flannery, the manager of County Wicklow, moved from the civil service to local government. His lectures and publications on town planning played an important part in the framing of the Planning and Development Act of 1963. D. A. Hegarty was city manager of Waterford and then county manager for Sligo and Leitrim. In 1946 he became general manager of the Dublin Port and Docks Board, and is largely responsible for a major port development plan published in June 1965. Among other activities, he has been chairman for the Irish Management Institute.

Another factor in the success of Irish local government has been the operation of the Local Appointments Commission, set up in 1926. Candidates for vacancies in local administration are examined by the commission which then nominates its choice to the authority concerned. Thus a chief clerk in a mental hospital can become city manager of Limerick: as was the case with M. Macken, now manager of Dublin city and county and the doyen of the managerial corps. This system allows promotion outlets for administrative talent at all levels, and the commissioners—three in number, appointed by government as 'fit and proper persons'—have kept local government appointments singularly free from political or other pressures.

There are two other important bodies in the orbit of local administration: the Vocational Education Committee set up in 1930, and the County Committee for Agriculture formed in 1931. The members of these are nominated by the respective county councils.

Legal System

The Irish legal system is almost a replica of the English. A man is presumed innocent until proved guilty; *Habeas Corpus* and trial by jury are operative; and offences against property generally rate harsher sentences than offences against the person. From the seventeenth century, the two systems were identical in statute, customs and professional practices. The same juristic

* Founded on a voluntary basis in 1957, the Institute of Public Administration became fully professionalised in 1960. It finances itself by selling courses to state departments and local authorities. Its work is invaluable in improving the standard of public administration. Tom Barrington, a former civil servant and, with Whitaker and C. H. Murray, a main initiator of it, is the present director. Another Watershed creation, the Irish Management Institute, is having a beneficial effect on the standard of management.

virtues and defects characterised both systems; and the same reforms, seeking to remove the latter, were applied on both sides of Saint George's Channel. Irish judges were appointed to the English bench and Irish barristers practised in English courts, while English judges received Irish appointments—though few Englishmen pleaded briefs in Irish courts, retained in the larger country by its richer market in litigation.

The only significant departure from English practice was the establishment of the illegal Sinn Fein courts in 1919. These included courts of land settlement and also circuit, district and parish courts. When the Free State was set up, however, the Irish returned to the English model, taking over the laws then in force. Although the Courts of Justice Act of 1924 altered the judicial system, the basic principles of the old system remained unchanged. The only major alteration came in 1933 when Fianna Fail abolished the right of appeal to the Privy Council in London. In harmony with the gradual liberalisation of the penal code which has taken place in Britain since 1945, Ireland in 1964 abolished capital punishment; or rather, it abolished it for all save political crimes. An IRA gunman who murders a policeman is still liable to the death penalty.

Judges can be removed only by a two-thirds majority in parliament. The courts system forms a pyramid with the Supreme Court at the apex. This is the court of final appeal, and it is also the juridical body to which the Republic's head of state may refer bills of which the constitutional validity is in question. It consists of six judges, including the chief justice and the president of the High Court. Immediately beneath it is the High Court, followed by circuit and district courts. The High Court can hear all cases which come within the jurisdiction of the lower courts. It ordinarily sits in Dublin save when, as the 'High Court on Circuit', it travels to one of the larger towns to hear appeals from circuit court decisions. There are nine such circuit courts. The district courts—twenty-four in number—have a limited local jurisdiction, although they do hear the preliminaries of more serious offences before sending them on to a higher court for trial by jury. These district courts replaced the justices of the peace system of the British administration: a system often characterised by eccentric judgements from men insecure in their tenure of office. District judges have to be lawyers of ten years' standing at least. Judges on the circuit courts, unlike district judges, must be drawn from the ranks of Senior Counsels. A Senior Counsel is the equivalent of the English Queen's Counsel. The legal profession, as in England, is divided into barristers and solicitors. Although 'Lord Chief Justice' and 'Lord Justice' are titles unknown to the Irish Constitution, a barrister would be ill-advised in the Republic's courts to refrain from addressing the bench as 'M'Lud'. As a former chief justice remarked over the wine in an English Inn of Court: 'We're a Republic now, so none of that Lord Chief Justice talk if you please. But you may call me "My Lord": we're not all *that* Republican, thank God!'

Armed Forces

Command of the armed forces is vested in the president of the Republic, who also commissions cadets to the officer corps. Control is exercised through the minister for Defence who is assisted, under the terms of the 1954 Defence Act, by a Council of Defence when this is required. This council comprises the parliamentary secretary to the minister for Defence, the secretary of the Department for Defence, the chief of staff, the adjutant-general and the quartermaster-general.

The amount apportioned to defence in the 1965 budget was just under £10 million. The establishments provide for a permanent defence force of approximately 13,000 (all ranks) for the army, navy and air force. Recruitment is voluntary, and in fact the normal strength of the combined services runs at three to four thousand below this figure. Due partly, perhaps, to the hitherto depressed state of the economy, the officer corps, like the civil service, has always been of high calibre. There are approximately 26,000 men on the reserve.

The bulk of the Republic's armed manpower is contained in the army. The air force is small, consisting of twenty-five aircraft and approximately 600 men of all ranks. The aircraft include Vampire jets, Chipmunks and Provosts; these are used for training purposes only. The force fulfills the important function of training pilots for Aer Lingus, the national airline. The navy has difficulty in crewing and maintaining its three British 'Flower Class' corvettes. The army's infantry section is armed with the FN rifle, the Energa grenade, the Gustaf submachine gun and the GMG bren, together with 84-mm anti-tank guns, Vickers machine guns, and 81-mm and 2-inch mortars. The artillery section (field, air and coastal) is supplied with British 25-pounders, French 75s and 120-mm Brandt mortars, along with some venerable 4·5 howitzers and 18-pounders for the field section. The Irish army's anti-aircraft division in 1939, curiously enough, had a higher percentage of anti-aircraft guns than the British army. Its present armament consists of modern Swedish Bofors and 3·7 heavy ack-ack guns. Coastal defence relies largely on a number of 6-inch guns. The armoured division is equipped with Churchill, Comet and Landswerk tanks and with Leyland, Ford and Landswerk armoured cars.

Officer cadets are trained through the Military College at The Curragh. After a two-years' course, they take service as second lieutenants. It was a detachment from this college which so impressed President Kennedy on his Irish visit that his widow signalised his regard for them by inviting the Irish government to send them to participate in the funeral at Arlington.

Promotion from first lieutenant to captain requires a further course (four months) at the Military College, and captains seeking further promotion are required to take a course of nine months' duration. The college is located in Pearse Barracks at The Curragh, where each of the seven barracks is called after one of the signatories of the 1916 Proclamation.

Central Financing

The Irish banking system came into being largely as the result of the efforts of a group of Belfast businessmen to get permission for banks other than the Bank of Ireland to issue notes outside a fifty-mile radius of Dublin. Legislation passed in 1824 made this possible, and in the following year the Hibernian, Provincial and Northern banks were founded. These, together with the Bank of Ireland, the National Bank, the Munster and Leinster Bank, the Royal Bank and the Ulster Bank constitute the major banking houses of the country, and are the eight 'associated banks' of the Central Bank.

The Central Bank, which does not deal with the public, is the agency charged with safeguarding the Irish currency, though in view of the latter's link with sterling there is not a great deal it can do on its own initiative. It is the end-product of a series of financial evolutions starting with the Coinage Act of 1926 which gave the Free State the right to issue its own coinage. In 1927 the Currency Commission was set up to administer the paper currency first issued in that year: the Saorstat Punt, which had, and still has, the same value as the English pound. (In Ireland, that is; in England there is for Irish, as for Scotch, banknotes a small discounting charge.) In 1929 the Commission took over the issuing of coinage as well. Five years later the Banking Commission was set up to examine Ireland's monetary and banking system; its recommendations (1938) led to the Central Bank Act of 1942 which replaced the Currency Commission with the 'Central Bank of Ireland'. This is the currency-issuing authority; it acts as the banker to the government and to the associated commercial banks, controlling in co-operation with them the volume of credit in the country. For example, its report for 1964-65 described its role in the credit squeeze as 'advice to the Associated Banks concerning their lending policy'. This advice was followed by every bank in the country, resulting in reduction of overdraft facilities and the curtailing of credit except for productive investment.

On May 3, 1965 the Central Bank's powers were extended by making it responsible for exchange-control. It administers the Tax Reserve Certificates (introduced in 1962 to encourage advance tax payments by regarding these as temporary tax-free investments) and the new type of National Bonds, first issued in 1965. These are redeemable at fixed future dates with a fixed premium, instead of being undated interest-bearing stock. Section I of the Central Bank Act of 1964 empowers it to deal in 'securities of any international or international financial institution' which is formed 'wholly or mainly by governments'. This has greatly widened the Central Bank's scope by allowing it to deal in securities other than those of the Bank for International Settlements, which was, under the 1942 Act, the only international financial institution in which the Central Bank could hold securities. The change was made to enable it to buy shares in the World Bank. It also performs, of course, functions like discounting exchequer bills, taking in non-interest-bearing deposits from public authorities and other banks, and advancing money to banks against the security of government stocks or bills.

The Central Bank's board consists of a governor, appointed by the president on the advice of the government, and eight directors appointed by the minister for Finance. He nominates five of these directly, and chooses the other three from a panel drawn up by the eight associated banks.

In March 1965 there were notes and coin in circulation to the value of £113,349,034. The external assets of Irish banks and of government funds on April 20, 1965 amounted to £224·6 million.

Social Services

The Irish health and social welfare services are not dazzlingly Beveridgean in their liberality. The social services are organised on the Plimsoll line notion that below a certain figure people should not be expected to live. Above this level they do not get too much encouragement to survive either. Although welfare service benefits were appreciably increased in 1965 (see Appendix II, Table 9), most sentient people rightly feel that there is still considerable room for improvement. Yet it must be said that the social services are not greatly below the level which Irish prosperity generally would lead one to expect. One of the main problems in regard to health schemes, social welfare and indeed income levels in Ireland has been and continues to be the fact that people in Ireland tend to expect the same levels of benefit as apply in Britain—a vastly richer country—without, until recent years, their making a significant attempt to earn these things.

As at present operated, the health scheme entitles the very poor to free hospital care and treatment. People whom a means-test rules out of this category but whose income falls below £1,200 per annum get hospital treatment at a reduced rate; they are also entitled to free maternity services and care for their babies. Treatment for infectious diseases and tuberculosis, and medical visitation in schools are free to everyone wishing to make use of these services, including the higher income groups who must, however, pay for all other forms of treatment. The Voluntary Health Insurance Board, a state-sponsored organisation, runs a very good health insurance scheme.

Non-contributory pensions (after stringent means-tests) are paid out of central funds to widows, old age pensioners, the blind and the unemployed, and in the shape of home assistance. The payment of social insurance is compulsory on a basis of contributions from worker, employer and state. This entitles the insured or their dependants to a higher rate of benefit. Parents in all income brackets are entitled to a monthly children's allowance.

The voluntary element in the Irish economy is still vitally important. The Church is active in education, and all rehabilitation work, for instance, is voluntary. Without the many charitable organisations there would be widespread hardship. The weekly shilling contribution to this football pool competition or that draw is a feature of the household expenses of almost all Irish homes. The most important of these fund-raising activities is the Irish Hospitals Sweepstake which contributes roughly 12 per cent of the amount spent on hospitals in the Republic. It has helped in the founding of 100 hospitals and 300 dispensaries, in addition to donations to other medical charities.

The Public Hospitals Act of 1933 set up a Hospitals Commission which inspects the national hospital situation and advises the minister for Health on the spending of the Sweepstake's contributions. Its accounts are meticulously audited, police supervise the draws, and irregularities in the Sweepstake's running are as unlikely as indecency in a cathedral chancel. But outside Ireland the Sweepstake is illegal in practically every country in which it operates. It has had to build up what must be one of the largest smuggling rings in the world.

This extraordinary organisation is controlled by Joseph McGrath who has been associated with the Irish Hospitals Sweepstake since 1930. Financially, physically and philanthropically he is one of the biggest men in Ireland. He found it hard to tell me off-hand even to the nearest fifty how many horses he owned. No one will ever know how much he has given to charity. At seventy-seven, he looks like everyone's dream vision of an Irish-American millionaire: bow-tie, light grey suit, voice harsh and eyes like shaded flamethrowers. Much of the success of the Sweep is due to him. He was destined to be an accountant but the 1916 Rising, in which he took part fully expecting to be killed, changed all that. Although he left politics after the Army Mutiny (described in chapter 3), he has always played an important part in the life of the country. (For a period he was head of the secret service.) The night before the first Sweepstake draw in 1930, he happened to read an account of the history of draws and lotteries throughout the world which demonstrated that every one of them had ended in fraud and disaster. McGrath swore a mighty oath that this fate should not befall his fledgling Sweep, and he has exercised the most searching control ever since. Talking to him and to survivors of the struggle for Irish freedom like him, it is easy to see what made the British willing to concede independence in 1921!

THE ECONOMY

By world standards, Ireland is not a poor country, nor an especially small one. Of the 100 members of the United Nations in 1961, thirty-one had populations of three million or less. Ireland's standard of living is in the top quarter of all the nations of the world. But in European terms, Ireland is small and among the poorer countries of the 'developed' world. Its economy is more dependent on a single market (Britain) than any other European country.* It has a high ratio of dependants to producers: seventy-four to every 100, as compared with fifty-three in Britain, fifty-seven in Italy and forty-eight in Germany. The country is still heavily reliant in balancing its budget on the universal popular indifference to cirrhosis of the liver and lung cancer. Without the revenue from alcohol and tobacco taxes (which in 1963–64 accounted for 30 per cent of budget income), the Irish exchequer would totter. Because of the proportion of the labour force in agriculture as opposed to industry, the tax basis is so low that in 1961–62 tax on personal incomes brought in only 4 per cent of the national income.

Under the Second Programme, overall economic activity is expected to increase to an extent permitting of a rise of 75 per cent in exports between 1963 and 1970. Since imports and exports represent the equivalent of 80 per cent of the country's Gross National Product, Ireland is almost helplessly reliant on external circumstances for her national growth-rate. The British 15 per cent import surcharge of 1964, for instance, was a heavy blow, both to the Second Programme's prospects and to national confidence. Even so, since 1958 (when Gross National Product was £600 million) the country has maintained a 4½ per cent growth in its GNP—affectionately known as Gross National Patrick. The official estimate for 1965 is £1,016 million. The balance of payments' deficit on direct trading has grown from £1 million in 1948 to nearly £31½ million in 1964. This gap would have been far greater had it not been for remittances from emigrants and other 'invisible' assets.

In real terms people of the Republic are now one third better off than they were in 1958. But every step in Ireland's economic advance has to be

* For Irish economic statistics in detail, see Appendix II, page 335 *et seq.*

worked for very hard. Although zinc and copper are mined in County Galway and there are coal deposits in Kilkenny and Tipperary, the country has no sizeable mineral resources. Ireland's main assets are the supply of intelligent manpower, temperate climate, limestone pastures and nearness to European markets.

Union with England in the eighteenth century killed off those Irish industries which competed with England's, and stifled the spirit of enterprise in the South. When the industrial revolution crossed Saint George's Channel, it was only in the North-East that new industries were established on any significant scale. In the South, the land system—with its attendant evils of insecurity of tenure and penalisation of all improvements by crippling rent-increases—made the accumulation of wealth impossible. Subdivision of holdings resulted in the creation of three times the present number of farms, over 80 per cent of which were less than fifteen acres in extent. Prior to the Famine of the 1840s, the average life-expectancy in Southern Ireland was twenty-nine years, and the staple diet of the great majority of the people was the potato. All this has left its mark on the economy of present-day Ireland. Moreover, the economic effects of the union with England were exacerbated by the way in which Ireland achieved its independence: the splitting away of the industrialised North-East from the overwhelmingly rural South.

The country areas' long despoilment of people and of local small industries, together with the concentration of economic activity in a few large towns, has led to a grave imbalance in the distribution of national wealth. This has important effects on the local resources available for such things as education and social services. Dublin, city and county, contains a quarter of the Republic's population. Cork, the major city and county in the South (and, Corkmen would have us believe, in the whole country), has ten times the population of Leitrim, which has the highest proportion of old people in the country (12·85 per cent as compared with Dublin city's 6·8 per cent). Taxes per head of population in Dublin are twice as high as in Mayo in the West. The capital earns 29 per cent of the national income, pays 33 per cent of all rates and 45 per cent of all taxes on incomes and for social security benefits. But bleakly beautiful Donegal in the North-West, where the population is only 4 per cent of the national total, earns but 3·1 per cent of the national income and pays only 2·7 per cent in taxes and social insurance contributions.

Agriculture

Farming is the major industry, accounting in an average year for roughly 65 per cent of the total of exports, and employing 35 per cent of the working population. The agricultural provisions of the Second Programme envisaged an annual increase in productivity of 4·6 per cent, but foresaw a fall of 1·8 per cent in employment on the land. There are roughly 289,000 holdings of over one acre in the Republic. Of these, only 10 per cent are 100-acre holdings or more, but they represent 36 per cent of the total area under crops and pasture. Nearly three-quarters of the total number of holdings are under fifty acres, but they account for only a third of the area under crops and pasture. The predicted national fall of 1·8 per cent in employment would mean 38,000 people fewer on the land by 1970 in the Western areas. In Connacht 37 per cent and in the counties of Leitrim, Cavan and Monaghan 29 per cent of the working population earn their livelihood on holdings of thirty acres or under. This is the category of holdings which has declined most rapidly, falling from 91,000 in 1930 to 73,000 in 1960. When the Congested Districts Board was set up in 1891, there were five million small farmers along the Western seaboard and its hinterland trying to scrape a living from 200,000 tiny holdings. Today Ireland has the lowest population density in Europe: 130 to the square mile.

The decline of the small farmer is a world-wide phenomenon and the trend is probably irreversible. But when an Irishman stands on a mountain in Connemara or Kerry or Donegal and looks down at the anguished beauty of a valley in which formerly there were hundreds of cottages and now are only half-a-dozen, he gets a kind of heart sickness. When he considers that in the few cottages still visible along the valley families averaging eight or nine children were reared for the cities of the world, he feels inclined to shake his fist at God and government. And still the drift from the land is going on—to the bigger Irish towns and to England and America. It is this which gives added urgency to industrialisation. Along with the ferro-concrete and the balance sheets, the establishment of a factory in a given area brings the benefits of technical competence and training to the people—particularly the young people—of the whole district, enabling them to have not merely the wish of the toast, 'Death in Eireann', but life in Ireland also.

However, despite agriculture's manifold difficulties, the targets of the Second Programme seem likely to be achieved. State aid to agriculture, which was running at just over £21 million in 1958–59, reached £52,391,000 in 1965–66. In particular, a heifer subsidy scheme has encouraged farmers to build up their stock so that there is now in the cattle trade a hitherto unknown freedom from the necessity of selling, whatever the market price be like. The cattle trade is so important to the national life that any marked fluctuation in prices has a corresponding effect on the standard of living. The problem of developing the Western districts has been tackled in a scientific programme initiated in 1965: a scheme which differs commendably from the 'dole mentality' methods of earlier administrations.

Whether or not it will stem the predicted flow of emigrants is highly prob-lematical. The merits of the scheme will, unfortunately, remain embryonic for some time, since the 1965 credit squeeze slowed it down.

A major difficulty in the way of improving agricultural methods arises from the large number of elderly people on the land. In Ireland eleven out of every 100 people are over the age of seventy, and an uncomputed but significantly large number of its aged population are small farmers. With the pitiful tenacity of age, they hold on to their land while their children slowly grow past innovation. However, it should be noted that, in view of the drop in emigration after 1961—caused by a general increase in prosperity—the Irish Central Statistics Office has forecast an increase of over 60 per cent between 1961 and 1974 for the numbers in the twenty to thirty age group.

The principal Irish farming organisation, the National Farmers' Associa-tion with its 138,000 members, evolved from an earlier rural organisation called Macra na Feirme (Scions of the Soil). Macra began in the early 1940s, mainly through the efforts of three men engaged in giving winter lectures to farmers under the auspices of the Vocational Schools, set up by the Vocational Education Act of 1930, and of the County Agricultural Committees set up under the Agricultural Act of 1931. These 'founding fathers' were: Dr Henry Spain of Kilmallock, County Limerick (an agricultural inspector); Steve Cullinan (a teacher of rural science in the Vocational School at Athy, County Kildare); and Frank Cronin (head-master of the Vocational School at Mooncoin, County Kilkenny). Deciding that the existing classes were inadequate, in 1944 they laid plans for some-thing more ambitious. Macra na Feirme was born the following year under the chairmanship of Patrick Kehoe. Its principal objective was to raise the level of farming know-how. Its meetings and classes throughout the country were well attended. But, being primarily educational, it could not cater for such problems as marketing and prices. Accordingly, between 1952 and 1954 negotiations took place among various bodies—mainly the Creamery Milk Suppliers' Association, the Beetgrowers' Association, and the Irish Agricultural Organisation Society (Plunkett's Co-operative creation)—which led, on January 6, 1955, to the formation of the National Farmers' Association (although the Creamery Milk Suppliers' Association has remained outside the NFA).

The NFA maintains a powerful lobby through its Oireachtas Subcom-mittee. For instance, it brought pressure on the government to introduce in 1964 more stringent precautions against German land-buying. But it is not affiliated to any political party. It caters for farmers of all kinds, yet in the nature of things it tends to be more representative of the views of the bigger farmers in the Midland and Eastern areas, for it is these which have the time and the education to devote to its efforts. However, it is firmly behind Fr McDyer's campaign in the West (see below, page 225) and gives support and encouragement to efforts to improve the lot and the working methods of small farmers.

The most widespread organisation in country districts is Muintir na Tire (People of the Land), with a committee in the majority of Irish parishes. Inspired by the example of the Belgian Boerenbond, Fr Michael Hayes founded it in 1931 as a parent body for a federation of rural producers, but in 1937 changed its character to that of a parish movement designed to make the country a better place to live in. Muintir's underlying principle—community development—is an excellent one, and the movement has done a great deal to improve social amenities in rural Ireland, especially in the field of adult education. But it cannot be claimed that it has had any appreciable effect on emigration or economic development. Even so, as a Protestant clergyman once pointed out to me, Fr Hayes by the time of his death in 1957 had become one of Ireland's first ecumenists in that Protestants as well as Catholics were, and are, always welcome as members of Muintir's local branches, even though its patron is an archbishop, its president a bishop and many of its officers are Catholic clergy.

The main rural organisation for women is the Irish Countrywomen's Association which grew out of the United Irishwomen, founded in 1910 by Lady Fingal who based her movement on one of Sir Horace Plunkett's principles: 'better living'. On its becoming the Irish Countrywomen's Association in 1934, the leading spirits in the new body saw to it that it was strictly non-political and non-sectarian. There was a general feeling that too many of the members of the United Irishwomen had got mixed up with the Blueshirt movement. The ICA has 24,000 members throughout the country. In many ways it corresponds to the Women's Institute movement in Britain, organising classes in domestic economy and handicrafts, and staging debates and discussion groups. It also conducts residential courses at its attractive country house at Termonfeckin in County Louth. Most of its members tend to be women who have already received a secondary or university education, so that in a sense it is preaching to the converted. But the ICA has certainly helped to brighten up rural life, and from time to time it brings pressure to bear on the authorities in regard to problems like the need for extending piped water to all farms. In September 1965, it was host to the World Conference of Associated Countrywomen. This brought so many countrywomen to Dublin that the hotels were almost too full of them to cope with the critics and camp-followers whom Bord Failte, the national tourist organisation, were attempting to bring over for the Theatre Festival as part of its campaign to attract visitors to Dublin!

Industry and Commerce

Between 1955 and 1964, some 200 industrial enterprises were set up, providing new jobs for 26,000 people and representing an injection of £48 million in new capital. The largest single source of this investment, providing 40 per cent of the total, is Britain. Germany has provided 19 per cent and the United States 15 per cent. Japan, Belgium, Holland and France have also made valuable contributions to the capital structure of Irish industry. The failure rate has been less than 3 per cent of the total. Even more encouraging has been the steady growth of new factories from year to year. In the period 1959–64, two factories were established for every one in the previous five-year period. The major enterprises set up with state aid have been: a light-aircraft factory outside Dublin; a factory for making precision-tooled components for aircraft and electronic equipment at Shannon, County Clare, and, in the same area, an important knitwear concern; and a large plastic-pipes plant in the northern part of County Dublin.

The incentives to open a factory in Ireland, available both to Irish citizens and to foreigners, include exemption from income tax and corporation tax on profits from exports for the first ten years; and thereafter a period of five years in which these taxes are gradually raised to the full rate. There is also a system of grants for assisting in the setting up of factories (in some cases grants can be as much as two-thirds and more of the cost of installation) and for the training of workers. A condition of such grants is that the factories concerned must produce goods for the export market.

The national plan for strengthening the economy has begun to show heartening results. Yet all is by no means plain sailing. The Committee on Industrial Organisation (described later) recommended in 1962 the establishment of growth-centres as against the scattered siting of industries, and some ministers have spoken in favour of it. But difficulties arising from the political implications have so far delayed decentralisation schemes. For instance (a hypothetical case): how does the government explain to the electors of Kerry that they are not going to get a new industry or a civil service department, when adjoining Cork has got both? What the effect will be of the social and economic implications of the changes entailed in such measures can only be guessed at. The published plans envisage the development of Waterford and Galway, to begin with, into 'strong towns' which will supply their hinterlands with the amenities of city life and prevent the country's lifeblood from being siphoned off into a handful of cities like Dublin, Cork and Limerick.

A feature of the economic scene which makes Ireland a curious blend of laissez-faire and socialism is the state-sponsored body. The processes by which the 'state companies' were set up were never referred to, or even thought of, as 'socialism'. The authority to establish them was sanctioned in Article 43, section 3.11 of the 1937 Constitution, which says: 'The State shall favour and where necessary supplement private initiative in industry and commerce'. The first such body to be set up was the Electricity Supply Board in 1927.

State-sponsored bodies may be divided functionally as follows: production, marketing, health, finance, communications, promotion, development, research—and the inevitable 'other functions': the Greyhound Racing Board, the Horse Racing Board, and the Foyle Fisheries Commission. This latter is jointly controlled by the governments of Southern and Northern Ireland. These bodies, all told, employ some 50,000 people (roughly one third of all people in government employ), and their total annual paysheet represents about 10 per cent of the sums paid out in wages and salaries in the Republic. Their combined assets in 1962 were approximately £230 million. As well as by function, there is the division by legal classification, and classification by economic sector: agriculture, tourism, transport, and so forth. Legally, the companies may be defined, generally speaking, as statutory corporations of two types. First, there are those set up by a specific statute: for example, the Electricity Supply Board, Bord na Mona (Turf Company) and Coras Iompair Eireann (National Transport Company). Secondly, there are those arising from the terms of a legislative measure in which such a development was foreseen but not specifically prescribed. Aer Rianta (National Airlines Holding Company) was established in this way under the terms of the Navigation and Transport Act of 1936.

Some were set up simply as the need arose or to meet a special demand— like the National Blood Transfusion Association. Others were created to fill a gap left by private enterprise: for example, the Irish Film Finance Company which advances money to film-makers, generally for short films. Yet others came into being to preserve an undertaking whose service was in the public interest but which was in danger of going bankrupt. Coras Iompair, for instance, was set up after the take-over of the old Great Southern Railway by the state in 1946 because it was going into liquidation. Irish Steel Holdings Ltd became a state-sponsored body for similar reasons. Lack of initiative on the part of private enterprise in the communications field led to the creation by the state of Aer Lingus (Irish International Airlines) and of the Irish Shipping Company, made necessary by the wartime shipping crisis. The character of a given state-sponsored body reflects very accurately the complexion of the times in which it was set up. In the period of the economic war with Britain between 1932 and 1939, when Ireland was striving to become as self-sufficient as possible, thirteen of them were created. Twelve came into being in the recovery period following the crisis of the mid-'fifties, whereas only seven were created between 1952 and 1957.

Some of these bodies are entirely state-controlled and financed, having sprung from branches of the civil service charged with carrying out government policy. Such a one is Bord Failte—literally, the Welcome Board: a typical example of the Irish gift for combining whimsy with commerce. Its senior executives are former civil servants, though its personnel is mainly recruited from the public in the same way as a private commercial enterprise recruits its staff. Some state-sponsored bodies have borrowed part of the capital needed for expansion from private sources. Both Bord na Mona and Aer Lingus have done this in recent years. A great and unresolved contention over the operation of state bodies is whether they should finance their development programmes out of profits (which would entail their building up reserves and hence of becoming independent of government control to some degree), or whether they should pay back the money advanced to them by the state to set them up. In some cases there are complaints that they have an unfair advantage over private enterprise in that they are able to keep prices artificially low to the consumer. To overcome this, certain checks have been imposed: for example, the Electricity Supply Board is debarred from damaging private electrical repair firms by undercutting prices. On the whole, this type of complaint is not widespread, though Coras Iompair Eireann runs a number of hotels, taken over from the old Great Southern Railway, which are technically in competition with private hotels.

It is also charged against the state-sponsored bodies that they attract a particularly good type of executive to the detriment of private industry. Job security and status have played a part in this, but the main reason has been that public service, opening up new vistas of national development, has attracted the idealistically minded manager with sights set on a wider horizon than a seat on a board. The chief executives of the bigger state companies are among the most important men in the country. General Costello (sugar), Dr 'Tod' Andrews (transport), Dr T. J. O'Driscoll (tourism) and Dr J. F. Dempsey (airlines) command respect which is on a par with, if not greater than, that accorded to a minister when they pronounce on a given issue. Such men are 'magnates' in the full sense, and disquiet is expressed from time to time at the extent of the powers they are able to wield. The Irish state companies, in fact, suffer from a problem common to many such bodies in other countries: ill-defined control. Outright state control is forsworn because of the fear that this would inhibit their operation and make it difficult to get resourceful and enterprising chief executives. The formula developed in practice is an uncertain balancing act between the companies, the civil service and the politicians. The question of control remains largely academic so long as a given company is providing an efficient service and pursuing an intelligibly far-sighted policy; but it is far from being purely theoretical and a good deal of discussion goes on in the Republic about the principles and the methods of control.

Very little information, in fact, is made available to the Dail about the activities of state companies, other than their annual reports. To analyse and make constructive criticisms of these would take up rather more than the quota of time, interest and expertise that is normally available in the Oireachtas. Furthermore, although the minister of the department concerned is the ultimate authority, ministerial intervention in the affairs of the companies tends not to go beyond the 'pressure level' of telephone calls, since to interfere openly in, or dismiss, the management of a state body would automatically make its running hesitant and over-cautious, and make executive replacement difficult. Sometimes the very efficiency of these bodies causes difficulty. Ordinarily they endeavour to show the main characteristics of good private enterprise: forward planning, efficiency, an attempt at profitability. Their activities under these heads may not, and often do not, coincide with the views of the civil servants who have the day-to-day contact with their running. Not all civil servants are Whitakers or Barringtons. On the whole the civil servants and the executives strike up a harmonious relationship; but not inevitably so, and civil servants can sometimes influence a state body either by dexterously manipulating red tape or by giving weighted advice to a minister.

Then there is the question of the 'national interest'—which often, in fact, is the politician's translation of sectional or personal interest. It might be in the national interest to take back a fishing boat from an inefficient party hack; but what about the political interest? A resolute state company will speedily give an answer to this question, but there is no definite answer as to who will always be right over a policy decision. The Electricity Supply Board unsuccessfully fought Lemass in 1953 over his direction to it to pursue a programme of increased investment based on his projection for future electricity demands. It was subsequently shown that Lemass was wrong, and that the ESB had got itself landed with a programme adding hundreds of thousands of pounds (exactly how much is not known) to the annual cost of electricity production in 1956–59. Of course, there are cases where the state body is not so prescient as the ESB was on that occasion. The boards controlling them are normally composed either of civil servants or of businessmen, trade unionists, professional people and the like, appointed by the government of the day for reasons which may not always be connected with their competence to judge in matters concerning the running of their particular state company.

Yet despite these difficulties, most of the state-sponsored bodies have been reasonably successful. Three of them at least—the Turf Board, the Sugar Company and the ESB—can be singled out as having not only provided excellent services for Ireland but also given examples to other countries which yearly draw experts from all over the world to study their working. Aer Lingus is one of the world's most successful airlines.

An important factor in Irish economic life in the last ten years has been the emergence of a new managerial class. Brendan O'Kelly, chairman of the Fisheries Board, is an outstanding example of the 'new men'. A low-sized Dubliner with a high IQ, O'Kelly played soccer for Ireland when a student at University College, Dublin (UCD), and then gained a scholarship to the Harvard Business School. He became chairman of the Board (Bord Iascaigh Mhara) in 1963 after a successful business career. He aims to treble fish-landings by 1970. In his first two years fish exports have gone up by 13 per cent (to the value of £2 million in 1964), and repayments on boats have increased by 25 per cent. O'Kelly has put an end to the days when fishing boats had as many as a dozen owners in two years. Newspapers seem to be perpetually reporting about fish. Traditionally, the stuff was what you ate on Friday and on fast days—and that was just about as much as most people wanted to have to do with it. But the Fisheries Board's activities and national fish-cooking competitions are making the Irish increasingly aware of the charms of fish as an everyday food as distinct from a pious mortification. The Board has increased its grants and advisory services. One of O'Kelly's first steps was to arrange a survey of the potential of the North Atlantic and of the Irish Fishing Industry through a personal approach to President Kennedy. Retailers have been encouraged to modernise their shops. A system of regional fish-distribution has been introduced in place of the old inefficient system whereby fish caught, say, in Galway Bay was sent to the Dublin market and then shipped back across country for retail sale in Galway. Shell-fish processing, bigger boats and—most important—a new spirit of confidence have given the Board and its product a fresh image. For me, this is summed up by the way the telephone is answered there now. Instead of a male voice saying in stern-voiced Irish, *Bord Iascaigh Mhara*, a charming girl now says, *B.I.M., Good morning!*

Until the Watershed, there was only a handful of firms which had any worthwhile export trade—principally Jacobs (the biscuit firm controlled by the Bewleys, a Quaker family) and the Guinness Brewery. Jacobs were one of the first firms to appoint young men to senior executive positions:

notably Gordon Lambert, an accountant who has revolutionised the company's selling techniques. Guinness is, of course, to Ireland something more than a firm: it is an institution. Eighty per cent of all beer and stout sold in the Republic comes from Guinness, amounting to £27 million—or 4 per cent of the national income. The company pays 25 per cent of the excise duty raised in the country (£8·4 million), and with 4,000 employees it is the largest private employer in Ireland. For 300 years the name of Guinness to the Irish people has signified benevolence. The company fed thousands during the Famine; and 'Uncle Arthur' (as the Guinness spirit of giving is popularly known) has bequeathed to the nation a beautiful park (Saint Stephen's Green in the heart of Dublin); Iveagh House, the fine mansion which houses the Department of External Affairs; hostels for the aged and wretched; and a tradition of good employment practices not always imitated outside the firm. The benevolence is largely a matter of the family's influence rather than of company policy as such. Along with its higher wages and almost total job security, the firm had a rigid caste system in which upper and lower grade staff did not mix. Protestants were almost invariably preferred to Catholics when it came to promotion. But this tendency has been halted in recent years. Its marketing director is Guy Jackson, born in 1923: a marketing genius who holds an Oxford degree in chemistry. He is one of the few international class tennis players produced by Ireland and is the captain of the Davis Cup team.

One of Ireland's greatest hopes for the future is the tourist industry: a source of national wealth with which the Irish were endowed without any effort on their part, at any rate at first. Compared with rationed, restriction-bound Britain, Ireland immediately after the end of the war was a land of ease flowing with milk and honey—and big juicy steaks. Visitors flocked to Ireland like flies to a jampot. Publicity and special services were unnecessary. But as Britain and the rest of Europe climbed out of the bomb-holes and began to live prosperous peacetime lives again, tourists became more choosy and particular. In response to the new situation, the Irish approach to tourism has changed radically; from the friendly lackadaisical to the (no less friendly) sophisticated.* The formation of Bord Failte weaned the Irish away from the 'I'll leave it to yourself, Sor' approach to tourism. Training schemes, grants for building and improving hotels and guesthouses, restocking lakes with fish, signposting beauty spots, and a massive advertising campaign—these have made a major industry out of the Irish scenery. The low population density means that, outside the immediate precincts of towns, a holiday-maker will be unlikely to share a mile-long

---

* In some cases the sophistication has gone a little too far. Throughout 1965 there was a good deal of public controversy about overcharging and bad service in hotels. It is to be hoped that the controversy will have the effect of removing its origin.

beach with anything except an occasional donkey. The visitor can spend a day in the hills of Wicklow, Tipperary, Connemara or Kerry without meeting a living soul. The vast reaches of the Shannon make the Norfolk Broads in East Anglia seem like a riparian slum.

Setting and Co-ordinating Targets

A highly significant development was the formation of two special bodies to speed economic development: the Committee on Industrial Organisation set up on August 30, 1961, and the National Industrial Economic Council inaugurated on October 9, 1963. The brief of the Committee on Industrial Organisation was governed by the assumption that: 'Searching, uninhibited and objective surveys of industries are the only kind worth undertaking as a serious preparation to the realities of participation in the European Economic Organisation'. The CIO took this brief to heart and reported in very blunt terms on excessive diversification, poor management, inadequate knowledge and deployment of modern business methods, low standards of design, vulnerability to competition by overseas producers, and a general unawareness of the imperatives of a competitive economy and free trade. To implement its findings, 'adaptation councils' were established in a number of industries.

The stimulus to modernisation given by the CIO has outlasted the dashing of Ireland's Common Market hopes. Its findings are being acted on by firms in widely different sectors of industry and commerce: firms like the Glenabbey Textile Company in Dublin, run by Colm Barnes; the merchant house of the MacDonagh family in the West; the Staffords of Wexford in the South-East, with interests in shipping and industry; MacMahons, the timber barons of Limerick in the southern Midlands; and further South, the Dwyers of Cork with their million-pound interests in wool and hosiery. (A church in Cork built by a member of the family is known locally as 'Andy Dwyer's fire insurance'.) Family firms are more important to the Irish economy than, say, to the English, for the small privately owned business was until recently almost the only form of enterprise known to the Irish economy—apart from a few great undertakings like Guinness's; and even Guinness in many ways is still a family firm. Unfortunately, there are no reliable figures available of the number or value of them, statistical science in Ireland not having yet solved the problem of evaluating their role, or even of defining them with precision. As the tendency towards the bigger unit develops in Ireland as elsewhere, the majority of them will decline in importance; but the decline will have a long way to go before it becomes noticeable.

The National Industrial Economic Council is a permanent body 'charged with preparing reports on the principles which should be applied for the development of the national economy and for the realisation and maintenance of full employment at adequate wages with reasonable price stability and reasonably long-term equilibrium in the balance of external payments'. A pretty tall order! But to give it its due, the NIEC has not balked at the heavy task set it. Its reports have had, and will in the future have, a profound effect on government policies.

Two in particular merit attention: the Report on Manpower, published in July 1964; and the Report on Economic Planning, published in June 1965. The Manpower Report has had a chance to show itself in concrete application. After the election in April 1965, a Manpower Authority was set up. Proposals have been made for retraining and resettlement, and a policy has been outlined for giving the worker job-satisfaction so as to improve his contribution both to the community and to his own work and life. The Report's emphasis on training and vocational guidance is of paramount importance to Ireland's coping with the problem of surplus workers on the land and not enough workers in industry. An even more far-reaching document, potentially, is the Report on Economic Planning of 1965, though at the time of writing its effects have still to show themselves. In setting out the need for more detailed planning, it marks the end of the 'programming' era. The need now is for much closer communication between employers and unions, and between departments of state with both sides of industry. Produced with government approval, and representing the findings of leading industrialists, civil servants and trade unionists, the Report on Economic Planning is a major policy-shaping document with implications for almost all aspects of national life.

Trade Unions

One of the key questions of Ireland's economic future is the role of organised labour in the setting and achieving of planning targets. The Committee on Industrial Organisation urged on the Labour movement the necessity of eradicating restrictive practices, which in old-established industries at least are as much of a problem for Ireland as for Britain. (Workers in newly founded industries are on the whole organised on 'industrial union' lines.) However, it did not find that union practices and attitudes had flaws so grave as to be capable of seriously impeding development of the economy.

The trade union movement in Ireland is guided—though not controlled —by the Irish Congress of Trade Unions, which negotiates with the Federated Union of Employers. There are almost 100 trade unions in Ireland, a great many of which are craft unions. As in Britain, there are cases of membership 'poaching', and demarcation disputes—in fact, all the problems which arise when unions are not organised on an 'industrial' basis, embracing all the workers in a given industry. There is also the further problem of contests within the same trade or job-process between British-based unions and native Irish unions. This situation arose with the setting up of the Free State. Many independent Irish unions came into being in the unrealised expectation that their British counterparts would retire from the scene with the same completeness with which British governmental agencies left the political scene—at least in the South.

Management and labour have shown signs of reaching agreement on common goals, notably with the signing of the National Wage Agreement of 1964. But this particular achievement will be difficult to repeat in the future. There are too many inequalities in the present wage-structure; and, although real incomes have risen since the end of the second world war, the cost of living is now almost as high as in Britain. Undue pay increases would put the extinguisher on Ireland's export hopes, but price control and a consistent incomes policy have not yet got beyond the blueprint stage.

The Irish Labour Court has endeavoured to cope with these problems. Set up in 1946 by the Industrial Relations Act, this is a state tribunal to which unions and employers can voluntarily refer industrial disputes. Its functions include the registration of agreements and the fixing of wages in certain poorly paid sectors of the economy. In general, it has been very useful, providing a medium of negotiation which enables the industrial dialogue to be formalised. But it can only make recommendations. The more sophisticated conditions of contemporary wage and union disputes have proved beyond it, and there have been suggestions that it should be reorganised.

The Irish trade union movement is, strictly speaking, non-political. Of the 330,000 trade unionists in the country, only about 50,000 are attached to the Labour Party through their membership of a small group of unions affiliated to it, the largest of which is the Workers' Union of Ireland. By the evidence of cold figures alone, the Labour Party would be a very weak political force; but in fact, whether affiliated to it or not, very large numbers of trade unionists support the party at election time. The Irish TGWU, with 150,000 members, pays the expenses of its men who stand as Labour candidates.

One of the movement's gravest handicaps has been the internal war between William O'Brien, who succeeded James Connolly as leader of the Irish Transport and General Workers' Union, and James Larkin and his Workers' Union of Ireland. Energies were therein dissipated which could conceivably have gone to building up a unified and more powerful Labour Party. To add to this handicap there is also the effect of Partition. The severance of the industrial North-East from the South of Ireland has deprived the Labour movement (in both parts of Ireland, let it be said) of the cohesion and common action which, elsewhere, make the industrial workers so much easier to organise than agrarian workers. But this situation is changing. The Northern unions are now affiliated to the Irish Trades Union Congress. These Ulster trade unionists fall into three categories: first, there are the members of British-based unions with branches in the North but not in the Republic; secondly, the members of Southern unions with branches in the North; and thirdly, members of unions which are exclusively Northern. All now, however, are affiliated to the Congress in respect to their Irish membership, Northern and Southern alike, and irrespective of any British connection. This is one of the 'quiet' developments which, as we shall see in chapter 12, have been taking place behind the ostensibly impenetrable folds of the Green Curtain.

The trade union movement in Ireland has tended to devote itself more to the grass-roots business of getting more money for its members than to any long-term social and economic planning. Although seminars and educational programmes are a marked feature of its activities in recent years, the effectiveness of communications between the leadership and the rank and file is not of a high order. In 1964 and 1965 there were strikes in transport, printing and building which owed at least as much to this factor as to any other cause. The trade union movement has some outstandingly able men: John Conroy, general president of the Irish TGWU; Fintan Kennedy, its general secretary; James Larkin, son of the elder James and, like him, head of the Workers' Union of Ireland; and Charles McCarthy of the Vocational Teachers Association, whose strong advocacy of a manpower policy was one of the determining influences in the setting up of the Manpower Authority. Leading officials of the Irish Trade Union Congress, like its joint secretaries, Ruaidhri Roberts and Leo Crawford, and particularly its research officer, Donal Nevin: a man with the brain of a computer and a heart of gold—all certainly are capable of fulfilling more lucrative roles in industry. Irish trade unionism has come to be grateful for their great services to it. But the idealism of these men and of many others in the trade union movement has yet to find the leader or the moment which could give it the coherent drive it needs to develop its full potential.

The Free Trade Agreement of 1965

The signing of the trade agreement between Ireland and Britain on December 14, 1965 placed the whole question of trade relationships between the two countries on an entirely different footing. It is generally referred to in Ireland as the 'Free Trade Agreement'. Its implications would appear to cast rather a quaint light over earlier political and economic labels, like 'Free State', 'Self-Sufficiency', 'Northern Ireland' and 'Republic of

Ireland'. This is not to suggest that it belittles them: rather that it deprives them of such pejorative undertones as they still retain.

The Agreement comes into effect on July 1, 1966, on which date Britain will abolish all tariffs between herself and Ireland, including the import levy. Ireland, however, is allowed a ten-year withdrawal period from her present tariff structure, beginning with a 10 per cent cut in July 1966. Between this date and 1980 Ireland will continue to make periodic cuts until all protective measures, including tax incentives, are abolished. (Exception is made for the Shannon industrial zone, which will have until 1983 to free itself from protection.) The agricultural provisions of the Agreement allow for what appears more than a 100 per cent increase in Britain's quota of butter imports from Ireland—from 11,000 to 23,000 tons. (Actually, since the Republic at present is already exceeding its butter quota, this will mean only an increase of 4,000 tons in real terms.) Ireland's exports to Britain of sheep, cattle, pig-meat and horticultural products will also be increased.

The Agreement represents a new and more hopeful relationship between the two countries. But it is also a calculated risk for the Republic. A country like Ireland must export or die; exports must grow from a healthy home market; and such a market in turn depends on a healthy employment situation. Initially, the Agreement will cause some dislocation and possibly a fall in employment. For example, the Irish car-assembly industry will not be able to survive unrestricted British competition. But the government is gambling on the expectation that the stimulus given by tariff cuts (which, of course, are additional to Ireland's self-imposed, unilateral 'Kennedy Round' reduction) will generate the dynamism which will enable Irish industry to withstand the shock of free trade and go on, after some initial turbulence, to prosper in the new conditions.

The brutal truth is that not only Irish industry but every sector of the national economy must be prepared for such an adaptation. In the world of today, an island with a total market of only four million people, living on the periphery of Western Europe, could wilt away unnoticed. Modern Ireland happily shows no signs of wilting away. The period of adjustment required by the Free Trade Agreement may be just what the country needs before taking the plunge into Europe and the Common Market, if and when this becomes again a negotiable politico-economic question.

8. CULTURE AND SOCIETY

Censorship · The Contemporary Scene
The Irish Ethos–Old and New

IN no field is the change which has come over Ireland since the Watershed more obvious than in social and cultural matters. Yet neither is there any field in which precise information to illustrate this change is more hard to come by. However, certain obvious and essential factors may be stated.

The first is that, being Catholic, Irish society (prior to Pope John) was inherently less prone to question itself than a Protestant society with its emphasis on individualism. The second is the effect of the Civil War. This poisoned the climate of opinion by perpetually wrong-footing every controversy through the refusal to consider issues in anything other than personal, political terms. The third factor is economic. It is not possible, financially, for an Irish artist to create solely for the Irish market—or else it is so difficult as to be well-nigh impossible. And then there is the fourth factor, which particularly affects writers: the censorship. The maladroit attempt to erect a cultural and intellectual greenbelt around Ireland, combined with the other factors and aggravated by the wartime isolation, meant that free and informed discussion in Irish public life was, until the Watershed, a rarity. The resultant inhibition of ideas was (and to a noticeable, though decreasing, extent still is) a major stumbling-block, not only to cultural development, but also to social progress. In a country which for generations had had a tradition of protest, the critical voice was muted to a whisper, and a race of Rubashovs grew up: perhaps not willing to die in silence but certainly prepared to live that way.

If a culture can be said to be the sum of the ways in which a people work and worship and express themselves, then the most representative form of the culture is that in which it expresses itself most distinctively. If talking is excluded, it is in her writers that Ireland has expressed herself most outstandingly. The enrichment of the literature of the English-speaking peoples by writers like Goldsmith, Sheridan, Wilde and Shaw is too well known to require emphasising. What concerns us here is the fact that, from the fall of Parnell, Ireland *needed* her writers. Until 1916 it was her writers who provided the most effective outlet for nationalistic feeling.

The IRB worked furtively, but the whole world could read the poetry of Yeats, Æ (George Russell), Padraic Colum, Katharine Tynan, Seamus O'Sullivan. In this awakening of cultural awareness, the Gaelic League grew and prospered, and the Irish Texts Society began to uncover sagas of an earlier Ireland. The plays of Yeats, Synge, Lady Gregory, Padraic Colum, Edward Martyn, George Moore, Alice Milligan, Douglas Hyde, and even of the 'realist' school of Lennox Robinson, T. C. Murray and R. C. Ray—all aroused a political as well as an artistic response. Yeats, after all, was a member of the IRB.

The cultural awakening of Ireland was essentially local in inspiration, but not entirely so. A fruitful initiative was made in 1918—the year in which the old Irish Parliamentary Party of Parnell and Redmond was extinguished—in the founding of the Irish Drama League with the object of bringing international authors to the Dublin stage. This seemed to mark out a wider cultural terrain for Irish artists in various fields, that of the theatre in particular. Ten years later, having brought Dennis Johnston to the public's attention, the Drama League made way for the partnership of Hilton Edwards and Miceal MacLiammoir. This heralded the great days of the Gate Theatre. In 1923 O'Casey's *Shadow of a Gunman* was first produced; *Juno and the Paycock* and *The Plough and the Stars* followed in 1924 and 1926 respectively. But by then Ireland, having won her independence, had suffered the Civil War and the amputation of Partition, had grown disillusioned and embittered. O'Casey's work was considered both nationalistically and artistically unacceptable. His distillation of the spirit of the country was unpalatable to a generation whose teeth had been set on edge by the sour grapes of frustrated nationalism. Already the Ireland of saints and scholars was on its way to becoming the Ireland of the hagiographers and censors.

It is almost impossible for a member of my generation to describe what the internal strife within Ireland meant to the psychology of the people. The comradeship, the national 'oneness' of the independence movement, was broken. I have seen hardened, cynical old men with tears in their eyes as they told how, instead of friendship, bitterness grew; instead of self-sacrifice, selfishness; instead of order, chaos; instead of progress, destruction. Art and politics diverged. Cathleen ni Houlihan, who at the end of Yeats' play of the same name had been transformed into a young girl 'with the walk of a queen', now became a shrewish beldame with a quarrelling family.

Symbolising this wreckage was the closing down of the great Irish publishing house of Maunsel, which had published the works of every major figure of the Irish renascence, Yeats excepted. From then on until 1951, when the Dolmen Press was set up, there was no Irish publishing company devoted solely to issuing imaginative literature on a commercial scale. This is not to denigrate the work of the Cuala Press, started as the Dun Emer Press in 1902 by Evelyn Gleeson and Elizabeth Yeats, the poet's sister. Its primary aim was to give employment and education to Irish girls. The Dun Emer Press became the Cuala Press in 1908 when Miss Gleeson left the venture. Yeats was its literary editor. Its printing style was informed by the theories of Emery Walker and William Morris. The Cuala Press published to 1946 and was the first to produce some of the best works of many Irish writers: Douglas Hyde, Lady Gregory, J. M. Synge, Katharine Tynan, F. R. Higgins, Frank O'Connor, Oliver St John Gogarty, Robin Flower and, of course, Yeats, together with writers of a later school, like Louis MacNiece and Patrick Kavanagh. But though widely admired for its beautiful printing, the firm's output in no case exceeded 500 copies of any edition. It now prints Christmas cards and does art work.

Since the people who buy limited editions are not the sort of people who send books to the censor for banning, the Cuala Press's work escaped the wrath of the slab-faced pig-buyers who for long have dominated Irish public taste. But writers seeking a more lucrative turn to their pen have, until very recently at least, gone outside the country for their publishers. Hence much of native writing for many years has come to the Irish public from outside sources, which made it suspect and with a high ban-potential. Whether a large-scale literary publishing house in Ireland would have defeated the censorship or been overcome by it, we shall never know.

It was literary periodicals, like the *Dublin Magazine*, *The Bell* and *Irish Writing*, which kept the flag flying. These are now defunct, though a worthy successor, *The Kilkenny Magazine*, is flourishing. Even so, until Liam Miller, then an architectural student in Dublin, founded the Dolmen Press in 1951, Irish writers lacked a literary publisher on a commercial scale between 1922 and 1951. I stress the word 'literary', meaning imaginative writing in fiction and verse. Some 'special interest' books do very well in Ireland. I conducted my own, highly unscientific, survey into what sells best in Ireland by the simple process of going round the leading Dublin bookshops to ask what their best titles were. They all gave the same four. One dealt with an unusual aspect of religion: Teilhard de Chardin's *Le Milieu Divin*. The other three dealt with Irish themes: *Thy Tears Might Cease*, a book about the Independence movement by Michael Farrell; *The Great Hunger*, by Cecil Woodham Smith; and *Oliver St John Gogarty*, by Ulick O'Connor. These are an exception to the general rule in Irish book-buying, for their sales can be measured in thousands rather than hundreds.

The sales of newspapers for such a small population are remarkably large,* but the hardcover sales of most novels are negligible. A hard cover book which in England runs from the middle to the top level in the booksellers' lists, will in Ireland normally not sell more than 500 copies. The consignment of John McGahern's book, *The Dark*, which was seized by the Customs in 1965, numbered 261 copies. An Irish author must, therefore, face up to three things not calculated to encourage him. In the first place, his countrymen do very little to aid him by way of buying his book. Then, not having bought it and possibly not even read it, they will set to with a will to discuss him chidingly, learnedly and futilely in Dublin's literary columns. But the odds are that the general public will pay small heed to this literary dissection for—and this is the third of the Irish writer's woes—in all probability the only widespread notice he will get in his own country is if he is officially regarded as a pornographer or as one of that great band of Irish writers who are accused of 'letting the country down'. This, of course, puts him in excellent company.

CENSORSHIP

By 1965, the Irish censorship authorities had assembled a list of works banned on grounds of indecency or obscenity since 1929 (when the first Censorship Law was introduced) which reads like a students' guide to modern literature. Hemingway, Faulkner, Thomas Mann, Sartre, Steinbeck, Sinclair Lewis, John Dos Passos, J. D. Salinger, Budd Schulberg, Robert Penn Warren, Ilya Ehrenburg, Truman Capote, Tennessee Williams, Scott Fitzgerald, James Baldwin, Alberto Moravia, Norman Mailer, Jack Kerouac, William Saroyan, Samuel Beckett, James Jones, Dylan Thomas, Graham Greene, Joyce Cary, George Orwell, C. P. Snow —with other well-known pornographers—peer at you from the 'index bannorum'. Irish writers like Sean O'Faolain, Frank O'Connor, Kate O'Brien, Liam O'Flaherty, Brendan Behan, Edna O'Brien and John McGahern might have felt put out had they not been put on it!

The Irish Catholic Church was the main inspiration behind the introduction of the censorship, but it was aided and abetted by a good many of the old-guard patriots, who in any case disliked the press because it had usually been hostile to them. For them the motivation was much the same as that which inspired the Cuban communists to shut down the brothels and the pornographic film houses when Castro took power: the zeal for a revolutionary purity which would sweep away all the nastiness of the old

* The newspapers with the highest circulations are: *Sunday Press* 422,486; *Sunday Independent* 348,042; *Irish Independent* 174,074; *Evening Press* 150,206; *Evening Herald* 142,338; *Irish Press* 123,553. (Average sales per issue for the six months ending June 1965.) The *Irish Times*, a 'quality' paper with an Anglo-Irish flavour and aimed mainly at professional and senior business people, has an average daily sale of 37,816.

regime and create a nation of shining idealism. The Irish, indeed, closed down the brothels in 1922 at the height of the Civil War. First things first! (Since then, you understand, vice in Ireland has been driven out, like the snakes before Saint Patrick's brandished crozier. If any is found still lurking, it has crept in from England while no one was looking.)

A student of literature can always get a permit to import any book he wants by making a special application to the minister for Justice. Anyone else can usually get the book from a friend in England or from Belfast. (Such books follow the same shifty route as birth-control appliances.) But the average reader's approach to literature is inevitably heavily coloured by the way in which it is regarded by society at large. Such a list as I have set out—in brief only: I could have gone on with it for umpteen pages—presents some of the greatest writers of this century as 'dirty', as purveyors of forbidden fruit. Hence in Ireland books have generally tended to be discussed, not on their merits, but as to whether they should have been banned or not. No allowance in law is made for the difference between a cheap magazine of depravity aimed at the puberty belt and the writings of a Nobel Prize winner.

The Censorship of Publications Act of 1929 set up a board whose function was to be the recommendation of books for banning by the minister of Justice. In 1946, the Act was amended to empower the board itself to ban books, and an appeal board was set up. For an appeal to be lodged against banning, six copies of the book concerned, accompanied by £5, must be sent to the board. Only the editor, publisher, author or a group of five members of the Oireachtas may submit an appeal. A book can be banned if more than one of the five-man Censorship Board disapproves of it. Two is a quorum for banning, three for approval. In the case of the Appeal Board, also consisting of five members, a simple majority suffices. The members of both boards are unpaid. Since 1957, the chairman of the Censorship Board (who is appointed by the minister for Justice) has been Judge Conroy, a practising judge of the High Court. The other members are a former High Court judge, a civil servant, a former District Court judge and a retired civil servant. Between 1950 and 1955, the number of books banned each year averaged 677. In the period 1960 to 1965, this declined to an annual average of 380. This smaller figure includes *The Bachelors* by Muriel Spark, *Catch 22* by Joseph Heller, and *To Feed the Hungry* by Danilo Dolci (sic!). However, the large drop in recent years in the total of banned works does indicate that a more lenient spirit is at work on the Censorship Board. The bulk of the material now banned is decidedly pornographic.

Judge Conroy, a rubicund, silver-haired Fieldingesque figure who described himself on British television (quite accurately) as 'something of a bawdy character', is in a large measure responsible for the change. Although a teetotaller and with a reputation for severity on the bench, he is the antithesis of what one would expect a censor to be. He studied in America on a Rockefeller scholarship, has five children and a generous hand on the whiskey decanter reserved for guests. Sitting in his comfortable Dublin home, I put it to him that Irish democracy, public and family life had been inhibited by lack of free discussion, and that the censorship was largely responsible for this. I regret I must censor his lordship's reply.

However, a little while later, after having blown many similar blasts of (no doubt) refreshing Limerick logic into my reeling Dublin liberalism, Judge Conroy went on to say that he would like changes to be made in the censorship laws to allow of the censors' taking account of changes in modern outlook. On the other hand, he would like to see the censorship intensified in regard to magazines, so as to be able to ban them permanently and not just for three months at a time, as is now the case. Judge Conroy thinks it a disgrace that a magazine like the London *Spectator* should sink so low as to carry family planning advertisements. He has no disagreement with the present policy in Ireland of banning books which advocate contraception or the unnatural prevention of birth.

The Censorship Board as at present constituted has the unpleasant side-effect of making informers of large numbers of the public. Most of the books read by the censors are referred to them by members of the public; in fact, all of the 537 titles examined by the board in 1964 came to it in this fashion. Others can be referred to them by Customs officials who catch sight of a book they don't like the look of in a traveller's suitcase. Brendan Behan's *Borstal Boy* was sent in by a Dublin author. Not satisfied with following the routine procedure of sending the book to the censorship office, he had it despatched by express post to Conroy's chambers. Advance publicity about a book in London or New York, or the printing before publication of some parts of it in magazines and newspapers, alerts the Customs officials who are empowered to seize consignments of books and send copies to the Censorship Board. I suggested to Judge Conroy that, in view of the large number of titles dealt with by his office each year, and of the fact that the Board has only one inspection copy for its five voluntary, unpaid members, marked passages rather than entire works are likely to be studied. He said that this was not the case. I accept the judge's statement on this point, of course, but one is curious to know why an appeal requires so many copies. It rather looks as if the extra copies may be provided in order to give the Appeal Board censors a more comprehensive idea of the book than was obtainable when it was first scheduled for banning.

Film censorship has existed since 1925. The Film Censor, unlike the censor of books, is paid by the state, and refuses to be interviewed. The present holder of the office is Dr C. Macken. The public until recently have not been told what films are banned. Usually one can only judge what these are by what one doesn't see. For instance, *La Dolce Vita* never emerged to bring the blush of maidenly pudicity to the cheek of Cathleen ni Houlihan, and two Peter Sellers' films—*Dr Strangelove* and *I'm All Right, Jack*—both aroused the censor's perturbation before being let in after long delays. The operation of film censorship has in the past made for hypocrisy in some ways. Two films produced at Ardmore (the Irish film studio in Bray, County Wicklow) were censored for showing in Ireland, although no official eyebrows were raised in concern at the thought of their being made at a profit to the economy and sent forth to corrupt people outside the country who had not the protection of the Irish Film Censor. The films were: *Of Human Bondage* and *The Girl With the Green Eyes* (which in fact was never shown in Ireland at all).

The most notable official action to liberalise the censorship system in films was taken in 1964 by the young new minister for Justice, Brian Lenihan, who came to the office at the age of thirty-four as a result of the reshuffle following Smith's resignation. One of his first acts was to Bomb the Ban! He sacked the old Film Appeal Board and brought in a younger body of men, one of the most liberal of whom was a Jesuit, Fr John Kelly.* The Film Censor, a recent appointment, had been wielding a rather eager pair of scissors, and Lenihan's action was unmistakably a gesture of official dissent from this policy. Some of his colleagues in the cabinet strongly disagreed with him over this, but the ensuing run of films was a great advance on what had gone before. To be fair to the state and the censors, the poor quality of the films shown was at least partly due to the lack of enterprise of the film distributors who did nothing to improve the system or the quality of the films shown in Ireland. The changes that have taken place in this field have been entirely due to public opinion.

THE CONTEMPORARY SCENE

The theatre is not subject to an official censorship, although the possibility of prosecution for obscenity cannot be ruled out, as was shown in the case of the (unsuccessful) *Rose Tattoo* prosecution. But the risk of legal action cannot be blamed for the present state of the theatre in Dublin. (Outside the capital, Cork and Galway are the only centres with a theatre exclusively devoted to putting on serious plays: the Group Theatre in Cork and the Taidbhearc in Galway.) With rising costs and the competition of television,

* Another Jesuit, Fr Donal O'Sullivan, is chairman of the Arts Council. Under his sur-veillance, it is playing a notable part in influencing public taste towards the contemporary arts.

Dublin, like most cities in the world, finds it difficult to support a flourishing, unsubsidised theatre life.

On top of this situation there is the unfortunate effect of the annual Theatre Festival. This shotgun marriage between culture and tourism has resulted in all new plays being kept for the Festival: a constipated fortnight of something like a dozen new openings in each week. Very few of these offerings to Thespis survive to light up the encircling gloom which resettles when the Festival ends. It has been suggested, in its defence, that the handful of playwrights and producers who have emerged into international recognition through the Festival—the writers Brian Friel and Hugh Leonard, and the producer, Jim Fitzgerald—would not have become celebrated without it. This hardly bears examination. These men would have made their mark in any case, as Miceal MacLiammoir did before the Festival was ever thought of. This does not prevent Festival propagandists from trying to claim his international success—a one-man tour de force, *The Importance of Being Oscar*, based on the life of Wilde—as a feather in the cap of the Festival on the grounds that it was first produced there. But it would have been produced with or without the Festival.

The Abbey Theatre was at the heart of the cultural and national resurgence in the early years of this century. But for some time now its only connection with its distinguished past has been the fact of its still being a theatre devoted to putting on plays. However, new hopes for the future have been stirred by the decision to rebuild it. (The theatre was burnt out in 1951, and thereafter it was housed at the Queen's, an old variety theatre.) These hopes have some justification, for in 1964 its list of shareholders was increased to allow some of the liberal spirits in the Irish artistic and literary world to be included among those exercising influence on the theatre's policy. Lovers of the drama in Ireland and the English-speaking world are awaiting with hopeful curiosity the fruits of the new regime at the Abbey. Its contribution to the 1965 Theatre Festival was Brecht's *Galileo*—which opened, appropriately enough, on the day the Vatican Council voted overwhelmingly in favour of religious liberty. So it does move!

Away from the 'legitimate' stage, something quite new was born in the mid-'fifties. Out of the long stale nights of a depopulating countryside, there developed an amateur dramatic movement. By 1960 this had caught hold to such an extent that the All-Ireland Final of that year represented the last stage of a nationwide competition involving 750 different acting groups. The most considerable playwright to emerge so far from this new movement is John B. Keane from Listowel, County Kerry.

Public opinion, albeit many people engaged in the arts think it has still a long way to go, is certainly becoming more internationally minded and enlightened. Although there is as yet only one widely circulating lay journal of opinion—*Hibernia*, a monthly magazine which publishes serious, outspoken contributions to Irish intellectual life—more of the country's newspapers are coming to see their role as stimulators of the mind and not as retailers of received prejudices. If I can blow my own paper's trumpet, the *Evening Press* deserves more credit for this than any other single medium of communication in Ireland. It was founded in 1954 purely as a commercial venture, though with an objective which laid stress on 'the truth in the news'. Under its present editor—Conor O'Brien, a thirty-seven-year-old Dubliner whose premature grey hairs could not have been won more honourably or in a better cause—the paper has consistently shown, in its news coverage, in feature articles and in its excellent letters' page, a valuable courage and initiative. The *Irish Times*, for all the incidental criticisms one can make of it, has also been foremost in giving a wider and deeper character to Irish public opinion and taste. A staunchly Unionist organ under the old regime, it has evolved into a valuable, and at times a vital, example of what a paper of integrity can achieve in a free society, even though its circulation is less than a quarter of that of the *Evening Press*. But whereas the exposed reactionary has found occasion to impute 'un-Irishness' to the Protestant-owned and -edited *Irish Times*, the *Evening Press*, being edited by an exemplary Catholic, has defied such needling obscurantism. Dublin does not have a monopoly of good newspapers. High journalistic standards are maintained, among provincial dailies, by the *Cork Examiner* and, among weeklies, by the *Kerryman* of Tralee, the *Nationalist* of Carlow, the *Connacht Tribune* of Galway, the Donegal *Democrat*, the Limerick *Leader* and the *Munster Express* of Clonmel.

The inauguration of the Irish television service (Telefís Eireann) in 1960 also opened doors, not perhaps so much in news reporting (which is still heavily susceptible of official influence) as in its discussion programmes. In particular, these are providing a forum for young people to say in public what they have for a long time felt. Programmes of the BBC can also be received in Ireland, and these have had a markedly liberalising effect. So much so that, when a chain of booster stations for Irish Television was set up, rumours were rife that one function they could have would be to blot out BBC transmissions.

Stories of this kind are almost impossible to check. Telephone tapping by 'them' is also frequently alleged, and, like the matter of the transmitters, has been raised in the Dail. My own view is that, if such a thing does ever occur, it is more likely to be the work of some overzealous civil servant than the consequence of official policy. Certainly Cosgrave, de Valera, Costello and Lemass have nothing in their records which would enable one to make a categorical assertion of this sort. But censorship and fear breed rumours and dark suspicions. A lady whom I greatly admire for her stand against injustice in the North wrote to me while I was writing this book asking me to confirm if I had got material she had sent me earlier, 'as there is a lot of interference with the post'. If there is, it is attributable more to the itchy fingers of a nosy postmistress than to official tampering with the British postal service.

In the event, Telefís Eireann has done remarkably well to establish itself so successfully. Apart from the BBC, it also has competition from Welsh and Ulster Television. A factor in its success is, as with the *Evening Press*, the number of young faces to be seen at work in all departments.

It may seem premature to speak of a contemporary literary renascence in Ireland against the backcloth of banning depicted earlier; but something near akin to it is occurring. The Mercier Press in Cork, Anvil Books in Kerry and Helicon Books in Dublin—all comparatively recent recruits to the publishing ranks—would scarcely be so flourishing if there were not. The modern development of paperback publishing has a lot to do with this. Although, as we have said, hardcover sales on the whole continue to be modest, the publisher of a good paperback expects to sell some 20,000 copies in Ireland.

The three big Irish houses publishing books in the English language*
—Browne and Nolan; Gill; and Hodges, Figgis—have mainly been concerned with religious and educational writing, much of it of excellent quality in matter and presentation. New ground, however, is being broken in the two last-named houses by the young inheritors of the family traditions, Michael Gill and Alan Figgis, both of whom are doing a fine job in design and also in selection of titles. Perhaps most credit for the literary revival of the last decade or so should go to Liam Miller of the Dolmen Press. He has reprinted the work of Austin Clarke, Ireland's leading poet and the only living writer to bridge the gap between the Maunsel era of publishing and today. Miller was also the first to publish Thomas Kinsella, the outstanding figure among the new generation of poets, ranking next to Austin Clarke and Patrick Kavanagh in the poetic hierarchy, so untimely bereft by the early death of Denis Devlin. Richard Murphy, John Montague, Richard Weber and Pearse Hutchinson all had their first poetry published by Miller's Dolmen Press.

Contemporary Irish writers now in their forties or late thirties, like Brian Moore, Aidan Higgins, John Montague and Pearse Hutchinson,

---

* These also publish some works in Irish. The role of publishing firms in the Irish language is described in chapter 9, pages 198-9 below. Considerations of space prevent my detailing the work of other English-language publishers, notably The Talbot Press (the importance of which can be judged by the frequency of its appearance in the Bibliography), and The Sign of the Three Candles, run by Colm O'Lochlain.

still tend to live abroad. But Miller's arrangement with the Oxford University Press, whereby he can use its overseas distribution facilities, has now given Irish writers access to an international cultural conduit whose fountain-head is in Dublin rather than in London or New York. There is hope that the new publishing opportunities opening up, coupled with increasing freedom from political, religious and social pressures, will cease to make 'silence, cunning and exile' mandatory on the Irish writer who aspires to be as freely creative, in his own generation, as Joyce, Shaw and O'Casey were, and Beckett still is: but only by leaving their native land.

Indeed, the theme in Irish culture today tends to be return, not exile. In sculpture, the most important of the younger generation is Edward Delaney, a Mayo man in his mid-'thirties who returned from the continent and now lives at Dun Laoghaire in a house he designed for himself out of two adjoining cottages. Brian Bourke, a remarkable young painter, depicts a Baconesque view of life after years of struggling for a living in London. It may not be a view which many of his countrymen will take to with any enthusiasm, but the significant thing is that he is now recording it among them, not abroad. John McGahern is still a controversial figure and he ploughs his furrow withdrawn from Dublin's social life. But he ploughs it in his native field, writing his novels at home in Ireland. Also home-based is another outstanding Irish novelist, John Broderick. It is the same with young poets like Brendan Kennelly, James Liddy and Michael Harnett; as it is with Kevin Casey, a playwright and short-story writer in his early 'twenties: an author of great promise. These men do not feel, as did many of their predecessors, that their muse will be chilled by the Irish mists of censorship and obscurantism. To them, as to others in Ireland, the mists are lifting.

Of course, the mists never obscured the work of the painter, Jack B. Yeats, who carried on with his inimitable depiction of his countrymen no matter what government came or went. Mainie Jellet and Evie Hone followed him and, though not of his stature, made reputations for themselves as painters which could hardly have emanated from a cultural graveyard. (To many, Evie Hone is perhaps even better known for her work in stained glass.) The 1940s were unmemorable, but the 'fifties saw a stirring which, in sculpture, yielded amongst others Oisin Kelly, Paddy McElroy and Hilary Heron; and in painting, the abstract artists Louis le Brocquy and Patrick Scott. Before the 'sixties are out, we will hear more of Noel Sherridan and Pat MacMahon, both abstract painters, though MacMahon works in metal also. Sherridan is still living in New York, but MacMahon is now working in his native Dublin.

As the Church is still the largest patron by far of the visual arts, it is here perhaps that we should seek for the real touchstone of current trends in this field. Turning quickly with a shudder from most examples of recent church architecture, but pausing with an admiring salute to the occasional structure exhibiting a new and enlightened taste, let us consider sacred art. Seven or eight years ago this was a field which, apart from the work of Ian and Imogen Stuart, sprouted little more than the tinselled thistles of 'repository art'. But new and vigorous blooms to the glory of God have begun to show themselves since Ray and Mary Carroll came home from Scotland. Artists in religious themes themselves, they have opened up a gallery in the hills overlooking Dublin where other artists as well show their work. At their table one will find a scientist, a Jesuit, a poet and a painter at one and the same time. Much railing will be heard against the slab-faced pig-buyers who still have a strong hold over the arts. You will hear similar complaints coming from Irish artists and writers in New York, in London, in Paris . . . in any number of the world's cities. The difference is that the Carrolls and their like are doing the complaining *at home*. Creative criticism, home-bred and home-expressed, is beginning to tell.

What does it have to tell against? These mists are lifting. What engendered them?

THE IRISH ETHOS: OLD AND NEW

There is certainly a centuries-old tradition of artistic activity in Dublin, even if it mainly lay in the popular Liffey-side sport of destroying one's neighbours' characters. But a great deal of Dublin culture has tended to be provincial British rather than metropolitan Irish. Resentful awareness of this was a leading motive in the Gaelic linguistic and cultural campaign, discussed in the next chapter. The Celtic Revival, however, made little headway among the ordinary people of Dublin whose amusements and tastes continued mainly to be derived from sources across the Irish Sea— though with the engaging sparkle of Irish wit and accent to give them a distinctively Dublin zest. The cultural nationalists comforted themselves with the dream of how different everything would be if only the British could be sent packing. Nationalism triumphed; independence came; the British went—and culture nearly went with them.

In the 1930s, in the mingled disillusionment and fervour of post-Civil War nationalism, the portcullis was lowered on the outside world. Within the citadel, the cultural gaze was turned inward and backward to some supposedly pure and blessed era in Ireland's past. The approved vision of Ireland in her ancient glory tended to set the closed fortress of her culture in a kind of Ossianic clearing, with about as much contiguity to reality as had Fionn and Ossian. Such influences as did penetrate to reach the rank and file were, ironically, almost exclusively Anglo-Saxon. The result is that, even today, Scandinavian design and German and French writing are practically unknown in Ireland. Popular taste in countless things—in furniture, pictures, decoration, objets d'art—is still basically Edwardo-Georgian with strong residual traces of Victorian forms, the whole decked out with frippery culled at random from the fairground-prize-ornament debasement of the 'modernism' of the 1920s.

Architecturally, Dublin for long was content to let the most beautiful parts of the city literally fall to pieces. It was not until sagging tenements in fine eighteenth-century streets stopped sagging and collapsed, claiming lives, that attempts began to be made, in 1963, to restore and rebuild. The pace of new building—although slowed down in 1965 by the credit squeeze emanating from Britain's financial crisis—reflects both the enhanced condition of the Irish economy and a new expansive spirit in the country. One of the most adventurous long-term building schemes in Europe is in progress at Ballymun on the northern outskirts of the city. But development is still patchy, and in the centre of Dublin the modern buildings dotted here and there look like new suits in a wardrobe of rags.

But the Irish wardrobe, in the literal sartorial sense, is now as modern as that of any Western country. When I attended Mass in New York in May 1960, what struck me most forcibly was the contrast between the smartness of the clothes and hairstyles of the American congregation and the drab look of most people in church at home. Today, at a glance, you could not tell the two congregations apart.

The character of Irish society, and hence of its culture in the broadest sense, has been markedly masculine. Irishmen as a whole seem at an early date to have developed an attitude reflecting both the common male readiness to avail of pleasure without responsibility, and also the direct converse of this: a kind of Sean O'Œdipus complex—a shrinking from sex as something shameful and a treachery to the maternal and sisterly love which is so strong a force in Irish family life. Irish children probably have the happiest existence of any children in the Western world. This is a wonderful and cherishable thing, but one of its corollaries can be, and all too often is, an excessive emotional tension within the family.

But the Irish attitude to sex is mainly conditioned by history. Before the Famine, the Irish married early, mainly—as an investigating commission from England found—as a relief from their poverty. Bishop Doyle, giving evidence before the Select Committee on the State of Ireland in 1825, declared: 'The wretched people say that their state cannot be worse when married than before, and hence they go together'. It is this which accounts for the 'population explosion' in the two or so generations before 1845. After the Famine, however, revulsion against the fate which befell large families during the disaster combined with the insecurity of land tenure to postpone the age of marriage for most Irish people. The coupling of man and woman in matrimony became more a matter of economic feasibilities than emotional affinities. Until the present decade, the depressed state of the economy, the tendency for couples when they did marry to have large families, and the lack of social benefits of a sufficiently large scale—all this tended to make for such inequality in the standard of living as between married and single men on the same income that the Irish male exhibited a marked reluctance to accept the responsibilities of wedlock. At the same time, women in rural areas showed a reluctance to marry farmers, large numbers preferring to emigrate rather than stay on the land.

Another factor in sustaining the male-orientation of the external aspects of Irish life is the privileged position within the average home which mothers give to sons. A man treated as a superior being in childhood and adolescence does not readily submit to the restraints and sharing of marriage. Or if he does submit for a time, they prove so irksome that, when the home becomes crowded with children and the wife grows dowdy and nerve-strained with running the home and striving to make ends meet, the husband asserts his prescriptive right from Adam to do as he pleases in avoiding the frustrations and hindrances.

The outlet for this, as for most personal problems in Ireland, used to be the pub. Perhaps I am being a little premature in saying 'used to be'. The Licensed Vintners Association estimates the total adult drinking population to be around one million—which doesn't leave too many adults on the waggon. The Pioneer Total Abstinence Association claims 400,000 members, but many of these are young people, priests and members of religious orders. There are no precise figures for alcoholics, but Alcoholics Anonymous estimates the total at 70,000. The Jellinek formula endorsed by the World Health Organisation would put the figure as low as 17,927. One way or another, allowing for the normal average of four lives' being affected —in addition to the drunkard's—by each case of alcoholism, even this lower figure represents a sizeable total for a small country. As an example of how the bucket of whitewash nearly supplanted the shamrock as the national emblem of Ireland, commend me the statement of Dr John F. Eustace, an authority on alcoholism in Dublin and medical officer to a number of Irish industries. He was quoted in the *Irish Times* for May 27, 1965 as saying that, during more than thirty years in industry, he had never seen a case in which absence from work was medically certified as being due to alcohol.*

---

* Suicide is also covered up as much as possible; which is why the Irish statistics for *felo de se* are the lowest in Europe. Unless a corpse is actually found dangling from a rope, some other verdict than suicide is usually sought and given. And sometimes even in such an unambiguous case a verdict of accidental death is brought in.

A further factor making for heavy drinking is the Irish tradition of hospitality which gave rise to the 'rounds' system. In any party of Irish drinkers, even one in which Mr Coogan may be drinking large brandies and everybody else only stout, each person is expected to buy their round of 'the same again': which not only increases the amount but also the cost of the drinking.

But changes are taking place even in that sanctus sanctorum of the Irish male—the pub. Up to the 'sixties, the average Irish pub was smoky and dirty, bare and coarse: certainly no place for a respectable woman. Now, in the large towns at least, a wave of soft lighting and snug carpetry is engulfing more and more of the pubs. Groups of women—no, bejasus! of ladies—are now frequently to be seen in pubs unescorted by men—though not yet, it is true, in country areas. And even in Dublin a party of people will normally still divide into two groups: the men here, the women there. Another notable change is to be detected in the reports of publicans that increasing numbers of young people now tend to drink only beer or soft drinks. The evidence of one's own eyes bears this out. While sharing in the world-wide tendency towards increasing adolescent violence, Ireland remains, among young and old alike, a wholesome, friendly society. The drug habit is still very rare indeed, although there are signs that the revolution in sexual mores has reached the island of saints and scholars. Even so, this has not yet attained the point where libertarianism replaces liberalism. Ireland is still close to the era in which publicising Christine Keeler's doings could justifiably be argued as spreading a liberalising influence.

Though perhaps it is too early yet to talk of a radical change in the status of women in Irish society, the entrance of the fair sex into so traditionally exclusive a male preserve as the pub is certainly a sign that male attitudes are beginning to change. Irishmen are even beginning to marry earlier! The Central Statistics Office forecasts that by the early 1970s the number of married men under thirty will have increased to around 60,000, as compared with the reckoning of 30,000 for 1961. Between 1958 and 1962, the number of marriages of men aged twenty-two and twenty-three went up by 36 per cent and 39 per cent respectively. The actual number of marriages contracted annually is expected to increase from the 1963 figure of 15,300 to 18,500 in the mid 'seventies, growing to 20,000 by 1980. The trends indicated by these figures reveal clearly the change wrought by greater affluence and by new social attitudes.

These latter can be seen at work in the easier mingling of the sexes in leisure activities and social amusements. Dancing has always been an enormously popular diversion in Irish life. Today 'ballroom' dancing is perhaps the most popular single (or rather, double) public activity in the country. Dance halls are habitually packed, and 'showbands' command the adulation and rewards that 'pop' singers receive in other countries. A leading Irish impresario calculated for me that, on a Saturday night alone, about £500,000 changes hands at dance box-offices. The enthusiasm for modernity has taken deep root among Irish young people. The old-style ceilis of the countryside are becoming rarer. With every passing year one is a little less likely to hear the lusty exhortation to begin the dance: 'Round the house and mind the dresser'.

Yet it cannot be said that Irish country life is appreciably less colourful with the decline of the old diversions. One symbol both of greater prosperity and of new forms of gaiety is the 'festival phenomenon'. There are now festivals of beer, of lobsters, of beauty, of drama, of oysters, of horse-racing, of angling—to name but a few. These jamborees can last from two days to as many weeks. Apart from attracting the persons and purses of tourists and city-dwellers, they offer country folk, in a modern form, the gaiety once provided by the sideshows and drinking which accompanied the old livestock fairs, now largely replaced by hygienic, but prosaic, marts. The week-long Festival of Kerry—which offers, amongst other things, horse-racing and dancing—eventually results in the choice of a pretty girl as the 'Rose of Tralee' and in the host-town's enrichment by some £300,000. The Wexford Opera Festival, bringing famous singers to the town, is an undisputed artistic success, even by international standards. The Beer Festival, which burst forth suddenly at Kilkenny in 1963, is simply a success. Another noted festival is the 'happening' of Puck Fair at the little town of Killorglin in Kerry: a seventy-two hours' stamina test in which the pubs stay open day and night and a goat is enthroned King of the Fair. Enough of ancient tradition and modern jollity here to smother the grumbles of the most gloomy *laudator temporis acti*!

Still going strong are the two great national relaxations of horse-racing and talking (still pretty strong entrenchments of the male ascendancy!). Of Irish horse-racing we need not speak: the results-boards and studbooks of the world proclaim the glory of Ireland's steeds and the prowess of the men who breed and back them. As for talking: Irishmen are still unsurpassed in this, even if they do make one another drink more than they should do in company—for fear of what each will say about the other when the party breaks up.

Increasing affluence; the setting up of an Irish television service, now carrying international material transmitted by Telstar and Early Bird; the increased news-coverage of some Irish newspapers; the ramifications of the Vatican Council; the visit of President Kennedy in June 1963—all these have played their part in liberalising the climate of opinion in Ireland. The country's libraries and cinemas now bear only an architectural resemblance to the same places a few years ago. A symbol of this change is the success of a discussion group called Tuarim (Opinion). Begun in 1954, it has now spread so that it has branches in the bigger Irish towns and in England. Tuarim, particularly under the chairmanship in 1963 and 1964 of David Thornley, a brilliant Trinity don, helped to make the Irishman's opinion something which he didn't necessarily have to keep to himself. In the schools, the short stories of Sean O'Faolain and Frank O'Connor have found their way into the senior English courses. The decision-makers in most sectors of national life are becoming much more approachable, much more available to comment and criticism (well, *gentle* criticism anyway!), particularly the younger generation among them. With one notable exception, the only people who refused to see me in connection with this book were over fifty.

The reader outside Ireland may wonder why I single out Kennedy's visit as one of the major influences in liberalising opinion in Ireland. It had a peculiarly Irish effect which is hard to explain. For the few days he was in the country it was possible to engage wholeheartedly, without cynicism or dissension, in honouring a man who was not only an Irish hero but also a politician. For too long in the island one man's admiration for a political figure has been another man's hatred. I trust I shall be excused a little sentiment when I say that it meant something inexpressibly moving to an Irishman to stand beside President Kennedy in the grounds of Arus an Uachtaran the day he planted the tree. This man's great-grandfather left Ireland during the Famine. The great-grandson of him was now president of the United States. The Arus used to be the Vice-Regal Lodge, the centre of Dublin's high social life under the British. After independence it eventually became the home of the president of Ireland. And here now was this descendant of stricken peasants planting a tree hard by one planted by Queen Victoria when she came to Ireland as the Famine was ending. A wind blew from Dallas and the tree died. But Kennedy's memory is strong: more steadfast than any tree could be; more enduring than the vicissitudes of parties or states. He helped to solder past and present together, and suddenly to make politics something which gave a future meaning to the present.

Kennedy inspired the world with the vision of the New Frontier. Among all the influences which are shaping a more adventurous and liberal temper in Ireland's cultural and social life, the quickening spirit of Kennedy stands in the forefront with the great soul of Pope John.

9. GAELIC MOVEMENT

Death of the Gael · The Revival that Failed: *Gaelic League;*
The Language Movement Today: Aims and Problems
Gaelic Culture–New Life and Old Rancour: *Gael Linn;*
Comhaltas Ceoltóirí and the Fleadhs; Gaelic Athletic Association

THE Irish language movement is, after Partition, the most controversial subject in Ireland. Its protagonists include some of the most dedicated, intelligent and likeable people in the state; they also include a vociferous element which periodically gives the language movement the appearance of having not only a lunatic fringe but also a lunatic core. Of course, this phenomenon is not peculiar to Ireland. A community's love of its language is a reasonable, and can be an admirable, thing: the language being, we might assume, a medium of communication. But, without going back further than this decade, there is evidence in plenty of its being an instrument of separation: massacres in Madras, riots in Ceylon, and tension between Flemings and Walloons in Belgium.

Broadly speaking, the policy-differences among supporters of the Irish language movement can be attributed to two fundamentally different attitudes co-existing within the movement. One wing of it is willing to take in outside influences and use them to enhance and propagate the language. Another wing is concerned with the de-anglicisation of Irish culture, regarding all outside influences as suspect. This gives their crusade the appearance of being against rather than for something. All the same, both wings share a great sincerity and a great cultural tradition.

DEATH OF THE GAEL

Before the coming of Christianity in the fifth century, students and scholars from all over Celtic Europe studied at the Druidic schools in Ireland. As Christianity spread, the monastic seats of learning incorporated Latin words into the language and Latin metres into the poetry. The poet was then, and for long continued to be, a considerable person in Irish life. He was the reflector and shaper, not only of its cultural character, but also of popular attitudes on public questions. In 575, for example, the High King summoned at Druim Ceatt a convention of 1,200 poets to show cause why they should not be banished for satirising him. Thanks to the intervention of Saint Columcille, the poets won the day.

The Norse invasions, beginning in 795, destroyed many of the monasteries, and with them went much of the vigour of Irish Christianity. While the coming of the Normans in 1169 brought a strengthening of Christian institutions in Ireland, the continental religious orders which followed the conquerors imposed a discipline nearer to that of Rome. Monastic education was reformed in a spirit quite different from that of pre-Norse Christianity. Yet in areas where the Irish chieftains retained their hold, the bardic schools of poetry survived. Indeed, the bardic tradition up to the sixteenth century did more than survive. Horace's well-known line, *Graecia capta ferum victoremque cepit*, can be applied as well to Irish as to Greek culture. Within two or three generations of their arrival in Ireland, many of the Anglo-Norman lords beyond the Pale had become more Irish than the Irish themselves, marrying the daughters of Irish chiefs who brought the Gaelic language and its bards into the castles of the new masters. In quicker time than the royal authorities in London and Dublin liked to contemplate, the scions of great houses like the Fitzgeralds were wearing Irish dress, speaking Irish as their first language and maintaining household bards, like any native Irish chief.

But the Reformation and its aftermath closed down the skies on Ireland. The bardic and the monastic schools decayed together, so that only wandering minstrels and hedge-schoolmasters survived. Irish culture and Irish Catholicism were vital citadels earmarked for destruction by alien civil and religious rulers aiming at the complete control of the land and people of Ireland. The Cromwellian 'final solution', the system of Anglo-Scottish plantations, the penal laws which made Irish an illegal tongue and presumed no such being as a Catholic to have legal rights—all these brought the culture of the nation and the mass of its people by the nineteenth century to the level of the kulaks in Stalin's Russia and beneath even that of the Bantus under Verwoerd.

And yet, vestiges of the poetic tradition were maintained. As late as the eighteenth century, courts of poetry at which bards judged each other's work were common in Munster and in parts of Ulster—most common in the now partitioned parts of that province. Certainly there was nothing written of the high calibre of the poetry of the eighth and ninth centuries: the age which saw the creation of the great Irish saga, *Tain bo Cuailgne* (the Cattle Raid of Cooley). But verse of great beauty was produced, its poignantly elegiac note expressing the despair of a beaten but unbroken people. The plight of the country is reflected in the 'Aisling' or dream poetry of bards like O'Bruadair and O'Rathaile. Ireland takes the form of a beautiful woman and appears to the poet in his sleep to tell of her miserable lot, but also, as a symbol of the Stuarts, to give him comfort. Misery is also the keynote of Raftery, the blind poet, and it is present in the verses of O'Carolan, although with him love and merriment predominate. The funeral of this poet in 1783 was made almost a national day of mourning in the Irish-speaking parts of the country. The people thought they were attending the obsequies of the last of the great poets.* But in his stead came Bryan Merryman, who was truly the last of the great poets. He died at the beginning of the nineteenth century: the century whose last years marked the Irish revival. Merryman's great work, the *Midnight Court*, was banned by the censors when translated into English. The poem tells the story of a Midnight Court at which the women of Ireland bemoan the fact that Irishmen marry late and the priests don't marry at all.

The main theme in Gaelic verse, occurring to a greater or lesser degree even in sagas of battles and heroic deeds, is one of lament: the lament of the old Druidic order at the spread of Christianity; or the lament of the *revenant* from the dead bewailing the plight of Ireland after the Flight of the Earls in 1647 had left the people without leaders, their traditional way of life in ruins.

By the beginning of the nineteenth century, the Irish language was spoken mainly in the poorer and more inaccessible parts of the country. The ports and the bigger inland towns all spoke English. Although many people in these areas spoke and understood Irish, it was the language of decline. The decline was hastened by the formation of the National Schools in 1831, a principal aim of which was the eradication of the Gaelic (in British eyes, the trouble-making) tradition. The school books prescribed under this system contained things like this:

> I thank the goodness and the grace
> Which on my birth has smiled,
> And made me in these Christian days,
> A happy English child.

And this:

> On the East of Ireland is England where the Queen lives; many people who live in Ireland were born in England, and we speak the same language, and are called One Nation.

* O'Carolan died on March 28, 1783 at the home of the MacDermotts of Roscommon. His end was in the highest bardic traditions. Feeling himself sinking, he called for his harp and played *A Farewell to Music*. Everyone present burst into tears, but the bard stretched out his hand for a cup of whiskey saying he must give it a 'farewell kiss'. As he did so he fell out of bed, which led him to remark that many men had had falls on the hunting field but only O'Carolan could have a fall on his death bed. His wake was Connacht's greatest. Tents were erected all round the MacDermotts' house for the vast throng of mourners. Sixty clergymen of all denominations streamed in and the whiskey poured down.

The Famine hit the poorer districts hardest, draining off through death and emigration the wellsprings of the Gaelic culture. With English the language of advancement, parents struggled to help their children to shed the retarding and stigmatising Irish tongue. The Church was less concerned with revivifying a dying language than with fighting Protestantisation under the National Schools system. (The Board administering the schools consisted of six Protestants and two Catholics.) In fact, throughout the nineteenth century—and indeed, into the twentieth—the Catholic Church as a world faith was to benefit enormously from the emigration from Ireland. This was the spearhead of the diffusion of Catholicism throughout the English-speaking world both in the shape of emigrants and of missionaries. As we shall see in chapter 10, the Irish missionary contribution to the Church has been outstanding among European countries— far greater, for example, than that of the larger Catholic nation of Poland. From the point of view of the faith, it was well that Ireland's sons and daughters spoke English as a native tongue. To the hierarchy, talk of reviving the Irish language must have seemed like putting stumbling blocks in the way of Providence.

A modern authority on the language, Dr Sean O'Tuama, has calculated that by 1883 not more than fifty people among the Irish-speaking population could write and read the language. The census figures given below show that at this date it was still the spoken language of a large number of people, but it was regarded as a badge of inferiority. Those few among the Catholic gentry who, by the beginning of the nineteenth century, still spoke the language made it clear to questioners that they had learned it from their servants—not their parents!

	DECLINE OF IRISH-SPEAKING	
	Speaking Irish Only	*Speaking Irish and English*
1851	319,602	1,204,684
1881	64,167	885,765
1891	38,192	642,053
1901	20,953	620,189
1926	—	540,802
1946	—	588,725*

These census figures show that the number of people (over the age of three) knowing nothing but Irish has died out altogether. They also indicate the number of those who now know Irish as well as English. The

* The current Irish-speaking population is believed to have remained more or less stable at the 1946 level, though for some curious reason the 1961 Census returns were never published.

necessarily simplified census questionnaire gives no indication, of course, of the degree of knowledge of the language among this latter category. It can range from complete mastery to the ability to speak merely a few phrases. It is, however, a safe assumption that today the literate knowledge of the language is more widespread than at any time since the sixteenth century.

But to supporters of the language movement, delight at the increase of knowledge of Irish among English-speaking Irishmen is marred by their awareness that this is, in a sense, an artificial revival of the language. For the language movement the great tragedy is the fate of the *natural* Irish-speaking districts in the West, South-West and parts of the North-West: the areas embraced in the common term, the *Gaeltacht*. Both the Gaeltacht Commission set up in 1926, and the Commission on the Restoration of the Irish Language, which presented its report in 1964, stressed the necessity for maintaining the Gaeltacht as a reservoir for the preservation of the language. Both bodies made recommendations for the siting of industries in these areas in order to retain the population there. But, being the poorest and most inaccessible parts of the country, they are the most prone to emigration and the least conducive to the growth of industry. Government encouragement has as a result tended to be verbal rather than practical. The fact is, people would not be living in these areas at all had not circumstances in the past—Cromwell's persecution and later the Famine—pushed landless and starving peasants to the Western sea-board where a living could be eked out by fishing.

The most recent figures available fix the numbers using Irish as a spoken language in the Gaeltacht areas at 85,547. All save a tiny fraction of these use English also. It is not the inroads of English as such but the composition of the figures which holds the real menace to the Gaeltacht. There is the very real prospect that, just as people in Dublin who, claiming to be bilingual, can muster up in fact only a few phrases of Irish, so eventually the people in the Gaeltacht will come to have only a residual knowledge of what is at present regarded as their first language.

In the summer of 1964, I stood with my family on the pier at Killeany on Inis Mór, the largest of the three Aran Islands, strongholds of old Irish ways, lying off Galway and in sight of the hills of Connemara. Inis Mór is one of the most poignantly beautiful places in Ireland—a grimly splendid mass rising from the sea, its steep slopes of grey rock checkered with tiny stone-walled plots which flicker into green life when sunlight and wind move over them. Countless generations of patient toil, of endless humping of sand and seaweed, have won those tiny patches of grass from the rocky steeps. Beneath us the young mullet rummaged through the silt of the harbour. Earlier, fishing on the Atlantic side of the island, we had seen a basking shark throw itself from the sea to free itself of lampreys. To the right lay Inis Meáin, where Fr O'Growney—one of the founders of the Gaelic League—had gone to learn Irish and where Synge went to learn English. Between us and the mainland hills of Connemara, shimmering bluely in the heat haze of August, there slowly moved the five Galway hookers which still bring turf to Aran. They looked for all the world like Chinese junks as they inched out of the horizon. The five Galway hookers! At the turn of this century there were a hundred of them. A few people on the island still catch the rockfish, mainly wrasse: a sea-perch, considered in Connemara as a great winter delicacy when split and salted. The islanders sell these 'Aran chickens' at £7 10s a hundred, buying the winter's fuel from the Connemara men in return.

Behind us lay the ruins of Arkin's Castle where the troops of General Reynolds took command of Aran in 1652 and kept guard over Galway Bay as Cromwell imposed his 'settlement' of Ireland after the siege of Drogheda.

> It has pleased God to bless our endeavours at Drogheda [wrote Cromwell after the massacre of the townsfolk] . . . The enemy were about 3,000 strong in the town. I believe we put to the sword the whole number. . . . I wish that all honest hearts may give the glory of this to God alone, to Whom, indeed, the praise of this mercy belongs.

'To Hell or Connaught' was the alternative he gave the native Irish as he commandeered their land. They could flee no further west than Connemara. Aran was used as a prisonhouse for priests, reliving in a grimmer sense its old tradition as *Ara na Naomh*, Aran of the Saints. Today the Irish are fleeing from Connacht—to England or America.

As we walked up the road from the harbour, my children—who attend one of the 183 schools in the Republic which use Irish as the normal medium of teaching—spoke in the native tongue with the children they met. The old people smiled at them and saluted them melodically, as did the exceptionally beautiful Aran children. But very few of those children will stay on the island until they are the same age as the old people. That night we gave a party. The teenagers and twenty-year-olds who came did the twist! They had learned it in the cities of England and America, to which they would be returning when their holidays were over.

Most people on Aran have neither love nor hate for the language. In this they are typical of the other Gaeltacht areas.* It is something they

---

* But, curiously, the people of the Connemara Gaeltacht, even when settled elsewhere in the country or abroad, tend to transmit the language to their children; whereas the emigrants from other parts of the Gaeltacht rarely keep up the language beyond the second generation.

have grown up with. They get some small grants because of it. These mainly take the form of a housing grant towards the cost of building a new house. Also, until recently, it was easier for a Gaeltacht fisherman to get a boat from the state than his English-speaking counterpart on the East coast. There are other benefits, like an annual bonus of £5 for every child in an Irish-speaking home, and an arrangement whereby bottled gas for lighting is supplied at reduced rates to Gaeltacht homes. But these grants coming on top of the traditions of the Congested Districts Board, have tended, I fear, to encourage a dole-mentality which has not been altogether beneficial to the character of some Gaeltacht people. Others just shrug their shoulders and say: 'Sure, what use is it to us once we leave Kilronan pier. They laugh at us in the shops in Galway if we don't ask for a thing in English.'

This remark contains the kernel of the Irish language controversy. There is no *practical* use for the language. Yet a large part of every child's school life must be spent in learning it, for a pass in Irish is essential to achieve the school-leaving certificate. Knowledge of the language is obligatory for anyone wishing to join the civil service, the police and the army. It is the same with the professions, since no one who is Irish-born can enter the universities without matriculating in Irish. At the setting up of the state in 1922, Irish was made the 'official language', and in the 1937 Constitution it became the 'first official language'. Most government printing and signposting is done bilingually in Irish and English—though no one reads the Irish.

Under Cosgrave, Cumann na nGaedheal made Irish compulsory for the public service and the armed forces in the belief that these bodies would soon be the agencies of an Irish-speaking state.* Time was to prove that the public services, like the letter boxes, had merely been painted green. As in the case of the letter boxes, the British symbols were still clearly visible. A special report published with the census returns taken in 1946 showed that, on average, out of every 1,000 Irish-speakers aged between ten and fourteen who had remained in the country since 1936, only 571 could still speak the language ten years later.

THE REVIVAL THAT FAILED

What has gone wrong? How is it that Ireland—proudly independent and

---

* In 1929 Cumann na nGaedheal introduced legislation, in the teeth of heated protest from the legal profession, requiring proficiency in Irish as an essential qualification for passing the bar examination. The profession objected that throughout the country there was not one legal text in Irish.

with a people more collectively conscious of their history and culture than, perhaps, any other in Europe—has become the world's great example of a language revival that failed ? To discover the answer, it is necessary to know something of the history of the language movement generally and of the Gaelic League in particular.

The Gaelic League

The foundation of the Gaelic League in 1893 changed not only the fortunes of the Irish language but also the course of Irish history. Through the League young men like Padraig Pearse, Eamon de Valera, Michael Collins with hundreds of others of their generation became fired with an enthusiasm for Irish culture which eventually lit the fires of Easter Week. Founded by Fr Eugene O'Growney, Dr Douglas Hyde and Eoin MacNeill, the League's objects were:

> The Preservation of Irish as the National Language of Ireland and the extension of its use as a spoken tongue.
>
> The study and publication of existing Gaelic literature and the cultivation of a modern literature in Irish.

Fr O'Growney was professor of Irish at Maynooth. His 'easy lessons' published in five textbooks were the primers of the nascent movement. His obsequies in 1903—surely one of the most impressive accorded any man, lay or cleric, observed as they were along a funeral route that stretched from Los Angeles where he died to Maynooth where he was buried—were to the revival movement what the funeral of O'Donovan Rossa had been to the Irish Republican Brotherhood. Dr Douglas Hyde subsequently became president of Ireland; MacNeill, as we have seen, was the man whose suggestion led to the formation of the Volunteers.

The League concentrated on the spoken aspect of the language to avoid wounding the susceptibilities of two other Irish language organisations which preceded it: the Society for the Preservation of the Irish Language (founded in 1876), and its offshoot, the Gaelic Union (founded in 1878). Both of these bodies were mainly concerned with the written, published word. Fr O'Growney was editor of the second organisation's official paper, the *Gaelic Union*.

The fissiparous tendency is characteristic of Irish organisations. The Gaelic League also had its early splits. A branch was set up in Cork to demonstrate that proud city's independence of Dublin,* while some Protestant Ascendancy elements who supported the Irish revival founded

* This feeling of suspicion towards Dublin is also noticeable in Belfast. The Cork and Belfast wings of the Irish cultural movement tend to see Dublin as the city of the Pale, almost as if it were still a stronghold of the Sassenach conquest set in a strip of enemy-held territory along the East coast.

their own Protestant Gaelic League. A diversion called the Celtic Congress also enfeebled the League for a time, but the splinter group soon lost its impetus. It survives today in a sort of Celtic twilight. The four pioneer organisers of the League—Tomás Bán Concannon, Peadar McGinley, Pádraig O' Siochfhradha (known as An Seabhac, The Hawk) and Peadar O hAnnracháin—strengthened the new movement throughout the country, and their example was subsequently followed by many others. The writings of Fr Peter O'Leary, embodying what he called 'caint na ndaoine' (speech of the people) presented to Irishmen a tongue they had forgotten. Two newspapers in particular benefited the League: *An Claidheamh Soluis* (The Sword of Light), edited by MacNeill and Pearse as the organisation's official organ, and the *Leader*, edited by D. P. Moran to propagate the notion of an Irish Ireland. This journal was not only concerned with the Irish language: under Moran it also did a great deal to further the cause of Irish nationality in the political field. It still survives today, edited by his daughter.

All this enthusiasm gradually forced Irish first on to the bottom step and then rung by rung up the educational ladder. In 1878 Irish was included in the syllabus for the Intermediate Examination, though less than 5 per cent of the pupils taking the examination presented it. In the following year the primary schools accepted it as an extra subject, albeit instruction in it at first was given outside school hours. It was the drive and diplomacy of Douglas Hyde which co-ordinated these cautious first steps into a triumphant march. The really important brake on the process of anglicisation was applied in 1906–7 when, for the first time, Irish was admitted as a medium of instruction in the Gaeltacht (though even today some of the old people there can neither read nor write the language). The final triumph under the Union was attained in 1908 with the setting up of the National University. Irish was included in the curriculum and both MacNeill and Hyde became professors at the new university.

But the political movement which sprang from the League frustrated its aims. Before it had had time to permeate the country, the League split in 1915 when an IRB-sponsored resolution was carried at the annual convention held in Dundalk. The resolution proposed that henceforth the League should adopt as one of its aims 'the independence of Ireland'. Hitherto the League as a body, though in favour of independence, had been strictly non-political. At the passing of the resolution, Douglas Hyde and a sizeable section of the membership, including most of those who hitherto had supported the Irish Parliamentary Party, withdrew from the League. In the subsequent rush of history, the language movement lost other great leaders. Pearse, Collins and Cathal Brugha were killed in action, while MacNeill, as we have seen, was discredited over the Boundary

Commission's findings in 1925. The League lost efficacy further through becoming associated, rightly or wrongly, in the public mind with one political view only: the Republican. Its president after the Civil War became a Fianna Fail deputy, and during the IRA internments in the 1939–45 war it elected one of the internees, Seán Og O'Tuama, as its new president.

Even so, the Gaelic League still exists as the 'Establishment' organisation within the language movement. With an office in Dublin and branches throughout the country, it is one of the four major Gaelic cultural organisations. However, most of the language's supporters never join any organisation. Although it is a popular belief in Ireland that people make fortunes out of the movement, most restorationists contribute generously in time and money to Irish cultural causes. The state is not less open-handed. In 1963 government expenditure on the language was between 0·2 and 0·3 per cent of the total state expenditure. In all, the sums spent on the language since the foundation of the state must be astronomical.

The principal newspaper of the language movement is *Inniu* (which means 'Today' although it is a weekly). The title is a tribute to the faith and energy of its creator, Ciaran O'Nuallain, who in 1943 was a little known Irish journalist and language enthusiast. He interested an organisation called Glun na Bua (of which he was then secretary) in the idea of starting a paper. Backed by its chairman, Proinsias Mac an Bheatha, the organisation published the first issue of *Inniu* in March 1943, as a monthly. O'Nuallain acted as editor, advertisement manager and sales officer. It became a weekly in 1946 and over the years has grown steadily in circulation, attaining today an average sale of 17,000 copies. Its principal writers and workers are Tarlach O'h-Uid, Padraig O'Gaora and Séamas O'Cathasaigh, who gave up his job in the civil service to work as the paper's manager. It compares well with English-language journalism and, for all the lack of enthusiasm on the part of advertisers, its sales increase each year. Even so, it could hardly survive without a government grant, made available since 1948. The ambition of O'Nuallain is to see *Inniu* become some day a daily in fact as in name. He may well succeed.

Glun na Bua came into being through a group which broke away from the Gaelic League in 1942: Craobh na h-Aiséirí (the Resurrection Branch), whose president was Gearóid O'Cuinneagáin. But O'Cuinneagáin wanted to found a political party, while the section which, under Proinsias Mac an Bheatha, eventually formed Glun na Bua wanted to spread the language by means of film shows, open-air classes and lectures. This it eventually did and succeeded, even during the war, in making a number of small films. The wing which followed O'Cuinneagáin formed itself into a political party called Ailtirí na h-Aiséirí (Architects of the Resurrection), contesting both local government and Dail elections. It failed to win any seats in the Dail but it had some success in municipal elections at Cork and Drogheda. The political thinking of the party, which for a time attracted quite a lot of support, was dominated by the vocational teaching of *Quadragesimo Anno*, and evinced an admiration for Salazar's administration in Portugal. A touch of anti-semitism also manifested itself in some of the party's followers. This, however, was more attributable to a pro-German feeling which became marked in the period of German victories than to any deep-rooted antagonism to the Jews. The party founded a paper, *Aiséiri* (Resurrection) which continues today under the editorship of O'Cuinneagáin.

The Language Movement Today: Aims and Problems

With a country divided by Civil War in the South and Partition in the North, it turned out to be much more difficult to revive the language than had been supposed. It was not possible for Cumann na nGaedheal to lower the portcullis and declare a reign of Irish throughout the country immediately on the setting up of the state. Ireland was unable to take the bold step made by Israel in making Hebrew the national language. With people of so many different languages in the new Jewish state, there was general agreement that there had to be one common tongue. But in Ireland there was already a common tongue, and this was not Irish. In the pioneer zeal of the return to the Holy Land, Israeli parents tolerated their children being badly taught for a generation so that the next generation would be fully fledged citizens of Israel, speaking Hebrew as their native language. In the disillusioned aftermath of Civil War and Partition, the Irish people as a whole had no such pioneer zeal; and more and more it became clear that the real mode of educational and professional advancement in free Ireland was still English.

The Knesset spoke Hebrew from the start. In the Dail and Seanad, however, the average percentage of Irish speeches in debates is 2 per cent. Nor does any significant proportion of leading politicians either speak Irish privately or have their children educated at schools where Irish is the sole medium of instruction. The figure of 2 per cent also holds good for the civil service's work. A commission was set up in 1937 to plan the extension of Irish throughout the public service, but the war intervened and the project was shelved. The change of government in 1932 did not materially alter the position, even though the restoration of the language is one of the major objectives set out in the constitution of Fianna Fail. Significantly, Fine Gael made it a plank in their 1961 election platform that, if elected, they would remove Irish as a compulsory requirement. This pledge did not succeed in getting Fine Gael into office, but it may have played a part in enhancing its electoral strength. (The party gained seven seats.)

In fact, although in recent years economic prosperity has brought with it an improvement in the popular attitude to the question, the people as a whole have not shown any strong feeling for the Irish language. All that can be discerned is a vague goodwill which falls short either of agitating for more money to promote its revival or of actually learning it. Douglas Hyde, the apostle of the movement, was defeated when he stood for the Senate in 1925, despite his work for the Irish language.

In the early days of the state, teachers were often only marginally ahead of their pupils in knowledge of the language. They were required to spend part of the summer holidays in the Gaeltacht. Instead of acquiring a love for the language, many of them came to detest it. Another aspect of the situation which caused resentful obstinacy to the urgings of the authorities was the fact that in the 'thirties and well into the 'forties promotion within the public services was not infrequently bestowed less on merit than on proficiency in Irish. Even today, medical appointments within the public service are dependent on a knowledge of the language.

The teaching difficulty has not yet been resolved. The report of the Commission on the Restoration of the Irish Language (1964) somewhat disingenuously states that 89 per cent of the Republic's teachers are qualified to teach Irish. This is strictly correct in that, in order to meet the demand for teachers, the Department of Education accepts a pass BA degree as sufficient qualification. But educational authorities say privately that an honours BA is necessary. All this bears most heavily on the children of the poor who are constrained to learn a language for which there is no day-to-day demand. If you come from the sort of family that can put its offspring through the university with a view to a civil service or professional career, Irish, though it may be a bore, is clearly a useful means to an end— like Latin under the humanistic system of education. But if you are the son of a small farmer hoping for a job as a worker in the nearest town, or a labourer who will have to emigrate, or the son of an artisan in Dublin or Cork, hoping to improve your lot by becoming a technician—what use is Irish to you ?

Among supporters of the Irish movement there is, however, another school of thought. This holds that there should be less stress on academic qualifications and more concentration on propagating a love for the language, and this, it is argued, will only be achieved by encouraging people actually to talk it, no matter how badly at first. This way of looking at things is a reaction against the rather snobbish attitude taken by a good many Gaelic Leaguers to people who spoke the language badly—an attitude which scared off hundreds of potential supporters for the language movement.

A major stumbling block to the spread of Irish has been the structure of the language itself. Irish is an indigenous tongue which is properly described in English as 'Irish'—*not* as 'Gaelic' or 'Erse', for these are Scottish derivations. Irish is divided into four linguistic periods: *Old Irish*, AD c. 700 to 950; *Middle*, 950 to 1200; *Early Modern*, 1200 to 1650; *Late Modern*, 1650 to the present day. Only fragments of old Irish exist in manuscript but, because of the unbalanced, over-romantic nature of the language revival in the nineteenth century, the usages of the other three periods were entwined in the vocabularies and dialects of the first Gaelic League teachers to spread the language. The results achieved often were akin to a blend of Chaucerian with contemporary English, with a whiff of the Anglo-Saxon Chronicle to add period flavour.

The voluntary teachers who went through the country spreading Irish dances and music as well as the language naturally disseminated whatever dialect they had themselves learned. But, albeit basically Irish—in the sense that the people who learned the language could claim to be speaking (as the phrase has it) 'through the medium'—the language thus spread varied considerably from county to county, and still more markedly from province to province—in the same way that, say, Yorkshire English differs from that of a Scottish Highlander. Spelling is also a problem. For instance, the word for a house may correctly be spelt ᴄɪ5 (tig) or ᴄeᴀᴄ (tshock). When the Free State was set up, an effort at standardisation was made with the introduction of the Cló Romhánach, or Roman script, for use in official documents. This mode of writing the language uses an *h* in the stead of an aspirate symbol. But for schoolbooks the Gaelic script, which has no *v, w, x, y* or *z*, was retained. There was a reversal to the Gaelic script in official printing after Fianna Fail came to power in 1932. But since then the Roman script has gradually come into general use—largely because it is ruinously expensive to get type and typewriters made with Gaelic characters (which, moreover, allow of no selection of type beyond capitals and lower case). After the war, the Litriú Nua, or new spelling, was first proposed. This is designed to bring spelling closer to speech and to establish a common form for the language throughout the country.*

Some such reform of the spelling is greatly needed. At the time of writing the same word can often be spelt in different ways in each province. These differences would not have made for undue difficulty had the emphasis on Irish teaching not been heavily grammatical, with scant

* Litriú Nua will not be fully in use until 1972. It was officially introduced into schools in 1962, but on a graduated basis: junior schools first, technical schools next, and so on.

concern for oral expression. This imbalance has now been recognised as such by the introduction since 1964 of oral examinations and language laboratories (though these are as yet only a handful) into the language promotion methods of the Department of Education.

But perhaps an even greater retarding factor has been the public image given to the entire movement by the behaviour of certain of its adherents —albeit these are moved by a genuine feeling and concern for the language. A university professor once told me that he regarded comment on the language as he would regard comment on his mother or father. Some language revivalists have allowed this kind of feeling to grow into something very like paranoia. The letter-columns of the newspapers are usually occupied with at least one controversy or other about the language. Some correspondents would earnestly seem to believe that Christ spoke Irish. (That agreed, there would still, I suppose, be quite violent disputation as to the dialect.) Many good souls are determined to prove that 'anti-national' elements—a phrase used *ad nauseam*—are running a 'campaign' against the language.

The sort of obfuscation with which the Irish language movement tends to surround itself is typified, I think, by a recommendation in the Language Commission's report of 1963 to the effect that the phrase 'compulsory Irish' should never be used; instead, the term should be 'essential Irish'. Many language supporters will not recognise the fact that their fellow country-men's objections to certain aspects of language revival policy are genuine, and not just inventions of the *Irish Times*. It is not being perversely Sas-senach to suggest that the enthusiasts are not wholly correct when they aver that there is no more compulsion involved in learning Irish than, say, English or mathematics. The problem is a difficult one and will not be solved by casuistry.

The founders of the language movement were entirely honest and democratic in their efforts. In a letter to John Devoy on the university situation, Douglas Hyde wrote (November 30, 1909): '. . . The question of *compulsory* Irish is not settled yet, and can hardly be settled, so far as I can see, before the end of February. . . . If we win, we have Ireland's nationality. If we lose, nobody will benefit by it. . . .' Hyde was clear about how he wished to 'win Ireland's nationality': by persuasion and democratic methods. In 1943 he created a precedent which has since been followed as occasion warrants. As president, he was instrumental in getting the courts to over-rule, for the first time, a bill passed by the Dail: legislation designed to increase the spread of Irish. He refused to sign the School Attendance Bill, under Section 4 of which parents who sent their children abroad to school might have been liable to prosecution for failing to have their children taught Irish. The Supreme Court ruled on April 15 that Section 4 was repugnant to Article 42 of the Constitution which guarantees the rights of the family. The section was deleted from the bill.

The adoption, following the Language Commission's report, of the epithet 'essential' does nothing to solve the problem posed by the fact that, though necessary to the getting of scholarships and passing examinations, Irish is not 'essential' in life after school or university. The only way to solve the difficulty is to recognise it frankly and seek to inculcate a voluntary love of the language rather than an enforced distaste for it. A hopeful sign is that the Commission also recommended that pupils failing their school-leaving examination because of bad marks in Irish should be given a second chance. This recommendation was adopted by the government, which also introduced a provision by which children of emigrants who have returned to work in Ireland are not compelled to study Irish.

Following the publication of the Language Commission's report in December 1963 all the language organisations in the country got together to mobilise public support for a nation-wide language revival campaign. They managed, in an uncöordinated, early Sinn Fein-like burst of enthusiasm, to get the support of local bodies and organisations of all sorts. These passed resolutions and inundated the government with advice and exhortation: mostly in English! While this was going on, a petition was organised under the slogan of 'Let the Language Live'. This collected 400,000 signatures in five weeks. Many of them, of course, belonged to schoolchildren, asked by their teachers simply to 'sign here'. Yet a response of 400,000 could not be achieved solely by such means. There is unquestionably a strong ground-swell of support for a sane, modern approach to the problem. In recent years, the Gaelic enthusiasts have succeeded in getting more public notice taken of Irish by Telefis Eireann and by public bodies like Coras Iompair Eireann, the nationalised transport company which now has place-names in Irish on its direction indicators. One notices signs of promotional activity almost every day.

Unfortunately, since many of the old guard revivalists have come by revolution to be on or near the seats of power, public controversy on the subject of the language can only be engaged in with impunity by people with private incomes. As a result of this unhealthily inhibited climate of discussion, it is only since 1964 that it has been possible for a consensus of public opinion to be developed in support of the idea of a government plan for the promotion of Irish based on the linguistic quantum now existing. It is rather melancholy to think that a realistic scheme for fostering Irish will get under way only as the die-hards die out.

And they really are die-hards. Much of the ardour which went into fighting for Irish freedom now goes into the fight for the language. People go to court rather than pay their radio licences if the necessary forms are not made out in Irish. An undue hostility to foreign influences (mainly to things English) and a concentration on the pastoral aspects of Irish culture have tended to create an uneasy vision in the public mind of what the country would be like if the Gaels ever controlled it. The concept of the Gael as propagated by the extreme wing of the movement is of a man approximately six feet and five inches in height, noble-browed and with the faraway look in his eye which comes through perusing Erin's past glories. His wife is serene, beautiful and the mother of eleven children. In view of the mandatory chastity of the couple, conception, it will be understood, occurs non-sexually—through the 'medium' as it were.

To be just, however, it must be said that, if many language enthusiasts display an excessive hostility to English influences, there are parts of the country where the Anglo-Saxon tradition is still strong and where one can encounter a no less strong animosity to Irish. One of the most rational and brilliant public servants in the country revealed to me accidentally that he spoke the language fluently. He never uses it, though, because of what he associates with it. Much of what seems to be the pernickety sensitivity of Gaelic culture supporters is a reaction against the continual rejection by some Irishmen of the fact that Irish is, after all, the official language of the country. Many officials in the public service arouse the justifiable ire of those who, having had their names registered in Irish as a gesture of nationality, receive correspondence which brusquely ignores this fact.

GAELIC CULTURE: NEW LIFE AND OLD RANCOUR

Gaelic culture, particularly its literature, is in reality much more worthwhile than the excessively heroic and virtuous vision of Gaelic Man might suggest. No book in Irish has ever been banned, despite the fact that some prose and verse in the language is far more mature and adult than has been found acceptable, until recently, by the censors of English-language publications in Ireland.

Apart from schoolbooks bought by the Department of Education, Irish language publishing subsists largely through the existence of An Club Leabhar, a book club of approximately 1,500 members, which guarantees a tolerable initial sale. The principal private firm is Sairseal agus Dill. Run in his spare time by Seán O hÉigeartaigh, a dedicated civil servant, the firm maintains for Irish-language books the high standards which other Irish publishers observe in their English-language works. It expects to sell about 3,000 copies of a good title. Of the other firms, An Clóchomhar Tta (a co-operative venture), Foilseacháin Náisiúnta Tta (controlled by the publishers of *Inniu*), and Cló Uí Mheara (founded and managed in

Nenagh by Pádraig O'Meara) are the most important. An Clóchomhar, in particular, has done some useful work. It published Dónall Mac Amhlaigh's *Dialann Deorái*, which was translated into English by Valentin Iremonger as *An Irish Navvy*; while another of this firm's books, poems by Maírtín O'Direaín, won the Irish Arts Council's prize of £300. There is also a government publishing house, An Gum, founded in 1926—a worthy but rather slow-moving establishment. Authors complain that it has taken from ten to fifteen years to publish a book!

Among writers in Irish there is at least one outstanding playwright, Mairéad Ní Ghráda. A number of other good writers treat of contemporary themes, the most notable being Maírtín O'Cadhain and Diarmuid O'Sullivan in prose, Séan O'Ríordáin and Máire Mac an tSaoi in poetry. Their general standard would not be far below that of, say O'Faolain or Frank O'Connor in English. Some of O'Cadhain's best work, particularly *Cre na Cille* (Dust of the Graveyard), a story in which the dead talk about their native village, would rank with either of these highly esteemed writers in English. Before writers such as these came on the Irish literary scene, the major works in the language were written about what was practically a neolithic way of life. Three of such works reached international stature: *The Islander*, by Tomás O'Criomhthain, *Twenty Years A-Growing* by Muiris O'Súileabháin, and *Peig* by Peig Sayers. O'Criomhthain's book was about a small Gaeltacht district in Kerry; O'Súileabháin and Sayers wrote about the Blaskets, a group of islands off the South-West coast, now void of people. Liam O'Flaherty, an Aran man, also became internationally known, but most of his most celebrated works, like *The Informer*, were written in English.

Unfortunately, much of what is published and broadcast in Irish is junk which would never come to eye or ear if pressures and subsidies were not so prominent a feature of the movement. One reason why Radio Eireann, for instance, is such a poor quality station is because of the high quota of mediocre Irish programmes it is forced to carry.

The Gaelic League has attracted much of the limelight and certainly most of the heat in the revival of Irish culture. But many loyally 'Irish' Irishmen probably attach at least as much importance to other movements within the cultural spectrum. Principal among these are Gael Linn, the Gaelic Athletic Association, and Comhaltas Ceoltoírí Eireann—all of which play a large part in Irish life. There are also all sorts of other smaller groups. One such seeks to spread Irish among the clergy; another propagates the sale of Irish Christmas cards; yet another promotes the wearing of a small ring which signifies that the wearer speaks and welcomes being spoken to in Irish.

Gael Linn

In an effort to co-ordinate the activities of the various groups in the cultural movement, Comhdháil Náisiúnta na Gaeilge (National Gaelic Congress) was founded in 1943. Three years later control of its executive council was seized by members of An Comhchaidreamh, a ginger-group of Irish-loving but apolitical students from the constituent colleges of the National University and from Queen's College, Belfast. Since its formation in 1936 this group has made the running in the language movement much as the Gaelic League had done earlier. The initiative for An Comhchaidreamh came from a civil servant, Máirtín O'Flathartaigh, then a student, who later became de Valera's secretary. The group included Tomás de Bhaldraithe (now professor of Irish at University College, Dublin, and editor of the most up-to-date Irish dictionary), David Greene, professor of Irish at Trinity College, Tomás O'Floinn (for a time editor of *Comhar*, the group's journal, founded in 1942), and Seán O hÉigeartaigh, the publisher of Irish books. *Comhar*'s early contributors included Liam O'Flaherty, Conor Cruise O'Brien and Valentin Iremonger. It published a series of sketches which Brendan Behan later expanded into *Borstal Boy*. At a meeting of the Comhchaidreamh at Cork in March 1953, Dónal O'Moráin successfully proposed the setting up of Gael Linn to deploy modern media for the promotion of the language: films, records, plays and so on.

Gael Linn is one of the major success stories of modern Irish culture. It began with a football pool with a capital of £100 and a working day of twenty-five hours. Today it has 1,500 organisers and is the biggest pool in the country. Under its auspices, the Damer Theatre gave Brendan Behan's play, *An Giall* (later internationally famous as *The Hostage*) its first production, and put on Mairéad Ni Ghráda's *An Triail*, a play about Irish attitudes to illegitimacy. Harold Hobson, the *Sunday Times* critic, thought it the best play of the 1964 Dublin Theatre Festival, and it has since been produced in Berlin.

Gael Linn's film-making activities include two important documentary films in Irish, built up by George Morrison from old newspapers and rare newsreels: *Saoirse?* (Freedom?) and *Mise Eire* (I am Eire). An innovationist composer, Seán O'Riada, who wrote the hauntingly beautiful score for the two films, became famous in Ireland as a result. He uses bowrans (a traditional tambourine-like instrument), spoons and pieces of bone in his compositions. Gael Linn also produces 'pop' records in Irish.

The organisation has supplied boats on easy terms for Gaeltacht fishermen, and sends young people to Irish-speaking areas on scholarship grants so that they can learn the language by living with families. Lest the reader should groan at the thought of yet another 'folksy', 'olde worlde crafte' body, it must be stressed that Gael Linn is very much concerned with *living* Irish culture and is a highly practical, 'with it' organisation. To dispel the Celtic twilight aura surrounding the language movement, it has established its offices in Dublin's most exclusive quarter, Grafton Street. Here, with all the accoutrements of a modern office, a staff of fifty smoothly transacts business in Irish. Dónal O'Moráin has been elected director for three-yearly periods since Gael Linn's inception by a board of twenty shareholders chosen from among people prominent in the Gaelic movement.

Comhaltas Ceoltoirí and the Fleadhs

But the most dramatic success of any of the Irish cultural organisations has been that achieved by Comhaltas Ceoltoirí Eireann (Traditional Music Society of Ireland), founded on February 4, 1951 simply to spread a love of Irish music. Aided by the world-wide upsurge of interest in traditional music, it now has branches in England, America and Australia. The Comhaltas organises musical fleadhs (festivals) on an intercounty basis. The winners of competitions at county level go forward to provincial fleadhs, the winners in which then compete in the annual All-Ireland Fleadh.

The Comhaltas was started by a group of traditional musicians who played regularly at the Pipers' Club, 14 Thomas Street, Dublin.* The first fleadh of any sort was held at Whitsuntide in 1951 at Mullingar. Fifteen hundred people attended. The All-Ireland Fleadh at Monaghan in the following year attracted some 10,000 people. The All-Ireland Fleadhs are usually held over the Whit weekend and in recent years, the organisers estimate, the average attendance has been over 100,000, most of them young people. Few visitors have any knowledge of traditional music (though this is spreading), but are drawn by the experience of listening to the various impromptu 'sessions' which spring up in the streets, in bars, in surrounding fields—in any place where a group of instrumentalists or singers pause. The feast of drinking and merrymaking which accompanies the music gives the fleadhs the air of an Irish Mardi Gras, and brings to the towns where they are held money amounting, the Comhaltas reckons, to between £250,000 and £300,000.

The fleadhs also bring thousands of young city-dwellers into the Irish countryside and to the wellsprings of their land's traditions (achieving in this, on the level of Gaelic culture, much the same revivification of country life as is created by the various festivals described in the previous chapter). The average Dublin labourer, for example, would normally undertake a

* This group consisted of Arthur Cannick, Leo and Tom Rowsome, Aidan McCloud, Jim Dowling, Ger Tuohy, Jim Christle, Paddy McElvaney and Sean Seery.

journey to Liverpool or Manchester or Birmingham more readily than he would go to Mullingar or Clones, Thurles or Gorey. Also significant is the liberalising effect of the fleadhs on moral and political attitudes. The Clones Fleadh of 1964 was one of the most successful and good humoured ever held. Thousands of besweatered boys and girls, undulantly proving it is the end that justifies the jeans, sang their way through the streets arm in arm, most of them oblivious of the official competitions taking place in the halls. One of the principal organisers of this free-and-easy fleadh was a priest, Fr Gallagher. The significance of this as an aspect of new attitudes in Irish life may escape the reader who is unaware that it was a former parish priest of Clones, Canon Marron, who enforced a rule that men and women should sit on different sides of the aisle in the local cinema.

Perhaps even more important is the entire divorcement of the fleadhs from politics. At Clones, for example, the Border runs a few hundred yards outside the town. Thousands of enthusiastic Northerners, many of them Orangemen, attended the fleadh. 'The fiddle knows no boundaries', is a favourite Comhaltas slogan. Sean Maguire, the leading traditional violinist, is a Belfast man, and Irish music is particularly strong in the North, though most of its leading exponents are based in Dublin. Leo Rowsome, the champion Ullean piper, the violinist brothers Kieran and Owen O'Rahilly, and Seamus Kane, all play at the Pipers' Club.

Unfortunately, as I wrote this, the fleadh movement came under a cloud partly because of overcharging at the Thurles Fleadh in 1965. Previously there had been trouble at the Mullingar Fleadh in 1963, the heat having induced a little mixed bathing *au naturel*. But the Thurles riots were more serious: they led to the closing of the pubs! No one was hurt but many young people, having paid excessive prices for their drinks, decided to get value for their money by lobbing bottles into the air. These incidents made headlines the next day. Tuam in County Galway, after the local clergy had made their views known, announced that it would not accept the All-Ireland Fleadh scheduled to take place there in 1966. (However, Boyle in Roscommon agreed to be host-town.) While fleadhs do certainly attract a hoodlum element, with little interest in traditional music or simple merrymaking, it would be a grievous pity if local avarice allowed these festivals of traditional music to go the same way as Saint Maelruain's Day which, degenerating into Moll Rooney's Day, became a sort of Donnybrook Fair of fighting and debauchery and, like the Fair, had to be suppressed.

Gaelic Athletic Association

Some stalwarts of the Irish culture movement would consider the fleadhs as 'lowering the tone' of the movement, and would look to the Gaelic

Athletic Association for reassurances that the hearts and thews of young Ireland were still sound. The Association is the biggest organisation of any sort within the movement, with more than 3,000 clubs in Ireland, 174 in Britain, some in America and a branch in New South Wales. An All-Ireland final for Irish football or hurling at Croke Park, Dublin, will be attended by numbers equivalent to, if not more than, the whole population of the Gaeltacht. The GAA is a tremendous social asset in rural areas both for players and followers of national games. Like the Comhaltas, it has done something to improve North–South relationships. A team from County Down in the North won the All-Ireland Gaelic football final in 1960—to the huge delight of the Unionists! (Some of the staunchest and most extreme supporters of the Gaelic cultural movement have been, and are, Protestants.) Winning an All-Ireland medal carries with it such kudos that many a deputy and not a few ministers have demonstrated that the road to the Dail lies through the goalmouth.

The Gaelic Athletic Association was founded in Thurles on November 1, 1884. Its inspirer was Michael Cusack, an Irish-speaking Clare man who ran a cramming establishment for aspirants to the civil service. Its inculcation of specifically Irish sports was a focal point for the awakening national awareness of the country. The British army then, as now, carried soccer and cricket wherever it went. Soccer in particular proved very popular in Ireland and many a young Irishman took the Queen's shilling through playing football with the British garrison. To combat this and to encourage the spread of Irish pastimes, the GAA introduced a ban on playing 'foreign games', breach of which entails dismissal from the organisation. Rule 27 of the Association defines foreign games as: cricket, hockey, rugby and soccer.* Rugby and soccer still shows traces of the British regime in the form of club names like Shelbourne, Palmerston and Lansdowne, but these (called anyway after the places where the clubs were founded, not after the Anglo-Irish figures of the same names) are about the only tangible evidence remaining today to give a colourable argument for the ban. But history plays its part in maintaining it. Unionist employers in the old days could be very objectionable to young workers who went in for 'subversive' games, and older people still tell stories of the RIC's breaking up games of Gaelic football and hurling.

The ban is a bitter source of controversy within and without the GAA,

---

* Gaelic football is played with fifteen a side. Substitutes are allowed—and needed! The ball may be caught, punched or kicked, but must not be carried for more than three paces or picked up directly from the ground. There is no offside rule. As with hurling, a match lasts for an hour, with a short interval at half-time. Hurling, also with fifteen a side, is played with a leather stitched ball and wooden sticks. The ball can be bounced on the stick, taken by the player and then hit by stick or hand under rugby-like goalposts to score a goal or over the bar to score a point. Gaelic football has a similar system of scoring.

since another rule prescribes the dismissal from the Association of anyone who 'promotes' foreign games: for example, by going to dances organised by rugby, hockey, soccer or cricket clubs. Local vigilante committees have enforced the ban by spying on backsliders. This tendency automatically to make an interest in things Irish synonymous with an exclusionist attitude to things non-Irish is deplored by liberal-minded Irishmen, and it tends to deter them from taking part in all Gaelic cultural and recreational activities. Since the Association's rules also prevent local clubs from raising funds by running dances and entertainments other than in the form of ceilis, changing-room facilities are rare save in the bigger centres.

The congress of the GAA decided at its Easter meeting in 1965 to retain the ban. This decision contrasted poorly with the gesture made on the same day by the former IRA general, Tom Barry. Hitherto one of the most die-hard Republicans, he delivered on Easter Sunday at Beal na Blath an oratorical tribute to Michael Collins, making honourable recognition of the fact that times had changed. The official report of the GAA in 1965 opened with a just encomium of the association's greatest secretary, Padraig O'Keefe, who had died the previous year after forty years of work, doing more than any other man to build up the GAA. But the section devoted to attacking those who criticised the ban was twice the length of the tribute to O'Keefe.

However, it would not be fair to write off the ban's supporters as a lot of reactionary 'Little-Irelanders'. Their sticking to its retention springs from a sincerely held belief in an Irish Ireland. Many of them speak Irish in their homes and conduct the GAA's business in the language. The situation at the time of writing is that it is accepted in GAA circles that thousands of its members regularly attend 'foreign games'—so many that it would be impossible to prevent them. All the same, when the vigilante committee of an unscrupulous county decides to report a player from a rival county team, that player can be, and is, suspended. In areas where the GAA is strong, suspension can often mean more than being sent off the field: it can entail impairment of the offender's social life.

The Gaelic Athletic Association is a great promoter of ceilis—the traditional dance and sing-song entertainment of the villages. These are most enjoyable when staged naturally in a holiday spirit in places like the Aran Islands. But prior to the growth of the fleadhs, outside such venues the word 'ceili' tended to conjure up visions of ringleted children in elaborate Irish costumes dancing in the rain on the tailboards of lorries: 'folk culture' of the forced, pretentious sort. I think the well-meaning but joyless image the word tends to invoke is best symbolised by a poster which appears from time to time in O'Connell Street: MONSTER CEILI RUN BY THE NATIONAL GRAVES ASSOCIATION.

However the GAA's 'die-hard' majority was greatly reduced at the 1965 congress as compared with previous years. It is confidently forecast within the movement that Rule 27 will be removed or amended in a liberal sense at the next congress in 1968. It is to be hoped so. The language and traditions of Ireland deserve better than to be etched with the rancorous symbols of animosities dating from unhappier times.

10. RELIGION

The Catholic Church: *Organisation; Status in Community;*
Education; Ethos of Irish Catholicism; New Trends, New
Problems; Church Leadership; The Future · The Protestants

THERE are two ecclesiastical establishments in Ireland both calling
themselves the 'Holy Catholic and Apostolic Church'. However,
with some rare exceptions, priests of the Church of Ireland
(Anglican) are chary, in the ordinary usages of their vocation, of applying
the term 'Catholic' to themselves and, strong in their attachment to
Reformation principles, follow the custom of the great majority of the Irish
people in identifying the term with the Irish Church (Roman). I do not
therefore have to make any special pleading for adopting, with suitable
adjustments to the Irish situation, the catena of definition of the Anglican
divine in *Tom Jones* who said: 'When I speak of religion, I mean the
Christian religion; when I speak of the Christian religion I mean the
Protestant religion; and when I speak of the Protestant religion, I mean
the Church of England as by law established'. In this chapter, when I
speak of the Church, I mean the Catholic Church as understood and
reverenced by the vast preponderance of Irishmen and Irishwomen
throughout the world.

This may seem a rather arch way to introduce the chapter on religion
in a book about Ireland. It is. But there is a reason for it. It is too readily
assumed that Protestantism is some weird, abnormal excrescence on the
national life. It is certainly *untypical* of the general temper of the Irish
people, and its institutional form was, in the past, certainly imposed on
them against their will and in harsh defiance of their passionate attachment
to the Roman Church. As an institution it was 'alien'. Yet many of Ireland's
greatest patriots—Wolfe Tone, Robert Emmet, Charles Stewart Parnell:
one could fill a paragraph with their names—were born of Protestant
families. And some of the greatest and most typical flowerings of the Irish
national genius—Edmund Burke, Oscar Wilde, George Bernard Shaw
to name but three—belonged to the Protestant tradition. Despite the
oppressions of the past, the present dismemberment of the island on
religious grounds and the caste-consciousness of some of them, the
Protestants are an accepted and valuable part of the Irish community.

The evidence of their presence is everywhere. Every sizeable village has two churches. The unwary foreigner, looking for Mass or a sight of Irish Catholicism in stone, wood and glass, will make for the more venerable of the two. He will recoil with amazement and perhaps with an oath flung at Irish perversity, for it will almost certainly be a Church of Ireland building. (To avoid making the mistake, remember that if the church is small, looks old and has a square tower, it is Protestant!) Though disestablished, the Church in communion with Canterbury retains most of the places of worship acquired at the Reformation, all of the churches built during the Ascendancy, and the full panoply of archdioceses and dioceses proper to a 'national' Church (even if, in many cases, it has been constrained to amalgamate sees). There are two cathedrals in Dublin. Both are Protestant. The cathedral of the Catholic archbishop is, strictly speaking, only a pro-cathedral.

Ireland exhibits the paradox of the 'old faith' worshipping in new buildings and struggling hard to house its priests and congregations in premises suitable for a majority religion, and the 'new faith' struggling hard to maintain for the minority religion the venerable externals of Christian antiquity. This point should be borne in mind when criticisms are made by people (myself included) who chafe at the expenditure of so much priestly energy and lay resources on building appeals, loan-liquidation and the like. To all intents and purposes, the National Church had, in material terms, to start from scratch only a little more than a century ago. It is to the National Church that we now turn, leaving further discussion of the Protestant Church to the concluding section of the chapter.

THE CATHOLIC CHURCH

To write about the Irish Catholic Church is perhaps the most difficult task a contemporary Irish writer can undertake. In other countries, religion may be no more (or no less) than what a man applies to his palms when he wakes up sweating with thoughts of eternity at two in the morning; or what occupies his mind when he wonders if, during a nuclear confrontation, he should shoot his own children. Irishmen, being human, also have such agonising moments of gloomy introspection; but religion for them is a continuing daily experience, not an occasional twinge. Although the ratio between Catholic laity and priests is not unusually high—558 per priest, including regulars; 861 to diocesan clergy alone*—Catholicity pervades the atmosphere. Conversationally, the Church takes the place of the weather in other countries. Until the Watershed, the tallest buildings in

* Cf. 314 in Malta, 454 in Switzerland, 494 in Holland, 507 in Britain, 862 in Spain. (Figures cited in *Annuncio Pontifico*, 1960.)

Ireland were almost invariably steeples. In Dublin mention of the arch-bishop is so frequent in conversation that it would seem wherever two or three Irishmen are gathered together, Dr McQuaid is of the company.

It is particularly difficult to write about the Church at this time of change, for no sooner does one make ready to assail some reactionary statement or attitude than one is confronted by some laudable effort at a new approach. For example: Dr McQuaid has for long been charged with bigotry—witness the annual admonition in his pastoral letters that it is mortal sin for a Catholic to attend Trinity College without special permission. Yet while I was writing this book, he personally brought a copy of the Vatican's decree on ecumenism to Dr Simms, the Protestant archbishop of Dublin, and dropped the reference to Trinity from the 1965 pastoral—although it is still necessary for a Catholic to obtain his permission to study there.

Then there is the problem of 'background reading'. Almost all lay writing on the subject up to the Watershed era was neatly divisible into two categories: the nauseatingly obsequious home-product and the bitterly hostile diatribe from the foreign observer or the native 'angry' abroad. What has since been produced, though revealing, is mainly scattered journalism. Since the Church shapes and censors the thought-moulds of 95 per cent of the nation, the blame for this lies largely at its own door in that it has not encouraged a healthier and more creative climate of debate. It is a sad commentary that as yet there is not one comprehensive study of the Irish Church (though there are two in progress as I write: one by an American professor, and the other edited by a Maynooth professor of history).

Until recently the Irish Church almost completely failed to recognise the fact that the layman who raises his voice in criticism is almost invari-ably a concerned Catholic. The atheist, the communist, the libertarian are on the whole content to keep their mouths shut, trusting that eventually under the pressure of 'abuses' every church in the country will cave in.

A home-based Irish writer trying to explain why this is so is faced with a number of problems. An Irishman feels more deeply about the Church than about anything else, and what begins in a spirit of calm objectivity can all too easily dissolve into pietas and fall into the first category of writing: the cloyingly complacent. Visions of his kindly clerical relations, his teachers, his priestly friends, the schoolmate who received the call and more than half-inclined him to follow his companion to the African mission fields—all these pull him towards uncritical conformism. But then, if he has any spark of conscience, anger will prompt him to heated dissidence when he recalls the island priest who drove a woman into a mental home by standing at her bedside three hours after she had given birth to an illegitimate child, denouncing her sin and completing the hysteria excited by the unbroken ostracism of an entire community during her months of pregnancy. The Irish evaluation of an hotel—'You'll know it's good if the clergy eat there'—rasps through his mind as he thinks of the portly priests all over the country who daily give the judgement validity.

The slothful dispensers of 'petrol pump pastoralism' stir his wrath further as he thinks of the 'lost generation' of priests—those ordained in the stagnant years during and immediately after the war—who comfortably assumed that the faithful would always continue to 'fill up' on their monotonous and irrelevant sermons. Meanwhile the emigrants streamed by in their thousands, many to lose the faith in London and Birmingham, almost all emigrating without any advice or any useful training from the one organisation in the country with the resources to supply such a service.* (Even today, a third of all schoolchildren still leave school at the age of 14.)

It is at this stage that you have to make up your mind about your intentions. It is all too easy to take a great human organisation with a suprahuman mission which has existed for many generations without competition and, by depicting the symptoms rather than analysing the cause, produce a general picture. Entertaining and infuriating, the picture will be valid enough as representing aspects, but hardly so as representing the whole scene. Or one can overlook the blemishes and go in for the pious-complacent style of writing. I have decided to do neither, but to try to describe, in a necessarily limited, impressionistic way, the Irish Church as I see it: not as the hagiographer would have it appear, nor yet as the debunker would portray it, but as it *is*. Since this may well expose me to the charge of being a leftist subversive from the hagiographers and a time-serving rightist from the debunking hatchetmen, I owe it to my readers and myself to make my interest clear. When it became known that I was writing this book, I was, of course, approached simultaneously by the American CIA and the Russian KGB. We decided in the end that, since Ireland was such a small country, I should accept the agency for both rather than put either to the expense of maintaining a rival to me. With this point made clear, my readers and I can proceed.

Organisation

Ireland is divided into four ecclesiastical provinces: Armagh, Dublin, Cashel and Tuam. These provinces do not exactly follow the boundaries of the geographical provinces. Armagh, the largest, takes in the Six Counties and parts of Leinster. The incumbent of the see of Armagh, by

---

* A partial exception to this charge is the emigrant service provided since 1942 by the archdiocese of Dublin. Other dioceses are beginning to follow suit and, of course, individual priests have always been an exception to the general rule. Even so, such laudable 'social' activity is primarily spiritual; and man does not live by prayer alone.

long tradition the Primate of All Ireland, is usually appointed a cardinal. Since 1922 there has been a faintly political tinge to this since it emphasises, in Catholic minds, the unity of the country. The archdiocese of Dublin includes most of Leinster, and its metropolitan is the Primate of Ireland.* It is the richest and most important archdiocese. Cashel roughly corresponds to the province of Munster in the South-West. Tuam, stretching from the North-West into the centre of the country, is the smallest ecclesiastical province. These provinces are subdivided into the unusually high total (for so small a country) of twenty-six dioceses. Nine are in Armagh, four in Dublin, seven in Cashel and six in Tuam. The population of all Ireland, by religion, is as follows:

Province	Catholics	Protestants
Armagh	968,000	932,000†
Dublin	988,000	92,000
Cashel	886,000	26,000
Tuam	440,000	7,000

The bishops meet twice yearly at Maynooth, in October and June. These, in effect, are the Church's 'board meetings' at which its organisation is planned. The four archbishops constitute a standing committee which meets more regularly. In his own diocese a bishop has autonomous power in administrative matters. In the unlikely event of a bishop's becoming a public scandal, the archbishop of the province concerned would have the obligation to report the matter to Rome, but he could not directly interfere in the affairs of the bishop's diocese. The differences in rank are more of status than authority, though a man with a particularly strong personality—like the present archbishop of Dublin—may exert a commanding influence. The cardinal, like any other prelate of his rank, has special status in the matter of faculties: he may hear confession anywhere in the world without applying for a faculty from the local bishop, and he also enjoys the distinction due to any senior executive through his being the chairman of the regular meetings of the hierarchy at Maynooth.

The appointment of bishops is by way of consultative advice to the Holy Father. A list of suitable candidates is prepared for the metropolitan by the bishops of the province. From this list the metropolitan sends his own selection, usually from three to five names, to Rome or, if requested, to the Apostolic Nuncio in Ireland. The final choice lies with the Holy See,

* This parallels the situation in the Anglican Church wherein the archbishop of Canterbury is Primate of All England and he of York Primate of England. In the case of both countries, the distinction is a rich example of medieval face-saving. It is proper to mention here that Armagh is also the senior see in the Church of Ireland and that there are two Protestant metropolitan provinces: Armagh and Dublin.

† The great majority of these, of course, live in Northern Ireland.

which may follow metropolitan advice or go outside the proffered list as it thinks fit. The state makes its views known through its ambassador at the Vatican. Parish priests are appointed by the bishop of the diocese in which they were ordained, and may not be removed from their cures without grave cause—which in practice means almost never.

The dioceses and parishes are all in the hands of the secular clergy. Maynooth College is the premier seminary of the Irish Church, and two-thirds of the Irish hierarchy are Maynooth men. There are seven other major seminaries. Clonliffe provides priests for the Dublin diocese; All Hallows in Dublin is purely a seminary for missionaries, mainly to Australia, America and Britain. The other five leading seminaries—Thurles, Wexford, Kilkenny, Waterford and Carlow—supply priests to their home dioceses as well as for the mission field. There is also the Irish College in Rome. There are no seminaries in Northern Ireland. A number of other seminaries ordain priests for particular orders—Jesuits, Benedictines and so forth—and there are the missionary societies which ordain exclusively for the mission field.

Status in the Community

Strictly speaking, the Church has no special legal status other than the rather vague status accorded by Article 44 of the Constitution: 'The State recognises the special position of the Holy Catholic Apostolic and Roman Church as the guardian of the Faith professed by the great majority of the citizens'. The Church depends entirely on the generosity of the faithful for its income, receiving no state grants other than those for education. Church property, except for places of worship and parish National Schools, is liable to taxation. Maynooth College, exempt until a decision of the High Court in 1934, must also pay rates and taxes. The clergy are liable to all the penalties for any breach of the civil law in exactly the same way as the laity. However, these penalties are not as likely to be enforced on priests as on laity. The Hunt case, for example, caused some considerable stir. As reported in the *Irish Times* for December 10, 1945, Hunt was a convert from Protestantism who bigamously married a Catholic after his conversion. He was prosecuted in the criminal court and received a suspended sentence. The priest who married him had been aware that Hunt's first wife was still alive, but performed the ceremony because, according to canon law, the first marriage was invalid having been a civil marriage contracted in a London registry office. However, no action was taken against the priest. This is a rare, but not a unique, case.

Church income is derived in various ways. A main source are offerings for masses: generally 10s or £1. (The Franciscans in Dublin are much sought after since from them a mass can be had for 5s. The friars get the masses said by their missioners.) There are also the Easter and Christmas offerings to the parish priest. Church door collections furnish a little revenue, as do baptismal and nuptial offerings. Those for baptism are usually only a matter of a few shillings, but marriage offerings can be quite large, reflecting the status of the couple and their families. Some priests are known to take nothing from a poor couple, others to name their own figure: quite commonly £10 and at times even £120. And, of course, there are the exceptional offerings from very wealthy individuals, especially in rural districts where, through lack of a central salary scheme, parish priests have to depend on such offerings for a large part of their income. This is the main reason why many country people get married in Dublin, applying for their letters of freedom through a Dublin curate and paying quite a small offering to the officiating town priest. Convents draw a considerable sum from the dowries of postulants. (There are approximately 5,000 nuns in Ireland.)

There are also occasional weird customs like that sometimes observed at funerals where the priest sits at a table in the church beside the coffin and the mourners demonstrate the depths of their feelings for the deceased by the extent of their donations to the priest—which are later read out from the altar. This custom survives mainly in the North and in the backward parts of the West.

The banks advance money at 5½ per cent for church building (i.e., at a cheaper rate than to the government or laity) solely on the moral force of a bishop's guarantee: which is reasonable since the hierarchy in Ireland is probably the most powerful in the world. Advances of hundreds of thousands of pounds are not uncommon. Occasionally parish priests become very wealthy through legacies or gifts. Wills of £30,000 and £60,000 have been proven in the name of priests in my own experience. (Much of such sums, of course, was left to charity.)

A priest's income is assessed at a fixed sum, and as a rule he is not pressed to amplify his return. But a priest's estate is subjected to a searching examination before his will is admitted to probate. A friend of mine, a parish priest of more than ordinary business acumen, was hauled before the revenue commissioners to explain the lapse of memory which had prevented certain profitable transactions from appearing in his return of income. The problem was settled with amity, the commissioner saying resignedly: 'We'll get it in death duties, anyhow.' To which my friend replied spiritedly: 'I don't give a particular damn what you get—when I'm gone!'

But, though even the most junior chaplain can seemingly soon afford a car, and most priests are manifestly 'comfortable', this is more the effect of prudent bachelorhood than of battening on the poor. What gives rise to exaggerated estimates of clerical wealth is the Irish Church's unnecessarily secretive attitude to all matters financial. It is easy to say, 'Father X is always looking for money', when Father X does not explain that the money is not for himself but for such-and-such charitable object.

The constitutional definition of the Church's status has been given. What does its status amount to in the life of the nation? Three comments made to me by people belonging to what one can call the 'intelligentsia' indicate something of the ambivalent attitudes about the Church among educated Irishmen.

> I think the old farmer who never bothers himself with questions about religion and just does what he is told has the right attitude. All this new talk is causing a lot of trouble.

> The Church will hold its present position in Ireland for ten years at the most unless it changes radically. Its future depends on the degree to which it changes to meet the new conditions.

> Jasus! Your man would have been excommunicated during the 'thirties!

The last speaker was an old Republican who had just listened to a paper delivered on 'The Responsibility of Wealth' to a social study congress held under the auspices of the archbishop of Dublin. The first comment came from an Irish journalist who had covered the opening sessions of the Vatican Council. The second was that of a professor at Maynooth. They should be kept in mind as we appraise the role of the Church in modern Ireland.

Practically all important public functions—opening of the Dail, of law terms, even of factories—are preceded by Mass. At official functions, the cardinal takes precedence over the prime minister, and the archbishops over his deputy. (Lest this should seem to some a monstrous token of 'priest-ridden' Ireland, be it remembered that the archbishop of Canterbury gives the pass to no one save the sovereign, the royal consort and the sons of an English monarch.) The great majority of Irish children are educated in schools run by the Church. Its places of worship are filled on Sundays. A priest is the most honoured visitor one can imagine to the home. His statement of income for tax purposes is accepted, as we have seen, without question by the authorities. In the Tilson case of 1951, the Supreme Court ruled that a promise made before marriage by a non-

Catholic spouse to have children of the union brought up as Catholics is legally binding.

Ireland is today the world's last 'non-post-Christian' society. This means that practically everyone in the country is either a Catholic or a Protestant. It means that, almost uniquely, the Church has not 'lost' the working class. It means that the last great political issue—Partition—is fundamentally a religious issue. It means that the churches of the majority faith are crowded, and that the minority faith makes great efforts to keep its places of worship still functioning. It means that the great centres of pilgrimage attract thousands of faithful every year: Croagh Patrick, a mountain in Mayo 3,000 feet high, climbed barefoot by old and young, women and children; Lough Derg, to whose holy isle pilgrims come from all over the country, and indeed from different parts of the Catholic world, to spend a night and a day, sleepless, fasting, bare-footed. It means that in the cities the great occasions of multiple sacrament, like Confirmation and First Communion, are attended by hundreds, and often thousands, of children. Above all, it means that there is a special reverence for and trust in the person of the priest. A joy inconceivable to non-Catholics possesses an Irish family when a son of the house enters holy orders.

Although some authorities say that the number of vocations is falling, the extent of the fall is not, at first sight, apparent. I tried to check the assumption current about fewer vocations by sending a questionnaire to secondary schools, asking them to compare the number of vocations in the final-year classes in 1965 with those in 1955. The figures returned represented a sample (twenty-five schools) too small for a representative assessment, but they revealed a marked characteristic: the number of vocations would, if anything, appear to have slightly increased; but the increase was as nothing in comparison with the general increase in second-ary school enrolments. I would hazard the opinion that more pupils seem to enter the religious orders which teach them or opt for a missionary order than enlist for diocesan work in Ireland.

The social background of those who become priests is as follows: small farming or rural labouring families, 30 per cent; working class families, 20 per cent; middle class families, 30 per cent; professional families, 20 per cent. Apart from priests loaned or on temporary duty, there are at the time of writing (autumn 1965) 10,885 Irish-born priests, nuns and lay workers in the mission fields of the world, together with a total of roughly 11,000 priests and nuns at their vocation in Ireland itself. In 1965, over 1,000 lay missionaries left Ireland for terms of duty, ranging from two weeks to three years, in Africa and in that other 'underdeveloped area', Britain. They went under the auspices of the Legion of Mary: a voluntary organisation founded in 1934 by Frank Duff.* It is now established in some 2,000 dioceses throughout the world, and is said to be increasing at the rate of fifty branches (called praesidia) every week.

Education

The Church controls education, and it is in this sphere that its most difficult phase of adaptation will lie. Almost all Irish education is denominational. The parish priest or parson is the primary school manager. He appoints the teachers and it is his responsibility to commission any new buildings, for which the Department of Education pays two-thirds of the cost. The state also pays the teachers' salaries. The National School system, established in 1831, was fought for and moulded by the Church until it evolved into its present shape. A teacher may not be appointed or dismissed without the local bishop's sanction. Apart from those run by Protestants and a few lay schools, most secondary schools are controlled by religious orders. The technical schools are exclusively state-controlled, though priests sometimes teach in them. They are not as well regarded as they deserve to be because of a sort of snobbish feeling against them.

Higher education in Ireland began with the founding in 1592 of Dublin University, commonly called Trinity. Sir Robert Peel in 1845 founded the three Queen's Colleges of Belfast, Cork and Galway. These were condemned as 'godless colleges' by Pius IX and the hierarchy. Cardinal Newman attempted to counterbalance them in 1854 by a Catholic University, but this was killed by a combination of the hierarchy's opposition and the British government's refusal to recognise its degrees. To cut the Gordian knot, Gladstone in 1881 set up the Royal University of Ireland to organise examinations for the students of the three Queen's Colleges and to confer degrees. In the following year, the Jesuits founded University College, Dublin. This lasted until 1908 when the National University was set up embracing the four colleges and 'recognising' Maynooth College's courses in Arts, Science and Philosophy. (Trinity had no familiarity with all these goings on!)

On the whole the primary system has worked well. (Ireland has a 1·6 per cent illiteracy rate.) Its main deficiency is that an old parish priest or parson may be unable or even unwilling to undertake the upkeep of the school. Although in recent years many bright new schools have become a most welcome addition to the Irish landscape, some National Schools are in a disgraceful condition. This has resulted in a number of school strikes

* Duff left the civil service to found the Legion. The Chinese Communists killed 10,000 of its Chinese members and imprisoned 20,000. In Ireland the movement devotes itself mainly to good works of all kinds. As a spokesman of the Legion said to me: 'Our efforts are purely spiritual—even if it only means dish-washing!'

in which parents refuse to allow their children to attend the school. The real problem arises in secondary education. In many parts of Ireland there are not enough secondary schools to equip the youth of the nation for modern conditions.

Both Church and State must answer for much of the blame for the situation which has arisen. The Church took over a task which it could not fully carry out, despite all the self-sacrificing devotion to duty of people like the typical Christian Brother. (Notwithstanding his sometimes over-zealous use of the leather strap on the palms of his pupils, he provides education for generations of Irish schoolchildren at a return to himself of less than the price of twenty cigarettes a week.) The State failed to honour its responsibilities in that it did not ensure all citizens equal, or even nearly equal, educational opportunities. Now both negligent parties are suddenly faced with the urgency of dealing with a problem made much more acute by the educational and technological demands of the movement to modernise Ireland. How the problem is resolved depends on the good sense and the liberal vision of both. Neither will find it easy.

There were 569 secondary schools in operation in 1964, as compared with 494 in 1959. Of these, forty-three were under Protestant management and sixty under Catholic lay management. The rest were run by religious (priests and nuns). The proportion of clerical to lay teachers has not altered appreciably from that obtaining in 1961, when of the 5,724 second-ary school teachers, 3,141 were priests, nuns or Christian Brothers. The Brothers, a dedicated body founded in 1802 by Edmund Ignatius Rice, concentrate on the teaching of Irish, and have tended to impose a strongly nationalistic, almost propagandist, imprint on their teaching of history. They account for 40 per cent of all the boys in Irish secondary schools.

Irish education has been run on the cheap. In 1963, 80 per cent of all attenders at voluntary schools in the Republic were paying an average of only £15 a year for tuition in day schools. Yet in that year—the only one for which comparable figures are available—both these and almost every other school in the country were not just full but overcrowded, with 84,916 pupils. In 1964, there were approximately 92,000: a notable increase over the 1948 figure of 48,559. Even more daunting are the figures for primary education in the National Schools, where 4,864 schools had enrolled 502,059 pupils. The country's 298 permanent Vocational Schools had 29,689 full-time pupils; when evening-class and part-time students are added, the Vocational Schools' total came to 101,424.

It is estimated that by 1976 there will be 160,000 students enrolled in secondary schools. Enormous though this expansion is, and allowing for the fact that many primary schoolchildren will not be of the type to benefit from secondary education, it is clear that the *opportunity* for such education is not going to be available for all, still less university education. In 1964 there were 8,155 full-time students in the National University and 2,964 at Trinity, a good many of the latter being students from abroad. (And here it is pertinent to speculate how long the Republic, wherein people are at last coming to realise that a university education should be something more than a status symbol, can afford to go on maintaining two separate universities in one city.)

It is argued forcibly that Britain is falling behind countries like Russia and America in education, particularly in technical education. Northern Ireland bemoans the fact of its not keeping pace with Britain. Yet in 1963 Northern Ireland, with less than half the population of the Republic, had over 10,000 more pupils in actual numbers attending secondary schools than had the South. I trust that the criticisms I have made of my country hitherto reveal enough objectivity to permit me the seemingly boastful statement that it is only native Irish genius which has prevented the educational situation in Ireland from turning her into a nation of cattle-drovers. But Ireland is now in the 'EEC era' wherein skilled men and women are at an urgent premium, and native genius of itself is no longer sufficient.

Until 1964 there were no state grants for secondary school buildings. State assistance was limited to capitation grants which, in 1965, were £14 per pupil at intermediate level up to a total of 100, and beyond this number £13 per pupil. Above the intermediate level the grant is £19 per pupil, whether attending day or boarding school and irrespective of the number of pupils involved. The state salary grants to registered unmarried secondary teachers, male and female—the unmarried category is the only one which need concern us here—are £470 rising to £1,070 over a period of sixteen years. An honours degree carries a bonus of £110 per annum.* The grants towards buildings introduced in 1964 apply, in practice, to those schools which a Department of Education survey concludes will have a minimum of 150 pupils within a reasonable period of time. In such cases, the Department will guarantee the loan which the builder of the school must first raise on his or her own initiative. The Department will then take responsibility for payment of 60 per cent of the total annual interest and capital repayments, but a deduction of from 5 to 10 per cent, approximately, from the capitation grants will be made towards this loan-assistance. Furthermore, the new school must guarantee by means of trustees that the building will be used as a school for at least 100 years. For Catholic voluntary schools in England, the period is from fifteen to twenty years.

---

* But only approximately 15 to 20 per cent of Irish secondary school teachers have honours degrees in the subjects in which they teach. The religious orders tend to appoint young deacons to teach classes before they are ordained. These young monks' goodness is unquestionable, but they are enrolled in their orders as priests—not as teachers.

A paramount factor in all these recent developments is the Church's concept of Catholic education. In his pastoral letter of 1961, Archbishop McQuaid quoted canon law on this subject:

> Catholic pupils are not to frequent non-Catholic schools or neutral schools or schools that are open also to non-Catholics. Only the Ordinary of the place where the school is situated is competent to determine, according to the instructions of the Apostolic See, in what circumstances it may be tolerated for Catholics to attend such schools and what safeguards are to be prescribed against the danger of perversion.

Taking the last consideration first: there is no means of verifying the widespread belief that, hitherto, if the bishop did not approve of a school's being set up in his diocese, then the Department of Education withheld state recognition and state assistance. It may simply be that this belief stems from the fact that the Department is not required to give any explanation for such refusals. But since a school must be in being for about a year, as a rule, before it is even considered for these grants, the would-be headmaster must obviously either be confident that objections will not result in the Department's withholding recognition, or else be a person of substantial independent means. As it is, the most tangible evidence of episcopal intervention one comes across is when a thriving lay school is suddenly confronted by competition by having a large school run by nuns or priests set down beside it. (It is very easy to prove this charge.) Such occurrences, however, could be set down to human competitiveness of the kind which we do not find abnormal in the case of supermarkets. The really serious defects of the system are fourfold.

1. The capitation system makes it desirable, from a business point of view, to site schools in or near centres of population. The result is that, while Dublin is well enough catered for, some thinly populated areas are short of schools. A Donegal child, for example, has approximately one third of the chances of a secondary school education enjoyed by a child born in Cork, Kerry or Clare.

2. The reason for this is not wholly ascribable to the capitation system. Some bishops in the past have refused to allow religious orders into their dioceses. There are none at all in the dioceses of Derry and Killala, and very few in the provinces of Armagh and Tuam—though here and there will be found schools of the Christian Brothers. Even the Brothers are not free to spread their wings as they might wish. They are ultimately responsible, not to the Irish hierarchy, but to their superior general in Rome, and are naturally very jealous of their autonomy. Bishops are no less so in regard to their authority. The result sometimes is that existing

schools of the Brothers are not permitted to be extended, or new ones are refused. In one diocese in the West, this circumstance meant that, since the bishop had no objection to nuns, three times more girls than boys in a certain county were receiving secondary education: a situation which continued until the mid-'fifties when a change of policy took place.

3. The most serious defect is that fundamentally the Irish educational system is grounded on privilege. This is the case, notwithstanding all the very many instances in which fees are waived for orphan children and for other deserving cases, particularly by the Christian Brothers: instances so frequent and typical of the kindly Irish temperament as to make cold statistical analysis of them difficult.

In 1960–61, the average expenditure on scholarships per person in the twelve to eighteen age group was £16 6s in Northern Ireland. It was 11s 3d in the Republic, where 2,746 scholarships from primary to secondary schools were provided for 76,843 pupils. Certainly, by 1964 the number of such scholarships had shown a commendable increase to 5,231, but in the same period the number of secondary school enrolments had grown by some 11,000. These scholarship figures, in practice, mean that, though the poor but brilliant pupil has a good chance of a free education, the poor but averagely talented child has not. Hence the state of his parents' pocket dictates that he will probably go to the Christian Brothers, who in 1965 increased their fees for the generality of schools run by them (they also operate more expensive colleges) to £20 a year for new secondary school pupils; existing pupils continued at the old rate of £12. The richer child goes to a college of the Jesuits, the Benedictines, the Franciscans, the Holy Ghost Fathers, or to some other of the more fashionable schools where he may or may not get a better education but where he will undoubtedly make better contacts.

Caste still plays an unfortunately large part in Irish education. A not uncommon situation exists in a Tipperary town where there are three convent schools, each with about 100 pupils. The fees of the most fashionable and therefore most expensive school are less than £40, and between the fees charged by the three of them the difference is about £10. But *vive la différence*! A pound or two more or less makes all the difference in 'status'. An amalgamation of all three would conserve resources and enable better equipment and courses to be provided. But something more powerful than educational principles is involved here: human nature, aided and abetted by the particularist tendencies of Irish religious education. In such circumstances as those obtaining in Tipperary, all this means that, allowing for normal wastage, each school is competing to provide final-year studies for classes of about half-a-dozen girls. The question of studying science or physics obviously does not arise—which brings us to the final defect.

4. In place of the specialisation in the last two years in English secondary schools, the Irish School Leaving Certificate calls for a minimum of five subjects, one of which—Irish—is obligatory. Most pupils take more than five and some take as many as ten subjects. The teaching time in the average secondary school is some twenty-nine hours a week. Latin and Irish normally account for nine of these, and religious instruction also has to be provided. The teaching of 'modern' subjects naturally suffers in consequence. Readers may draw their own conclusions from the fact that, in a predominantly agricultural country, biology is not, at the time of writing, a subject on the approved secondary school curriculum. One need say no more about the provision made for mathematics—so essential to technological advancement and all the sciences—than to indicate that in 1963, out of a total of 680 mathematics teachers, only thirty-three were honours graduates. However, big improvements were foreshadowed by the introduction in 1965 of new courses in mathematics both for schools and universities.

In the late summer of 1965, a high-powered committee, working under the auspices of OECD, finished a survey of the Irish educational situation. At the time of writing, its report was awaited. Clearly many of the problems I have indicated will have fallen within the committee's purview, and it is a safe assumption that it will have remedies to suggest. Another reasonable assumption is that the present minister of Education will act on them. At the same time, a hierarchy composed of twenty-seven individuals will not be unanimous in its approval of the recommendations and the minister's actions—and not necessarily because of 'Church politics'. Already there have been clashes between Bishop Browne of Galway and the minister for Education. There is, certainly, the problem of what changes in education may mean to vocations. A survey of 250 schools and colleges conducted in 1961 by Fr Jeremiah Newman of Maynooth (see Appendix IV) showed that out of 24,339 pupils surveyed between 1956 and 1960, 3,189 went on to the priesthood. But these are the sort of adjustment problems which must be overcome if Ireland is to be shoehorned into the twentieth century.

Before Dr Michael Hillery was appointed minister for Education in 1961, the Department's job was conceived of as little more than a plumber's. But in an important interview in *Hibernia* (February 1964), Hillery described his, very different, concept.

> I have to take the initiative all the time. More and more the state is coming out as the only body that is geared to take the initiative, and the Minister now has to be somebody planning and pointing the way,

instead of just going round with an oilcan keeping the machinery in order.

Hillery is a doctor from Clare with a reputation for intellectual toughness—and physical brightness also: he plays golf off a four handicap and is a judo expert. His transfer in 1965 to Industry and Commerce aroused from a senior civil servant the comment: 'It's typical of this country that we should think that a man like that is more valuable in Industry and Commerce than in Education'.

His method of taking the initiative was to set up comprehensive schools (which are expected to come into operation in 1966), each managed by a committee composed of a representative of the bishop, of the local educational authority and of the minister. The committee is intended to select the teachers. Hillery's original intention was to break through the expected wall of clerical disfavour by siting the comprehensive schools in areas where there were no existing schools. In the *Hibernia* interview, he said: 'I have to realise that, while voluntary bodies as we call them, have done an excellent job for the country and will continue to do so, there are areas where they have not supplied the service, and the state will have to take the responsibility of supplying this educational opportunity for everybody'.

When Hillery left the Department, there were widespread suggestions that this was the end of the New Departure. But when I spoke with his successor, George Colley, in July 1965, I found that Hillery's policy was unquestionably government policy also. Another of the 'new men', Colley is equally dedicated to change. He comes of a prominent Republican family and has an internationalist viewpoint, strengthened by a term with the Council of Europe. This he combines with a keen devotion to the national culture: in the Colley household of parents and seven children, Irish is the language of ordinary conversation. He talks of his job with an attractive, infectious logic.

> We must improve our system if we are going to progress. I'm talking to priests and educationalists every day telling them what our plans are and what the need is. But in the last analysis, it's my job. I have the power to enforce the rules. The fact that they haven't been enforced doesn't mean that they won't be in the future.

He discussed with me the teaching of history, and said frankly that he was not satisfied with the way history was taught in most Irish schools, particularly the history of the nineteenth century. 'The whole country was shaped then. Everything we have came from Parnell, the Fenians and the Land League.' This is certainly an area in which reform is overdue, and I would have considered the interview well spent just to hear him say that.

The inflammatory teaching of Irish history has brought young men into the IRA and to their deaths. But it is going to be difficult to give the *full* story of this period in Church-run schools and still maintain the benevolent, patriots-encouraging image of the Church which is current in such schools. After all, the much-denounced Land League's first blow for peasant-rights was to make a parish priest reduce his rents!

Ethos of Irish Catholicism

It is surely one of the great paradoxes of modern religion that the Irish Church, with one of the greatest missionary traditions in Christendom, should have a particularly inward-looking Catholicism. Two young priests leave the same seminary on the same day. One goes to the missions; the other stays in Ireland. Both have the same quotients of idealism and self-sacrifice. The missionary comes back five years later with these qualities enhanced. The man who stays at home is better than average if he has not lost some of them, and in the process acquired something of smugness and a remoteness from the human problems of the poor, and even of the rich.

Some experts ascribe the inward-looking character to traces of Jansenism which made their appearance after the foundation of Maynooth and the employment there of French professors driven from their country by revolution. Jansenism—the theological residuum of a small and unrepresentative part of the writings of Jansenius, bishop of Yypres in the early seventeenth century—manifests itself in a censorious, holier-than-thou attitude. This is all too prone to find a Tartuffe-like justification for its actions by virtue of its practitioners' claim to have a special devotion for, and insight into, the mind of God. Certainly, the landscape of the Irish Church is littered with evidences of this spirit. But Maynooth has only been opened since 1795: a short span in the existence of an organisation catering for eternity. The reasons may go back even further.

The Romans never came to Ireland. Christianity, therefore, came to the country later and to a different soil than elsewhere in Europe. Irish Christianity was practically the only Christianity in Northern Europe during the dark ages. It is in these times that the continuing tradition of Irish missionary activity began. The ethos of Irish religion was from the start severe: witness the descriptions of its early monastic settlements and its purgatorial tradition. Up to, and indeed after, the Reformation, it was the one unifying force in a country ravaged by invasions and quarrelling chieftains: self-centred petty rulers who, if they had had enough common sense and patriotism to compose their squabbles, would not have given the English the chance for seven, let alone seven hundred, years of dominance.

The penal laws gave the Church an extra dimension of martyrdom. But underlying its dogged survival against oppression was a no less dogged and continuing particularism: a strong streak of conceit arising from its severance from the mainstream of European Catholicism and from its proud remembrance of the time when it was the only light in the West amid the encircling gloom of pagan barbarism. Pope Adrian, like his predecessors in Saint Peter's Chair during the long hagglings over Celtic versus Roman usages and rites, saw the Irish Church's lustre as a dim, uncertain light. The hope of reformation in that Church prompted his approval of Henry II's Irish expedition in 1171, the beginning of the 'seven hundred years of oppression'. It could perhaps be argued that Innocent XI may have had something similar in mind—if his thoughts were free for a moment from the nightmare notion of Louis XIV as master of all Europe— when he gave his endorsement to William of Orange's expedition to wrest control of the three kingdoms from the Catholic king, James II. The shameful breach of the Treaty of Limerick by the English made the Supreme Pontiff an aider and abettor of the near-destruction of Catholicism in Ireland. Emotionally, devotion to the Holy See continued strong; but during the eighteenth century, in the day-to-day life of the beleaguered Irish Catholics, Rome was remote, unhelpful.

The Church was in a highly disorganised condition at the time of the foundation of Maynooth and the Act of Union. Its rise to political influence was achieved, not by the hierarchy, but by a lay politician. It is with Daniel O'Connell's great and successful campaign for equal civil rights for Catholic subjects of the Crown that the new era dawned for the Church. Even so, its geographical position continued to have theological, or at least disciplinary, implications. When Cardinal Cullen returned from Rome in 1849, part of his ultramontane zeal undoubtedly arose from his confusion of Fenianism with Mazzini-type republicanism, but part also owed itself to widespread irregularity within the Irish Church. Archbishop MacHale's province, for example, was one in which Roman discipline cast but a faint shadow. Cullen differed sharply from MacHale and nationalist-minded members of the hierarchy, like Nulty of Meath, in placing disestablishment of the Church of Ireland and the Catholic control of education ahead of finding a solution to the land problem. This led to the curious situation in which, by leading a campaign for disestablishment and the separation of Church and State, Cullen—the arch-ultramontane—was in fact postulating the establishment of a 'Free Church in a Free State': a theory which had been specifically condemned by Pius XI in the Syllabus of Errors of 1864. To Rome at that time such a separation meant the secularisation of Church property.

Thus the 'tone' of the Irish Church continued to differ from that of

Roman, continental Catholicism. Though an ultramontane disciplinary character has been a strong feature of Irish Catholicism since Cullen's day, the hierarchy, representative of the educated, guiding (almost governing) class of the country, has at times shown what seems something very like—dare one say it?—a Gallican spirit. The arrival of the first Papal Nuncio, Mgr Robinson in 1929, was praised with faint damns. Similarly, the Irish hierarchy's meagre contribution to the Second Vatican Council can be explained in terms of its feeling that most of the problems discussed were no concern of Ireland's.

This passivity regarding what agitates mankind, however, is not always extended to home affairs, at least not up to the time of the rumpus over the Mother and Child scheme in 1951. In this respect the Irish hierarchy reminds one of the character in Anouilh's *Waltz of the Toreadors*, of whom his wife said: 'The general is a man of peace, except of course in the conduct of home affairs'. Its tendency to appear a conservative body, making its presence felt by occasional Jehovah-like pronouncements against modern thinking and attitudes, is also largely influenced by the fact that the average Irish bishop has grown out of touch with 'home affairs'— except in the higher realms of Church policy. Approximately half of the present hierarchy had no pastoral experience before being presented to their sees. Life in suburbia is different from that seen through the windows of a comfortable study in Maynooth.

Yet, remarkably, it is in Maynooth and places like it that the battle for the Catholic mind of Ireland is being fought out. Any liberal-tempered, modern-minded layman who pushes his way through the traditions clustering round the door will find in Maynooth as lively and critical a collection of clerics as exist anywhere in these islands. Such men are waiting until the old guard passes on. They do not say in public the things they say in private, their reason being that they do not want to cause schism or even hurt the feelings of the older men. An understandable reserve, perhaps; but the trouble is that there will not necessarily come a day wherein their words will be acceptable unless the men who say brave things in private also make use of press and television to give the new answers. If the reforming spirits in the Irish Church are not careful, the story of 'le Catholicisme du type irlandais' may become the old, old story of too little too late.

Diocesan clergy are generally from comfortable middle-class families. The poorer aspirants to the priesthood usually enter the missionary orders. Hence, in the upbringing and outlook of large numbers of parochial clergy there is at the outset a cleavage between themselves and the bulk of those to whom they minister.

Other factors are also at work in creating an 'attitudes-gap' between the temper of the Church and the temper of modern Ireland. The flight from the land has intensified the contrast between rich and poor counties. For many a dedicated, socially conscious priest, the local resources for creative action are pitifully inadequate. Moreover, the rosary-saying parish of old is gone or going. In its place there is the 40,000-strong Dublin grouping of television watchers. Many rural parish clerics have allowed the change to overwhelm them. The evils of dancing; the duty of young people to contribute to the upkeep of their pastors; sinful pictures and magazines; the priceless heritage of the faith—these were (and often still are) the burden of the pastoral guidance ringing through the unheated yellow-walled churches where the men sat on one side of the aisle and the women on the other.

Yet the Irish priesthood has not lacked men of a different stamp. To illustrate what might have been done by more of his brethren, there is the example of Fr James McDyer—the 'communist priest'—curate of Glen-columcille, one of the most northerly and beautiful valleys in County Donegal, and himself the son of a small farmer.

Fr McDyer is in his early fifties: a brown-eyed six-footer with crew-cut greying hair and a crisp approach. After ordination he spent ten years in England where he was appalled at the number of emigrants and their frequent loss of faith. On his return to Ireland he was sent immediately to Tory Island because he knew Irish. There he spent four and a half years: a sharp change from his former cure in Brighton. He had little to do and indeed could do little on the bleak, emptying island, but he saw at first hand why Irish rural Catholicism, based on automatic and unthinking acceptance of things as they were, did not long survive the impact of England's great cities. As well as the religious concern this aroused in him, it also struck him as unpatriotic that so many Irish people should leave their homes and everyone accept this as a matter of course. The country was emptying west of a line drawn from Lough Swilly in the North to Bantry Bay in the South, an area comprising all Connacht and parts of Ulster and Munster—and what was anyone doing about it?

He started from the assumption that improved social life would keep potential emigrants at home. In this he was following in the footsteps of Fr Hayes of Bansha, County Tipperary, who had started Muintir na Tire (see page 154 above) in 1937 with the object of making country life more attractive. He began by building a local hall with the help of thirty volunteers. It gave a focal point for local life, but emigration still continued. He then turned to other projects, founding a knitwear factory and starting an agricultural show. His most far-reaching venture was to get 112 small farmers whose holdings—ranging from ten to thirty-five acres—

were contiguous, to amalgamate them and form a co-operative to grow vegetables. The produce is grown and marketed under the auspices of the Irish Sugar Company under the general management of General Costello, a champion of the small farmer for all his association with a big state company.

Fr McDyer is attempting to prove on a small scale what he believes could be done all over the country. 'I want to cut out this nonsense of slaving from dawn to dusk in backward discomfort. A farmer need only work eight hours a day [he works sixteen to eighteen hours himself]. Within the limits of his earning power he should have the best of everything—best design, best food, best clothing and so on.' His knitting factory, the kind of project dear to 'the tall man', was got going through interceding with de Valera. It has succeeded in keeping sixty girls in Glencolumcille who would otherwise have emigrated. 'That's something', he says; 'but there's an entire generation of men aged between thirty-five and sixty who have no women and no hope of mates'. He is frankly autocratic. His ambition is for a new type of Sinn Fein approach to the country's problems.

> I don't know about democracy. It's a Protestant idea. Lots of deputies debating and talking. I just try to serve God. No one can serve him enough. My method is to propound a list of projects with the emphasis on the 'pound'. I give every man on my parish council a job. Now, I say, I'll not expect success at the end of the month, but I will expect *action*. . . . I've nothing against modern dancing, but the dance halls could be in Miami or Montmartre. I'd like to see our native culture reviving. Collins, Griffith, Brugha and Lynch were great men and their example should be followed.

Fr McDyer's crusade has not yet either been widely emulated by his colleagues or generally welcomed by economists. Where fellow-priests have followed his lead, a tricky problem has arisen in many cases. McDyer's approach is scientific. Vegetables are grown because the valley's soil is suitable; knitting is encouraged because it is a traditional skill in the area. But other priests, moved by the publicity attending his efforts, have attempted vegetable-growing and knitting in their parishes also, often in circumstances so utterly unsuitable that the Department of Agriculture, alarmed at the prospects, clamped down, I understand, on grants and aid to projects similar to McDyer's. On top of this, the subsidiary of the Sugar Company—Erin Foods—which markets vegetable produce, showed enormous losses in 1965.

The Second Programme provides for a decline of 17 per cent in the total rural population and an increase of 43 per cent in the numbers of cattle. Fr McDyer is trying to reverse this trend. 'But', said one of the senior government planners to me, 'suppose he succeeds and we get a whole lot of Glencolumcilles all round the country? What's going to happen to planned development then?' This is easier said in Dublin than in Glencolumcille. If he can succeed and inspire others to a 'scientific' approach, he will have not only an economic but a psychological triumph to his credit.

A 'Save the West' committee launched in 1963 at Charlestown, County Mayo, has the support of a number of bishops in furthering aims akin to Fr McDyer's. But in other parts of the country the attitude of the people could be summed up by the farming expert who told me: 'The West's been declining for a long time. But now, when their Lordships see that their congregations and their dues are falling, and the government tells them they are going to fall still more, they start getting worried.'

The innuendo about the financial factor is significant of an undertow of criticism running beneath the great broad stream of Catholic devotion. It illustrates how, in such an overwhelmingly Catholic country, a man of my informant's position should be so misinformed about the hierarchy's motives through its almost complete lack of sensible concern for 'public relations'. But one must take into account the apathy of the people—what Fr McDyer calls 'invertebracy': lack of confidence in themselves and prevalence of the dole-mentality. He himself concedes: 'I wouldn't have got my particular slant if I hadn't been to England. It doesn't grow in Ireland.'

Why doesn't it grow? For the answer one must, as for practically everything else in Ireland, go back to Saint Patrick. Whether Ireland's patron saint was one man or two or even more has still not been resolved by the learned, but what is not in doubt is that his multiple arrival in the fifth century gave Christianity deep roots in Ireland. There is no word for 'hello' in Irish; the greeting is 'Dia duit' (God be with you), and the reply is 'Dia's Muire duit' (God and Mary be with you). The Irish tendency to make a woman the figure of Ireland not only results in the lovely poetic names for the country—*Eire, Banba, Fodhla, Cathleen ni Houlihan* and *Roisin Dubh*, Dark Rosaleen—but also probably explains the prevalence of the devotion to Mary in Irish Catholicism.

What Saint Patrick, a slave from Britain, established was strengthened by the lords from Britain. The penal laws of the Protestant Ascendancy took the priest into the deep embrace of the national soul. Spiritually, nationalistically, politically and educationally, Catholics were second-class citizens in their own land. They could not vote for or sit in the Irish parliament, nor join the army or navy or administrative service. Owning fire-arms was forbidden them; a horse, no matter how valuable, if intended

for sale had to be offered to a Protestant for £5. The laws also aimed at
degrading the people. A woman who took service without informing her
employer that she was pregnant was liable to be whipped through the
streets (though—Christian leniency!—not until two months after her
confinement). Priests were officially restricted in numbers and in their
movements. The heads of unauthorised priests and bishops fetched good
prices to anyone delivering them to the authorities. The hunted, fugitive
priest became a mystical symbol of defiance and comfort as he raised the
Host above a mass-rock in the open air.

The Church was the Nation, the Nation the Church. But gradually
during the course of the nineteenth century the utter identity of the two
was disturbed. The opening of Maynooth College in 1795, inspired by the
Younger Pitt's desire to make Irish Catholics less susceptible to godless
French republicanism, was a first step toward separating Nationalism and
Catholicism. Under the Union, which most of the hierarchy supported on
grounds of ecclesiastical policy (the might of England which had oppressed
the Church could now be cajoled into removing that oppression), the
Church as an organisation came out of the shadows. And the policy seemed
justified. O'Connell's tremendous energy and courage won Catholic
Emancipation in 1829. An increased endowment for Maynooth in 1846
made clergy and hierarchy easy in their mind vis-à-vis England.

It also made them hostile to the disruptive activities of the Young
Irelanders and the Fenians. Individual priests sided with the peasantry in
the struggle against starvation. Practically the entire land reform movement
stemmed from the formation of a Tenants Protection Society in 1849 by
two priests: Fathers Thomas O'Shea and Matthew Keeffe of County
Kilkenny, out of whose activities developed in 1852 the Tenant Right
League. One of its leaders, Father T. W. Croke, later became archbishop
of Cashel and patron of the Gaelic Athletic Association. But the Church as
a body felt that it stood to lose rather than gain from anything which might
lead to an armed rebellion. The underlying notion of an independent
Ireland aroused in particular the opposition of the ultramontane archbishop
of Dublin, Cardinal Paul Cullen, who returned to Ireland in 1849 after
twenty-nine years in Rome. As we have seen, to him nationalism was
synonymous with Italian radicalism and he regarded Gavan Duffy, the
founder of the Young Ireland movement, as an 'Irish Mazzini'. (Dis-
heartened, Duffy left Ireland for Australia in 1855.)

The chief practitioner of the Land League's most successful weapon—
boycotting—was a priest, Father John O'Malley. Nevertheless, Archbishop MacCabe of Dublin (gamely opposed by Archbishop Croke of
Cashel) became a cardinal on the strength of his fulminations against the
League. The hierarchy, after some shilly-shallying while it awaited the

reactions of the English Nonconformists (then key supporters of Glad-stone's Irish policy), took sides against Parnell when the scandal of the O'Shea divorce case broke and he refused to give up the leadership of the Irish Party. Church leaders as a whole by this time endorsed Home Rule, but saw no prospect of gaining it if Parnell carried its banner after the alienation of the English Nonconformists. Though remaining, most of them, devout Catholics, the radical nationalists after the 'betrayal' of Parnell viewed the Church's leaders with suspicion, amounting at times to contemptuous hostility.

In Parnell's time, the clergy formed the political machine in the greater part of the country, running meetings, attending to organisational details and so on. The hierarchy's first major political intervention on the side of nationalism after the O'Shea period was its declaration against con-scription in 1918. But its denunciations against militant republicans in 1922, 1931 and 1956 were not noticeably efficacious. To those denounced, its condemnations could be treated as lightly as the thunderbolts hurled against the Fenians. If the local priest refused the sacraments, there was always a 'patriot priest' within reasonable reach to minister to the devout militant (just as there was a priest in the GPO with the 1916 rebels, whose leaders were given the last rites by Capuchin friars before execu-tion).

Most of the old clergy had been Redmondite. In the official history of the independence struggle authorised by Cumann na nGaedheal, Pearse Beasley describes how, at a meeting one evening, a Redmondite priest drew a gun on Patrick Pearse and threatened to blow his head off. Later, on December 13, 1920, Dr Colohan, bishop of Cork, put the Volunteers under the ban of excommunication and instructed his priests to refuse them absolution. A friend of mine, now a venerable parish priest, used to subedit Colohan's pastoral charges so that when delivered from the pulpit they conveyed exactly the opposite from what his bishop intended. Eventually my friend went on the run himself, with the IRA, from both Colohan and the Black and Tans. All the same, despite disregard of his strictures—particularly by the regulars—Colohan and other bishops like him had a powerful effect. In his book, *B'fhiu an Braon Fola* (It was worth the Bloodshed), the late Seamus O'Maoileoin, one of Michael Collins' agents, describes how Collins sent for him to meet him in Tipper-ary, and asked him how the excommunication was taking effect. 'If the priests were with us, things would be better', said Collins. 'If I had my way, that —— of a bishop would be shot. There is neither sense nor reason in shooting poor, uneducated idiots as spies and letting people like the bishop of Cork get away with it. According to the rules of warfare, any civilian aiding the enemy is a spy. But I suppose our political friends would never agree to it.' Colohan survived!

We have then a curious paradox: a Faith revered by its adherents beyond the devotion given to any other Church in Christendom (with the possible exception of Poland); and a Church whose authority in matters of politics can be shrugged off with little difficulty by those whose radical nationalism conflicts with the hierarchy's 'moderate' line. This does not mean, of course, that the Church is a broken reed when a particular political question is involved. Far from it. As we have seen, its opposition to the Mother and Child scheme was crucial in defeating Noel Browne. And in 1939 its pressure was sufficient to make the Labour Party remove the phrase 'Workers' Republic' from its manifesto. Nor has it been unuseful to the Republic of Ireland, in terms of international relations, to have strong advocacy of moderation against extremism coming from so important a force in the national life.

The picture of a calculating, British-sympathising clergy selling out their countrymen for the sake of Church politics does not altogether bear close examination. Yet those who want to bring such an indictment can squeeze a colourable justification for it out of the Church's relationship with British authority. Part of the 'deal' involved in the setting up of Maynooth College was that the sovereign should be prayed for morning and evening. The bargain seems to have been kept by the Church—except that the prayer, *Domine salvum fac Regem*, was solemnly given out, and responded to, as *Domine salvum* whack *Regem*! Eventually the prayer was quietly dropped.

Today, generally speaking, the Church avoids all reference to its 'fellow-travelling' period in the nineteenth century, and instead harks back to its penal-time tribulations. One of Cardinal Conway's first public speeches after consecration in 1965 made reference to the attachment to the Mass formed among the Irish people 'in the dark days of the penal times'. An old parish priest whose generosity and Christianity I am particularly well placed to appreciate replied, when asked how the ecumenical movement was progressing in his parish (which is not in Ireland): 'The two Anglican ministers are making great overtures about religion, but I'll wait until they scrape the blood off the Mass Rocks before we talk religion as we understand it'.

Traits such as those discussed in this section have been intensified in our day by other factors: the wartime isolation, which had a stultifying effect on the Church in as much as it kept in Ireland hundreds of priests who had been ordained for the mission field; the fact that up to the end of the 'fifties Fianna Fail administrations were largely composed of men who had been excommunicated during the Civil War; a genuine desire to withdraw from the political arena*—all played a part in restricting the contribution, if not the status, of the priest in the community.

New Trends, New Problems

But, paralleling the Watershed in other spheres of national life, new trends in Irish Catholic thought began to appear in the 'fifties. Notable expressions of a fresh outlook began to be voiced in the better religious magazines: in *The Furrow*, edited from Maynooth by Dr J. G. McGarry; in *Studies* (an Irish version of the French *Etudes*), published by the Jesuits in Dublin and edited by Fr Burke Savage; in *Doctrine and Life*, edited by a Dominican, Fr Austin Flannery; and in *Christus Rex*, the organ of a clerical sociology group and edited by Fr Jeremiah Newman of Maynooth. Generally—apart from the arts criticism in *The Furrow*, which is some of the best in the country—these were carefully phrased articles, written mainly for priests and keeping to fairly 'safe' areas.

Then came the Council. Pope John perhaps meant more to Ireland than he did to most countries—politically as well as religiously. In a keynote speech on social and economic policy delivered to Fianna Fail delegates on October 7, 1963, Sean Lemass said:

> ... The Encyclicals of Pope John are of enormous help, because they remove doubts and uncertainties, and give to all mankind the benefit of a clear guiding light. In these modern days, no nation can operate in isolation, and social progress anywhere depends in some degree on progress everywhere. It is therefore true that the universal understanding and application of the social teachings of Pope John can help every nation, including Ireland, in their effective application. For the Irish Government, I can say that Ministers keep these Encyclicals at hand for constant inspiration and reference when working out their plans to accelerate the application of the social policy which we are seeking to develop. ...

The effect of Pope John's lead was remarkable. Suddenly, a little valid criticism began to be uttered by laymen instead of being left entirely to priests discoursing to priests, or discounted as 'anti-clericalism' (the contemporary equivalent of the all-silencing epithet of 'communism' of recent times), or—worse still—drowned in disgruntled gurglings in pubs. The criticism was not an incitement to laicisation or the sacking of churches. In Ireland, such dissidence is never directed at dogma (with the possible exception of the birth-control issue). The most virulent critic of the Church on a liquidly articulate Saturday night will invariably reel into

---

* Decree 21 of the Maynooth Synod of 1956, the current source of local legislation for the Irish Church, specifically forbids the use of the pulpit for political purposes.

last Mass the next day. Indeed, with the advent of evening Mass, he will as like as not bow the knee with his objurgations still hot on the tongue.

The criticism now freely expressed has centred mainly on the secular clergy. The regular orders, being concerned with education and missionary activity, are expected by people to be withdrawn, and are justly admired for their educational work. Some orders—notably the Jesuits, with a series of 'advanced' lectures at their house at Milltown, County Dublin, and the Benedictines, with their annual Liturgical Congress at Glenstal in County Limerick—are pioneers of the liberal ethic. The Jesuits, in fact, exemplify the all-embracing nature of the Church in Ireland. In the self-same area they run both one of the most exclusive day schools in the country and also a workers' college for the sons of trade unionists!

The main trouble lies in the fact that there is no retiring age for priests. The average country parish priest is far more likely to make news in the local paper when his solicitor tells a district justice that Father X wishes to object to the granting of a licence for dancing after midnight than for his running some McDyer-like enterprise. Young priests may not become McDyers without the permission of the senior priest in the parish and the result tends to be inaction. The fact that parish priests may be, and often are, men of untold private charity, does not prevent their public image from being one of an extreme conservatism.

The Church is badly organised. Every diocese in the country, except the few with a large centre like Dublin, has shown a marked drop in population since 1901. Yet every diocese has shown an equally marked increase in the number of priests, with the result that there are sometimes not enough in the city parishes and too many in the country. In Dublin an old priest from the country is faced with a task that is sometimes beyond him. My own parish priest is seventy-two. He runs twenty-one church committees, is reducing a parish debt of over £100,000—and has half a stomach left him. He maintains two large churches, a large school and a number of parochial residences. Part of his parish is in a poor neighbourhood plagued by juvenile delinquency. Denunciations against vandalism failed to rectify the situation. After some heart-searching he started a teenage dance club. The crime rate dropped appreciably.

But against this one must set the case of the parish in another part of the city where the priest was, literally, moribund. He had an alcoholic brother, a doctor, who used to give him the injections needed to make him sit up and sign documents for the layman who handled the parish's business affairs. Injection accomplished, the brother would be given a bottle of whiskey, and the business affairs of the parish continued somewhat less profitably than they might have done. This is, of course, a bizarre and unrepresentative example, but—in an extreme form—it illustrates what is a general difficulty arising from the great age of many parish priests.

Pope John and Cardinal Bea, both in their late seventies when the Council began, certainly demonstrate that age of itself is no impediment to great energy and reform. But the average old parish priest, reared in the mental climate and against the inward-looking background described earlier, finds it difficult to get in tune with parishioners who have got beyond *Mater et Magistra* and *Pacem in Terris*. The sermons of such priests tend to bore rather than inspire. They and their curates are immersed in the multifarious fund-raising activities for new schools and churches necessitated by the great rash of new housing schemes around Dublin, Cork and other large towns. Moreover, there is growing irritation among many laymen at the fact that, whereas the normal household mortgage is from twenty to thirty years, bishops expect to have their churches paid for in a third of that time. (Hence the low interest rate on Church borrowings.)

The burden of money-raising is, in Dublin parishes, being eased by the introduction in 1965 of a professional fund-raising agency. Its system of planned giving may help to introduce a better sense of communal feeling by arousing a greater sense of responsibility among the laity in the running of the parish. The planned giving campaign is having the usual teething troubles. People complain that collectors press them to 'give something more', and a keeping-up-with-the-Jones attitude has increased some people's contributions beyond what they can reasonably sustain. I know of one area in which the local doctors contribute £3 10s a week. Even so, the new system—if it becomes general—should give the quietus to the custom which still survives in some churches of having 'fashionable' sections— usually in the centre of the nave or near the altar—entry to which means larger contributions to the collection than from the working-class sections, usually at the side or back of the church. (New churches are being designed on 'classless' lines: a good example of the effect of church architecture on more than the eye.)

But even where the fund-raising burden is eased by planned giving schemes, the priests often get bogged down in the mechanical business of conducting the sodalities and confraternities which proliferate around city churches. The laity taking part in these activities are mainly the pious middle-aged. The young people who attend are usually there because their parents make them go. The mothers of Ireland are the real strength of the Church. The anxiety of younger priests and progressive theologians is that, when free of parental influence, such young people and their children may not participate in the communal life of the parish church. Today's Catholicism is not allied to a great national struggle as it was in the past, while the all-pervasive influence of modern media of communications does not bear any marked impress of a concern for spreading the Word of God.

The current unease about the teaching of catechetics is such that when Fr Hofinger, the celebrated catechist, visited Ireland in July 1964, he attracted what he said were the largest audiences he had found in nine world tours. There is nothing wrong with the enthusiasm of the teachers. The trouble lies in the catechisms themselves: cumbersome compendia of theology framed for the exigencies of an earlier day. Not only is there a lack of printed knowledge; there is also a lack of knowledge in the minds of the educated professional classes who should, by virtue of their standing, be the upholders of the Faith. One of the most bitter complaints of concerned young priests is the ignorance of matters doctrinal displayed, for example, by a good many doctors on questions like birth control.

There is a great urge on the part of the younger clergy to get to grips—as individuals, not as authority-figures—with their congregations. In country villages the parish priest is the traditional figure of authority, ranking before the doctor and the bank manager. But the practical need for status of the old kind does not exist today, and the priest is no longer the major *sympathetic* authority-figure in any parish. When my father was a boy in Castlecomer, County Kilkenny, the parish priest, Fr MacNamara, negotiated all marriage settlements and dealt with the Land Commission on behalf of the people. Today Castlecomer does not need this service, so devotedly and unstintingly given. What it needs is an industry. While this book was being written, a local mine closed down, putting 300 people out of work: which for Castlecomer was equivalent to pulling the plug out of a bath of water. Yet in all fairness to the priests who carry the heat and burden of the day, it must be said that much of the task they are charged with is not necessarily of their own seeking. Transformed as Irish life is from the past, there is still in many areas a paucity of people with the education, the opportunity and the *willingness* to take on leading roles in society. The priest is looked up to; he is also a jack-of-all-trades conveniently at hand. Priests and curates automatically find themselves chairmen and patrons of the local Gaelic Athletic Association club and of whatever other local bodies there may be. Not that this position is regulated solely by respect for the cloth. The clergy's power is so real that, before the holding of a beer festival in Kilkenny or the introducing of legislation in Dublin to increase drinking hours, those concerned will automatically first seek the approval of the bishop of the diocese.

Yet, for all this, the problems of most Irish parishes have hitherto existed uninfluenced by the clergy except in so far as offering opportunities for institutional charity. There are, of course, many outstanding exceptions to this criticism, but it must be said that the attitudes of a 'social elite' clergy are not always conducive to successful grappling with social problems on house visitation. Mind, this criticism cuts both ways. The prestige attached to having a priest in the family produces a moral pressure on some seminarists, not with an inherently strong sense of vocation, to persevere and be ordained rather than face the stigma of becoming a 'spoiled priest'—as those who bravely try and then honourably withdraw are still referred to in Ireland. Some young clergy have an excessively academic attitude—denounced by a priest friend of mine as the insignia of the 'I-was-hungry-and-ye-founded-a-study-group' brigade. On the other extreme is the type represented by the young curate who told me that he approaches home visitation on the principle that 'I only have to start talking about soccer and the wallpaper, and I'm in'. How far from 'in' he is really is only discovered by the seminary-insulated young celibate when he visits a house where the door is opened by a strained woman holding in her arms a child with a dirty nappy, six other children clutching her skirts, beds unmade and dishes unwashed. Many a young priest is so unnerved by such a confrontation that the urge for house visitation dies in him.

As a result of too much organisational activity in the towns and not enough in the country, Evelyn Waugh's young man who suffered from 'doubts' would not find the atmosphere in the average presbytery conducive to solving his problems. But, happily, the situation is changing—if slowly— as younger priests begin to develop a new pastoral approach.

Church Leadership

The people who control the Church are, of course, the bishops. It is to them that clergy and people look for guidance. Their pastoral letters delivered throughout their dioceses at the beginning of Lent set the key-note for Irish Catholicism. Up to *circa* 1964 it was not an inspiring note. They were couched in the *Quadragesimo Anno* language of subsidiarity and vocationalism, and seemed especially intent on drawing attention to the dangers of ballroom dancing, 'keeping company', the wearing of shorts by young girls and mixed cycling clubs. But of social questions there was little mention. (A notable exception was Dr Duignan, bishop of Clonfert, who died in 1953. He submitted a social insurance scheme to the government in 1944, but it was not proceeded with.)

However, as the Second Vatican Council progressed, the pastorals slowly swung into line with the new thinking. The Irish hierarchy at Rome began to vote in the 'progressive' lobby. Unfamiliar words like catechetics, liturgy, theology, suddenly entered the vocabulary of the laity. Religion began to mean more than going to church on Sunday and not eating meat on Friday. Throughout the country, middle-aged and elderly, slightly

bewildered priests manfully tried to convey to their parishioners the meaning of the changes in the Mass and the reasons for them. One began to
notice the word 'Christian' being used rather than 'Catholic' or 'Protestant'
—and this is, I believe, fundamentally more important than the fact that
some prelates have visibly still failed to respond to the new spirit in the
Christian world.

What are members of the hierarchy like as individuals? As a rule few
people in Ireland know much of them outside the circle of their official
contacts and a handful of senior clerical colleagues—which is a pity, for an
Irish bishop (or an Irish parish priest for that matter) is generally a
humble, shy man with a good sense of humour: not the browbeating,
forbidding character he is often supposed to be. But the system shuts the
episcopacy off from their flock, and they tend to hear only what their
entourage believes they want to hear. The archbishop of Dublin, Dr John
Charles McQuaid (who was a regular—of the Holy Ghost order—before
his consecration) is a particular sufferer in this regard. I have spoken to
people who know him: prominent trade unionists, members of the government; they generally agree that he is a charming, shy and very holy man.
His initiative has created the greatest complex of charitable institutions
in the country: hospitals, schools, boys' clubs, rehabilitation centres for
unwed mothers and for potential suicides. But, because of his reserved
manner, he has got less credit for all this than if he had just occasionally
walked down O'Connell Street and bought a few threepenny ice-creams
for the kids. In the word used by himself on April 24, 1965, his public
image was that of an 'ogre'.

So much unfavourable comment has percolated through the clerical
grapevine about the Church's image that Dr McQuaid decided something
special needed to be done. His decision seems to have been prompted by
the affair of the two Vatican Council *periti* (experts). In December 1963
Fr Gregory Baum (an Augustinian, converted from Jewry, who now runs
an ecumenical centre in Montreal) and Fr Courtney Murray (a Jesuit who
acts as adviser to the American hierarchy) were expected to give a lecture in
Dublin. It became known—such things are never announced—that there
was some objection to their speaking in Dublin. At any rate, Fr Murray
never came, though Fr Baum did give some private talks in Dublin and
public addresses in Maynooth, Carlow and Belfast. There was an outcry
at the fact that two people who symbolised so much of the new and
attractive thinking of the Church should appear to have been hindered
rather than helped in addressing audiences in Dublin. On January 31,
1964 Dr McQuaid set up a commission to examine 'the image of the
Church in Dublin'. The commission's findings, of course, were kept
secret (well, *almost* secret), but in the event a public relations officer was

appointed: Mr O. G. Dowling, a Dublin journalist. The office was duly opened on April 25, 1965 'in accordance with the Vatican's decree on mass communication'. It was the first such office in the world.

In preparing material for this book, I was able to interview three prominent members of the Irish hierarchy: Dr Michael Browne, bishop of Galway (the major town in the West); Dr Cornelius Lucey, bishop of Cork (the second city of the Republic); and Dr Birch, bishop of Ossory, whose diocese has Kilkenny as its chief centre.

1. Dr Michael Browne

Known to the irreverent as 'Cross Michael'—possibly because he signs himself ✠ *Michael*—Dr Browne was formerly a professor of moral theology at Maynooth. After a brilliant academic career, he was appointed bishop of Galway in 1937 at the age of forty-two, which made him at the time the youngest bishop in Ireland. He has travelled widely—in Europe, the Middle East and America—and is a noted controversialist who has made front-page news in Irish papers several times in his career. His principal controversies have been with local authorities in Galway over the building of another school; with Lemass over vocational education; with the present minister for Education over the new plans; and, of course, with proponents of the Mother and Child scheme, in which dispute he and Dr McQuaid played leading roles. He is a fine-looking, florid man over six feet tall. His speech is accented in the English upper-class fashion and embroidered with Latin quotations. One of his favourite publications is the BBC's *Listener*: 'It's the best for giving the educated Anglican viewpoint'. We met in an elegant Dublin hotel where he talked forcefully, but always pleasantly, for nearly two hours. Here are some of the principal matters we discussed.

Would Ireland lose the Faith in a materialistic age? 'Young people say these things, but they don't have a clear view of their country's history. The same sort of thing was said in the days of the Veto, the Fenian crisis and after the fall of Parnell. It was a commonly held belief that after independence Ireland would be no longer Catholic.'* What of the charge that there was a strong vein of superstition and unthinking acceptance in Irish religious practice as compared, say, with continental Catholicism? 'You

* In fact, the numbers of secular priests have increased from 2,967 in 1910 to 3,798 in 1961; and non-diocesan clergy, who in 1911 numbered 759, fifty years later numbered 2,180. In 1906, there were 2,417 churches as compared with 2,574 in 1961. Many of the new churches, however, were built with the generous assistance of Irish emigrants in America and elsewhere. It is a moot point whether the dwindling populations of some of the rural districts in which a number of these churches were built would themselves have provided the funds. In the past ninety years, the population of Ireland has fallen by 23 per cent; during the same period the number of priests has risen by 87 per cent.

know the story about the Frenchman who was asked if he was a Catholic?
*Are you a Catholic? But yes! Do you eat meat on Friday? Certainly. Do you
go to Mass every Sunday? Non: je ne suis pas fanatique!* That's the kind of
thing you get over there. The French and Italians have problems we
simply don't have here. It comes to this. Which is more important: a
church with a thousand peasants attending Mass, or one professor? They
sneer at us for attendance at Mass. But what are we to do? Give these
things up?'

Church architecture. I asked him how it was that whereas in one part of
his diocese (Ennistymon, County Clare) he had built a church of the most
advanced design, his new cathedral (opened by Cardinal Cushing in
August 1965) was a twentieth-century variant of the Byzantine style. 'That's
the sort of thing that young people say. A large church *can't* be macabre.
You can't reproduce the sort of thing you get in a small church like
Ennistymon in a cathedral. In the old days a cathedral used to be the
poor man's bible. You can't just go putting in any horrible colour—like
your tie!'

Influence of television. Dr Browne had just made headlines by his criticism
of Telefis Eireann's attitude to religious programmes. I gathered that he
did not watch television very often, but he had happened to see a programme in which three laymen and only one priest had appeared. 'Three
to one. Now that wasn't fair, was it? . . . You journalists and television
people are the people that count nowadays. You tell us what to do now.' It
hadn't struck me that anyone would imagine that the panel might seem a
case of one against three since the programme was a discussion, not a
confrontation. But in every discussion on religion since the station opened,
the Church has come in for some criticism, and this probably weighed
with his Lordship.

Birth control. 'Women get interested in this stuff from the papers. Most
of it is written in America and they think it's great. Of course, an awful lot
of women are going out to work to pay for the telly and that sort of thing,
and this makes some of them want small families.'

Emigration and the land question. Dr Browne felt that the state's attitude
was Dublin-based rather than orientated towards the poorer districts in
the West. He proposed the radical solution that land should be entailed,
and cited a case to prove his point. A man had married and come back
from England to invest his savings in his mother's farm. There had been
a row and he had taken his mother to court in an effort to get his savings
back. The judge had had to rule against him, saying 'this is a court of
law, not justice'.

Mother and child scheme. 'That was a tragedy—a young man like Browne
with an ordinary degree becoming a minister.' The bishop took his

particular stand on the issue of the right to choose a doctor. To him the fact that a non-Catholic doctor might have the care of Catholics in maternity cases could have led to an infringement of Catholic teaching. He said in reply to a question that, if a similar situation arose in the future, he thought the hierarchy would probably stand up for its rights in the same way.

Second Vatican Council. He found it a remarkable Council convoked at a time when no enemy threatened 'like Luther'. He thought it right that mankind rather than merely Jews should share the blame for Christ's death. But, in view of this, he felt it was not fair to blame only Catholics for the Reformation. 'If not the Jews for Christ, why Catholics exclusively for the Reformation?' In answer to a question, the bishop said that the reason why so little was heard from the Irish hierarchy at the Council (up to the end of the second session) was because they had obeyed to the letter the conciliar strictures about not talking to the press. And in any case the Irish delegation was located in the Irish College on the other side of Rome and hence did not easily come into contact with the press. He asked me what I thought of the Council. I said that, frankly, being Irish, I didn't think anything of it or consider that it could be relevant to me personally when it started, but that I was thrilled as it went on. 'There you are', he said, 'you young people don't realise how the Church can change.'

Dr Browne had never been interviewed before, apart from a visit from the late Dr Halliday Sutherland who had called to enquire how he dealt with illegitimacy in his diocese. Their meeting was not fruitful! I found him a very fair-minded man. During our talk we discussed a public figure whose career had been tremendously advanced by his marriage. This I flippantly opined to be the principal reason for the union. The bishop thought I was serious and was horrified at my cynicism. However, mutually satisfied that neither of us had two heads, we parted amiably and he kindly invited me to call on him again whenever I was in Galway.

2. Dr Cornelius Lucey

The bishop of Cork is a tall man with short-cropped hair. He has an energetic, driving walk and a gentle voice. His hobby is gardening and he goes on holiday to Italy with three priest friends each year. Cold print makes his pronouncements about government policy (usually about the plight of the small farmer) sound more Jehovah-like than he does when speaking. In conversation he is a most gentle, reticent man—yet politicians regard him as the archetype of the commentating Irish bishop. This estimate of Dr Lucey was given public prominence following a difference of opinion in May 1961 between the bishop and a fellow Corkman, Jack Lynch, then minister for Industry and Commerce. After a Confirmation ceremony in the parish of Rath and the Islands in impoverished West Cork, the bishop said: 'West Cork wants no hand-outs from the dispensers of patronage in Merrion Square* or elsewhere. It wants Justice, elementary Social Justice.' The minister politely chided him in the Dail, citing an authority on moral theology to point out that the pastoral authority of bishops extended to faith and morals but not to matters political and economic. Lynch, a former hurling star, is a devout Catholic and his courteous but firm rejection of clerical intervention is one of the more significant aspects of relations between Church and State in recent years.

But, whatever his manner of expressing himself, Dr Lucey's feelings for the small farmer reflect the deep disquiet of a large section of the community. He is himself one of ten children of a small farmer. Whether sound or not, his ideas are sincere. He reminded me that the Second Programme projected that 36,000 people will have left the land by 1970. This he declared to be an 'iniquity'. 'In any other country in the world these people would leave to go to cities within their own borders, but in Ireland it means they will go to another country.† There are 200,000 small farmers in Ireland. The government is paying £39 million a year in agricultural subsidies. Why can't they give each small farmer a weekly income instead?'

Before meeting Dr Lucey, I spoke with a bank manager in Cork who commented adversely on the parsimonious, investment-wary attitude of Irish small-town businessmen. 'A decent labouring man I know in Skibbereen', he said, 'is just after getting work with a local gombeen man who I know for a certainty is worth near £100,000. The unfortunate labourer is delighted with his "good job". Six pounds a week he's getting. Six pounds a week! For maybe ten hours a day.' In Skibbereen Dr Lucey's proposal would be more intelligible than in the office of a government economist.

He received me in his two-storey brick house overlooking the city of Cork, one of the loveliest in Ireland. On the hills circling the city lies the rosary of churches he built over a period of nine years at a cost of one million pounds. We spent the afternoon talking, and after tea served by nuns with a cake made by his sister, I took my leave with his blessing for my wife and children. We didn't get on to a plane of intimacy but the reserve between us was, I felt, the result of the difference in our ages and outlook rather

---

* Dublin's 'Whitehall', formerly the city's most fashionable residential quarter.

† There is complete freedom of movement between Ireland and Britain, and most Irish professional qualifications are accepted on the other side of Saint George's Channel.

than of any desire on the part of this holy and dedicated churchman to avoid my questions, which he answered fully and frankly.

Censorship. Dr Lucey would prefer to see a system whereby the author and distributor of a suspect book were tried before an ordinary judge and jury. If the jury found it 'not filthy', as it were, then let it circulate freely. If otherwise, then slap on a fine or a prison sentence. Such would be the expression of the will of ordinary people as opposed to that of a select few.

Birth control. 'Do you think', he said, 'that people who have had too many children through irresponsibility are going to be more responsible in their use of contraceptives? The Church isn't opposed to control. It's the means which are used she is concerned with. Anyone who wants contraceptives in this country can get them if they want them.* There will always be some people who want to avoid having children. But no one wants to give away a child when it arrives. The Whites say the Blacks have too many children, the rich say the families of the poor are too big, and so on.'

Irish newspapers. 'Of course, the *Irish Times* has blackened us all over the world. They've distorted what I said sometimes and they put headlines on stories like "Bishop attacks such-and-such a thing". That makes it look as though the bishops are going round the country beating everything down with their croziers.' I asked why did he not write and complain if he felt he was being misrepresented. 'I've never written to a paper in my life', he said.

Second Vatican Council. 'The Council is all right for a week or so, but it doesn't seem so interesting when you are watching it. A lot of the problems they discuss are of no interest to us. The Jews, religious liberty . . . we already have it here. The only time there's any trouble, the Jehovah's Witnesses cause it. Our people don't want them.' In perhaps giving the impression that he is not greatly concerned with the things which interest fellow Catholics overseas, Dr Lucey may have done himself an injustice in the mind of the reader. In fact, shortly after our meeting he flew to Peru where he adopted a parish, making himself responsible for its supply of priests and religious facilities.

Freedom of speech. 'I'm all for freedom of speech.' Though suspicious of the word 'liberal', Dr Lucey showed himself genuinely in favour of open discussion on important issues. Clearly somewhat puzzled that anyone should ask such questions, he was equally clearly prepared to answer them.

---

* Most people, whether Protestant or Catholic, get them sent under plain wrapper from England or Belfast. In the bigger Dublin parishes—and for all I know in some of the country parishes also—the younger priests are advising women that, if they want to use the various pills, it is a matter for their conscience. A modern Irish mother may find herself prescribed five decades of the Rosary and triplets at one confessional, and *Enovid* at another.

Bishops and the community. He deprecated my estimate of their power. 'The Church's power is indirect. If we tell people to do or not to do something, they'll tend to ignore us. We are all very small now with the Council. People forget that the Church is everyone; we're only officers.' He said he found it difficult to mingle with people in the sense of walking around the streets, because he would be stopped every few yards by someone wanting to kiss his ring. Ordinarily he uses Confirmation ceremonies as an opportunity to meet his flock and to make any pronouncements he thinks necessary.

Will Ireland stay Christian ? 'Of course.'

Church funds. 'There's no difficulty in getting money for the building of churches. But people tend to regard payment for school buildings as the state's responsibility.' He collected the money to build his churches by means of a levy on each family, collected by voluntary helpers.

Irish language and culture. 'I like them and support them because they're ours.'

Dr Lucey's remarks about the *Irish Times* and his not writing to newspapers may surprise some readers who assume that everyone in Ireland bows at the wave of a crozier. In fact, it is the climate of opinion, a morbid concern for 'pious ears', rather than any set of actions on the part of clerics which newspapers have to contend with. Apart from occasional eccentricities,* bishops and priests seldom if ever make their presence felt.

3. Dr Peter Birch

The Church as a whole is taking another look at itself in the social field. The Irish Church runs the orphanages, the rest homes and the other charitable institutions without which the poor of Ireland would be miserable beyond imagination. But in the matter of day-to-day domestic misery caused by gaps in social legislation, ignorance or drink, the Church hitherto has not matched its institutional endeavours. Some bishops are rectifying this. One such is the bishop of Ossory. Dr Birch is of the current Maynooth vintage. He was appointed co-adjutor in 1962, and then (when the old bishop died) became in 1964 bishop of this predominantly rural diocese but which also includes the large town of Kilkenny with its brewing, leather works, bakeries and hotels. Its site on the River Nore makes it a pleasant town.

He is a tall, stooping man with a fatigued appearance who smokes incessantly. He reads widely, taking in the better English and Irish news-

---

* Like the case of the members of an order who claimed that a brief agency report in a Dublin paper—to the effect that members of the order's Italian sister-house had been arrested on a smuggling and manslaughter charge—was proof of malice on the part of those who edited the paper.

papers and *La Croix*. His residence is an unpretentious, rather shabby two-storey house outside Kilkenny. I found him completely approachable, and if we disagreed in a matter he would argue his point with force but without the slightest hauteur.

Social problems. 'It's a pity in some ways we haven't got a Communist Party here so that we would sit up and do something about the gaps in our social legislation.' Some of the things Dr Birch mentioned in this context were orphan institutions where the children never saw an adult eating. He gets people to take the children out so that they can see how a cake is made, where eggs come from, what a normal home with pictures on the wall looks like. Other problems are more taxing: for example, malnutrition. The bishop believes there is more of this than people suspect: the old age pensioner who lives alone; the wife left in the squalid home by her drunken labourer husband, expecting her eighth child; the poor home with a mentally defective child who seems to destroy all initiative in the family. Keeping up with the Joneses, paying for the TV and the car, and skimping the money spent on food for the children in order to have these 'nice things'—these, he believes, are common causes of malnutrition. The situation is made worse by popular attitudes. 'People say of a woman, "Why should she be helped? She's got £8 15s a week." But she will also very likely have eight children. Some standards of charity are just middle-class notions that are out of date.'

He 'abhors amateurs'. He sends girls to Holland to be trained how to live and work in homes which need help, pass on their knowledge to the occupants, and then move on to the next house. With no time for vague do-gooders, he has a great appreciation of the value of experienced voluntary organisations and works through bodies like the Legion of Mary and the Society of Saint Vincent de Paul. He is particularly appreciative of the practical work they do, making furniture, papering and decorating rooms and teaching housewives how to cook. 'There's no use preaching at a family if the wife is sitting in squalor with eight children and the man can get more comfortable surroundings in a pub.' He has formed a committee of local businessmen whom he has asked to raise £250,000 ('There is no problem getting money') for amenity buildings and projects like providing scholarships for girls in orphanages to enable them to complete their education.

Dr Birch is one of the few churchmen I have met (they usually exhibit the general Irishman's mistrust of women) who volunteers a good opinion of nuns.* In the diocese of Ossory they are especially valued when it comes to ticklish cases like bringing help to people in their homes who would

---

* In fact there are more nuns than regular clergy in Ireland (about 4,000 to about 2,012). They staff hospitals, visit the sick in their homes, run schools and care for the aged.

normally prefer to do without it rather than have their neighbours know of their circumstances.

Young people and 'indifference'. 'I find that young people are wonderful. This is a very stimulating time. A lot depends on how things are done and on who does them.' The bishop described how some of his young voluntary workers have brought their own beds to the homes of old people, moving in with them to give them company, seeing to meals and household chores. He mentioned the case of a young nurse who, under an 'adoption' scheme, had an old man to look after. One evening on her way home from a dance, still in her ball dress, she called at his house to see how he was. She found him dying. She sent for a priest, stayed with him till he died, laid him out at the hospital, then went straight on duty without sleep and without saying a word to anyone.

The bishop cited another case as an example of a situation in which the Birch formula did not work. Before going to the Vatican Council in 1964, he arranged a job for a drunkard whose wife had had five children in six years. To minimise his temptations, the voluntary workers took the man to work every morning, accompanied him to and from lunch, which they prepared, and brought him back again at teatime. At the same time the mother was also taught how to cook. When Dr Birch returned from the Council, however, he found the man had gone on the drink again and had lost his job. The house was filthy and the mother was expecting twins. Attention was then concentrated on the mother. 'She's very proud now of her brown bread.'

Censorship. 'There must be some censorship. Books have sensuous passages put in them to make them sell. These are very disturbing for young people. The only true censorship is the judgement of the mature mind. People in Dublin who've been to universities think their standards apply all over the country. It's not like that for young people down here.'

Bishops and the community. Dr Birch finds it difficult to get around to his friends now that he is a bishop. 'People go to too much trouble for me and if I call to one and not another it causes jealousy.' Hence he tends to keep his personal contacts to his workers, colleagues and family. There is also the inhibition some members of the hierarchy experience, particularly the younger ones, which makes them hesitate to say or do anything that may seem either a reflection on their colleagues or an effort to boost themselves.

Changes in Ireland. What strikes him most forcibly is the change in people's attitudes. 'They're as helpful as ever they were, but they're more independent. If they don't like what you are doing they'll very soon let you know.' Emigration has meant that he has had to move some curates from certain parishes. 'They were trying to run a car and pay a housekeeper on £6 a week!' He also finds that he is granting more and more dispensations for young people to marry outside the Church.

In the course of the interview I suggested to Dr Birch that the hierarchy could make use of television. A little while after, he said in an after-dinner speech that, as farm labourers obviously could not live on their wages (£7 15s a week), the state should pay the same amount as the farmer to them. I telephoned him and invited him to discuss the question on television. 'What will I bring down on my head?' he asked. But he drove to Dublin and did the interview which—since it involved night driving, and his eyesight is poor—was no easy matter for him.

'Which is more important: a church with a thousand peasants attending Mass, or one professor?' In that sentence lies the entire Catholic debate in Ireland. Dr Browne's view is clearly and honourably stated, but the young men in the seminaries and some of those who teach them feel that Ireland is running out of peasants and something else is needed than the traditional approach.

Unlike England, where voluble Anglican prelates vie with the bishop of Woolwich in stating their television theology, Irish divines do not normally allow their conflicts, if there are any, to break out of the religious quarterlies. But the tensions between the new thinking and the old suddenly appeared in a popular, mass-circulation newspaper, the *Irish Independent*, when Dr Browne took issue with Fr Enda MacDonagh (who now holds the chair at Maynooth formerly occupied by the bishop) over the report of a lecture Fr MacDonagh had given to the Maynooth Union on August 25, 1964. Calling for a renewal in the approach to the teaching of theology, the professor was reported to have said that 'too much moral teaching concentrated on what a man should not do in a particular area of life without any very developed understanding of what he should do . . . '. As reported, he went on to say that moral theology 'as it has been developed and presented in our manuals seems to be much more a combination of Aristotelian ethics and canon law than theological reflections on the biblical account of Christ'.

Four days later (August 29) the correspondence column of the paper carried Dr Browne's reaction. He singled out the Aristotelian reference.

I sincerely hope that the reporting is not correct, for in my opinion it is a gross exaggeration and gives a false and misleading impression. It would lead many to think that Catholic moral theology as expounded and approved in authorised manuals does not give adequate place to the teaching of Christ and that the clergy who had been trained on these manuals have consequently not given the true and full teaching of Christ. Such an impression would reflect gravely on those who authorised the use of the manuals.

Fr MacDonagh amplified his statement in a reply on September 1, but he did not say that there had been any misreporting (which would have been an easy way out of the controversy). There the unprecedented exchange ended. Since the teaching of theology is at the very root of the 'Catholicity' of Catholic Ireland, the fact that such a public exchange of different views should have occurred is highly significant. (MacDonagh was chosen to accompany his bishop as a *peritus* at the final session of the Vatican Council.)

The Future

An ominous thought occurred to me as I prepared this chapter for the press: how close, religiously speaking, the parallel is between the present ferment of younger clergy on the side of liberalism, with older priests clinging to conservatism, and earlier political developments in Ireland. When the Second Vatican Council has gone into history, will the urge for change perhaps die out after a few years—just as it did in Irish politics after the attainment of independence? If the future bears out the analogy, then this time the Church will lose. The world will be bereft of a powerful influence for good, and Ireland of something far more deeply based and indigenous than her language even: her soul. For, albeit often exasperating, sometimes cruel, frequently misguided, the Church *was* Ireland for several centuries and Ireland was the Church. In many ways this is still so.

There is no longer a *status quo* to accept as the years roll on and youthful idealism grows disillusioned. Today's prize, and even more so that of tomorrow, is this intangible thing: the mind of man. Juke-box Man, Telly Man, Sputnik Man, Shop Steward Man, Educated Man—all mortal man, mortal man. He may answer to 'Sean' or 'Paddy', but what will he pray to? Will there be any place at all in his life, in his wife's or in his children's for prayer?

This is the challenge which faces the Irish Church today—not the old confrontation between Protestant and Catholic, or even the more recent confrontation between Christian and Marxist. It is hard for the older priests to say, in effect, that the old authoritarian attitudes of calm certitude were wrong. It is difficult for the younger priests to accept that Yves Congar is someone whom Patrick of the Paperbacks next door speaks of with the same frequency and respect once reserved to the priest as the sole occupant of the theological field. It is nearly impossible to explain to the older laity what has happened to the canons they were reared by, or to break it to some of the younger ones that freedom of conscience is not translatable as licence.

The real problem is not so much *how* to overcome these complexities as to get it accepted that they *must* be overcome. A priest, whether 'conservative' or 'liberal', is still fundamentally a good man. But in many ways the Irish Church of the past, and to some degree still today, is the Church Juridical. This may suffice in an age when the priest is the only educated man in a backward, rural community. It will not serve in the age of the education explosion. The future of the Church Juridical depends almost entirely on the extent to which it can make itself the Church Charismatic.

THE PROTESTANTS

I have devoted so much space to the Catholics because, of the Republic's 2,813,341 inhabitants, Protestants number only about 130,000. The Church of Ireland (considered as 'Low Church' by Anglican standards) accounts for three-quarters of these. Presbyterians with 19,000 have three times the total of Methodists and outnumber the Jews by six to one. Baptists, Lutherans and Jehovah's Witnesses all told amount only to 1,487.

The Protestant community has a historical background of prosperity. The Church of Ireland itself, disestablished by Gladstone in 1869 and since then a self-governing branch of the Anglican communion, has investments of £16 million. Most of these, however, are not freely negotiable since they are earmarked for specific purposes. A Church of Ireland parson is paid £850 a year and is provided with a house and travelling expenses.

The Protestant community was the backbone of the Union, maintaining it, let it be said, with the help of 'Castle Catholics' (wealthy toadies to the Establishment). At the same time, as we mentioned earlier, it also provided leaders of Irish independence like Wolfe Tone, Robert Emmet, Thomas Davis and Charles Stewart Parnell, and—in more recent times—Douglas Hyde, Erskine Childers, Robert Barton, the Countess Markievicz and Ernest Blythe. The Co-operative movement of Sir Horace Plunkett, the great literary tradition of Goldsmith, Wilde, Shaw, Synge, Yeats and most of the creators of the Abbey Theatre, sprang from that same Anglo-Irish Ascendancy which suborned the squalid, starving, landlord-shooting peasantry.

Theirs was a world of fine country houses, for the great ones, and of pretentious (and often ruinous) emulation of that world by the lesser gentry among them. The Royal Dublin Society's annual horseshow in the capital, apart from its serious purpose as the country's major trade and agricultural event, still serves as an opportunity for the chinless wonders of England to join their braying kin in Ireland in throwing icecubes at waiters. (To be just, even the Catholics among them—there are indeed such—are somewhat given to a bold, uninhibited comportment in public places: witness the fears aroused in the summer of 1965 for the safety of Mr Harold Wilson's life, apparently in forfeit to the jesting whim of an Irish peer.)

Most Protestants would be highly insulted at being thought un-Irish. Talking to a Church of Ireland clergyman, I noticed that he referred to Lemass as 'our man' and to Captain O'Neill as 'their man'. The only two occasions when I ever heard a round of applause in a Dublin cinema (cramful with Catholic wild Irish!) were after an interview of Brendan Behan by Eamonn Andrews, and after the wedding film of Queen Elizabeth.

When people talk of a 'very Protestant-looking man', they mean a distinct type: fair-haired, neat, usually with an upper-class English accent—and prosperous. Out of every 1,000 Protestants, sixty-five are in executive managerial positions, and eighty-three are professional men or top-level technicians; whereas the Catholic proportions are nine and forty-three respectively. A fifth of all farms over 200 acres are Protestant-owned. There are, of course, poor Protestants also; out of 17,500 engaged in farming, 4,000 own farms of less than fifty acres, while many are agricultural labourers.

The Protestants in the Republic are a declining minority: a fact which is frequently used to arouse sectarian fears in the North. In 1911, the number of Protestants in Southern Ireland was 327,171; by 1926 the figure had fallen to 220,723 and went on dropping. By 1946, the Protestant community was reduced to 169,000; and at the time of writing there are some 40,000 fewer. Dublin, which had 77,000 members of the Church of Ireland in 1888, had only 35,000 in 1957. On the opposite side of the country, in County Clare, the number of Church of Ireland children between the ages of two and four in 1961 was six: three boys and three girls—which may be a reassuring balance from the viewpoint of mixed marriages, but not for the prospects of repopulation. There are only eight Methodists in Clare.

Forty closed churches have been demolished in the Republic, and ninety more are scheduled to go. Most Protestants cluster in Dublin (re-enacting in a sense the earlier historical withdrawal to 'the Pale'), where the Church of Ireland Representative Body has its headquarters.* In the North of

* The Representative Body is the organ of government of the Church of Ireland, following its reorganisation at disestablishment. The Church has a general Synod composed of three orders: bishops, who sit as the 'upper' house, clergy and laity representatives, who sit together as the 'lower' house.

Ireland, the picture is quite different, the Protestant population staying more or less static at the following totals:

RELIGIOUS POPULATION OF NORTHERN IRELAND

Presbyterian	413,006
Church of Ireland	344,584
Methodists	71,912
Others (Baptists, etc.)	97,929
Catholics	498,031

These figures reveal the Presbyterians to be the majority Protestant denomination in Ulster: the religious effect of the heavy Scottish immigration there in the seventeenth century.

Despite the fact that its greater strength is in the North, the Church of Ireland prefers to make its headquarters in Dublin—although, as was noted earlier, by historical tradition the Ulster city of Armagh is the seat of the premier metropolitan of the Church of Ireland as well as of the Catholic Church. Its decision to make Dublin the effective centre is partly because the Church thus affirms its Irish character as against the markedly Scottish character of the North; partly because there is a feeling that Dublin is still the capital of the whole island, whatever the vicissitudes of twentieth-century politics; and partly also because the city offers the best tension-free meeting point between the North and the South. This means, however, that the Church of Ireland has half of its clergy in the South to care for only a third of its flock. There are well-filled churches in Dublin, but at country services there are often less than a dozen people.

The other denominations have the same problem. Of the fifty-one Presbyterian clergymen in the Republic, half are in Dublin. The rest of the flock is so thin on the ground that in one case (in the West) the incumbent is drawing £1,110 a year for ministering to six people (though in the holiday season his congregation increases).

The desire to cling to the old parishes has led to a crisis in Protestant education in the Republic where, in 1963, there were 9,300 children in Protestant primary schools and 5,520 in some forty secondary establishments. Many of these schools are in a poor state of repair and are understaffed. Of the 400 teachers in them, 100 are Catholics, and often a single teacher takes separate 'classes' drawn from a group of perhaps twenty children of different ages. The Church Representative Body has ruthlessly reassessed its educational requirements. In July 1965 it proposed a drastic scheme whereby all the Protestant denominations would combine in a regrouping and improvement of educational facilities. Such an amalgamation could only do good. It might possibly be a first step towards a genuinely national system of education. The present denominational division keeps

Protestant and Catholic children apart while growing up as citizens of the same country.

One sometimes encounters a certain superciliousness on the part of Protestants in regard to the efforts being made by the political leaders of the majority community towards a new Ireland. One Protestant managing director I interviewed said:

> Oh, I suppose this country will always give a living to about four million. The British seem to have this curious guilt complex towards Ireland. You can always play on that, and of course you'll have the tourist trade to fall back on. The British need the Irish labour pool, too, though they don't care if they take in Irish or Jamaicans.

For him, 1916 was not so much a highroad to independence as the point when the 'poor-ye-shall-always-have-with-you' mentality of Catholic administration ('Look at Sweden compared with Spain', etc.) began to spread its influence to Irish social questions. However, the social statistics of Ireland under Protestant control (as described in chapter 1) are nothing to shout about—except it be in protest. And for all his rather disdainful aloofness (*you* will have the tourist trade to fall back on!), he chooses to live and keep his much-needed expertise in Ireland despite the offers of better jobs elsewhere.*

The principal points of dissatisfaction encountered in Protestant circles are, as one might expect, the censorship and contraceptive restrictions (usually on the grounds of principle, since both in practice are easily overcome), and the effects of the *Ne Temere* decree dating from the Council of Trent in 1564. In Ireland this is interpreted as meaning that the children of a mixed marriage shall be baptised and brought up in the Catholic faith. As we have seen, the judgement in the Tilson case has made this law of the Church binding in the eyes of the state also.

The Protestant community is closely integrated at the top and pretty closely at the middle level of society. A certain alarm at the pictures-of-the-Sacred-Heart, grassroots Catholicism of the working-class majority in Ireland tends to segregate the pin-ups-of-the-Royals element among the Protestant working-class, particularly in the rural areas. Protestants feel that in the field of ideas—e.g., librarianships in rural districts where local taste might not approve a Protestant's choice of books—they do not have a good chance of promotion in the public service. This is a widely held belief, but my own experience in journalism and television leads me to think that, however justifiable this belief may or may not have been in the

---

* It may be remarked in passing how the tone of his references to Britain faithfully reflects the calculating reserve towards John Bull's homeland which has been a marked feature of the Anglo-Irish community for generations.

past, it is certainly no longer justifiable. Much of the credit for the initial success of the *Evening Press* was due to its first editor, Douglas Gageby: a Protestant. In Telefis Eireann, some of the best interviewers and executives are Protestants, while one of the most brilliant producers is a Jew. Irish society is far more tolerant in this way than it is generally given credit for. In fact, there are a number of prominent former communists (and the odd present-tense member of the party) scattered about in the newspaper and television worlds.

However, for these and other reasons, young Protestants have tended, wrongly, to assume that there would be no openings for them in the Republic. So much so that the Protestant archbishop of Dublin, Dr Simms, issued a booklet in 1959 demonstrating how many callings were in fact open to them. The Protestant emigration has stemmed from two causes: one political, the other economic. In the first place, the major exodus of the 'twenties was certainly prompted by the fears aroused by the change of regime in 1922. Secondly, having greater resources and training, the Protestants find it easier to emigrate than most Catholics do. Protestant emigration in the 'fifties was five times greater, proportionately, than Catholic. A background of inherited wealth and property means that the average Protestant is psychologically geared to thoughts either of a 'good job' in Ireland or of emigration. He is not disposed to take whatever is going if it does not suit him. If he goes to Britain, the ties of history and often of family mean that most Protestants arrive in London or other big cities to take up a pre-arranged job and to live in pre-arranged accommodation.

Certainly, a good many Catholic emigrants have friends and relatives on the other side who are able to make smoother their introduction to a new life in Britain. But even at the close of the 'fifties one could still see Irish-speaking Catholic labourers from the West of Ireland standing at Holyhead with placards round their necks plaintively inscribed: 'Put me on a train to . . . '. The callousness of most Irishmen to this phenomenon is typified by the reaction of a brilliant young architect who, six or seven years ago, laughed as he told me how funny such a group from Connemara looked as they stood on the quay at Holyhead patiently waiting for someone to read their pleas for guidance. 'Did you help them?' I asked. 'Are you mad? I wouldn't have anything to do with those ejits.'

The irritations Protestants in Ireland feel—at least, those which have a genuine basis—should eventually disappear. The Vatican Council has already indicated that the doctrinal interpretation which gave rise to the Tilson judgement may be abrogated. And Rome's celibate theologians, having exhaustively considered how many angels may legitimately dance on the head of a birth-control device, are presumably also going to relax the present strictures on 'family planning'—if not tomorrow, then the next day. Such changes in Catholic practice will, by the way, place the Irish government in the interesting position of having to alter the laws of the state if it is to act according to the spirit of Article 44 of the Constitution and 'recognise the special position' of the Catholic Church in Ireland.

There are only four Protestant deputies in the Dail: three Church of Ireland members and one Methodist. Erskine Childers, son of the Republican leader executed during the Civil War, is a minister. Maurice Dockrell, one of the Church of Ireland deputies, was Lord Mayor of Dublin in 1960–61. Protestants get a good proportion of the religious programmes on Telefis Eireann. When a Protestant religious adviser for television was appointed as opposite number to the Catholic adviser, Fr Romuald Dodd, he was promptly christened 'The Man Who Got Even With Dodd'.

There are approximately 3,500 Jews in the Republic: some of them very wealthy, others quite poor. There is a Jewish deputy in the Dail: Ben Briscoe, whose colourful father, Robert, was an IRA leader who became a deputy and Lord Mayor of Dublin. The Jews are not yet admitted to most golf clubs, and—in at least one case I have direct knowledge of— are not allowed to be members of an exclusive rugby club. This sort of restriction is not typical of the regard in which the Jewish community is held, its members on the whole being generally liked; but it does tend to make them react by withdrawing into their own sporting clubs and encourages in them a touch of the chip-on-the-shoulder mentality. Their business instinct is a little disconcerting sometimes: as when, on plunging naked into a shower after a match against a Jewish team—Carlisle—on their home ground in Dublin, a muddied Catholic oaf finds it necessary to put a penny in the shower-meter!

The ecumenical movement is developing at a rate which would have been inconceivable prior to the Vatican Council. Catholic priests have addressed meetings of Protestants; clergy of the Church of Ireland and of the Presbyterian and Methodist communions have written both in Catholic and each other's magazines. The old 'ghetto' attitudes are noticeably crumbling. Ireland is perhaps unique in that, for her, the catalyst of ecumenical change is goodwill, not communism.

One of the most potent generators of this life-giving spirit is George Otto Simms, archbishop of Dublin and Primate of Ireland in the Anglican communion. A lithe six-footer in his mid-fifties, skin stretched tight over high cheekbones, eyes and features animated with intelligence, he is visibly a man of great powers. His manner is a rare combination of strong personality and diplomatic ease. One of his achievements during a Homeric career at Trinity was to take a double moderatorship (the equivalent at

Cambridge and Oxford of a double first) in classics with ancient history and in political science. He is one of the world's great experts on the Book of Kells: the earliest and finest example extant of illuminated Celtic manuscript, the original of which is kept in Trinity College Library.

We met in his comfortable house in the quietly fashionable suburb of Dartry. With Dr Simms was his wife Felicia, in whose family there are Jesuits as well as Anglican divines. They have five children. She is a tall, gracious and kindly woman with a very good figure, wearing her hair severely tied back. The archbishop carried in the coffee-tray himself, setting it down on the table at which, a brass plaque thereon complains, 'Gladstone plotted the Disestablishment of the Church in 1869'.

Dr Simms, unlike a good many clerics in the Church of Ireland, is neither a Mason nor an Orangeman. But his father signed the Ulster Covenant. 'Strange how they all came in for that', he mused. He said he would like to see Ireland united, but he thought the only way to end Partition was—and here he echoed Gladstone some eighty years ago—through a 'union of hearts'. Many formerly die-hard Catholic Republicans would now agree with him. He would like to see Ireland becoming more internationally minded and taking a greater place in Europe.

I remarked, à propos of the Gladstonian table, that disestablishment was a good thing for all concerned, it being a bad principle to have any religion subsidised by the state. The archbishop smiled kindly on my naïveté and said: 'I don't suppose it seemed like that to them at the time!' He added that he did not regard his Church as being part of an Irish 'minority', but as the Irish representative of the world-wide Anglican communion.

We conversed generally for about an hour, during which he went out of his way to mention kindnesses shown him by Dr McQuaid. The prelate whom some consider as a 'bigoted ogre' had been Dr Simms' first caller when he moved to his new home. He also lent his Protestant vis-à-vis some books about the Council. 'I thought they'd be conservative, but in fact they were all very critical of the Curia.' There is more of this kind of unobtrusive interchange among people who are apparently poles apart than one might suppose. For instance, Dr Simms frequently has long telephone conversations in Irish with President de Valera.

After our conversation, the archbishop helped me into my coat and escorted me down the stairs. He expressed interest in the book I told him I was going to write. 'You know', he said, 'my wife's uncle wrote a book once. The IRA blew his house up.' *Absit omen!*

But one must not imagine that all in the Irish religious garden is now lovely. Change is not easy for either side yet. When an English professional fund-raising service was introduced into a large Catholic parish in Dublin

I am familiar with, it had good results. But the clergy noted a widespread complaint among the parishioners, summed up by one stalwart of the Faith: 'I don't like the idea of Protestants collecting money for the Church'. To many Irish Catholics, the Protestant is still the person about whom they were warned in their Christian doctrine class at school: 'If a Protestant asks you about such-and-such a thing, tell him so-and-so'. One was not taught hostility, but in a small community a warning about 'the others' from the clergy is enough to keep in being the barriers erected by history and communalism.

It is possible that lay members of the Protestant community may be more reluctant even than their Catholic counterparts to entertain a genuine coming together of the denominations. There is still a markedly condescending 'West British' attitude among a good many in the community, while the merest hint of 'popery' can still arouse strong feelings in many Protestant breasts. A Church of Ireland parson found himself harried by violent protests from his flock when one of his more high-minded parishioners wanted to put RIP on a tombstone.

I should like to conclude this necessarily impressionistic and sketchy account of religion in Ireland with a short comparison. During the Tenant Right League days, Frederic Lucas—editor of the *Tablet*, then as now a leading Catholic lay magazine in England—came to Ireland to join on the tenants' side in the struggle for the land. The opposition of Archbishop Cullen eventually wrecked his efforts. In 1964, another brilliant English journalist, Michael Viney—a young non-Catholic who had also fallen in love with Ireland—wrote a series of articles in the *Irish Times* on illegitimacy. It was a frank account of what the Irish do and do not do about this problem. The present Catholic archbishop of Dublin, who is responsible for much of the rescue work for unwed mothers and their babies, directed his vicar-general to write a letter to the paper congratulating the writer.

It would be wrong to take too much guidance from such straws in the breeze. But the barometer is set at 'change' and the wind is blowing in the right direction, even if many liberal-minded Irish Catholics feel it is not yet blowing at sufficient force.

II. *THE IRA*

Political Characteristics · First Phase 1926–36: *Spanish Interlude*
Second Phase 1939–46 · Third Phase 1956–62 · The IRA Today

THE Irish Republican Army has given Ireland more publicity abroad than any other organisation in the country. Although the makers of this publicity have changed in personnel over the years, all IRA members have one thing in common: since Ireland's independence their activities have always been as unwelcome to the government in Dublin as to that in London. The ruling circles in Ireland today are proud to recall the exploits of what is called the 'Old IRA'—the men of 1916–23. The 'New IRA' must only be referred to in newspapers as 'an illegal organisation'.

Death has reduced to a matter of inches the weekly notices which used to appear in the local and national press telling the survivors of the struggle for independence where to meet and where to march to for this funeral or that anniversary of an old comrade-in-arms. But the 'illegal organisation's' activities get banner headlines. Young men inspired by Connolly's social teaching and Pearse's romantic nationalism continue to pursue the Grail to which generations of Irishmen and Irishwomen have dedicated themselves: an Ireland free and prosperous from the Glens of Antrim to the Ring of Kerry; an Ireland of thirty-two united counties.

The IRA withdrew recognition from the Second Dail on November 14, 1925. Its army council objected to the proposal that Sinn Fein deputies should take their seats in the legal, 'Treaty' parliament. Up to this time, the IRA men had regarded Eamon de Valera as president of their underground Republic, Sean Lemass as its minister for Defence and Frank Aiken as its army's chief of staff. This divergence split the Republican movement into two sections: Fianna Fail, led by de Valera, which came overground and formed a constitutional party; and Sinn Fein, which still regarded the Treaty as an illegal compact between the British and Irish 'compromisers', a compact imposed by force; and saw the surviving members of the Second Dail as the legitimate government of the Republic —a sort of home-based government in exile. The IRA now became a military organisation dedicated to the establishment of a Thirty-Two Counties Republic, and pledged itself to give allegiance to any democratically elected government which would attempt (simply to attempt was accepted as a sufficient test of its *bona fides*) to function as the government of such a Republic.

Despite frequent changes of personnel and leadership, the Irish Republican Army has continued to exist to the present day—in much the same way as any regular army renews itself. Its supreme authority is the army convention in session. This convention openly selects twelve men who are representative of the various army sections: the company, the brigade and the general headquarters. These twelve in secret conclave then select seven men, who may be drawn either from among the twelve or from outside this 'electoral college'. The seven men thus secretly chosen form the army council and control the IRA.

Up to the outbreak of the second world war, the leadership was generally of high intellectual calibre. Thereafter, though its sincerity and idealism continued unaltered, the IRA's organisational and leadership quality dropped. At the time of writing (autumn 1965) the organisation is quiescent, a cease-fire having been declared on February 26, 1962. During its first—and best-led—period (the ten years following the breach with de Valera in 1925), the leadership was composed of men who had been active in the Independence struggle against the British, in the Civil War, or—in some cases—in the 1916 Rising. Maurice Twomey, Peadar O'Donnell, Michael Price, George Gilmore, Frank Ryan, Sean Russell, Jim Killeen, Sean MacBride and George Plunkett were all gifted men. Had they chosen (as, in fact, MacBride eventually did), all could have become prominent in constitutional politics, in business or professional life.

POLITICAL CHARACTERISTICS

In its first phase, the IRA concentrated on building itself up with the aim, as George Gilmore told me, of 'having another go'. But within the organisation there was from the start an undercurrent of dissension between the element symbolising the old Fenian tradition (represented by Maurice Twomey) and the 'left' led by Peadar O'Donnell, George Gilmore, Frank Ryan and Michael Price: men inspired by Connolly, Mellows and by socialist principles. The precise degree of the IRA's 'leftishness' at any particular time is a recurring theme of Irish political discussion. Through Peadar O'Donnell, the IRA was certainly linked by association with the campaign against the payment of the land annuities to the Pro-Treaty government of Cumann na nGaedheal. (See pages 75–7 above.) But O'Donnell failed to get the IRA to support the campaign he launched in Donegal in 1924. Fianna Fail, the constitutional opposition party, took it up; the agricultural depression of the late 'twenties and the 'thirties made the campaign to retain the annuities an important factor in Fianna Fail's victory in 1932.

However, the IRA did take a step towards giving itself a socio-political identification with the formation of Saor Eire at a meeting held at No. 35 Great George Street, Dublin, on September 26, 1929. Its objects included, as well as to 'organise and consolidate the Republic of Ireland', the achievement of 'an independent revolutionary leadership for the working class and working farmers' aiming at 'the overthrow in Ireland of British imperialism and its ally, Irish Capitalism'. The only tangible result of Saor Eire* was to get itself outlawed under the provisions of the Public Safety Act of 1931, and denounced as communistic.

The IRA, in fact, has never been communistic as a body, although it is certainly the sort of organisation to which communists would be attracted. But communism has made very little headway in Ireland. The Irish Workers' Party has approximately seventy card-carrying members; most of these seem to be people of modest mental calibre who talk about the 'bosses' and fumblingly follow last year's Moscow line. There are perhaps some half-dozen really able activists. But on the whole the more cerebral Irish communists seem to be affected by the 'fat communist' syndrome: paid jobs in the trade union movement, promotion to which tends to weaken extremist zeal and to divide loyalties. All the same, a curious thing is worth noting in this context. I find that, after the 1956–62 phase of IRA campaigning, a number of the more *simpliste* types who had taken part in the raids had become communists and are now working for the Communist Party in Britain. Their metamorphosis would appear to have occurred after the Catholic hierarchy's condemnation of the raids: a striking example of what can befall a fervent activism not rooted in intellectual judgement.

The Marxist movement in the North is openly known as the Communist Party, but in the South it was known, until March 17–18, 1962, as the Irish Workers' League. At a conference held at that time the name was changed to Irish Workers' Party. Some idea of its flavour may be gained from the irate comment of Dave Bowman, representative of the British Communist Party at the 1962 meeting. He noted in his report that the bulk of the delegates seemed more concerned with the restoration of the Irish language than with such matters as the Common Market and NATO. A very proper British Marxist viewpoint! But most Irishmen, of whatever party, would agree that this was a highly suitable order of priorities. After all, the 1916

* Saor Eire's executive committee consisted of: Sean McGuinness, Fionain Lynch (deputising for McGuinness, who was in prison), Sean Hayes, Maire Laverty, Helena Maloney, Sheila Dowling, D. McGinley, Michael Fitzpatrick, Sean MacBride, Michael Price, Peadar O'Donnell, David Fitzgerald, M. Hallisey, P. McCormack, T. Kenny, L. Brady, N. Boran, J. Mulgrew and E. Maguire.

Rising must surely be the only one in this century in which 'bourgeois' nationalism succeeded in infiltrating the Marxists. The Irish Republican Brotherhood took over Connolly's Citizen Army, not vice-versa.

This may have been one of the factors which made abortive the trip to Russia in 1924 taken by Sean Russell and other Republicans with a view to getting Soviet aid for the cause. In the party was a man sent on behalf of the more cautious elements in the movement to keep an eye on the others. A splendid old character who later joined Fianna Fail, he told me the scheme for Soviet help foundered on the fundamental divergence between the Red and the Green concepts of the meaning of the word 'revolution'. The Russians, it seems, were chary of handing over their machine-guns to 'comrades' who strongly objected to being addressed as 'communists'.

The 1962 meeting of the Workers' League/Party laid much stress on the need for disseminating socialist ideas 'in the spirit of Connolly and Larkin'. This sort of 'front' usage by Marxists of the two men's names has generally meant that neither of them has been properly appreciated in his own country. Connolly and Larkin, of course, were both Marxists in the sense that they believed the class struggle and revolution to be the means for achieving victory for the workers. But they were Catholics, not atheistic materialists, and both received the last sacrament before they died. This double image of Connolly—Marxist and Irish Catholic—is not without its value to the communists, who associate his name with groups in Britain controlled by them which aim at attracting Irish emigrants.

Apart from the Soviets which blossomed briefly in the 1921–23 period (mentioned on page 73 above), the most determined Marxist effort was made in the election of 1927. Jim Larkin, his son James and John Lawlor contested seats in Dublin as candidates of the Irish Workers' League. Lawlor and the younger Larkin split the leftwing vote, which led to the defeat of Thomas Johnson, leader of the Labour Party, and of one of his colleagues. Jim Larkin was elected, but soon unseated on the grounds of his being an undischarged bankrupt. Six years later, on March 29, 1933, there was a riot in which the headquarters of the Revolutionary Workers Group (a communist section of the IRA) were set alight. Some say this was the work of enthusiasts in the Saint Patrick's Anti-Communist League; but the riot probably had as much to do with Civil War animosities as with Vatican versus Kremlin. Members of the Army Comrades' Association were involved, it seems.

On June 11, 1933 a body openly calling itself the Communist Party of Ireland emerged into the light of day with a paper, *The Irish Workers' Voice*. This body was involved in the Bodenstown riots at Wolfe Tone's grave in 1934 and 1935. But, except for a period during the second world war, few either in the IRA or out of it ever showed much enthusiasm for a political movement which logically meant flying the Red Flag instead of the tricolour sanctified by Easter Week. The CPI disappeared from the scene before war broke out in 1939, but the Irish Workers' League remained in the field and advanced in prestige and strength when Russia entered the war. It became, if not fashionable, then at least not markedly unpopular. Its worst moment, so far, came with the Russian repression of the Hungarians in 1956. There was a near-riot by demonstrating students at a Dublin bookshop run by one of the League's oldest supporters. Members of the League (now the Irish Workers' Party) have contested elections under various socialist labels. The political impression they make is exemplified in the experience of Michael O'Riordan, a Dublin bus conductor, who finds that his passengers, while willing to board his vehicle, are not inclined to fellow-travelling.

It is sometimes said that the small Marxist group in Ireland has served a useful purpose in that it has injected new economic ideas into the Irish body politic. This is perhaps true to some extent. But my own observation of the movement is that its better brains become 'fat communists' as they move up promotional ladders in the trade unions, journalism or civil service, and quietly abandon their earlier Marxist fervour.

The major phases of activity of the IRA after the Civil War were: from 1926 to 1936; from 1939 to 1946; and from 1956 to 1962.

FIRST PHASE: 1926–36

This was the period when the IRA was at its strongest, both numerically and in leadership. It had then certainly 15,000 and possibly as many as 30,000 members. In this phase it was using the weapons which had been dumped at the cease-fire ending the Civil War. Sean Russell, director of munitions of the IRA, had moved most of the arms from these dumps to new hide-outs, so that when the army council was set up it had the use of a sizeable arsenal, including a shipment of Thompson submachine-guns which had arrived from America too late for use against the British. But there was little or no ammunition for them in IRA stores.

But this time, however, the Irish people as a whole were sick of terrorism and gunmen. By persevering in building up its strength while refusing to give wholehearted support to the agitation against annuities or to give itself a social raison d'être, the IRA lost what chance it might have had of becoming a political power in the land. The fact of its being an armed and secret organisation maintained on a voluntary basis led inevitably to killings which alienated public sympathy still further. Its embroilment in gang warfare with the Blueshirts siphoned off much of its purpose and made it an easier target for government retaliation. The coup de grâce to this phase was delivered by the formation at Athlone on April 8, 1933 of a break-away group: the Republican Congress.* The leading spirits in the Congress were expelled from the IRA, and supporters of the two rival organisations clashed at Wolfe Tone's grave on the annual pilgrimages there in 1934 and 1935.

The Republican Congress was anti-fascist, anti-imperialist, anti-Fianna Fail, anti-Cosgravite. Its main asset was its paper (*Republican Congress*) edited with fire and brimstone by Peadar O'Donnell. But the Congress itself split within six months of its formation. At a meeting of its national executive on October 1, 1933 Michael Price and Norah Connolly O'Brien dissented from their colleagues on the issue of whether to concentrate on forming a united front against imperialism of workers in every walk of life or whether, as Price desired, to form a Workers' Republic. The Congress was potentially a powerful movement, but it never grew strong enough to contest elections. Even if it had, it is doubtful if the Irish people would have departed from the fierce loyalties of the Civil War legacy to support a leftwing splinter group. Although George Gilmore succeeded in getting some support for the new group in America, trade unionists fought shy of it, and the organisation's newspaper, *Republican Congress*, was dead by the end of 1935. The same year saw also the demise of *An Poblacht*—killed by official action. During much of this period it appeared with large blank spaces showing where some specially abrasive prose had displeased the police. The *Republican Congress* simply faded away through lack of support.

Even so, activities such as these made Irish politics very lively in the 'thirties. As mentioned earlier, both in 1934 and 1935 Wolfe Tone's grave at Bodenstown was the scene of near-riots among Republicans during the annual pilgrimages. In addition to the encounters between Blueshirts and IRA men (described in chapter 4), there were gatherings of the unemployed and protest marches of the jobless in which IRA men participated on their own initiative and without the support of the army's leadership. In these years, Frank Ryan's tall figure was one of the sights of Dublin, haranguing fiery meetings which usually concluded with the ceremonial burning of the Union Jack.

But there was, and still is, a darker side to the Republican movement. On the night of November 14, 1926, twelve police barracks were attacked

* The Republican Congress's manifesto was signed by the following (the dagger-sign indicating members of the Saor Eire executive): Mrs Connolly O'Brien, Michael Price,† Sean McGuinness,† Patrick Lynch, Thomas Maguire, Sheila Humphries, Maire Laverty,† Brian Corrigan, Eithne Coyle, Patrick Norton, Seamus McCann, Joseph Doyle, Robert Emmet, Patrick Gralton, John Joe Hoe, Michael Feely, George Gilmore,† Sean Mulgrew, Peadar O'Donnell,† Liam Kelly, James Cahill and Peter Doolan.

and two unarmed policemen killed. The Free State's minister for Justice, Kevin O'Higgins, was assassinated on Sunday July 10, 1927. As was said in chapter 3, there was never sufficient evidence to bring charges against anyone for the killing. This must be borne in mind by the reader. The fact that, in a city like Dublin where almost everything becomes public knowledge after a time, no one breathed a word about the killers is in itself strong evidence that very few men took part, and serves to confirm Eoin MacNeill's statement that he saw only three men at the scene of the crime. The murder has been variously attributed to the IRA and to people involved in the army Mutiny. There was never any evidence to support either of these theories. I have been able to establish that the IRA officially had nothing to do with the killing, nor do I think that any of the mutineers were involved in the crime. I am inclined to subscribe to the following account which was given me by a man who could hardly have been better placed for learning the truth. I have been able to make a check on some circumstantial details which bear out his version.

There was, it would appear, no plot of the IRA as an organisation to murder O'Higgins. But there were not a few men in it who thought he would be better dead. My informant explained: 'If some woman at a meeting would shout out: "What about the seventy-seven executions", O'Higgins would say something like: "You're wrong, ma'am; there were more than that shot". So these two fellows decided that there'd be more than that shot, all right.' The 'two fellows' is not inconsistent with MacNeill's statement, assuming the third man to be the driver of the get-away car referred to earlier. The murderers' purpose was made easier of accomplishment by the purely fortuitous circumstance that O'Higgins' guard did not accompany him to Mass that Sunday morning. The murderers apparently stole a car, lay in wait, shot him, and drove off. One of them fulfilled another engagement he had planned for that day, and drove to the South where he played in a Gaelic football match. I have checked my informant's story in this particular. The circumstantial evidence for it is such that I should be putting fourteen men, some of whom may still be alive, under suspicion if I revealed what match and what team (which was the winning team) I believe he played in. The second man was subsequently killed when the pair of them were sent out on an 'official' IRA execution and their plan misfired. If my information is right in leading me to believe that the third man, the driver of the car, was later killed in a road accident, there would thus be only one man alive who knows the true story: the football-playing murderer.

I asked an ex-IRA man (not my informant for the account given here) whom I had reason to suspect knew something about the killing, if he had been involved in it: 'No', he said, 'but it was a frightful nuisance. Myself

18—ISTR

and the brother were planning to kidnap himself and Cosgrave that month, and the killing put paid to the whole scheme. We weren't going to shoot them at all—just knock them on the head and keep them as hostages!'

The severe legislation which followed the murder of O'Higgins, and the public reaction against the killers, restricted the IRA's activities until January 1929. Then a campaign of intimidating jurors began. It was designed to prevent juries from bringing in verdicts of guilty in cases where IRA men were brought to court—usually for illegal drilling. The campaign resulted in several deaths, including that of Superintendent Curtin who was shot outside his home in Tipperary after giving evidence in a case of illegal drilling. The authorities met the situation by drastic public safety measures, including the setting up of military courts and the adoption of a cat-and-mouse policy; IRA suspects were picked up at frequent intervals, jailed, released, and jailed again.

The cry of 'release the prisoners'—always a potent political incantation in Ireland—now began to sound in Fianna Fail's favour. As the general election of February 1932 drew nigh, the IRA threw itself behind Fianna Fail. Promises to sack unpopular judges and to abolish the Criminal Investigation Division of the police force were made from some of the party's platforms. As it turned out, however, the rabble-rousers were disappointed. True, David Neligan (Michael Collins' old friend, the then head of the CID) found himself shunted off to the Department of Lands; and General O'Duffy was dismissed from government service. But there was no general purge under Fianna Fail. Democracy won out over partisan vengeance by the new leaders of the country. The importance of this for the future—which is to say the Ireland of today—cannot be over-emphasised.

The 'release the prisoners' cry was, however, answered. Frank Aiken's first official act as minister for Defence was to drive to Arbour Hill barracks on the day the new Dail was approved (March 9, 1932) and, with the minister for Justice (James Geoghan), make arrangements for the release of the IRA prisoners. Of these, the most celebrated were Frank Ryan and the Gilmore brothers, George and Charley. The latter had been arrested following the discovery of the famous arms-dump at the Hell Fire Club in the Dublin mountains. But George went behind bars in circumstances which even Cervantes could not have invented. He was caught near the Pine Forest (near the club) by two police officers. While one went to fetch reinforcements, the other remained sitting on his chest. Giving a sudden twist, George Gilmore managed to reverse the position. The policeman suggested that they while away the time by discussing astronomy. Since such a discussion, to be properly conducted, would have entailed looking upwards, and since he felt that circumstances required him to keep his gaze directed on the man beneath him, Gilmore made a counter-proposal: that they discuss botany, discourse on which would have a downward-looking character. After some time, the policeman complained that his face was a mass of rashes from his brushing against stinging nettles in their earlier struggle. Gilmore, having asked and received the officer's parole not to attack him, went for some dock leaves which, carefully applied, soothed the stings. When the reinforcements arrived, the IRA man put up a tremendous struggle before being finally taken away. He could have got free, but he was afraid that, in searching for him, the police might find his brother Harry who was in the vicinity guarding a dump. (The police officer, ex-Superintendent O'Reilly, verified this story. He told me, 'Give George my regards'.)

George and Charley Gilmore refused to accept prison clothes, with the result that, apart from towels, both went naked during the winter of 1931–32. Their barred cell-windows had no glass. Because of their extreme intransigence, they were refused all reading materials. However, the prison chaplain overcame this difficulty by purchasing out of his own pocket the complete works of Thomas Aquinas. George Gilmore, a dedicated socialist, would probably have preferred other literature had the choice been allowed him, but both he and Charley were highly appreciative of the chaplain's kindness. Such intransigence not only made things difficult for the authorities but also kept up morale and gave the incarcerated a certain 'militant initiative'.

The Military Tribunal was abolished on March 18, 1932, and de Valera made known his intention of making a *Sean na Scuab* (perhaps best translated as 'a stuffed dummy') of the governor-general. But the IRA were unimpressed. Their attitude was still that of the men who had seized the Four Courts. Fianna Fail was not the party of their heart's desire by any means. In *An Poblacht* of March 12, Maurice Twomey wrote: 'Fianna Fail declares its intention to chop off some of the Imperial tentacles; every such achievement is of value and will be welcomed. Notwithstanding such concessions, the Irish Republican Army must continue its work.' The organisation went on with its recruiting. It allowed some of its members to break up Cosgravite meetings, others to conduct a boycott of British goods.

The election of 1933, as mentioned in chapter 4, was largely a trial of strength between, on the one hand, the Army Comrades' Association and Cumann na nGaedheal, and, on the other, the IRA and Fianna Fail. The ACA and the IRA fought it out with knuckleduster and cosh in clashes which became more frequent when General O'Duffy, dismissed in February from his post as commissioner of police, was installed as leader of the Blueshirt movement in July. It became obvious that the ordinary, unarmed police force was unable to deal with the situation. To counter the Blueshirts, the government on August 12, 1933 formed the s division (the 'Broy Harriers'), recruited from Anti-Treaty members of the IRA. Ten days later, the Military Tribunal was set up again, this time by a Fianna Fail government.

But this did not immediately improve the situation. On October 29, 1933 a man called O'Reilly was beaten to death after having been denounced in *An Phoblacht*. An old man died on January 3, 1934 after being struck on the head by a Republican supporter. The worst outrage of this period occurred in Dundalk where, on February 8, a bomb was thrown into a Blueshirt supporter's house, fatally injuring his mother and maiming two children. General O'Duffy's leadership and his campaign for non-payment of rates were disrupted. On August 13, 1934 a boy called Lynch was shot dead by members of the s-division (Broy Harriers) of the police force when the Blueshirts attempted to break up a cattle sale in Marsh's auction yard at Cork. Before this, the Blueshirts had been cutting down telegraph poles and felling trees in a countrywide campaign to prevent sales in distraint of rates from taking place. The shooting of the boy Lynch was condemned all over the country. At the subsequent court hearing (of a case for damages brought by the boy's father: the shooting as such was never brought to court), the s-division was censured by Judge Hannah (April 5, 1937) as 'an excrescence on the regular body of the police'.

The IRA now began to feel the effects of Fianna Fail's strategy. In the first place, the political system was clearly becoming markedly more Republican than under the previous Cosgrave dispensation. Secondly, there was the effect of the Military Tribunal, in the use of which de Valera's government had the support of the opposition: support denied government when Cumann na nGaedheal was in power and Fianna Fail in opposition. The prisons were now filled with 'unconstitutional' Republicans, imprisoned by 'constitutional' Republicans. Thirdly, there was the effect of a Pensions Act, introduced by Fianna Fail on August 1, 1934, which gave pensions to those who had fought on the Republican side during the Civil War. This weaned a considerable number of the older militants from the activist ranks of the IRA. Many younger IRA men and intending recruits were attracted to the Volunteer Force (known as Aiken's Volunteers) which the government set up as a constitutional outlet for youthful ardour.

Three particularly shocking killings completed the alienation of public sympathy although they were, in fact, carried out without the knowledge or sanction of the army council. Richard More O'Ferrall, a young man aged twenty-one, was fatally shot on February 9, 1935 as he tried to prevent a group of armed men from taking his father away to maltreat him in some way. The IRA had been asked by some of the tenants to intervene in a land dispute on the Edgeworthstown estate for which More O'Ferrall senior was the agent. In March 1936, Admiral Somerville of Castle-townsend, County Cork—a veteran old salt of seventy-two—was shot dead because he had been in the habit of giving advice and references to anyone asking for them with a view to joining the British navy. A month later, on April 26, a young man called John Egan was murdered in Dungarvan, County Waterford. He was a former member of the IRA, and it is believed that he had refused to take part in the Somerville killing.

The whole country was outraged, and the government struck hard. In June 1936 the IRA was declared to be an unlawful organisation; the annual pilgrimage to Wolfe Tone's grave was banned; and Maurice Twomey, the army's chief of staff, was sent to prison. Stern governmental logic had forced Fianna Fail into the same attitude towards its old ally as Cumann na nGaedheal had once been driven to adopt towards the militant founders of Fianna Fail.

Spanish Interlude

After Twomey's arrest, the focus of IRA activity changed for some two years to Spain. About 200 Irishmen took part in the Spanish Civil War on the Republican side (as against the 700 or so enlisted in O'Duffy's detachment on the Franco side). Most of the Irish who fought for the Spanish Republic were IRA men. About forty of them, in a mainly English company, took part in the battle of Lopera. After ten days there were only sixty-six left out of the whole company of 120. Going into battle on the first day, the Irish sang the old Volunteer song: *We're off to Dublin in the Morning*, and shouted: 'Up the Republic'. 'You know', said Frank Edwards, one of the survivors, 'I think they meant the Irish Republic'. I think so too.

Most of the IRA men who fought were following Frank Ryan's example. Ryan is remembered in Dublin as a likeable man. An Irish Marxist with more courage than political acumen, he was to die in Hitler's Germany as an honoured guest of the Nazis.

In the battle for the Ebro in 1938, Ryan was captured by a group of Mussolini's troops. (Unlike these troops and Hitler's, both Ryan's men and O'Duffy's pro-Franco regiment were genuine volunteers.) The Italians at first hoped to exchange him for one of their captured officers, but the exchange negotiations broke down and Ryan was handed over to the Spanish Nationalist troops. He was immediately sentenced to death for 'mass murder and arson', and thrown into the condemned cell of a Spanish dungeon with eighteen other prisoners. Every morning for nine months, nine of his fellow prisoners were taken out and shot and a fresh nine put into the cell. It was de Valera who saved his life. An American journalist had been allowed to talk to the prisoners taken after the Ebro Valley campaign, and his report mentioned that a former Irish editor was in Franco's hands. It was realised in Ireland that this must be Ryan. De Valera sent Franco a telegram asking him to spare Ryan's life. But at the time no one knew if the telegram had changed Franco's mind—least of all Frank Ryan, who scratched his name on a comb, hoping that on his way to the firing squad he would be able to slip it to a prisoner who might survive to tell Ireland of his fate.

It was not until after the end of the Spanish Civil War that a sister of Michael Price's in the Red Cross discovered that Ryan was still alive, whereupon de Valera arranged for a Spanish lawyer to plead for his release. The only result of this was to get his death sentence commuted to life imprisonment: a mitigation of doubtful lenity for Ryan whose health had broken down to the point where he seemed a dying man. But then a German friend of his from student days, Captain Hoven, suggested to the Abwehr (the German secret service) that it would be a shrewd propagandist move to arrange for Ryan's release. Eventually, the head of the Abwehr, Admiral Canaris, became interested; it was finally arranged between de Valera, Canaris and the Spanish secret police that Ryan should 'escape' from a lorry on the way from one prison to another. Not knowing about this plan, Ryan stayed aboard the lorry and duly arrived at his new prison. A second 'escape' was staged. Still uncomprehending, Ryan was bundled over the French frontier at Irun-Hendaye in mid-July 1940. Two days later his liberators took him to eat at the Tour d'Argent in Paris. Prematurely aged at thirty-eight, Ryan had become almost deaf in prison; the Germans had great difficulty in getting him to comprehend the plan which brought him from a life-sentence in a Spanish cell to the elegant cuisine of the Tour d'Argent.*

SECOND PHASE: 1939–46

With Twomey's arrest, Sean Russell became chief of staff of the IRA. He was a man with the soldier mentality which requires specific authority for every action. So as to safeguard himself from the only criticism which really weighs with IRA men—that of their fellow Republicans—Russell persuaded the remnant of the Second Dail, now a very small number†—

---

* For further details of IRA relations with the Germans, see below pages 270–1, 273–4 and 276.

† This group was: Sean O'Ceallaigh, Count Plunkett (father of a signatory of the 1916 Proclamation), Brian O'Higgins, Mary MacSwiney (a sister of Terence MacSwiney), Professor Stockley and Thomas Maguire (one of the signatories of the Republican Congress's manifesto in 1933).

to vest its authority in the army council. On December 8, 1938 the *Wolfe Tone Weekly*, a Republican paper run by Brian O'Higgins and a number of other members of the Second Dail, carried an account of this transfer of power. Thus was re-established the formal link of the IRA with Sinn Fein, a link which exists to the present day. Thenceforward the IRA has recognised its army council as the only lawful government of Ireland.

The new leadership of the IRA was not slow to exert its authority. On January 11, 1939 it sent an ultimatum to Lord Halifax, foreign secretary in Neville Chamberlain's government. Four days later the ultimatum was made public. It called on Britain to withdraw 'her armed forces, her civilian officials and institutions, and representatives of all kinds from every part of Ireland'. It was signed by Sean Russell, Peadar O'Flaherty, Lawrence Grogan, Patrick Flemming and George Plunkett. The following day the bombing campaign in England began. Scotland and Wales were not regarded as hostile. It was reasoned that, since England alone was responsible for the Border, the new fight against her should be carried out on English soil. A shrewd enough move, this detachment of Wales (despite Lloyd George) and Scotland (despite Scotch Unionists like Bonar Law) from complicity in the dismemberment of Ireland.

It should be said at this point that Russell's initiative was not approved by the more clear-thinking Republican elements. George Gilmore, for instance, had written in *Easter Week* (another ephemeral Republican journal) on April 16, 1938 to urge the IRA to take no action which could benefit Germany, as a militant campaign against England would. In the light of the subsequent IRA contacts with the Germans, Gilmore's argument merits recording. The impending war would offer an excellent opportunity for Ireland to leave the Empire and declare herself a Republic. England, he argued, would be in no position to stop this. But, having declared their complete independence, Irishmen should 'line up our Republic with the democratic powers against fascism. It would put the Irish Republic where, I think, all true Republicans would wish to see it: as a friend of democracy instead of as a tool for fascism. . . . When we think of the effects it could have on the Six Counties problem, it opens up possibilities that are almost dazzling.' But the prospect of re-enacting the old drama of 'England's difficulty is Ireland's opportunity' was much more dazzling to the more headstrong spirits in the IRA. It was these, not men like Gilmore, who dictated the course the organisation was to take on the eve of and during the second world war.

To understand what motivated these men, a grasp of IRA theology is necessary. The IRA man's world outlook is one which gazes backward to Wolfe Tone and the United Irishmen of 1798. The successors to the periodical of that name launched by him, and published from generation to generation under different names and different editors, have the same unchanging refrain: 'The British are maintaining Partition. The Treaty was a trick and a betrayal. Cumann na nGaedheal were British agents. De Valera betrayed the Republic when he turned his face from the Second Dail after having led it throughout the Civil War. The police are enemies. The courts must not be recognised, since pleading in them to any charge means recognition of the unlawful state which set them up.'

The police are the ever-present enemy. Atrocity stories proliferate against them. The name of Oriel House, wherein the CID had its head-quarters during the Cosgrave era, ranks with that of Belsen in the young IRA man's inherited memories. His is a world of midnight tramping on lonely hillsides, of secret drilling, of absolute loyalty and immaculate purity. Apart from the occasional thug who inevitably crops up in such a movement, the typical IRA man is a quiet, affable character who leads a life of Carthusian virtue both in speech and private conduct, and with a scrupulous dedication to religious observance from which all the Church's denunciations of his organisation cannot budge him. Ireland's history—its grimmer parts—are as familiar to him as his own name; Ireland's Gaelic culture is his inspiration. Republicanism and the Irish language are the two issues on which a young Irishman will defy and upbraid a bishop. Arguments against taking human life will not move him. As one of the leaders put it to me—a man who had taken part in several raids and spent a number of years in prison: 'They said Pearse was wrong in 1916. If we're wrong today, then de Valera and Lemass and that crowd in Fianna Fail were wrong not to accept the Treaty.' The line runs back to 1798 and beyond. It traverses both logic and history, jobs and family ties. 'You know', said another leader (a man who holds his present job—one far below his abilities—only because his employer ranks his services to him higher than his political proclivities), 'a man can ruin his life in the Republican movement'.

He can also lose it. Between 1936 and 1963, forty-one IRA men died as a result of hunger strike, imprisonment, hanging and premature explosion. Yet of all those who have taken part in raids, only two have been killed in Border raids. Sean South was shot dead in a raid on Brookeborough police barracks in Northern Ireland on January 1, 1957. A companion of his on that raid, a lad of nineteen called Fergal O'Hanlon, was wounded in the stomach and left in an abandoned cottage to die with South's body beside him. The rest of the raiding party had also suffered wounds. Faced with a thirty-mile trek in mountain country before reaching the Border, they had to leave O'Hanlon behind.

I know three of the men who took part in the 1939 campaign. All of them now are exemplary citizens. We will call them Tim, Tom and Terry. Tim was eighteen in 1939: a fresh-faced lad with fair curly hair whom an English jury acquitted because it seemed ludicrous to charge him with terrorism. He was deported and later interned in Ireland. Tim was working in London and became involved with the IRA through going into Mooney's in the Strand for a glass of lemonade—he didn't drink, but thought he might meet an Irishman there. He did—a friend from his home town. 'Hello, Tim', said the friend; 'I didn't know you had got directions too'. 'I haven't', said Tim, 'but if there's anything going on I'd like to be in on it'.* A week later, Tim was in charge of bomb-making for the London area, confecting the explosive material in his digs in Highbury. He stirred the 'Paxo' in one of his landlady's saucepans. This was a mixture of potassium chloride and candle grease which was apt for demolition purposes when set off with a charge of gelignite or dynamite. If arson were the thing required, Tim made up a preparation of black iron oxide, aluminium powder and sugar. The charge was sulphuric acid in a halfpenny balloon. The acid took about two hours to eat its way through the balloon, whereupon it ignited the sugar which in turn ignited the iron oxide and so made a blaze.

Another timing device much favoured by the IRA was a farthing filed on the bias and affixed to the hammer of an alarm clock. When the clock went off, the farthing on striking closed a circuit to a detonation charge. Army manuals recommend that pliers be used in creating this particular infernal machine. Tim used his teeth. His English landlady accomplished far more than the English courts when she discovered his materials and patiently flushed hundredweights of it down the WC. (Her other paying guest was a British soldier!)

Tom joined because his is an old Republican family. This young man spent the early days of the war in Dublin compiling, under orders, a list of 300 names, including those of anti-German IRA leaders. The list, differentiating among 'safe', 'doubtful' and 'unreliable', was for the use of the German authorities once they landed in Ireland. He was later interned for four years in The Curragh. The third young man, Terry, joined the IRA after attending a lecture on the life of Wolfe Tone, given to the Wolfe Tone Society by a man who afterwards became a famous judge in Ireland. The boy, inspired by the discourse, tried to do his duty for Ireland and went to prison in The Curragh for four years. There are many Men-Who-Never-Gave-Lectures in Irish society. The Wolfe Tone Society is still flourishing, as are certain ceili dances, sporting organisations, schoolteacher groups and societies like Cumann na mBan and the Fianna Eireann—all of which

* Such is Ireland that Tim knew his friend was in the IRA—in the same vague way as a lad from a small English town would be aware that a friend in another part of the town played football.

continue to exert influences which may yet cause some future Fergal
O'Hanlon to put away the biography of Wolfe Tone, or Emmet, or
Pearse, or Brian Boru, and reach for a rifle to die for Cathleen ni Houlihan.

The way history is taught in some Irish schools has had an appreciable
influence on IRA recruitment. In fact, I would go so far as to say that there
are young men in early graves because of the flame-hot impress on
their minds of the interpretation given them at school of their country's
history. The minister for Education told me in 1965 that he was not satisfied with this teaching. Yet as he spoke, impressionable teenage boys in the
schools run by a prominent teaching order were still using a history
book containing lurid illustrations of British troops hanging Irish insurgents.

Terry, I think, would still be likely to fall in if the trumpets sounded in
the morning. But Tim and Tom wince when they recall those days.
Indeed, Tim told me that he would inform on his own son if he thought
that prison would keep him out of the IRA. Many parents in Ireland felt the
same way during the outbreak—which is how a good many young men
found themselves in The Curragh out of harm's way.

It was the devotion of the IRA to the past rather than to the realities of the
present which prevented the bombing campaign in England from becoming
a serious factor in the second world war. Had contact with the contemporary situation been established through prior liaison with the Germans,
and had the campaign been synchronised to coincide, say, with the blitz,
anything might have happened. But this is perhaps to judge matters with
the benefit of hindsight. In fact, during the 'thirties Hitler was neither
thinking of invading England nor of encouraging espionage in Ireland
against England. Contact with the IRA was forbidden to German agents.
Two Germans who had IRA contacts through their studies in Ireland,
Helmut Clissman and Jupp Hoven, had both volunteered to give help to
the Abwehr in developing links with the IRA, but their offers were turned
down.

The Germans realised too late the utility which a good many in the IRA
could be to them. And when this did dawn on them, they showed an
extraordinarily maladroit appreciation of the situation. When the bombing
campaign began, a German–American journalist called Oscar Pfaus was
sent to Ireland on February 3, 1939 to make contact with the IRA—through
General O'Duffy! The Germans' subsequent IRA policy continued on this
level of incompetence and achieved nothing beyond adding to the difficulties of de Valera in maintaining neutrality. A number of Nazi spies
were dropped in Ireland but were picked up almost immediately. One who
escaped the net for some time—the brave and honourable Dr Herman

Goertz—put the final touch of futility to the whole episode by committing suicide before being repatriated at the end of the war.

However, Dublin being Dublin (to this day anyone wanting to contact the IRA need only put four pennies in a public telephone and ring the *United Irishman* for an appointment), Pfaus—after being balked in his approach to O'Duffy—eventually met Maurice Twomey, Sean Russell and a number of other IRA leaders. The IRA decided that some contact with Germany might be politic, and sent James O'Donovan to Germany to establish links with the Abwehr. O'Donovan, a munitions expert in the struggle against the British, had retired from the IRA at the end of the Civil War in which, of course, he had taken the Anti-Treaty side. In 1939 he held a comfortable job with the Electricity Supply Board, but when Sean Russell approached him to come out of retirement, he resumed his bomb-making classes for young IRA men. His most famous pupil was the late Brendan Behan. (Anyone appraising Behan's literary achievements might bear in mind that Russell's bomb-making establishment in Killiney was his preparatory school and the prisons of England his university.) It was O'Donovan who drew up the Sabotage Plan (the s plan) directed at power grids and stations, factories and communications. These ostensibly were the objectives throughout the campaign against England.

Following Pfaus's meeting with the army council, the Germans hoped that the IRA would create enough trouble in the North-East of Ireland to draw off British troops from the theatres of war. Certainly, throughout the war the IRA were a constant source of worry, both in Dublin and London, and served to exacerbate Irish–British relationships. But, though policemen and civilians also were killed, the campaign's prospects for success rested so heavily on factors like Tim's landlady's saucepan (and the good lady herself) that in reality it was never a serious threat. If it had been, things would not have been very pleasant for the land the IRA sought to serve: the British seizure of Ireland would have been a near-certainty. British and Irish alike have good cause to thank Heaven for the general ineffectiveness of the IRA's campaigning. For example: my friend Tim and a fellow arsonist, a man of thirty-five, decided to burn down the National Gallery in Trafalgar Square. They made their plans and their balloon bombs. The young, innocent face of Tim smiling pleasantly above his open-necked white shirt would have been a certain passport to success in placing the bombs. But the older man, a plumber, decided to call the attempt off: not that he had any regretful feelings about the paintings—the worth of which he had not the slightest appreciation; but he reasoned that 'there's too many tiles in the place for it to burn properly'.

Even so, for all that it failed dismally of its object, the campaign at its launching bid fair to set all England by the ears. It broke on a bewildered country with a series of explosions, most notably in Birmingham, Manchester and London. In July 1939 the Prevention of Violence Bill was introduced in the House of Commons to deal with the situation. In moving it, Sir Samuel Hoare, the Home Secretary, gave details of the outrages which had taken place since January. There had been 127 incidents involving one death and fifty-five hospital cases. Six IRA men were in prison. The police had seized two tons of potassium chlorate, 1,000 detonators, seven gallons of sulphuric acid, four hundredweight of aluminium powder and fifty-five sticks of gelignite.

The campaign had aimed to destroy property without taking life—though this was hard to appreciate by a British citizen put in peril of his life by explosions in pillar boxes and public lavatories. But the decision to deal with the situation by the Prevention of Violence Bill (presented on July 24 and passed in swift order from Commons to Lords to receive the royal assent on July 28) seems to have given an ugly turn to the IRA's plans. While the debate was in progress, two fresh suitcase explosions occurred at King's Cross and Victoria stations. The first fatally injured one man (his legs were blown off) and badly injured two others. The Victoria explosion maimed five people. Both did considerable damage. The bill compelled the Irish in Britain who had been born in Ireland to register with the police like any other non-British nationals, curtailed their entry and provided for the deportation of suspected persons. The railway station outrages intensified police activity and hundreds of Irishmen were sent back to Ireland.

There followed an even bloodier outrage. On August 25 at Coventry an explosion killed five people, wounded seventy others and caused great damage. Coventry was later to know a greater frightfulness than this, but the circumstances of that explosion shocked to the very core an England which was still at peace. The bomb had been left on the carrier of a bicycle leant against a wall in the middle of a shopping street crowded with people: men and women of all ages, young girls and boys, and mothers with babies in their prams. Two IRA men, Barnes and MacCormack, were hanged on February 7, 1940 for their part in the explosion. It had been intended to blow up a power station, but the rider of the bicycle had been delayed on his way there. As detonation time approached he panicked, left the bicycle against a wall and fled away. His identity remains unknown: to the English, that is. It is generally held in IRA circles that neither Barnes nor MacCormack had anything to do with this particular explosion.

With the Coventry explosion, the bombing campaign reached its climax and thereafter fell away. Restricted in scope by intense surveillance in England, in Ireland the IRA was curtailed by new legislative measures. The Offences Against the State Bill became law on June 14, 1939. It enabled the government to reintroduce the Military Tribunal for the third time and provided for the internment of prisoners without trial. A Treason Bill, prescribing the death penalty for acts of treason, had become law on May 30. This fresh legislation was necessary because the new Constitution had made no provision for such crimes.

An internment camp was opened at The Curragh in County Kildare, while in Northern Ireland a prison ship was anchored in Lough Neagh in which over the war period hundreds of IRA supporters were locked up. The camp was opened under the terms of the Emergency Powers Act which was passed into law on January 4, 1940 as a direct reaction to the IRA's most daring and brilliant achievement since the end of the Tan War: the Magazine Fort Raid. The fort, situated in the Phoenix Park in Dublin, held the bulk of the ammunition with which the Irish army would defend the country in the event of an invasion. At 8.35 p.m. on December 23, 1939 the IRA raided the fort, locked up the guard and got away with 1,084,000 rounds of machine-gun and rifle ammunition—all without a shot fired or a drop of blood spilled. The ammunition was intended for the Thompson machine-guns acquired in 1926 from the Civil War arms dump. But after the most intensive police and army search in the history of the state, the greater part of the ammunition was recovered within a week. The arrests and internments following the raid sapped the strength of the organisation. An extraordinary internal controversy, described later, finished it off as a serious force of subversion for the duration of the second world war.

Sean Russell had gone to America early in 1939 to raise funds and support for the campaign against England through the agency of Clan na nGael. His place as chief of staff was taken by Stephen Hayes. Russell made world headlines when the Americans locked him up in Detroit before the arrival of King George and Queen Elizabeth. No fewer than seventy-six members of Congress of Irish descent signed a protest demanding an explanation from Roosevelt: a symptom of the reaction among their Irish-American constituents. The royal visit over, Russell was set at liberty. But by the spring of 1940 his visa had expired; he faced deportation and The Curragh. He made contact with German circles in New York, and it was eventually arranged, with the aid of Admiral Canaris, that he should be smuggled to Genoa and thence travel to Germany. He arrived in Berlin on May 3, 1940.

Of all the conspirators and agents provocateurs whom the Germans assembled at the wheels of their war machine, Russell and Ryan were two of the most unusual. Ryan refused to speak to a German acquaintance for three days after he had told him a dirty story. Russell amazed the Nazis by spending his time in a 9 a.m. to 5 p.m. routine devoted to studying the latest sabotage techniques, regular attendance at Mass and, like Ryan, no dissipation whatever. The two of them did not meet until August 4 when the Germans decided to take what they considered was the 'risk' of introducing them to each other. Ryan they regarded as a communist who should, by definition, be anathema to Russell. But to the Nazis' surprise, the pair nearly wept with joy at the meeting. 'Isms and 'ocracies' mean very little to Irish Republicans: the cause, Ireland, is their fundamental belief. The next day, Ribbentrop, the German foreign minister, saw Russell in the presence of Canaris and grudgingly gave his approval to a plan to send the Irishmen back to Ireland to do whatever Russell decided was best for his cause—on the general theory that what was good for that cause could only be bad for England. It was an extremely looseknit arrangement about which Ribbentrop, who disliked the Irish as a race, was unenthusiastic. But the pair left Wilhelmshaven on August 4 in a u-boat seconded to special service by Admiral Doenitz. Twenty-four years before, Roger Casement had set out on a similar mission: as ill-fated as theirs was to be.

By August 14, Russell was dead, apparently from a perforated gastric ulcer. He died in Frank Ryan's arms when the submarine was 100 miles west of Galway. Russell had been put in charge of the operation. Ryan, who knew nothing about the details, returned to Germany. This fortune-battered idealist died in Dresden from pleurisy and pneumonia on June 10, 1944—tormented with pain, lonely and broken-hearted.

To the end of the war, the name IRA remained something to conjure with among the Irish people. Shootings, executions, hunger-strikes and prison break-outs occurred spasmodically every year until 1946.* A typical incident was that of August 16, 1940 in which two IRA men—Paddy McGrath and Tom Harte—killed two policemen who were about to arrest them. Both Harte and McGrath were subsequently hanged. These four deaths were completely unnecessary, since the worst fate that could have befallen the IRA men would have been internment for the duration of the wartime emergency.

The Special Branch police had a grim time of it. In another incident earlier that year, on May 7, two of them—Gardai MacSweeney and Shanahan—were machine-gunned as they drove on a motor bicycle to deliver mail to Sir John Maffey, the British government's representative in Dublin. Though riddled with bullets, they managed to draw their revolvers, beat off their attackers and save the mail. Both lived and were promoted

---

* Altogether, if we exclude the deaths of Ryan and Russell already mentioned, twenty-six IRA men lost their lives between April 1939 and May 1946. Nine were executed; five killed in gun battles with police on both sides of the Border; six died in prison hospitals; three died on hunger-strike; two were killed in mishaps with guns or bombs; and one was shot by military police in The Curragh. Between 1940 and 1942, six members of the Irish police force were killed, usually in cases where IRA men resisted arrest. All told, since the foundation of the state, sixteen policemen have been killed as a result of IRA action.

for their courage. On top of activities like this, the IRA also operated a radio transmitter during the early days of the war. It went on the air at teatime and caused a good deal of perturbation by the plausible evidence it gave of the great strength of the organisation.

But by June 30, 1941 the IRA had destroyed itself internally. On that day, a group of IRA men from the North kidnapped Stephen Hayes, the chief of staff who had succeeded Sean Russell. They accused him of betraying the organisation to the Free State government—as both the IRA and the Nationalists in the North continue to refer to the authorities in Dublin, for them (as for the Unionists also!) the capital of only twenty-six counties. Sean MacCaughey was the master-mind of this strange episode in IRA history. He was to die on hunger-strike in May 1946 at Portlaoghaise prison. MacCaughey had succeeded Hayes as chief of staff; his old leader gave evidence against him at his trial, himself being sentenced to five years' penal servitude under the emergency legislation. Hayes is still alive, residing in the South of Ireland: a solitary, pathetic figure.

According to a sensational pamphlet, Hayes on being kidnapped and under interrogation confessed to having passed on all the IRA's plans to the government. De Valera's administration, in the weird reasoning of the pamphlet, was held to be responsible for a series of lurid misdemeanours, including the bombing campaign in England: the Irish government was alleged to have sponsored the bomb outrages in order to put pressure on the British to settle the Partition question. At the same time, it was also held culpable of the death of Sean Russell, who was supposed to have been shot at Saint Nazaire by a British agent, acting on information received from the Irish government! Hayes' statement opens with the words: 'This confession . . . has been made voluntarily by me'. In view of the fact that Hayes was savagely beaten and starved during his captivity in the hands of men of his own organisation, this admission may be disregarded. He claims that he wrote everything required of him in an attempt to buy time until he could escape. He was interrogated and threatened with death in six different houses which, as far as one can gather, were in a radius of over fifty miles. Marched by night over fields and bogs, he ended up in Terenure in the south of Dublin. From here he managed to make his escape and gave himself up to the authorities. The appearance of the legendary chief of staff of the IRA in a Rathmines police station, a cloud of treachery about his head and chains around his legs, asking for police protection from his own men—this cracked the organisation's morale. There ensued a period in which the IRA had a new chief of staff every few weeks. The prisons and The Curragh continued to fill with IRA men.

The security police, moreover, caught every one of the ten foreigners who sought, with varying degrees of inefficiency, to spy for the Axis. The most notable of these, Captain Herman Goertz, landed in Ireland in 1940. He managed, through the help of Republicans who were not members of the IRA, to stay free for nineteen months. Goertz had nothing but contempt for the wartime IRA. In his book on the wartime links between the IRA and the Germans, *Spies in Ireland* (the best source for this period), Enno Stephen quotes Goertz as saying: 'Nothing more than weakening intrigues and exchanges of fire with the police was achieved. . . . The IRA was outmanoeuvred and overwhelmed by men who had an exact knowledge of all its methods. . . . The IRA's intelligence system was as primitive as that of children playing cops and robbers.' Goertz was certainly right about the 'exact knowledge' of the police. The Irish force has comprehensive and detailed information about IRA personnel and plans.

This we can see with the advantage of hindsight. But at the time, the British and American authorities were unaware of the weaknesses of the IRA, and it is argued, not unintelligently, by sympathisers with the organisation, that the fear of an IRA 'fifth column' was a deterrent to any possible plan for an Allied invasion of Ireland during the war. Certainly, if the Irish government's intelligence service and containment policy had been relaxed, the IRA would have been a much more formidable force than it actually proved to be.

THIRD PHASE: 1956–62

Disgusted with the gang warfare into which 'the Army' had degenerated, some IRA elements arrived at the same decision come to by Fianna Fail twenty years earlier. They went overground, became constitutional and supported Clann na Poblachta. This party then proceeded to go up like a rocket—coming down, as we have seen, like a stick in 1951. But by that time the IRA, with a tenacity possible only in an organisation which produces men willing to die on hunger-strikes for their beliefs, had again attained a position of some strength. Open drilling was once more common by 1952. Although the organisation now had less than 1,000 members, its new paper, the *United Irishman*, increased its sales from week to week.

By the end of 1953, the Republican movement had a number of new groupings within it and a rising tide of support without. The principal body was Sinn Fein: the political and constitutional arm of the IRA. During the 1957 raids, a police officer making an arrest made a pertinent comment on Sinn Fein when he asked an objecting Republican: 'Would you mind telling me when does the Ard Comhairle of Sinn Fein (central executive) cease its meetings and the Army Council begin?' Sinn Fein was based in Dublin, though its activities extended around the country. Another grouping was Saor Uladh (Free Ulster), founded in 1953 in the

North by Liam Kelly of Pomeroy, County Tyrone. Saor Uladh favoured
force as a means of reuniting the island. Its military arm was Laocra Uladh
(Warriors of Ulster). Kelly had the unusual distinction of being elected
to the Stormont parliament, first as an MP and then as a senator, and also
of becoming a member of the Seanad in Dublin. He was charged with
making a seditious speech during the 1953 election campaign, and was
sentenced to imprisonment in December of that year when he refused to
recognise the jurisdiction of the court. Released in August 1954, a demon-
stration to welcome him home ended in what became known as the
Pomeroy Riots. Fifty people were taken to hospital.

Kelly's movement was supported in a number of its activities by a
dissident section of the IRA led by Joseph Christle: a Dublin lawyer well
known throughout the country for his prowess as a cyclist. Christle's group
was dissatisfied with the backward-looking, Second Dail mentality of Sinn
Fein, while being unaware of the IRA leadership's plans for a new major
campaign. Common to all the plans of extreme Republicans was the
determination to strike at the administration of the North-Eastern counties.
The upshot of it all was that in 1956 there were five groups launching
attacks, verbal and otherwise, on the long-suffering Six Counties: Sinn
Fein, Saor Uladh, Laocra Uladh, the IRA proper and Christle's followers.
Saor Uladh and the Christle group got together to burn down six Customs
posts along the Border on Armistice Day (November 11) 1956. This was
greatly to the irk of the 'official' IRA which had laid plans for beginning its
campaign on December 12.

Christle organised one of the most audacious forays of the entire new
outbreak: the rescue on February 12, 1959 of James Andrew May Murphy
of Castledermot, County Kildare, from Wakefield prison in Yorkshire.
The money for this—as for so many other blows against 'Tyrant England'
—came from Clan na nGael in America. A large number of men and
women from Ireland were involved in the affair at its various stages.
Murphy was serving life imprisonment for his part in the Arborfield raid
(see below). Christle arranged for another Irishman, Pat Donovan, to be
sentenced for a phony hold-up so as to plant him in Wakefield prison. At
the time it held two prominent Greek Cypriots and the atom spy, Dr Klaus
Fuchs. Fuchs taught Murphy to play chess and coached Donovan for his
GCE examination (which he subsequently passed). The IRA's offer to include
him in the escape in return for these kindnesses presumably struck the
scientist as excessively generous, for he declined. The London Agreement
signed by Makarios meant that the Cypriots would soon be released any
way, so they also declined. It had been intended to release Joseph Doyle—
serving a life sentence for his part in the Arborfield raid—but his health
had given way under the strain of imprisonment. Fuchs drew up a plan of

the inside of the prison from which a Dublin architect made a model. Murphy was duly 'sprung' and flown back to Ireland from Glasgow. In the end the exploit did not allow for Donovan's release and he served his four-year term. Murphy was upset when, on release, he found that one of his rescuers was a man who, a fortnight earlier, had signed a form in The Curragh camp promising loyalty to the state. Helping prisoners to escape was no way of keeping one's word, Murphy felt.

All that any person interned in Ireland at any stage of the new campaign had to do to be free was to sign this declaration. Even so, were it not for the fact that the government got control of the situation, thereby making it possible to release the prisoners without peril to the state, most of those young men would still be locked up. Both Laocra Uladh and Saor Uladh are now defunct. Laocra Uladh lost an important leader—Brendan O'Boyle, a Dublin jewellery salesman—when a bomb blew up in his car not far from Stormont telephone exchange on July 5, 1955.

Prior to the 1956 campaign, the 'official' IRA had carried out raids for arms on British military barracks in England and Northern Ireland. A raid led by Joe Christle on Armagh barracks in May 1954 was successful, a quantity of rifles being seized. Not so the raid on Omagh the following October; nor did the IRA retain any of the arms seized in a daring and well-organised raid on Arborfield barracks in England on August 13, 1955. Recruits and new support came in the wake of the publicity given to these raids. Sinn Fein meetings in Abbey Street, Dublin, ended with scores of young men enrolling in the movement.

Nor was the IRA dependent on raids for armaments. Following a tradition that dates back to the Fenians, money flowed in from American sympathisers mobilised by Clan na nGael, whose support for the Republican movement is in direct ratio to the prospects at any given moment of 'getting England out'. Collections and donations in Ireland also yielded large sums. Considerable quantities of rifles and submachine-guns were purchased in different parts of the world—particularly in Paris and Manchester—and were smuggled into Ireland. Moreover, the IRA could call on dumps of arms hidden all over the country from earlier conflicts. If present-day IRA sources are to be believed, there is a disquietingly large number of arms-caches still secreted around the Irish landscape. The communiqué of February 26, 1962 which ended the campaign, said: 'All arms and other materials have been dumped'. Dumped—not destroyed.

IRA bomb-making has never been noted for its efficiency. During the campaign, in 1957, a premature explosion killed five young IRA men in a cottage on the Border, intent on yet another Armistice Day exploit. But police vigilance prevented the distribution of a most ingenious variety of hand grenade: a line of cigarette lighters made from old grenade cases which the IRA discovered were on sale in Tokyo. They got through the Customs in sizeable quantities, but were seized when the police found that a gentleman in Dublin was taking the flints out and putting detonators in.

As we have seen, from 1953 militant Republican policy underwent a change in tactics. Like the lesser groups, the IRA decided that henceforth attacks would be directed solely against 'the British occupation in the North'. From then onward it was forbidden to IRA men to fire on the police or military of the Twenty-Six Counties. Guns were to be carried only on raids directed against the Six Counties. If it became necessary to retreat back across the Border, arms were to be dumped. The offensive cost Northern Ireland the lives of seven members of the Royal Ulster Constabulary and £700,000 in outright damage. Apart from an increased expenditure on the regular police force amounting to £270,000, the cost of maintaining a force of special constabulary known as B Specials ran to some £500,000 a year. In the South, the extra security measures taken by the Republic cost an average of £350,000 a year. The attacks on the North also necessitated the re-opening of the detention camp at The Curragh and the reintroduction in July 1957 of the disagreeable Part Two of the Offences Against the State Act, providing for arrest and detention without trial. By the end of 1957, 100 people were interned in the South and nearly 200 in prison or internment in the North. Another measure of the government in Dublin made it an offence to use the term 'IRA' in newspapers; an 'illegal organisation' was the term prescribed—and insisted on.*

The number of men engaged in the actual fighting was around 200. They operated in flying columns, sleeping in the open or in dug-outs, continually on the move and often enduring great hardships. It is not easy to say which body was where at a given time, but the bulk of the active personnel was made up of untrained young men whose distinctive regional accent made them easily identifiable by the Northern police. In all, six lives were lost. The few British-trained soldiers were an inadequately small leavening in the general body of IRA combatants. The fact that the first Northern policeman to be shot was a Catholic drew away a good deal of Nationalist sympathy in the Six Counties. Another factor in the lack of support from the minority over the Border was the calm handling of the situation by the Unionist government at Stormont. The Northern authorities acted with great forbearance and succeeded in restraining the wilder spirits among the Orangemen from reprisals against the Nationalists in Ulster and from counter-attacks across the Border. If these had taken

---

* This often has strange effects on a reporter's prose style. In a report in a Dublin evening paper following a raid in the North, a girl was solemnly quoted as saying: 'Mother, take cover! It's an attack by members of an illegal organisation.'

place, a situation would have been precipitated which could very possibly
have led to open conflict between North and South. This possibility was not
absent from the calculations of the IRA leadership. A cardinal point in IRA
policy was the possibility that a major outbreak would arouse such interest
in the United Nations that the Border would be abolished under international pressure.

At this point a puzzled reader may well ask how it was that militant
Republicanism, in such moral and organisational disarray in 1946, became
such a strong force again by the mid-'fifties? And what was the Southern
government doing to let all this happen? The answer to the first question
lies partly in the new IRA leadership. Men like Tomas MacCurtain (whose
father, the lord mayor of Cork, was shot by Crown forces during the
Independence war), Charles Murphy and Tony Magan were dedicated
and efficient organisers: men of the second generation of militant
Republicanism.

The answer to the second question is more complex. Clann na Poblachta's recent background made it especially difficult for the Coalition in
which it was a partner to deal with the IRA. From 1948, police co-operation
across the Border broke down, and though it was obviously functioning
again by 1957, the period of non-collaboration was of great benefit to the
campaign preparations of the IRA. When Sean MacBride and the remnant
of his party moved the No Confidence motion which finally brought down
the Coalition, his action not only brought Fianna Fail back to power but
also opened the way for more vigorous action against the trouble-makers.
It was easier for the homogeneous party of de Valera to quell the extreme
Republicans than it was for the 'tessellated pavement' of an all-party
alliance kept together solely by opposition to Fianna Fail.

But any Irish government, whatever its party complexion, in dealing
with the IRA is engaged in damping down a fire in a smoke-filled room in
which, somewhere, there is an open can of petrol: a wrong step and the
whole lot goes up in the spreading flames of martyrdom. On the Easter
Sunday of 1940, de Valera was called a traitor by a woman in the crowd as
he laid a wreath on the grave of the men executed in 1916. She was a sister
of one of them, Joseph Plunkett. At that moment her brother Jack was on
hunger-strike in Mountjoy prison. The incident would have been hardly
less embarrassing had W. T. Cosgrave been the prime minister laying the
wreath. Both he and de Valera had followed Joseph Plunkett's leadership
in 1916.

At any moment, admiration for an act of bravery or sympathy for a
young man's death in the cause of Ireland can touch the deep feelings of
the nation's heart. The funeral of Sean South in 1957 was almost a day of

national mourning. Thousands of people followed the cortège from the point on the Border where the body was handed over, through its long roundabout route to his native Limerick where he was buried. In Dublin the hearse halted in Parnell Square; a group of clergy said the Rosary which was responded to by a huge crowd. The outburst of militancy gave renewed support to Sinn Fein. In the March election of 1957 Sinn Fein candidates, under the stimulus of the raids, polled a total of 66,000 votes, despite their announced intention of not serving in the Dail if elected. In the Northern elections on May 26, 1955 Sinn Fein candidates won 152,310 votes—thereby almost obliterating the Northern Ireland Labour Party. Two of the party's candidates for the elections to Westminster in that year —Philip Clarke and Thomas Mitchell—were successful, but were subsequently unseated by court order as convicted felons (they had been captured after the Omagh raid for arms). In the South, county councils passed resolutions condemning their ten-year sentence and praising their bravery.

When the Catholic hierarchy condemned the raids, the IRA issued a circular informing its members that any IRA man who was refused the sacraments would be accommodated by priests sympathetic to the cause. This promise was kept. Indeed, some young priests offered to fight. During the campaign the police found it necessary to call on the principals of certain schools in the Republic to warn them that the propagandist influence of some members of their staffs was sending boys into the IRA. There were fears in official circles that some young officers in the Irish army might become sympathetic to the IRA, if only because (before the UN recruitment of Irish troops) they had almost nothing to do. An attack on the Border could be a good deal more attractive to a lively young officer than the garrison routine of a small, virtually non-combatant army.

Yet in the end, the patient firmness of the North and the resourceful containment policy of the South broke the back of this third major outbreak of IRA campaigning. As early as January 8, 1957, its working plan, known as Operation Harvest, was captured. It gave a list of targets in Derry, Tyrone, Fermanagh, Antrim and Belfast. These included BBC transmitters, bridges, oil refineries, radar stations, RUC barracks, and the destruction of the North's transport and communications system. Nothing like the full programme of sabotage was achieved. The campaign had passed its peak by 1959, and when the cease-fire came in 1962 the IRA was militarily powerless.

But its activities grievously damaged relations between North and South. The B Specials—an armed force of young part-time militia established in the North in 1920—unwittingly wounded or killed innocent travellers and fellow comrades in dozens of trigger-happy incidents. These nervy ambushes made travel in the North a hazardous business, particularly at night in the Border areas. Roads were spiked and cars stopped and searched as a matter of course. The death of Sergeant Ovens of the RUC in August 1957, which led to the arrest of a group of young men the following November, was a focal point of especial bitterness. Ovens, the father of three children, was blown to bits when he kicked open the booby-trapped door of a disused farmhouse. He had been lured there by a telephone call informing him that there were IRA men in the house. The young men were tried, and two of them—Kevin Mallon and Francis Talbot—were eventually given long sentences after a trial in which allegations were made against the RUC of extreme brutality in the extraction of confessions.

THE IRA TODAY

The campaign's failure, the influence of Pope John on Catholic–Protestant relationships, increasing prosperity and the Lemass–O'Neill talks have helped to dull these memories. Yet the IRA itself is far from extinct, although at the end of 1965 it was certainly in a quiescent period compared with the 1956 campaign. When O'Neill repaid Lemass's visit by coming to Dublin for lunch with him in February 1965, the news was not announced until late afternoon in case the IRA should block the road between Dublin and Belfast. The road blocks and riots at Mountmellick which followed Princess Margaret's visit to the district that same month gave evidence of a certain amount of life still left in the IRA.

However, it has lost a good deal of the support it once had from professional people and students. The former will presumably continue to perform services like sheltering a wanted man, subscribing to collections or attending ceilis and lectures. But for the latter, the main point of student entry into the organisation—the IRA branch organised from students of the National University—has been disbanded, partly through official pressure and partly as a matter of IRA policy. Students are frowned on in the movement because they tend to drop out too easily. They also are inclined to organise activities of a prankish nature which get publicity but jeopardise official IRA plans. A case in point was the taking of a picture in the Lane Collection from the Tate Gallery in April 1956. This made world headlines. The ensuing police activity very nearly resulted in the capture of a more serious-minded section of the IRA which was in England at the time, making preparations for a sterner exploit, which did not come off.

Sinn Fein had a split on June 16, 1965 when Sean Caughey in the North announced that he was setting up another organisation—the Irish Union—to secure limited objectives like the reform of local government franchise. He and his supporters differ from the Dublin-based Sinn Fein on the issue of *de facto* recognition of both Irish governments. The Dublin group, led by Tom Gill, Thomas Mitchell, Eamonn MacThomas and Sean Brady, still favours a policy of non-recognition.

As the organisation grows weaker, it becomes in a sense more dangerous. Local units acting unofficially tend to take unauthorised action to show that the organisation is still a force to be reckoned with. Not all the shootings in the campaign against the North were authorised. It cannot be assumed that the IRA will remain quiet. The statement of February 1962, declaring the third campaign ended, also said: 'The Irish Republican Army remains intact, and it is in a position to continue its campaign for the occupied area indefinitely'. This is not entirely bravado. In the summer of 1965, the IRA introduced the new tactics of firing on British warships as they pay courtesy visits to Irish ports. Some young men were arrested in connection with one such incident. The subsequent court proceedings gave rise to demonstrations and near-riots, regarded with such concern that the British Admiralty called off the visit of a gunboat to Cork planned for October 12. My IRA sources inform me that the fiftieth anniversary of the Rising will be made memorable by a series of demonstrations.

Sympathisers with the organisation's aims are by no means lacking in Ireland and elsewhere. In May 1965, the South–O'Hanlon Irish Republican Club was formed in New York, one of its objectives being 'to bring the plight of Ireland under British rule to the attention of the people of the United States'. Among the attractions at a dance sponsored by this organisation was a draw for a handbag and a wallet 'made by prisoners in English jails'. The proceeds were devoted to helping 'the Irish Republic Movement in Ireland'.

12. THE NORTH

The Origins of Divided Ireland · State and Economy: *Governmental*
System; Agriculture, Industry and Welfare
Religion and the Northern Mood · Political Parties:
Unionists; Labour; Liberals; Nationalists · Terence O'Neill
Old Prejudice, New Sensibility: *Discrimination; A New Departure?*

IRELAND'S is the history of the grief agreed upon. Nowhere is this
borne out more fully or more frequently than in the six North-Eastern
counties of Antrim, Down, Armagh, Derry, Fermanagh and Tyrone.
Known during the Home Rule crisis before 1914 as Ulster, they are
nowadays more often referred to in the Republic as 'The Six Counties': a
term which infuriates the Unionists who describe them as Northern Ireland.

The level of physical contact between North and South is low. The
average Southerner does not go North either for holidays or day excursions,
although trains run speedily and frequently between Dublin and Belfast.
The Northerner comes South more readily. A casual ear cocked in a Dublin
restaurant or a Southern holiday resort will ordinarily pick up a considerable volume of Northern cadences.

Before the advent of Pope John and the meetings between Lemass and
O'Neill, the image in the South was of 'the Black North': the land of a
grim, unsmiling, bigoted people whose capital city was as unlovely as the
scenery was unremarkable. In the North, the Republic was generally
depicted for propaganda purposes as a poverty-stricken, priest-ridden,
lackadaisical land of darksome popery. In fact, however, the average
inhabitant of the island, particularly of the younger generation in the
South, went his way without ever thinking about Partition unless a bomb
or a bigot suddenly burst in on his awareness. Even before the recent
indications of a 'thaw', a surprisingly large number of people on both sides
not only felt favourable to conciliation but also took what action they could
to try to improve matters.

Stormont, the parliament house of Northern Ireland, is a magnificent
white stone building: so huge and dramatic in its assertion of determined
perdurability as to arouse in sensitive Southerners uneasy reflections about
Thousand-Year Reichs. A little closer inspection yields the discovery that,
unlike the Dail in Dublin, there are no armed guards in sight. The sternest

figure one sees is the large bronze image of Carson. His back is to the Northern legislature, his gaze fixed on Cave Hill whereon in 1795 Wolfe Tone and his fellow United Irishmen—Russell, Nielson, Simms and MacCracken—swore 'never to desist in our efforts until we have subverted the authority of England over our country and asserted our independence'. Their intention was to form a 'brotherhood of affection, a communion of rights and union of power among Irishmen of every religious persuasion, and thereby to obtain a complete reform of the legislature founded on principles of civil, political and religious liberty'.

The interpretation of what befell this 'brotherhood of affection' will depend on whether one looks at Irish history from an Orange Unionist or a Green Republican position. Only the outcome is indisputable: the division of Ireland. Some readers may feel they have had quite enough of history in the first chapter. They must buckle to and absorb some more. Without at least a rough-and-ready grasp of the twists and turns of Irish history, the present severance of the island will seem an inexplicable compound of folly and malevolence. It may be one or the other, or both— but it is not inexplicable.

THE ORIGINS OF DIVIDED IRELAND

The Norman presence in Ireland began when Dermot MacMurragh, the king of Leinster, enlisted, with the permission of Henry II of England, the aid of a group of Norman barons against his rival chieftains. When Mac-Murragh died, Richard de Clare—'Strongbow'—who had married the king of Leinster's daughter, Aoife, gained control of that kingdom. To the alarm of Henry, this opened up a vista of Norman barons with strong independent power based on their Irish domains. To dispel this nightmare, in 1171 he landed in Ireland, his venture blessed by Pope Adrian, and received the submission of the barons and the Irish chieftains.

To the extreme Republican, this is where 700 years of English oppression began. I asked a contemporary IRA leader who had helped me with information for this book, if his knowledge of Republican affairs went back to the 'thirties. 'It goes back as far as Strongbow', was his answer. Even so, the 'Irishified' Norman barons and the native chieftains were not completely crushed, despite the near-extirpation of the house of Fitzgerald by Henry VII after that family's espousal of the anti-Tudor cause of Lambert Simnel and Perkin Warbeck. Risings against the English authority were endemic throughout the sixteenth century, the last being that of Ulster's 'Great O'Neill'—Hugh O'Neill of Tyrone who finally submitted to James I on the latter's accession in 1603. O'Neill's submission was the end of the Gaelic order and the signal for 'plantation' to begin in earnest. Plantation was a kind of 'pioneer colonisation', with the indigenous occupants of the land regarded with something akin to the tenderness shown to hostile Indians in the Americas. Six Ulster counties were handed over to 'undertakers' to be colonised by Protestant settlers. Many of these came from Scotland, bringing with them the Presbyterian religion.

The ensuing rebellions were put down with the ferocity common to the period. Brutality begot brutality. When in 1641 the Irish rose in rebellion as Civil War broke out in England, the memory of past oppressions, coupled with the recent loss of the lands in Ulster, provoked them to visit bloody vengeance on the Protestant settlers. By the time Cromwell landed in 1649 to restore 'order' in Ireland, the South had risen also. Irish grievances and devotion to the Stuart cause combined to produce a kind of royalist nationalism, Ireland in her despair cherishing the Stuarts as she had earlier cherished the House of York after 1485. Cromwell had to deal with the threat of a royalist springboard for attacks on the new parliamentarian regime in England. But he also felt impelled to avenge the 'massacres of 1641'. Genuine fear (the English at this period were in a state of near-panic at the thought of the royalists' unleashing on them a vast army of 'wild Irish') was exacerbated by religious hatred. Cromwell's soldiers went forth with fire and sword against the Irish like the Israelites against the Amalekites. If the massacres of Protestants by Catholics are still a bitter living memory to many Northerners, Cromwell's reprisals have burnt a deep, still-raw brand in the collective mind of the South.

Perhaps the most heart-rending of the ironies of the common history of the two islands is the grim rhythm whereby whatever served to promote liberty in England was the instrument of tyranny in Ireland. The curtailing of royalist absolutism in the execution of Charles I broke the Irish hope of the Crown as a fount of justice in a barren land. The Glorious Revolution of 1688 which made England safe for representative government made Ireland the haven for religious and economic despotism. With William of Orange invited to England as the Protestant Defender (albeit supported by the Pope who dreaded the hegemony of the Most Christian King, Louis XIV), the one hope for the Catholic Irish lay in supporting the deposed Stuart, James II, when he landed at Kinsale in March 1689. But any prospect that the Irish Protestants might acquiesce in a Stuart monarchy for Ireland (a very remote prospect, indeed) was killed by the confiscation of the estates of 2,000 Protestants by the Jacobite parliament in Dublin. With militant Catholicism now in the ascendant, the Protestants were beleaguered in a handful of towns. The Jacobite forces hoped to overwhelm the resistance before help could come from England. But the apprentice boys of Londonderry shut the town's gates in James' face and withstood with grim, implacable courage the harrowing privations of a fifteen-weeks' siege. The English 'army of liberation' landed. The dethroned king—tugged one way by the interests of Ireland, the other way by his ambition to regain England—proved no match for his supplanter when the two armies met by the Boyne on July 12, 1690. When his army wavered, James fled the field, leaving behind him as hostage to his ruined fortune the life and liberty of Catholic Ireland. The Protestant victory gave the Northerner of today his hero and symbol: William of Orange, 'Good King William'.

The Jacobite cause was crushed, Catholic Ireland broken in body and spirit. But the memories of the grim years, shut up in fortified towns beset by bands of Catholics waiting to destroy them, had quenched whatever glimmer there might have been among the Protestants of a spirit of tolerance and partnership. *Vae victis !*—this, and the determination to keep 'the heads of the papishes under our feet', governed the Williamite settlement of Ireland. The Protestant administration of the penal code can be understood, if not forgiven. As Edmund Burke said, it was 'a machine . . . as well fitted for the oppression, impoverishment and degradation of a people and the debasement in them of human nature itself, as ever proceeded from the perverted ingenuity of man'. But it was not only a system wherein a minority rode roughshod over a majority; a minority within the minority ruled the roost over all. With the Catholic subdued, the Anglican was free to discriminate against his erstwhile Presbyterian ally. This factor is of fundamental importance to the understanding of the political character of the North up to the middle of the nineteenth century. Indeed its consequences endure still. Scratch an ardent Orangeman and you will find hostility to Catholicism conjoined with a worried scepticism towards England: an uneasy pugnacity which keeps sharp look-out for the first hint of a 'betrayal from over there'. There are times when Orangemen are more truly Sinn Feiners than anyone in the South. 'Ourselves *Alone*' is a feeling which nibbles at the edge of the awareness of many in the North. This feeling goes far to explain the hectic extremity of the Ulster reaction to Home Rule before the first world war. It is in large measure the product of what one might call, parodying Bossuet, the 'alienations of Protestantism'.

It was against this Anglican dominance over Catholic and Presbyterian alike that Wolfe Tone struck. By the last generation of the eighteenth century, the Irish Protestants under Grattan had established a largely independent parliament in Ireland, but had done nothing to rectify the wrongs of their Catholic countrymen. Tone, born in 1763 of a Protestant family from Kildare, wrote: 'The Protestants (i.e. Church of Ireland men) I despaired of from the outset because they had an "unjust monopoly" of power, and it was not to be supposed that they would lend themselves to any venture which might lessen that power'. He thought it unnecessary to address himself specially to the Catholics. Since 'no change could make their political situation worse', he counted 'upon their support for a certainty'. The Dissenters, he decided, were 'patriotic and enlightened', and it was to them he addressed in September 1791 his pamphlet, *An Argument on Behalf of the Catholics of Ireland*.

Within a month of its appearance, societies of United Irishmen were formed in Dublin and Belfast. Protestant privilege responded with the Orange Societies, formed 'to maintain the laws and peace of the country and the Protestant Constitution'. The Orangemen grew out of an earlier organisation, the Peep-O-Day Boys: a semi-agrarian, semi-religious body which sprang up in the North out of resentment at the take-over by Catholics of holdings vacated by Presbyterians emigrating to America under the pressure of discrimination by the Established Church. As a counter to the Orangemen there emerged the Catholic Protection Society, popularly known as The Defenders. These derived from the Whiteboy societies: agrarian combinations which, in reaction to the cruel oppressions of the penal code, engaged in acts of savagery and terrorism. Defenders and Peep-O-Day Boys fought a two-day battle at The Diamond in County Armagh in September 1795. The Catholics were beaten, and the Battle of The Diamond joined the larger encounter on the Boyne in the incantatory rites of militant Orangeism. The first Orange lodge was formed soon after the Battle of The Diamond. The Peep-O-Day Boys, with government collusion, commandeered the lands of the defeated Defenders.

Ever since that affray at The Diamond, the Orange Order has served as an elite corps whenever 'retributory action' against Catholics has been felt necessary. The Order has pervaded business and political interests to such an extent that today practically every Protestant in the North who has a job of any consequence is an Orangeman. All members of the government of Northern Ireland are Orangemen. Indeed, for someone who is not a Lodge member to become a Unionist candidate is still a feat almost as prodigious as a Negro's getting selected to contest the senatorial elections for Alabama. Of the 712 delegates to the Unionist Council, 122 are nominated by County Grand Lodges of the Orange Order. Although enlightened Unionist opinion regards the Order as something of an incubus, most Unionists in conversation reveal a respect amounting almost to sacrosanct reverence for the traditions of the Order. Most of them, however, do nothing more within the organisation than indulge in a tremendous day out on the Twelfth of July—the anniversary of the Boyne battle.

Although set back by Wolfe Tone's ill-starred rebellion, the growth of liberal and humanitarian ideas in England eventually brought to an end the penal code, moved thereto by Daniel O'Connell's great agitation of the 1820s. But whereas in England the granting of equal civil rights to Catholic citizens of the United Kingdom meant a Protestant majority's recognising, with small cause for apprehension, the rights of an English minority, in Ireland it raised the bogy of Catholic domination over an Irish minority. The growth in the South of support for Home Rule increased this minority's fears, which were intensified by the alienation of interests as there developed in Ulster during the nineteenth century a Protestant industrial society. Sharing the 'go-ahead' outlook of their equivalents in England, the middle class and the skilled artisans in Ulster became divorced, not only in religious but also in economic and social attitudes, from the mass of the Catholic population. This divorce accentuated the political differences developing between North and South. By 1886, when (as had already occurred several times during the century) Protestant–Catholic rioting broke out, the lines of battle were firmly drawn.

Well aware of the depth of Protestant feeling, the Conservatives in England saw in the Home Rule issue a golden opportunity for overthrowing Gladstone's Liberal administration. Seizing this opportunity with both hands, Lord Randolph Churchill wrote (in a letter to his friend, James Fitzgibbon): 'I have decided some time ago that if the GOM* went for Home Rule, the Orange card would be the one to play'. He went to Belfast and played it, giving the Orangemen the slogan that echoes yet: 'Ulster will fight; Ulster will be right'. Tory opportunism, Liberal vacillation and Orange intransigence combined to pave the road to the 1916 Rising. If it was right for Belfast to fight, then Dublin could claim an identical right.

Yet it was not this fell conjunction which made the road from the Rising so bloody. Appalled at the way the Irish problem was developing, Asquith added to his responsibilities as prime minister the duties of chief secretary for Ireland, going to Dublin. While there he inspected a detachment of imprisoned Volunteers at Richmond Barracks, describing them as 'very good-looking fellows with such lovely eyes'. Seeing post-Rising Ireland through their eyes, Asquith realised that the Home Rule proposals, shelved at the outbreak of war in 1914, would no longer satisfy the new generation of Irish nationalists. With the intention of restoring the Irish Parliamentary Party's control over the South, he asked Lloyd George to try to arrange for a settlement between Redmond and Carson which would separate the North from the South and introduce Home Rule in the latter. There seems to have been a vague feeling that a Celtic radical from Wales might prove sympathetic to Celtic radicals in Ireland. Lloyd George accepted the commission† and succeeded so well in it that by mid-June

---

* I.e. 'Grand Old Man': a term of affection among Liberals, of sardonic contempt among Conservatives.

† By so doing he missed going with Lord Kitchener on his fatal voyage to Russia in HMS *Hampshire*, sunk off the Orkneys on June 5, 1916.

both Nationalists and Unionists had agreed that Home Rule should be introduced straightaway in the South, with the exclusion, until the end of the war, of the six Ulster counties from the jurisdiction of the new Dublin parliament. It was understood by all parties that the final relationship between North and South would be determined by a conference to meet after the end of the war. Pending the outcome of this conference, Redmond's party was to continue to sit at Westminster.

But this settlement was destroyed by Conservatives in England and Unionists in the South—notably Walter Long, Lord Robert Cecil and Lord Lansdowne. Leaders of the Conservative Party who had supported Ulster but who now endorsed the Lloyd George interim settlement—Balfour, Bonar Law, F. E. Smith (the latter two men outstanding before the war in breathing fire and brimstone against the 'disloyal' Liberal government)—were thus in the curious position of being aligned with their erstwhile enemies: Redmond, John Dillon, Joseph Devlin and the rest of the Nationalist Party. It was now a fight between the claims of Northern and Southern Ireland against those of a 'wider imperialism' which regarded Orangemen as only a slight cut above Catholics, and the claim of England to dispose of North and South as superior to the claims of either.

The Lloyd George settlement of 1916 had much to recommend it to three groups: to the Redmondites who saw control slipping away from them; to the Orangemen, who saw their abhorrence of rule from Dublin acknowledged; to the War Coalition leaders, like Asquith, Lloyd George and Balfour, who saw the dangers of the effect of the Irish problem on American public opinion and on the conduct of the war. But the Catholic population of the Six Counties found no cause for rejoicing in the settlement. When Lord Lansdowne (more concerned perhaps about his extensive estates in the South than about imperial unity) told the Lords, in effect, that the South would continue under military rule by the British commander, General Maxwell, and that the Six Counties would be permanently excluded, the Redmondite leadership threw up the sponge in despair. Their followers had been tried to the uttermost and would take no more. The Nationalist Party withdrew its endorsement of the scheme. The subsequent policy of drift under the Coalition government in England brought the Black and Tans to Ireland.

STATE AND ECONOMY

Governmental System

The North today derives its boundaries and its Constitution from the second of Lloyd George's Irish initiatives: the Government of Ireland Act of 1920. As mentioned in chapter 2, the provision in Article XII of the Treaty, allowing the North to opt out of Southern jurisdiction on presentation of an address to the king, was speedily availed of. The Boundary Commission provided for in the Treaty resulted in the London Agreements of 1925, which left the Border in much the same form as it had been delineated in the 1920 Act. This Act also provided for

[a] Council of Ireland with a view to an eventual establishment of a Parliament for the whole of Ireland, and to bringing about harmonious action between the parliaments and governments of Southern and Northern Ireland and to the promotion of mutual intercourse . . . to providing for the administration of services which the two parliaments mutually agree should be administered uniformly throughout the whole of Ireland.

It went on to determine the machinery whereby, if the two parliaments agreed, a single parliament might be established by assuming the powers of the 'Council of Ireland'. This Council remained but a notional body, however, and was given its quietus in the London Agreements which abolished it. This was felt at the time by some Southerners to be a grievous blow to the hope of a united Ireland. But if a law depends for its application on the support which those liable to it are prepared to give it, the idea of the Council was 'bad law' in Orange eyes before the ink was dry on the royal signature of the 1920 Act.

Control of navigation, defence, trade, foreign policy, air and postal links is reserved to Westminster. Taxes raised in Northern Ireland are paid directly into the United Kingdom Treasury. But in practice Westminster leaves legislation on matters directly relating to Northern Ireland to the competence of Stormont. In practice there is what amounts to a 'federal' relationship between Britain and Northern Ireland.

The British Crown is represented by a governor. Stormont today consists of a House of Commons with fifty-two members and a Senate with twenty-six. Twenty-four of these are elected by the House of Commons by proportional representation; the lord mayors of Belfast and Londonderry sit in the Senate as *ex-officio* members. The elected senators serve for an eight-year term, half of them retiring every four years, though they may be re-elected. The Senate may continue in being even if the lower house is dissolved. The Senate's powers are analogous to those of the House of Lords vis-à-vis the House of Commons, with this difference: if a bill passed by the Stormont Commons is rejected in two successive sessions by the Senate, the governor-general of Northern Ireland is empowered to convene a joint sitting of both chambers, wherein a simple majority of those voting serves to determine the matter. Northern Ireland elects twelve members of parliament to Westminster by the British electoral system, and these members—with very rare exceptions—take the Conservative whip. The constituency boundaries for the Westminster members are reviewed by the United Kingdom Boundary Commission.*

The North's legal system is similar to England's. As a part of the United Kingdom, appeals from its Supreme Court are made to the House of Lords, not to the Privy Council as is the case with most legal systems in the Commonwealth. The North appoints its own judges. Although, as I have said, the special guards at Stormont are unarmed while those in the Dail carry weapons, the Royal Ulster Constabulary is an armed police force, unlike the Garda Siochana (Civic Guard) in the South. This detail is symptomatic, along with the Special Powers Act, not of a police state but of the greater underlying tension in Northern society as compared with the South.

The local government system is the same as the British. Northern Ireland is divided into eight major administrative areas: six county councils and the two county boroughs of Belfast and Londonderry. The county areas are subdivided into ten boroughs, twenty-four urban districts and thirty-one rural districts. The county councils provide major services like education, health and welfare. In its rural districts, each county council is also responsible for rating and planning, libraries, public works and roads—apart from trunk roads which are the responsibility of the government. The borough and district councils, both urban and rural, are responsible for water supply, sewerage and cleansing services (the latter an important service in the tidy North). Under the general aegis of the county council, rural districts look after minor roads, while borough and urban district councils are also the planning, rating and road authorities for their areas. Belfast and Londonderry as county boroughs combine the functions of county councils and urban districts, but police, civil defence and fire services are centrally administered—with the exception of the Belfast fire service which is run by the city council.

The system of public finance in Northern Ireland is to all intents and purposes identical to that obtaining in Britain. Indeed, fiscally and economically it is as much a part of the United Kingdom as Wales is, and in the formal sense it would be erroneous to regard Northern Ireland as a 'separate' economy. As we have noted, revenue raised there (local taxes apart) is paid directly into the United Kingdom Exchequer, and cannot be withheld for local purposes except by specific authority of the British Treasury. The North's supply services are financed by means of Stormont's annual Appropriation Acts, based on estimates prepared by the

* For discussion of electoral arrangements for Stormont and local government bodies, see below page 321 *et seq*.

various public departments and approved by the Ministry of Finance. Taxation and postal services are directly controlled by Whitehall. The posts on the Border are manned and controlled by the British customs service. Out of the revenue paid into the United Kingdom Treasury, the latter deducts and retains a sum to cover the cost of running UK services in Northern Ireland. The balance, known as the 'Residuary Share of Reserved Taxes' is returned to the Northern exchequer. The Joint Exchequer Board—consisting of one representative each of the Treasury and of the Northern Ministry of Finance, with a chairman appointed by the Crown—determines the amount of the Reserved Revenue, the cost of the common services incurred by Northern Ireland, any special financial dealings between Stormont and Westminster, and the amount of the 'imperial contribution'.

The 'imperial contribution' is Northern Ireland's payment towards the cost of those services which are for the general benefit of the United Kingdom. These services are: National Debt charges and administrative costs of the National Debt commissioners; naval, military and air force expenditure, including pensions and allowances; the Civil List; the running costs of the British parliament; Foreign, Commonwealth and Colonial services; the Royal Mint; and official trade services outside the United Kingdom. The amount of the imperial contribution has fluctuated since the setting up of Northern Ireland. It was £16 million in 1956, but only £3½ million in 1963–64. One of the steps the British took to reassure Northern Ireland when in 1938 they renounced rights over ports in the South was the signing of an agreement with the Northern government in respect to its finances. Britain guaranteed that, if ever a deficit arose in the North's exchequer—other than one caused by Stormont's introducing higher social service expenditure or lower taxes than in Britain—this deficit would be met by the United Kingdom Treasury. With this went a pledge to pass on to the North the same rights to subsidies as those enjoyed by British farmers, and also to introduce social and other benefits step by step as they were introduced in Britain.

In 1964 the monies made available to Northern Ireland out of the United Kingdom Treasury in regard to National Insurance payments, welfare benefits and agricultural subsidies amounted to £44 million. It was estimated by the Hall Committee, reporting in 1962 on the Northern economy, that if the North had paid its share of the cost of imperial services on a population basis rather than on the basis of taxable capacity, it would be liable to pay a far greater share than it does in fact pay. In 1955–56, for example, when its assessed share was £16 million, it would have been liable for £55 million. Thus, in a sense, it may be said that maintaining the North costs the British taxpayer something over £100 million annually.*

Commenting sourly on this circumstance, a Northern politician said to me: 'The North is like an ex-mistress whose charms have faded but who must be kept on the payroll because a paternity suit would be embarrassing'. In the sense of 'direct' financing, this may be true. But the North, having a fair share of the beauties of Ireland, has in recent years discovered, like the South, a new and increasing source of revenue: the tourist trade. This was estimated to be worth £20 million in 1965.

Agriculture, Industry and Welfare

The largest single industry, as in the South, is farming. The North's 46,000 farm units in 1964 employed 101,000 people. As we have mentioned earlier, the Northern farmer receives all the benefits of British agricultural subsidies and development schemes. Such help makes the Northern farmer incomparably more productive than his Southern counterpart. The output per farm in the North is almost double the average output in the Republic. The Northern productivity figure of £59 per acre for grass and crop output, as compared with £19 in the Republic, is a figure which speaks for itself, even when due allowance is made for the South's having to cope with the poor areas of the Western seaboard.

Until recent years, the industrial scene in the North was dominated by two traditional industries: linen and shipbuilding; but both of these have been adversely affected by post-war changes. One of the major problems confronting the Harland and Wolff shipyards, and now also the aircraft manufacturing firm of Short Brothers and Harland, is how to keep their highly specialised design and technical teams during contraction. Since the war shipbuilding has been in a difficult condition everywhere, but Northern Ireland's difficulties have been particularly grave since shipbuilding is its major heavy industry. The loss of designers and technicians inflicts more serious damage in the long-term than the temporary laying off of 1,000 yard workers. Such losses have occurred over the last five years; but, though serious enough to cause worry, they have not yet been of an order to cause panic.†

Engineering industries in all employ 48,000 people. Contraction in the linen industry has very largely been offset by the North's ventures in

* This is a rough estimate. One thing which the British link has not enabled the North to do is supply people like me with up-to-date statistics!

† The comparative statistics for the monthly averages of unemployment in 1954 and 1964 are—Northern Ireland: 1954, 7·0 per cent, 1964, 6·6 per cent; Irish Republic: 1954, 8·1 per cent, 1964, 5·7 per cent; Britain: 1954, 1·3 per cent, 1964, 1·7 per cent.

satisfying the demand for man-made fibres. Big English concerns like Courtaulds have set up subsidiaries, and the making of fibres like *Acrilan*, *Terylene* and *Ulstron* has created jobs for some 6,000 people. The Northern woollen industry employs 1,800. Altogether the highly diversified textile industry in the North employs approximately 45,000 people. The rest of the 197,000 male and female workers employed in manufacturing and processing industries are spread over: construction (30,000); food, drink and tobacco (27,000); and clothing (23,000).

Since 1945, a series of Stormont measures, designed to aid industry, has created approximately 55,000 new jobs. These measures fall into four categories.

1. The *Industrial Development Acts* (1945–53), under which grants and loans are made to factories newly established in the North. Such help is given either towards the cost of new plant, machinery and building, or towards the expense of transferring existing equipment to the North for a new plant there. 2. The *Capital Grants to Industry Acts* (1954–62), under which the government gives grants to firms to stimulate capital investment. This assistance takes the form of a grant to firms each year amounting to a third of their annual expenditure on new building or on new plant and machinery. 3. The *Industrial Advice and Enterprise Act of 1964*. This makes grants available to firms which employ consultants to advise them on business and industrial efficiency schemes, and also to defray the cost of replacing obsolete plant and buildings. 4. The *Aids to Industry Acts* (1961–64). These among other things provide a system of fuel subsidies. For example, during 1964, the government grants towards meeting fuel costs represented the following percentages of total costs: coal and oil, 14·5 per cent; gas, 11·5 per cent; electricity, 7 per cent.

These measures have been largely responsible for increasing industrial productivity in the North by 23 per cent per head between 1958 and 1963. Firms attracted there include: Michelin Tyres, Ford's, Carreras Tobacco, du Pont, British Oxygen, and Associated Electrical Industries. Over 160 new industries have moved to the North since 1945.

We have already seen the disparity between official assistance to agriculture as between North and South. Since it is an important point in the case against assimilation with the South, as the South is at present politically constituted, and since at the same time it is an indication of the North's financial dependence on the United Kingdom, the 'benefits of the Union' merit further description.

Personal income per head is, on average, 38 per cent higher in the North than in the South. In 1963, the figures were: Republic, £244;

Northern Ireland, £336. In the same year gross fixed capital formation was £78 per head in the North as against an estimated £47·2 in the South. The North's population is less than half that of the South, but the number of secondary school pupils in 1964 was 95,000 in Northern Ireland as against 85,000 in the Republic. In 1963 university expenditure in the South was 17s per head; over the Border it was 48s 9d. Subject to a very lenient means-test, practically any Northern youngster with the requisite educational qualifications can get free university education. But in the South, although it is hoped to treble the figures by 1970, there were in 1965 only about 700 university scholarships and bursaries available, and all these were awarded on the basis of competitive examinations or tests.

In 1965 unemployment and sickness benefit for a married couple in the North amounted to £6 10s; in the South it was £3 12s 6d. Retirement age in the North is sixty-five, and for a married man the pension benefit is £6 10s; in the Republic, old age pension is not granted until the age of seventy, and the current rate for a married man is £4 17s. Children's allowances in the North are 8s a week for the first child and 10s a week for each subsequent child; in the South the payments are 10s a month for the first child, 15s 6d a month for the second child, and 26s 6d for each subsequent child. The health service in Northern Ireland is part of the British system and confers benefits far greater than those yet possible in the South. There are further discrepancies; for example: the North's maternity grant of £22 as compared with the South's £4, and the Northern grant of £25 towards burial expenses, which has no equivalent in the South. The number of houses built with state assistance rose in 1964 to an all-time record of 8,046 in the Republic. Even so, the North exceeded this total with 9,516 houses.

Of course, nothing comes of nothing, even under the benign paw of the British lion! The North, if it gets many benefits from the connection with Britain, has also to pay taxes at the full United Kingdom rate; and these are appreciably higher in general than in the Republic. The weekly contributions under the National Insurance scheme for those who have contracted out of the graduated pensions scheme (there is no similar pensions scheme in the South) are 15s 4d for employers and 16s 1d for employees. In the South the contribution is 5s 11d each. It should also be said that the benefits obtainable in the Republic are achieved through its own unaided efforts. Those in the North, despite commendable efforts made towards self-sufficiency, are made possible only by virtue of the fact that Lord Randolph Churchill's successful playing of the Orange card in 1886 has left the British taxpayer eighty years later contributing £100 million a year for the privilege of maintaining twelve Tory members at Westminster.

All the same, the over-riding reality remains: social benefits are far higher in the North than in the South.

RELIGION AND THE NORTHERN MOOD

The Northern climate of opinion derives its tone from religious differences. But today the situation is in flux following the Lemass–O'Neill talks: the most outstanding manifestation of an ecumenical spirit which was already beginning to be discernible. On both sides it is agreed that tension is slackening. Even granting the deep residual suspicion of Catholics and the discrimination against them in certain sectors of Northern life—understandable in the light of history if reprehensible in a modern democratic society—a far better spirit of co-operation is noticeable.

Rural Protestant and Catholic neighbours have traditionally helped each other at harvest time. In country districts generally co-operation has for long been more evident than dissension—except round about the time of the Twelfth of July celebrations, when Orange bigotry makes for a month or two's coolness each year; or when IRA raids make Nationalists suspect in the eyes of Unionist neighbours as aiders and abettors of terrorists. The curse of it all was that past annual outbreaks of fighting in Belfast between Sandy Row (Protestant) and Falls Road (Catholic) made any extension of this basically rural neighbourliness impossible. The shipyards were a strong area of conflict, although the serious rioting there would only be a memory in the minds of the older workers.

It does not require IRA raids or deliberate Orange incitement to keep tempers on edge, for the Northern situation is prolific of sources of tension (trivial-seeming enough to the outsider) which sometimes cause fights and nearly always give offence. The Nationalists' refusal to rise for the toast of 'The Queen' or to stand at the playing of *God Save The Queen* is highly offensive to the Unionists. The term Fenian, one of praise in the Nationalist vocabulary, is one of deep opprobrium in that of the Unionists. To say 'Six Counties' instead of 'Northern Ireland' makes Unionists flare up, and the converse is true for Nationalists. The term 'non-Catholic' is also potentially dangerous, as is the use of Derry by Nationalists and Londonderry by Unionists; while, in polite circles, the Protestant emphasis on *Roman* Catholics makes Catholic hackles rise. The Unionists point accusingly to the 'priest in politics' whenever a Father So-and-So is seen to be presiding at a Nationalist committee meeting—although curiously Nationalists don't retort the charge when Protestant clergymen are seen walking in Orange processions.

And then there are the occasional happenings in the South which give ammunition to Unionist die-hards. There have been none since 1960, but the Mother and Child scheme was a magnificent and continuing source of propaganda to some trouble-shooters in the North. The affair in 1960 concerned the issuing of a summons against two priests and a layman for assaulting a Jehovah's Witness who had been distributing tracts in Wexford town. The three defendants were found guilty of 'technical assault', and were put on probation. But the fact that they were found guilty tended to be overlooked in the light of the judge's comment on the Jehovah's Witnesses: 'I regard them as engaged in a calculated conspiracy against the peace of the country, and that peace I must help to preserve'.

To balance the record, however, it has to be said that, when the Witnesses held a large convention in Dublin during June 1965, no one interfered with them. When it was suggested that some people might, the Legion of Mary wrote to the papers to say that it was the duty of Christians, however much they might disapprove of its ideas and practices, to receive the sect with charity. In the event, the immersion ceremonies made front-page pictures and were given a sympathetic press coverage unmarred by any 'incidents'. In fact I can testify that some exemplary Catholics extended hospitality to them.

It is not just wishful-thinking, I believe, to hold that the day of such happenings as that in Wexford is over and done with in the Republic, and that the end to similar bigotry is drawing near in the North. If one wants to, one can still seek out and find ugly incidents, but increasingly it is the pleasant ones which predominate. For instance, in 1963 a lecture was arranged by the Irish Association at Queen's University, Belfast, on the life of Saint Colomcille. Church of Ireland bishops sat on the platform with the lecturer, Fr John Ryan, a Jesuit, and with the Catholic bishop of Down and Connor. The grace at the dinner preceding the lecture was given by the Moderator of the Presbyterian Church: which in Belfastian circumstances was a benediction on something more than physical food. The new spirit exemplified by this is beginning to inform the social, as well as the specifically 'religious', attitudes of liberal-minded men in the different denominations. A body which has done good work in recent years is the Churches Industrial Council. This is an interdenominational organisation of clergy and laity which works unobtrusively to eradicate discrimination in industry. Its most notable success so far has been the part it played in the discussions which smoothed the way for the official recognition by Stormont in 1964 of the Irish Congress of Trade Unions as a negotiating body and as one from which labour representatives can be appointed to government commissions. The Congress has member-unions on both sides of the Border, but its headquarters are in Dublin. Thanks to the work of enlightened lay and clerical opinion, this latter fact is no longer a stumbling-block at Stormont.

Even so, certain obvious difficulties must not be brushed aside. The ruling party is entirely Protestant. The police force is regarded by Catholics with such reserve that only 12 per cent of the Royal Ulster Constabulary are non-Protestant. Its entire 'B' (special) Force is Protestant—which perhaps is not surprising since its function is to defend the state against 'Catholic terrorists': i.e., the IRA raiders. But other examples of the over-whelming ratio of Protestants to Catholics are hard to explain save in terms of discrimination. This is most noticeably the case in regard to employment opportunities and to public appointments. To take an example from the health and welfare services: in Fermanagh, where Catholics out-number Protestants in the order of 27,291 as against 24,322, fifteen of the twenty members of the County Welfare Committee are Protestants, while the administrative staff has fifty-nine Protestants and only fifteen Catholics.

Yet, apart from the Mater Infirmorum Hospital,* which to Catholics is a symbolic test of the sincerity of official protestations of goodwill towards the minority, one would have to be painstaking indeed to find evidence of discrimination in the running of the health services. (Though, as we shall see, in other fields Catholic grievances are real enough.) The British social services, as mentioned earlier, have been introduced in Northern Ireland as part of a definite step-by-step policy since the setting up of the self-governing province of Northern Ireland. This policy has been pursued irrespective of whether the government in Britain has been Conservative or Labour. By their support, whether real or notional, of Nationalist policies which aimed at the overthrow of the system that made these benefits possible, Catholics in the North left themselves open to the charge of insincerity. Protestants were not slow to point out that, while complaining about the government which administered these services and about their not getting their fair share of what was going, the Catholics were quick enough off the mark in accepting the benefits.

This aspect of the Northern problem was signalised by a controversy in June 1956. In that year, the Unionist minister of Labour, Ivan Neill, introduced a bill to extend to the North a recent British increase in

* The Mater Hospital, as it is generally called, is the only Catholic teaching hospital in the United Kingdom. It is excluded from the payments made under the Northern Health Service founded in 1947 because, since it is run by nuns, the Catholics are unwilling to put it under secular control. Though it treats Catholic and Protestant patients alike, the government has not yet devised a method for bringing it within the range of Health Service grants by means of the de Valera formula of 'external association'. It raises its income through a football pool.

children's allowances. This nearly resulted in a divergence from the 'step-by-step' policy since the Unionists attempted in the bill to give fourth and subsequent children less than the benefits conferred in Britain. But opposition, led by liberal Unionists and by a general enlightened attitude among Protestants, was strongly voiced against a proposal which would have had the effect of discriminating against Catholics, who almost invariably have larger families than Protestants. This opposition was so powerful that on June 12 the prime minister, Lord Brookeborough, announced that the benefits would remain in step with those obtaining in Britain. Blatant as this discriminatory manoeuvre was, the tendency for some Catholic propagandists to regard the wombs of Catholic mothers in Northern Ireland as an agency for the advancement of the faith, makes the die-hard Unionist ruse understandable if not justifiable. There is far too much talk in Catholic circles in the North about 'outbreeding the Protestants' as the correct way to deal with them. Talk like this has to be seen in the light of cases like one I have personal knowledge of. Two cousins, both IRA suspects, were interned during the 1956 Border Campaign: one in the North, the other in the South. The family of the one in the North got every conceivable benefit conferable: educational, health, even unemployment assistance. The Southerner's family never got a penny.

The Catholic community as a whole is bedevilled by a reluctance to play a part in new developments—not out of stubbornness so much as out of a lack of the leadership which can quell old fears and set new objectives. It is widely hoped that Cardinal Conway, consecrated in March 1965, will prove himself such a leader. He is a Belfast man with a reputation for being able to combine a liberal approach with a respect for the traditions of the country. He made three of the total of five interventions by the Irish hierarchy during the first two sessions of the Vatican Council and a good speech on religious liberty in the third. By virtue of being a cardinal and the chairman of the hierarchy's biennial meetings at Maynooth, he is in a position to exert administrative as well as prestige influence over the Catholic community in both parts of the island.

For Northern Catholics, who are far more influenced by their clergy in their social relationships than are Protestants, the great problem, as in the South, is how to get a better education for their children. Catholic secondary education in both parts of Ireland is provided through voluntary schools subsidised by a variety of fund-raising activities, and primary schools are run on the manager system. (See page 215 above.) The following table, taken from a survey made by the *Belfast Telegraph*, shows what proportion of Catholic children in the North get as far as grammar school and university.

SCHOOL POPULATION 1963–64

Type of School	Catholics	Protestants
Primary	89,181	101,084
Secondary Intermediate	22,811	35,291
Grammar	12,466	23,712
Teacher Training	698	1,105
University	1,006	3,765

There are strong complaints about overcrowding in Catholic schools. Some primary schools operate a shift system: one class in the morning, one in the afternoon. The manager system comes under fire for preventing the development of parent-teacher committees (a fault in the South also), and there is increasing pressure for introducing something on the lines of the British 'four and two' committees, which would allow the managing authority to nominate four representatives and the public authorities two. This would enable Catholic, like Protestant, schools to receive 100 per cent grants for heating, lighting, cleaning, maintenance and teachers' National Insurance contributions. It would also pave the way for sympathetic consideration by the state of requests for other grants, such as help towards building costs, which the 'four and two' system does not provide.

It would, of course, mean a major break with Irish Church practice. But Catholics have to face the fact that their children do not press up the educational ladder at the same rate as the children of Protestant families. If a wholesale reappraisal of the Catholic approach to this problem is not carried out, Catholics in the North as a community will continue to be 'have-nots', more concerned with getting a fair share of unemployment assistance than a fair share of executive positions and high-skill jobs. The present Catholic–Protestant relationship is at least as much dependent on scarcity of economic opportunity—which in turn depends on lack of higher education—as on any other factor. The Church, therefore, is faced with the necessity of relinquishing some of its clerical prerogatives in order to increase the citizenship capabilities and opportunities of its lay members.

This seemingly simple positing of the problem is, however, complicated by the fact that many good Catholics genuinely fear that such loss of control would lead to discrimination against them by the Unionists. A young priest said to me: 'At least this way we can give a job to a Catholic teacher. I think we've bitten off more than we can chew, but if anyone said that in public the bigots on both sides would pounce. What we really need here is an O'Connell: a leader who will sweep away the barriers and lead us to freedom.'

Such a leader, to do any lasting good, would have to take a strong stand against the practices and attitudes of the majority community which, as we

shall see later, contrive to deny full democratic representation and equal
economic opportunity to the minority community. But he would also have
to rally his co-religionists against their own practices and attitudes which
derive almost as much from a 'ghetto' mentality as from Protestant discrimination. The nature of the problem has been well defined by G. B. Newe,
one of Northern Ireland's leading Catholic laymen, who is among other
things the secretary of the Northern Ireland Council of Social Service.
Discussing in *Christus Rex* (spring 1964) the prevalent attitude among
Catholics to serving on the various Health and Welfare Committees, he wrote:

> We seem to be not at all interested in either the existence or the work
> of such committees. Often it is alleged that these committees are
> carefully selected by 'the powers that be' so that we, who are an
> important section of this community, are deliberately excluded from
> their counsels. Even if it could be proved that this is so, *is it the whole
> story?* Can we *honestly* say that we are eager to assist the community
> in this kind of work? If we do take part, are we found to have the
> qualities required in these fields? Are we good 'stayers', really and
> sincerely interested in the good of *all* members of the community,
> including that vast majority who are not of the same faith as our-
> selves? . . . In the great majority of instances, a Catholic boy appears
> for interview with, not a chip on his shoulder, but a blinking log!
> Many Catholic youngsters are predisposed to failure, and the attitude
> is, to a great extent, cultivated in the schools, and in some schools in
> particular. I fear that it is said openly: 'Because you are a Catholic
> you are not likely to get a job'.

This courageous criticism by a prominent Catholic poses the problem of
religion and the Northern mood in its most intractable form. In many
fields of employment, Catholics definitely do find it difficult to get jobs
or higher promotion from existing jobs. But equally there is among many
of them a spirit of frustration and defeatism which inhibits them from
making the effort needed to take advantage of and extend the opportunities
that are available to them.

What we may call 'institutional' discrimination is discussed later. No
less important is the discrimination practised by both groups in everyday
life. Whereas the Northern Protestant's attitude expresses itself most
clearly in *de jure* discrimination, the Catholic's is exerted in *de facto* discrimination. Catholics give jobs to Catholics and limit business transactions, ranging from the purchase of ten cigarettes to six-figure deals, to
their co-religionists. Both Catholic and Protestant auctioneers are expected
as part of their service to their communities automatically to notify co-
religionists of impending sales of farms or premises. So widespread is this

practice that a Dublin friend of mine, commenting on the state of affairs in the North among both communities, said disgustedly: 'Don't mind talk about abolishing the Border. What we want to do is build up a great big high wall around the place and keep *all* the bastards up there!'

What is so hard to bear is the mean pettiness of so much of Northern life. The slow housing of Catholics is the biggest single complaint of the minority community. It may be clear enough to the political strategists that it is dangerous to give the permanency of a good home to a family which is treated by its own side as a counter in the politico-fertility game which, if won, will put the allocation of houses firmly into Catholic hands. It is not so clear to the ill-housed people themselves: for instance, to the family of thirteen living in a Nissen hut at Clogher, which sees childless Protestant couples getting houses while the only provision made for its existence is the wall built before the hut to hide the unsightliness from the passers-by. Outside Asia, there are few areas in the world which stand to benefit more than Northern Ireland from a slackening in the rigidity of Catholic birth-control regulations.

It is hard for an ecumenically minded Catholic layman to make a second speech advising his co-religionists to recognise Stormont as the *de jure* government, when his first speech caused him to lose business, including business with convents. The Protestant clergyman who differs politically from all other Protestant clergy in his town must wonder if he had fought on the right side when on Armistice Day he is the only cleric not invited to the ceremonies: he who lost a brother in the war against Nazism and is himself the only clergyman in the town who, before taking holy orders, fought in that war.

POLITICAL PARTIES

The state of the parties in the Northern House of Commons following the Stormont elections in November 1965 was: Unionists thirty-six; Nationalists nine; Northern Ireland Labour Party two; Republican Labour two; National Democrat one; Liberal one; Independent one.

Since the passing of the Government of Ireland Act in 1920, there has been only one real question in Northern politics: whether the North has the right to exist as part of the United Kingdom. The Unionists say that it has, the Nationalists that it has not. Labour only showed signs of making up its mind on this question in 1949; while the Liberals have been damned by both extremes: by the Unionists for being 'disloyal' to the Union, and by the Nationalists for 'betraying' Home Rule. Sinn Fein's 'a pox on both your houses' attitude has complicated the picture in the post-war years.

The question has been embittered by two intertwining factors: fear and privilege. Much of the former stems from apprehension at losing the latter; but a good deal of it goes straight back to the days of James II and William of Orange, and indeed to back beyond them.

Unionists

The Unionist Party is predominately Protestant. While this makes it prone to beat the religious drum for political advantage, it has to be remembered that its chief political opposition comes from a predominately Catholic party. Although this opposition finds itself exclusively Catholic more by circumstances than by conscious choice, its fundamental proposition from the start has been that the Unionist government had no legal right to its jurisdiction. It has not been easy, therefore, even if the will to do so were there (and this at times has been questionable), for the Unionist Party to act as if it were the strophe to an antistrophe in a well-ordered political drama of the British or American type. Its right challenged to be on the stage at all, it has out-Heroded Herod in hogging the scene.

The Unionist Party is an ally of the British Conservative Party (some of whose local associations are still called Unionist, notably in Scotland), and its members at Westminster accept the Conservative whip. Its fundamental planks are of the old Tory platform: religion and the existing Constitution. But the Unionist umbrella manages to cover a much greater diversity of opinion than the party's monolithic structure might lead one to suppose. As early as the mid-'twenties, when the Border was new and was firmly established only in the resolve of its advocates, a group within the party was already showing signs of divergence. Three prominent Unionists—District-Inspector Nixon of the RUC, Tommy Henderson and William Wilton—sat as Independent Unionists and opposed the official party line on unemployment and housing, and on social questions generally. In 1938, a group with similar views—the Progressive Unionists—was formed within the party. But it was in 1943 that the most striking example of divergence occurred. A palace revolution overthrew J. M. Andrews, who had succeeded Lord Craigavon (formerly Sir James Craig) as prime minister on the latter's death in November 1940. In a reshuffle which dispensed with all but one member of the existing cabinet, Sir Basil C. Brooke (later Lord Brookeborough) became prime minister, a post which he held for twenty years. A curious feature of the new cabinet—curious, that is, in the light of oft-repeated Unionist strictures about the role of priests in Southern politics—was the inclusion in it of two clergymen: Professor R. Corkey, minister of Education and leader of the Senate, and the Reverend Robert Moore, minister of Agriculture. The struggle between the contending forces within the party matured over the Christmas season of goodwill and broke into public view when the House resumed early in the new year. The stated issue of the Brookeborough group was the need for an intensification of the war effort, and for increased concentration on social and economic questions. After votes of confidence and all the other symptoms of waning support, Andrews finally resigned on April 28, 1944.

The 'permissive' element in Unionist Party discipline is subject to rather confusing fluctuations. For example, in 1959 it showed a decidedly illiberal character when it disowned Montgomery Hyde, an independent-minded Unionist MP at Westminster, because of his 'advanced' views—notably his opposition to capital punishment and his advocacy of the return of the Lane Collection to Dublin.* Yet the same year saw a different side of the Unionist coin. Sir Clarence Graham, chairman of the Standing Committee of the Ulster Unionist Council, and Brian Maginess, then attorney-general, were reported as being favourably disposed towards the admission of Catholics to the Unionist Party. Maginess, who had always been a liberal influence in Northern affairs, was quoted as saying at a Young Unionist political seminar at Portstewart: 'To broaden our outlook means no weakening of our faith. Toleration is not a sign of weakness, but proof of strength.'

But up to the time of writing there were few Catholics in the Unionist Party. The most noticeable spirit shown in the 1964 (UK) election campaign was the petrol in the flaming bottles which were hurled (with more enthusiasm than deliberation) in the constituency of West Belfast. Riots broke out over the exhibition of the Republican tricolour in the election headquarters of the Republican candidate. The Rev. Ian Paisley, leader of the Free Presbyterians—a fundamentalist sect which is so fundamental that it would never get off the ground were it not for his inspired demagogy —threatened to lead a protest march to the Sinn Fein headquarters. The Unionist authorities showed such hesitation in dealing with the affair that, by the time the flag was commandeered by the police, an ugly atmosphere prevailed over the entire city. No lives were lost in the disturbances, which continued for a week, but the fact that the Unionists won a seat which they were expected to lose lent some colour to the view that Unionist party strategists nurtured a secret joy over such a classic combination of raw emotionalism and rabble-rousing religious fervour.

To understand the divergencies and conflicting attitudes within the Unionist Party one has to take note of its broad social basis. If the description would not give unpardonable offence to the Unionist leaders (and to

* Sir Hugh Lane intended his fine collection of Impressionist pictures to be housed in Dublin. But the codicil in his will to this effect was unwitnessed. When he was drowned in the *Lusitania* in 1916, the pictures were installed in the Tate Gallery in London. After forty years of wrangling, by a happy compromise in 1961 part of the collection was restored to Dublin.

the Nationalists, who would tear me apart for blasphemy), one would say
that it was a sort of Christian Democratic Party as the term is understood
in Catholic Italy. It embraces Anglican conservatism, represented by the
landowning, shipping and textile barons; the more radical Dissenter or
Presbyterian tradition of the Scottish settlers; and the urban working class,
who belong to many Protestant sects. These latter give the Unionist Party
a claim to being regarded as the world's most outstanding example of
working-class Toryism. The Unionist Labour Association was founded as
long ago as 1914 by Carson and J. M. Andrews. Only those workers who
are trade union members may belong to it.

At the time of writing, the Unionist cabinet is composed thus: *Prime
Minister*, Captain Terence M. O'Neill; *Finance*, Herbert Kirk; *Home
Affairs*, R. W. B. McConnell; *Health and Social Services*, W. J. Morgan;
Agriculture, H. W. West; *Commerce*, A. B. D. Faulkner; *Development*,
William Craig; *Education*, William Fitzsimmons. J. L. O. Andrews is
leader of the Senate and minister without portfolio.

Fitzsimmons owes his ministerial post to a cabinet upheaval in 1965.
Ivan Neill resigned as minister for Finance and leader of the Commons on
April 2, following which there was a general reshuffle. The resignation of
Neill has been variously ascribed to personality clashes between him and
the prime minister, and to a reputed move by the Presbyterian business
community, led by Faulkner, to gain a larger, if possible dominant, influence in Unionist affairs. Neill, representative of the self-made man
tradition, was said also to be seeking to improve his political position.
If so, then it would appear he was outmanoeuvred by O'Neill, who may
moreover have seen the rebuff to Neill as a salutary warning to the ambitious Faulkner. Were it not for Captain O'Neill's comparative youth, for a
politician, one could say definitely that Faulkner should go further, for
he is one of the ablest men in Northern political life.

Labour

The Labour movement in Northern Ireland has had more off-shoots than
the Northern Ireland Labour Party has at present parliamentary members
(two). To name but a few of these splinter groups, there is: Commonwealth
Labour, Independent Labour, Republican Labour, Independent Dock
Labour, Eire Labour and O'Sullivan Labour. This confusing picture
becomes a little clearer if one bears in mind the two basic attitudes governing Northern politics: Pro-Partition and Anti-Partition. Before 1949, the
Northern Labour movement as a whole was Anti-Partition (without
decisively committing itself) in the sense that a united Ireland was a major
aim of the Irish Labour Party founded at Clonmel in 1912 by Connolly
and Larkin. But already by 1942 a growing feeling that it should accept the

status quo led the conference of the Northern Ireland Labour Party* to declare 'that there should be no change in the constitutional position of Northern Ireland without a democratic vote of the people of Northern Ireland'.

Caught between the Orange Unionists (Tories) and the Green Nationalists (Tories also), the Northern Ireland Labour Party's vote has always been susceptible to erosion, being vulnerable to charges from both sides that it is weakening the traditional allegiances. The party decided to accept the inevitable in 1949. On April 9 of that year, a special conference was called following the disturbances caused by the South's declaring itself a Republic. This conference declared: 'That the Northern Ireland Labour Party believes that the best interests of Northern Ireland lie in maintaining the constitutional links with the United Kingdom'. The principal behind-the-scenes organiser of this motion was Harry Midgley. One of the oldest and most respected members of the Labour movement, he had sat at Stormont as 'Commonwealth Labour'—that is, a Labour MP loyal to the Crown—but during the last war he turned Unionist and entered the cabinet in 1943. On a card vote of representatives of affiliated union members, the resolution was carried by 20,000 to 800. Its principal opponent was Jack Beattie, probably the Northern Labour movement's greatest figure. He represented West Belfast at Westminster until 1949. The 1949 General Election was the most bitter of the post-war election campaigns in the North. Borne forward by the emotional revulsion from the South's becoming a Republic, the Unionists swamped the opposition and were returned with the same majority they had had after the 1921 election: Unionists forty, others twelve. All nine of the Labour Party's candidates were defeated. The fear of being brought under the sway of Republican Dublin was enough to bring Northern politics back to the banks of the Boyne.

The Northern Ireland Labour Party was also totally unsuccessful at the 1953 election. In 1958 it managed to pick up four seats, but two of these it lost in November 1965, including that of an outstanding member, David Bleakley. Frank Hanna, the Independent Labour member for Belfast Central, one of the most respected and experienced trade union lawyers in the whole of Ireland, retired before the election. Labour in the North, as in the South, has never been in step with the true heartbeat of the electorate. The variously styled Labour candidates who remain outside the NILP attract support which is almost wholly personal, with a dash of nationalism.

---

* The Northern Ireland Labour Party came into being in 1924. The Northern and Southern parties are separate bodies. But the former is now associated with the Irish Trade Union Congress, not with the TUC in London, and is responsible to its own party conference.

The Labour movement as a whole in Northern Ireland has not shown itself capable of generating enough radicalism to wean away the large working-class vote of Belfast from the seductive music of the Orange drum. Some idea of the character of Labour in the North can be gained from the fact that in 1964 NILP representatives voted against opening children's playgrounds in Belfast on Sundays.

Liberals

The Liberals, to destroy whom that infamous 'Orange card' was played in 1886, have been trumped by it in Ulster ever since. A party which tells the people that Carson and Sinn Fein were both wrong cannot hope to thrive in the biting Londonderry air. Yet it has not lacked attractive personalities. The Rev. J. B. Armour used to electrify the Presbyterian General Assembly with his pleas for religious toleration. When he died in 1928, his fiery opponent on the Nationalist side, J. W. Devlin, declared: 'A great light has gone out in Ulster'. Armour, who was born in Lisboy, County Antrim, in many ways typified the best qualities of the radical Dissenting spirit of the North: a spirit which, if North and South ever do genuinely end their Cold War, will give a valuable jolt of vigorous questioning to the rather conformist temper of the South. He studied at Cork University where he acquired a sympathy for the Catholic viewpoint which led him to support Gladstone's and the later Home Rule efforts in the teeth of Carsonism. He died without receiving either the religious or the political honours which would have fallen to a man of his integrity—he refused to sign the Ulster Covenant—in times of less malice and uncharitableness. In a sense, his life symbolises the Liberal fate in Northern Ireland. The party was unrepresented at Stormont until 1961.

In that year Sheelagh Murnaghan, a hockey international in her youth, was victorious in the Queen's University constituency. The party's most colourful spokesman is the Rev. Albert McElroy, the Non-Subscribing Presbyterian incumbent for Newtownards. He is a man of Armour-like fortitude who, before Sheelagh Murnaghan carried off the prize, had fought the good, but lone, fight for Stormont. He gives prestige and strength to the party's organisation in circumstances which could hardly be more daunting. In a political arena where even organised Labour can command only two seats in the all-consuming fight between 'Pape' and 'Prod', the Liberals would need a combination of electoral reform and a revolution in popular attitudes to reach even double figures.

Nationalists

Until the Lemass–O'Neill talks, the Nationalist Party in the North existed more as a protest movement than as a disciplined and unified political party. Its only planks seemed to be the denial of the validity of the existence of Northern Ireland as a state, and the exposure of injustices perpetrated against Catholics. But as a young and liberal priest said to me in Belfast: 'Say what you like, they were the only people who spoke for the minority. If they hadn't been there, bad and all as they were, things would have been far worse.'

The Nationalists' support is almost exclusively rural and comes from the poorer parts of the country. In constituencies where the Unionist Party is particularly strong, the Nationalists (being single-mindedly *anti* rather than *pro* any social or economic programme) have so far failed to contest elections at all. This has led to campaigns in which as many as twenty-seven seats (out of a total of fifty-two) have been uncontested. The Nationalists did not recognise the Stormont parliament when first elected. But after the Boundary Commission's findings made the Border a fixture, the Nationalist leaders—Joseph Devlin and George Leek—took their seats. At that time Devlin, through his leadership of the old Irish Parliamentary Party element, was in control of the Nationalist representation on Belfast city council. A section of the Belfast party was pressing the leadership to resolve the anomaly of taking seats on the Belfast council (which implicitly recognised the Crown's jurisdiction) but not in Stormont, where alone effective action could be taken against discrimination against Catholics. Accordingly, out of the ten Nationalists elected, two took their seats in 1925, three more in 1926, and four more in 1927. But, though recognising that some constitutional platform was better than none, the Nationalists in a sense continued to deny the validity of the regime by refusing to become the official opposition, even though they were the largest group in parliament after the Unionists. The only concession they made to the *status quo* was to build up a not very efficient election machine in 1928.

In so far as they have any discernible social policies, the Nationalists are conservative-minded, which subjects them to the taunt of 'Green Tories' from Labour supporters. They have also tended to internal disunity for local or personal reasons. It was not until the aftermath of the Lemass–O'Neill talks that the air cleared sufficiently to allow of the formation of a centralised party and the drawing up of a manifesto.

However, even before the talks took place, there were indications of change within the Nationalist movement. Though the Nationalists differ from Sinn Fein in that they are willing to take the Oath of Allegiance to the Crown which is necessary to enter parliament, from 1955 onwards there has been manifest collusion between them and Sinn Fein. In that year the Nationalists withdrew from contesting elections for Westminster, leaving the field free to Sinn Fein. (Two Sinn Feiners were, in fact, elected to Westminster in that year, but did not take their seats.) This collusion has made their constitutionalism highly suspect in the eyes of Protestants and of the more progressive-minded Catholics. Since 1955 it has become a well-established factor in Northern politics that Sinn Fein (illegal in Northern Ireland, but not illegal in the United Kingdom) will fight the Westminster elections, the Nationalists the Stormont elections. What is more, in some areas—most notably in Tyrone and Fermanagh—the same election workers assist both parties. This 'yes-we-are-no-we're-not' relationship may have been meaningful to old-guard supporters of the movement who retained memories of the old Irish Parliamentary Party's attitude towards Sinn Fein, but it repelled young liberal-minded voters, Catholic and Protestant, and on polling day made Unionists of many of them.

A growing realisation of the futility of this kind of politics prompted the creation in December 1959 of an organisation called National Unity, which pledged itself to work for the unification of the island through the 'consent of the people of Northern Ireland'. National Unity's growth was aided by Lemass's speech in the Oxford Union on October 1959. He proposed a federal solution for Partition: a Northern parliament to continue in being with the powers conferred on it by the 1920 Act, with an All-Ireland parliament to exercise, in respect to the North, the powers at present exercised by Westminster. This proposal was reminiscent of the 'Council of Ireland' idea mooted in the 1920 Act. Though glancing backwards, it did represent an advance—albeit one totally unacceptable to Unionist minds. Its main significance was that the idea of force could finally be dropped from Nationalist ideology. A crucial conference was held at Maghery, County Armagh, on April 19, 1964, attended by Nationalist members of parliament, senators and supporters of all kinds. After slashing attacks on existing Nationalist policies, the Nationalist Political Front was formed to promote a unified movement.

The Front's main motivation was frustration at the lack of progress by the Nationalist movement. When the link with Sinn Fein became obvious, there began to develop a ground-swell of opinion among younger Nationalists which eventually took shape in the conviction that All-Ireland unity would only be achieved by the abandonment alike of the Sinn Fein policies and of those represented by the existing Nationalist organisation, such as it was. Frustration burst into something like rage when a Nationalist MP was completely outclassed on a BBC television programme by a Unionist minister. The issue discussed should have been a 'sitter' for a Nationalist: discrimination against Catholics in the North. It was made clear to the Nationalist old guard that it would no longer suffice to admonish the younger spirits in the old style, which could be summed up as: 'Go home, learn Irish, and leave the rest to the Catholic birth rate'. Accordingly, on June 2, 1964, the Nationalists chose a new leader: Edward McAteer,

Stormont member for Derry. Even so, in December 1964 McAteer, though supported in their different ways by liberal-minded Nationalists like Patrick Gormley MP, and Senator J. G. Lennon, was still appealing for a 'big effort at all levels and in all sections to end or diminish the feudin' and fightin' image that has won for us such damaging notoriety'. A series of Orange and Green talks initiated by McAteer had broken down that month because the Green was rebuffed over the constitutional position of the Orange. But McAteer's position became easier when Lemass in effect recognised the North's claim to autonomy, and on February 2, 1965 he became leader of the official opposition at Stormont. All the same, the Nationalists' attitude to Stormont is still that of Fianna Fail to the early Cumann na nGaedheal Oath: notional assent only.

TERENCE O'NEILL

Captain the Right Honourable Terence Marne O'Neill, PC, DL, MP, prime minister of Northern Ireland, is a smooth, courteous, modern politician: Eton, the Guards, very pleasant, very tough. Unless one happened to be an unemployed Londonderry Nationalist, it would be hard to dislike him. And even a Nationalist would have to admit that O'Neill and his family have earned their place in the Unionist establishment. His father, Captain the Honourable Arthur O'Neill, who represented Mid-Antrim at Westminster, was the first MP to be killed in the 1914–18 war. Both of the prime minister's brothers were killed in the second world war, in which he served with the Irish Guards. He is a direct descendant of Sir Arthur Chichester, who was James I's Lord of the Plantation in Ulster. The surname O'Neill—perhaps the proudest name in the earlier history of Irish rebellion against England—came into his family tree by marriage.

Captain O'Neill's cousinship is bewildering, but revealing, in its ramifications. He is a nephew of Lord Rathcavan who, as Sir Hugh O'Neill, represented Antrim at Westminster from 1915 to 1949, was a founder-member of the Conservative 1922 Committee (the powerful caucus of backbench parliamentarians), and the first Speaker of the Northern Ireland House of Commons. He is also the nephew of Dame Dehra Parker who represented South Derry at Stormont from 1920 to 1931, when her son, Major Chichester-Clark, took over the seat. On his death two years later she repossessed it, became minister of Health, and retained the seat until 1959 when she bequeathed it to her grandson, Captain James Chichester-Clark. The present member for South Derry, O'Neill's cousin, is Unionist chief whip at Stormont. Cousinly relations are also enjoyed by Phelim O'Neill who represents North Antrim at Stormont, by Robin Chichester-Clark who goes to Westminster on behalf of Derry County, and by Henry

Clark who attends to the interests of North Antrim in the same place. Captain O'Neill became a member of Stormont in 1946. Minister of Home Affairs in April 1956 and of Finance in the following September, he succeeded Lord Brookeborough as prime minister in March 1963.

I found him a relaxed, disarmingly frank person to interview. The style of his administration is informal. His private secretary, Jim Malley, met me in the hall of Stormont Castle (the prime minister's official residence), jacket off, hand extended. When I asked 'What'll I call him?' the reply was: 'Oh, call him anything you like'. Malley—a former squadron leader who spends his summer holidays in the Republic and is self-deprecatory about his performances as a bomber pilot in the RAF—acted as go-between while the historic Lemass–O'Neill talks were being negotiated.

O'Neill does not sound or act like a man who, if impelled by his own choice rather than by history, would have become the head of a party which has maintained itself in office for forty-five years assisted by gerrymandering and discrimination. Given the background of him, his achievement in meeting Sean Lemass on January 14, 1965 was, in Irish circumstances, an event which in the international field could only be equalled by Mao Tse-tung's receiving the Pope. In London it is said that Harold Wilson prompted the meeting; in Dublin that Lemass made the gesture foreseeing Labour gains on the Irish political front; in Belfast that O'Neill needed to pull out a card to trump his chief rival, Brian Faulkner, the able and restive minister of Commerce. These reasons may all be true and may have helped, but of themselves they would not have sufficed to promote the meeting.

The talks began through discreet overtures initiated by the ubiquitous Whitaker. He, O'Neill and Malley had been meeting each other at World Bank meetings ever since O'Neill had been Finance minister. Away from the envenomed atmosphere of Irish politics, a friendly relationship was established which encouraged Whitaker to make soundings in the close circles of both prime ministers. O'Neill stipulated that Lemass would have to come to Stormont first before he would go to Dublin. Lemass, to his everlasting credit, agreed to this. And so, for the first time in the history of the two states, the prime ministers of North and South officially met in Ireland. Until very recent years, the utmost that enlightened Southern opinion could publicly concede to the North was *de facto* recognition; *de jure* was out of the question. The Constitution of the Republic claims jurisdiction over all thirty-two counties, and the Republican viewpoint, shared by many of Lemass's senior colleagues, is that legally the North does not exist, being simply a British-garrisoned police state which maintains itself by trampling on the rights of the Catholic minority. Lemass, of course, had fought against acceptance both of the Treaty and of the Government of Ireland Act which sanctioned Partition.

This meeting was an act of political heroism for both men. Less than a month after the first meeting, while public opinion was still in a state of marked but uncoördinated pleasure, O'Neill paid a return visit to Dublin (February 9). While the reverberations of this were still making the air tingle with expectation, the gap opened in the Green Curtain became a highway. To frustrate any dangerous IRA or Orange protest, exchange visits between Northern and Southern ministers took place with such frequency that by midsummer 1965 the newspapers hardly bothered to record them.

During my interview with him, O'Neill revealed a good sense of humour—although it is perhaps typical of the upper-crust Unionist in him that when he had occasion to use a French phrase or sentence, his accent was impeccable, but when he told a story involving a take-off of some Southern politician, his Southern accent was execrable. He spoke to me with a candour which could be taken as proceeding either from a sense of unassailable superiority or from an honest belief in the justice of his cause. On the basis of his record and of the impression formed of him during our meeting, I would be inclined to believe the latter.

Bigotry. The prime minister denied that it was inspired by the ruling class, but agreed that it was a fact. Even though he and his colleagues try to get employers more readily to take on Catholics for jobs, he finds that foremen and other Protestant employees react with hostility to acceptance of Catholic workmates.* This is true, but I could not resist putting it to him that the fact that Orange lodges traditionally whipped up bigotry every Twelfth of July might have had some slight influence on the attitudes of Protestant workers. He countered this by pointing out (which is true) that no group in the country had been so loud as the Orange movement in pledging the support so necessary to the success of his talks with Lemass. I rather provokingly mentioned that both of his predecessors were on record as having made sectarian speeches. He visibly stiffened and said testily: 'Well, I haven't made any'. Indeed he has not, and I could see a doubt gathering on his strong, open face about the wisdom of letting this fang-toothed IRA journalist within biting distance!

Status of Northern Ireland. How did he feel about the North's not being able to have a foreign policy of its own? 'The very rich Canadian province

---

* Trouble can be caused in various ways, i.e. by Protestants decorating their work-benches for the 'Twalfth' or for a royal visit; by Catholics doing likewise on the Feast of Our Lady—and so on. This kind of friction is now officially frowned on, for more and more foreign industrialists are stipulating an end to such disruptive incidents as a condition of their bringing in new industries.

of Ontario has no foreign policy', he said. 'Yet its status gives it no sense of inferiority. Why should Northern Ireland feel ashamed at having the same attitude as Ontario ?'

Did not a man of his sophistication and calibre feel hurt at having his country referred to in articles abroad as a sort of John Bull's Portugal ? 'Of course I feel hurt, especially as the situation here is so unfairly and inaccurately described.' And here he made a point which he repeated a number of times during the interview: that all the talk of discrimination, bigotry, differences of outlook and so on, was already being—and to an increasing extent would further be—rendered less significant by growing affluence, modern communication, the spread of the ecumenical spirit, and the memory of Pope John. I would have travelled a good deal farther than the distance from Dublin to Belfast to have heard the prime minister of Northern Ireland praise a Pope.*

The effect of the South's contraception and censorship laws on the North's attitude. This, he thought, was confined to a very few people: 'a handful of intellectuals around Belfast'. Such matters were not at all an issue in the rural districts.

Southern politics. Captain O'Neill stressed the importance to the North of there being a strong government in power in the South in order to check the IRA. He had great respect for de Valera's ability to keep order, even if he disagreed fundamentally with his attitude towards the Border. He regarded the emergence of Clann na Poblachta as 'a disaster'. Here he was reflecting the reaction of the North both to the declaration of the Republic and also to the all-party Anti-Partition campaign of 1949 (described above, page 96), which brought together for a time militant Republicans and leading constitutional politicians in the South. O'Neill felt that part of the £50,000 collected to promote the campaign was used to put up Sinn Fein candidates in Northern Ireland. The belief is firmly held by many Unionists that practically all parties in the South at some time or other have had connections, direct or indirect, with Sinn Fein activities in the North. But, of course, Sinn Fein recognises neither the Dail nor the Northern parliament as *de jure* authorities in Ireland.

The prime minister was fascinatingly forthcoming about the incautious public utterances of certain Southern politicians whose fire-breathing denunciations against the North have been worth an incalculable number

---

* Whether it is still used in its pristine splendour, I cannot say, but the old Orange toast went as follows: 'To the glorious, pious and immortal memory of King William III who saved us from rogues and roguery, slaves and slavery, knaves and knavery, popes and popery, from brass money and wooden shoes; and whoever denies this toast, may he be slammed, crammed and jammed into the muzzle of the great gun of Athlone, and the gun fired into the Pope's belly, and the Pope into the Devil's belly, and the Devil into Hell, and the door locked and the key in an Orangeman's pocket'.

of votes to the Unionist Party when served up for the digestion of an alarmed Northern electorate. He regarded all talk of Dublin's right to rule a Thirty-Two Counties Republic with complete, and vividly expressed, scorn. But he volunteered praise of Lemass, Whitaker and some of the younger politicians, notably Jack Lynch.

The Catholic birth-rate. This he regarded as a major source of tension. Northern Protestants see the numbers of their faith in the South dropping. Fearing that the same thing can happen in the North, they react by strengthening their old 'give-way-not-an-inch' policy. I mentioned that recently the numbers of Protestants in the Republic had begun to rise and that it was of great concern to the Church of Ireland in the South that a great deal of what it considered to be needless emigration had taken place. He repeated what he had said earlier: that with increasing affluence and the spread of goodwill, this problem also would prove less intractable.

Newspaper coverage of events on both sides of the Border. 'I'm afraid that both sets of newspapers have been rather naughty. They have seemed to publish only what they thought their readers wanted to read.' In this he is largely right. Prior to his meeting with Lemass, newspapers North and South, with some honourable exceptions, tended to give the impression that on the one side there existed a squalid, poverty-stricken enclave of Rome, and on the other side an unemployment-stricken, bigoted police state. O'Neill was at pains to point out that, despite the IRA raids, the frontier between North and South was unguarded. No troops confronted each other; save for customs checks, men of goodwill could pass freely in both directions.

The importance of symbolism. 'To use that much overworked word "loyalty", the Union Jack is the flag we are loyal to. To us the Tricolour is the flag of the IRA.' If ever I needed an illustration of the evils that accrue when men start hating each other for the love of God, I got it then, drinking tea in that comfortable drawing-room. Captain O'Neill had been wounded in serving under the Union Jack. Though used by Unionists as a party emblem, it is the flag under which his father and two brothers had died, fighting for something more than a party. Yet to me the cross of Saint Patrick in the Union Jack flying over Stormont is a symbol of the dismemberment of my country, while the Tricolour, the flag which draped my father's coffin, symbolises its union: green for the Gaels of the South, orange for the men of the North, and white for peace between them. But if to me the Union Jack is a symbol of party, so is the Tricolour to Captain O'Neill: a banner of riot and subversion which can be prohibited under the Flags and Emblems Act of 1954.

But Captain O'Neill is as Irish as I am. (Well, nearly; his family came 300 years after mine, though they did better for themselves!) He shares the admiration of Southern Irishmen for John F. Kennedy and for Jacqueline Kennedy, whose picture hangs above his fireplace. And he is proud of the fact that Ulster Presbyterians were George Washington's best troops in the fight for American independence (even if his ancestors drove them from Ulster!).

The suggestion of a tripartite agreement on Partition. He said bluntly that there was no question of the North's taking part in any such agreement. Any suggestion of tripartite talks 'raises the spectre of the 1925 Agreements and all that sort of thing'. There it is in a nutshell. In the South, the 1925 Agreements embodying the findings of the Boundary Commission were regarded as a betrayal and a surrender, and revulsion against them destroyed the political career of a good man, Eoin MacNeill. In the North, Protestant fears had reached near-panic level when Sir James Craig went to London, for the tripartite negotiations involved the possibility that, under British pressure, the North might place itself under Dublin.

Among older civil servants in Dublin and Belfast—men who were in a position to know something of the manoeuvrings that took place between the three capitals during the early days of the second world war—I have met with the view that at this time Northern public opinion was thought to have reached a stage, because of the war, where a solution to Partition might have been achieved. The British certainly are known to have made some overture on the basis of the Free State's allowing the Royal Navy the use of its ports. But Sir James Craig's obduracy, it is claimed, forced Britain to abandon the scheme. If this British offer be true—and evidence for it must, of course, await the release of official documents, if there are any—it must be said that such a climate of opinion in the North, which is held to have encouraged this plan to solve the Partition question, no longer exists today.

The post-war social legislation of the Labour government in Britain (which the twelve Unionists at Westminster voted against!) ushered in an era wherein the enhanced standard of living for the mass of people in the North, quite apart from historical influences, has ruled out—at least for the present—any possibility of getting the man-in-the-street to accept unity with the South. When Captain O'Neill or any other Unionist talks about unity, he means unity with the United Kingdom. 'Unity' on the Border issue, if it means any diminution of the North's autonomous position, is translatable as 'surrender'—and 'No Surrender' has long been an Orange war-cry.

North and South have until very recently seen the issue simply as a question of who should have authority over the Six Counties. Where the present prime minister of Northern Ireland has made a significant advance from this point is in his open acknowledgement of the economic benefits which the North receives from the British connection. Hitherto these were officially regarded as a secondary issue.

OLD PREJUDICE, NEW SENSIBILITY

The plain truth about the North today is that the secret wish of most Northern Catholics is not for union with the South (entailing a fall-off in social benefits) but for an end to discrimination and for a fairer share of the Northern spoils. This truth may be unpalatable to us in the South, but it has to be faced.

Discrimination still exists, despite the vastly improved atmosphere following the Lemass–O'Neill meetings. In this respect, the appearance of the Northern scene differs like that of a mountain when seen on a gloomy wet day and on a day of warm sunshine. The difference is climatic: the mountain remains. Still, the question of how long it will remain in its present shape is, all-praisedly, at last a subject for validly hopeful speculation. The Northern mood is certainly changing; this change has already been pointed out and I hope to be able to give a further indication of it presently. But pleasure at the development of a more hopeful new mood must not make us overlook the evidences of the old mood which are still all too discernible in the North. It is still difficult for Catholics to believe that the Promised Land has been reached, especially if they live in the western parts of the province.

Belfast is a polite, prosperous and well laid-out British city. Aesthetically, architecturally and culturally, it has more in common with, say, Bradford or Manchester than with any town in the Republic.* Dubliners usually try to avoid spending the night there; Northerners on the other hand apparently feel a party has begun once they set foot in Dublin. However, it is not its lack of party spirit, whether real or imagined, which gives Belfast its special standing. The city holds half of the population of Northern Ireland and half of its industry, while most of the rest of the country's people and industrial activity lie around Belfast in the triangle formed by the eastern counties of Down, Armagh and Antrim. In 1963, the numbers employed in manufacturing by firms with twenty-five workers or more, classified by counties and county boroughs, were as follow: eastern region, 160,392; western region (Derry, Fermanagh and Tyrone), 28,773. The

---

* However, Gaelic Leaguers, Republicans and others that I know in Belfast say the city is far more characteristically *Irish* than Dublin, and say that it looks like Cork—which it does, architecturally. When I say it seems to me more British than Irish, I am thinking of its 'atmosphere'. The opinion of Northern Nationalists on this matter is very likely to be sound, though it is just possible that emphasis of the Irishness of Belfast has a political significance.

same sort of imbalance exists between the eastern and western regions of the Republic. Unfortunately, despite the new spirit developing in Northern Ireland, it is not possible to believe that the Northern imbalance arises from quite the same factors as condition that of the South.

Discrimination

The western counties are predominantly Catholic, the eastern predominantly Protestant. The North's development policy in recent years has given the Catholic population reason to believe that development is being concentrated in the eastern region so as to maintain the Unionist supremacy at the expense of the three western counties. Between 1963 and 1965 four things in particular served to strengthen this belief.

1. Londonderry, the second largest city in the North with 54,000 inhabitants, is also the principal Catholic stronghold in the western counties. Before 1964, Londonderry (county and city) was served by two rail links. As an economy measure (an Irish extension of Beechingism) one line was closed. This was the link which served Londonderry County and the other western counties of Tyrone and Fermanagh. These areas now have no railways whatever.

2. The government proposed to build a new town in County Armagh, appointing as its chief designer Geoffrey Copcutt, the English town planner who worked on Cumbernauld New Town near Glasgow. On August 13, 1964 he resigned his post, saying: 'I think there are better regions, environmentally and strategically' for such urban development. He urged that Londonderry be developed 'as a priority'. The government, however, is sticking to its plan for building the new town between two existing centres, Lurgan and Portadown (both Unionist), which are only four miles apart and which, Copcutt claims, only require a 1,000-yard expansion of their existing diameters in order 'to provide the equivalent total population set for the new city'.

The new town is to be called Craigavon after the North's first prime minister: the Unionist leader who made the celebrated claim that Stormont was 'a Protestant Parliament for a Protestant People'.* True, there have been a number of protests among liberal-minded Unionists at what they feel to be an unduly provocative name for a venture which was supposed to symbolise the 'new look' Ulster. Another aspect of the plan for the new town—cost of which is estimated to be £140 million—is the fact that the projection for school requirements allows for only five voluntary (i.e. Catholic) schools. Although at present Catholics account for only slightly

---

* Though it should be remembered that at the outset of his regime he appointed a Catholic chief justice and a Catholic permanent secretary to the Ministry of Education. His offer to reserve one third of the places in the RUC was withdrawn, because, it is said, Catholic applicants did not come forward.

more than a third of the North's population, their higher birth-rate means that 48 per cent of all primary schoolchildren are Catholic. With insufficient schools for their children in Craigavon, Catholic fathers are not likely to flock there in great numbers for jobs.

3. As in the South, the government at Stormont has put much of its hope for the future in planned economic development. In October 1963, Professor Wilson of Glasgow University was appointed economic consultant to Northern Ireland. He and a team of government economists produced a development plan in February 1965—the Wilson Report—which was adopted by the government. It recommended the creation of 65,000 new jobs by 1970, and the investment of £900 million in the private and public sectors to improve industry, housing (for which a target of 64,000 new houses was set), education and services of all kinds. Except for the last in the list, the growth-centres specified in the report were nearly all within one thirty-mile radius: Lurgan, Portadown, Bangor, Newtownards, Antrim, Ballymena, Carrickfergus, Carnmoney, Larne—and Londonderry. The report justified these siting arrangements by saying that 'some internal migration is the only alternative to industrial stagnation, unemployment, and the outward movement of people from the region: a less desirable form of migration'. The Catholic belief that the western region was being discriminated against was strengthened by the rather cursory inclusion of Londonderry: the only western site mentioned.

4. This belief was further intensified by another report: the Lockwood Committee on Higher Education, published in February 1965. This recommended that the new university for which the North, and Londonderry in particular, has for long been agitating, should be sited at Coleraine in County Antrim. Once again the eastern region had been chosen for a major venture in national development. The terms of reference of the Lockwood Committee were: 'To review the facilities for university and higher technical education in Northern Ireland having regard to the Report to the Robbins Committee, and to make recommendations'. Nothing was said in its terms of reference about recommending a site, and it was assumed that, as in England, this would be a matter for the government in consultation with the University Grants Committee. But the view is widely held in the North that it was conveyed to the committee in the course of its deliberations that it would be proper for it to recommend a site for the new university. This assumption, it is argued, is borne out at least in part by the letter with which the Lockwood Committee prefaced its report: '. . . We subsequently found that it was not possible to deal with the academic problems of a new university outside the context of general location . . .'.

Anywhere else this explanation might reasonably be accepted. But not

in the North. An unprecedented protest movement was launched in
Londonderry, in which liberal Unionists joined with the opposition parties.
On February 18, shops, business premises and schools in the city closed
down, and a motorcade of 1,500 vehicles drove the ninety miles to Stormont. The protest was unavailing. In the ensuing debate, the issue was
made one of confidence in the government. Of the thirty-three speakers in
the debate, only five spoke in favour of Coleraine: the prime minister, the
minister of Education and three other Unionists. Two Unionists abstained
from the vote; two Unionists voted with the opposition, which was solidly
united against the proposal. The government carried the day, although
with thirty-two Ayes against twenty Noes, the majority was one of the
smallest ever known at Stormont.

The main objection to the Lockwood Committee's report was threefold.
In the first place, there had not been a single Catholic on the committee.
Secondly, Coleraine has a population of only 12,000 while Londonderry
has 54,000—which makes the latter, the opposition contended, a more
appropriately sized place for a university. Thirdly, the 'academic problems'
mentioned in the report would have been made more easily soluble by the
selection of Londonderry, since that city already has the only university
college outside Belfast: Magee University College, which is a recognised
unit of Queen's University with over 200 students. The controversy over
the new university became explosive when Dr Robert Nixon, Stormont
member for North Down, alleged publicly that a cabinet minister had told
him that prominent Unionists in Londonderry as well as members of the
government were behind the proposal to site it at Coleraine. Nixon was
expelled from the Unionist parliamentary party. A petition with 15,000
signatures called for a public enquiry into his allegations. It was rejected
by the prime minister.

Whether the university-siting or any other planning venture is directly
conditioned by political factors is debatable. Proximity to Belfast and hence
to the main communication routes with Britain is a major attraction to
British and foreign industrialists. For example, a Dutch businessman,
Rolfe Schierbeek, has brought a man-made fibres plant to Antrim town
which, when in full production by the end of 1966, will employ some 1,200
people. He has sited it at Antrim on the understanding that certain conditions be met: improvement of the communications with Belfast; conversion
of the town into a smokeless zone; provision of facilities for higher education for the children of his employees. In view of the fact that, before
Schierbeek appeared on the scene, Antrim was a town of only 1,979 people,
the alacrity with which Stormont has met his demands is understandable.

Understandable to an outsider, I mean. The woe of the North is that it is not so easy to accept such planning as being governed by purely technical considerations if one happens to be a Catholic living in the North. The cause of the deep suspicion of whatever the government does arises from the application of that electoral device which takes its name from its inventor, Governor Elbridge Gerry of Massachusetts. The Unionists of Northern Ireland have few equals in the applied science of gerrymandering. While the franchise for the twelve Northern seats at Westminster is the same as that obtaining in Britain, the elections for Stormont (both houses) and for local government councils are conducted under the provincial Electoral Law Act of 1962, which in turn consolidated the provision of the Electoral Law Act of 1929 under which proportional representation was abolished. It must unfortunately be said that the Unionist speeches of the time and the subsequent use of gerrymandering make it quite clear that the reasons for seeking the abolition of proportional representation were the same as those which inspired its retention in the South: PR safeguards the rights of minorities.

According to the census report, the population of Northern Ireland in 1961 was 1,425,462. By normal adult suffrage, the electorate for representation at Westminster numbered 891,107. According to the latest Electoral Register (that published on February 15, 1964), which retains the special business and property votes abolished elsewhere in the United Kingdom, the 'domestic' electorate is composed as follows:

STORMONT ELECTORS

Adult suffrage	885,514
University second vote	13,763
Business second vote	12,663
Total	911,940

LOCAL GOVERNMENT ELECTORS

Residents and spouses	648,417
Business second vote	6,467
Company votes	3,894
Total	658,778

Even when eked out by business and company votes, the local government electorate is smaller by some 220,000 voters than the Westminster electorate; in short, there is large-scale disenfranchisement in local representation. In County Antrim, for example, there are 66,929 Catholics out of a total population of 273,905. The country returns two Unionists to Westminster: a reasonable enough result in view of the Protestant strength there. It has seven seats at Stormont; these are all held by Unionists: not quite so reasonable!

Of course, results of this kind can be achieved even in elections where the rectitude of the voting system is unquestionable—as the British Liberal Party knows to its grief. But their psychological effect in Northern Ireland, where 'personation' is so much a feature of electoral practice that all parties treat it as the Eleventh Commandment, is to make Catholics believe that the system in all its aspects is directly and deliberately contrived to their detriment. This is particularly so when there is a large discrepancy between the numbers of electors in the various constituencies. Mid-Down, for instance, has 41,402 electors. This is the largest constituency. The smallest is the Dock division of Belfast, with but 7,612. Both have equal representation in parliament. The university vote, abolished in Britain in 1949, gives the 13,763 graduates of Queen's not only a voice in the election of the members in their home constituencies, but also their four university members. The business vote in Stormont elections, granted to the owner (and spouse) of premises valued at £10 or over, is heavily weighted in favour of the Protestant community among which the majority of property-owners are to be found.

It is over local government elections that strongest criticism is made. In Stormont elections, the number of successful Unionists, though disproportionate to the party's overall strength, is not so disproportionately large as in local government elections. It is these which make one wonder if the British taxpayer, be he Conservative, Labour or Liberal, would lend himself to the system obtaining in Northern Ireland were he consulted. But perhaps this is an otiose question. The burden of representative government is doubtless such that certain matters tend inevitably to be 'reserved questions'.

There are seventy-three local authorities in the North with a total of 703 electoral divisions. These authorities, being organised on the council-and-committees systems, are—electoral questions apart—too numerous and too ineffectual to supply the needs of a modern community. Their structure is the result of various legislative measures passed between 1840 and 1898. To an antiquated administrative system are added the dubious complexities of the electoral system for local government.

Business and company votes count in local elections. Adult suffrage does not. The general vote is confined to the occupier of a house and his wife. Occupiers' children over twenty-one, and any servants or subtenants in the house, are excluded from the local franchise. The Unionists defend this on the grounds that democracy should mean something more than the mere counting of heads; property should have some rights also. The British-framed laws requiring adult suffrage for Westminster and Stormont elections do not enable the Unionists to enshrine their doctrine in the process for electing members to parliament. But they have autonomous control of 'local affairs'. Denied the larger hope, they make the best use of the more limited opportunity. The system is weighted in favour of those who already own property. A young married couple living with their in-laws may not vote for a councillor who might be expected to help them get a house of their own. A Catholic family living in a flat will hardly be comforted by the sentiments of Professor Corkey, a Unionist senator, who said in the Senate on October 8, 1964: ' . . . The parents of large families should be fined for having so many children'.

The local government system reaches its most questionable level in Londonderry town. It is divided into three wards: North, Waterside and South. The population (1961 census) is: Catholic, 36,049; Protestant, 17,695. There are 19,870 Catholics over the age of twenty-one, but the franchise qualifications enable only 14,325 of them (including 257 company votes) to vote. Of 10,573 Protestants over the age of twenty-one, 9,235 (including 902 company votes) have the suffrage. This would appear to give the Catholics a disproportionately small, but still a decided, majority on the council. Not so. The wards are drawn in such a way that they return twelve Unionists and only eight Nationalists.

The North Ward contains 6,711 voters divided two to one in the Unionists' favour. This ward returns eight representatives: six councillors and two aldermen. All eight are Unionists. The Waterside Ward has 5,459 voters, divided in much the same proportion relative to party strength. It returns four representatives: three councillors and one alderman. All are Unionists. The South Ward contains 11,390 voters, of whom 10,130 are Nationalist supporters. It returns eight representatives: six councillors and two aldermen. All are Nationalists. So, North and Waterside wards total 12,170 voters and yield twelve Unionist representatives as against South Ward's 11,390 voters and eight representatives.

The mayor is a Unionist and controls the allocation of public housing. Catholics believe that houses will be allocated to them quite readily in the South Ward, but only sparingly in the other two, so as to preserve the Unionist ascendancy. But the Unionists have a serious problem on their hands. By 1965 all the land available for building in the South Ward had been used up and the corporation refused to extend the city boundary. What happens next is one of the most absorbing subjects of speculation in all Ireland.

Of the total number of houses built in Londonderry since the end of the war, Catholics have received 2,212 and Protestants 924. This is not so equitable as may appear because, while the proportion of unhoused Protestants was insignificant, there were in 1965 over 2,000 Catholic families awaiting houses on the city's list. If this is taken in conjunction with the fact that, of the 177 employees of Londonderry Corporation, 145 were Protestants earning a total of £124,424 and thirty-two were Catholics earning a total of £20,420, one begins to understand why the Catholic third of the population of the North yielded almost 58 per cent of the emigration between 1937 and 1961. Emigration is the reason why, despite the higher Catholic birth-rate, the ratio between Catholic and Protestant in the North has remained almost at the level obtaining when the Government of Ireland Act was passed in 1920.

Londonderry city is as shabby as Belfast is tidy. Apparent everywhere is the ironic evidence of an underprivileged Catholic majority in the town which withstood one of the great sieges of history in defence of the Protestant liberty of the subject. Its British 'provincial' architecture (its reflection of London is confined to its name) makes it look un-Irish to the Southerner, while the North, for its part, seems to be saying it does not want it any more. It is a NATO base; and 5,000 of its people find employment in making shirts, collars and pyjamas in the ugly Victorian factories which dot the town. There are a number of smaller industries, but there are almost no tourist amenities. The principal attraction, apart from salmon fishing, is the old wall of Derry against which King James broke his heart.

Edward McAteer, the leader of the Nationalist Party, looks down on this uneasy, unhappy city from a pleasant hillside villa where he lives with his cheerful, hospitable wife and their ten children. An accountant and travel agent just turned fifty, he is a tall, handsome man with iron-grey hair and bushy eyebrows. Over the telephone he had said: 'You're writing a book? Come up and we'll pour a drop of hemlock in your ear.'

This is rather what I had expected he would do, given the circumstances of his native city and his own background. His brother Hugh, chief of staff of the IRA at the time, created a national sensation in 1943 when he appeared on the stage of the Hippodrome Cinema in Londonderry during a performance. Edward McAteer had advised me to apprise myself of the contemporary situation in the city by consulting the history of the Honourable Irish Society which administered the Londonderry Plantation in the early part of the seventeenth century. In addition he had sent me pamphlets he had written in the days of the all-party campaign in the South against Partition. In one of these he advised Catholics to get as much as they could out of the Welfare State and then 'act stupid, demand explanation, object —anything at all that will clog the Departmental machinery'.

But he turned out to be a friendly, rational man, and as concerned in his own way to do as much for better relationships as Captain O'Neill in his. Before the Lemass–O'Neill talks, McAteer himself had been groping his way from the standpoint of grimly pointing out the warts on the North's face towards an attempt to come to terms with the condition of which they are the symptom. As was mentioned above (page 311), he initiated a series of Orange and Green talks which petered out during 1964 because the Green would not acknowledge the constitutional position of the Orange. The realities of life in Londonderry stifled all efforts at overcoming the unreality of refusing recognition to Stormont. He looked out over the drab, divided city, and said: 'We've had to abandon our proud dream of trampling the Tricolour in their faces. It's not easy to change. Though some of us have been twenty years at Stormont, in that time we haven't spoken to our opposite numbers except on the floor of the House. In the restaurants we never even had a cup of coffee together. And then there's the gerrymandering. The only way, I suppose, is Pope John's way—through a union of hearts.' He pointed out hopefully some improvements in the climate of relations which had occurred even before the Lemass–O'Neill talks: the fact that rioting in the 1964 elections had been confined to a small area of Belfast instead of spreading as it would have done a few years earlier; the fact that the Border Campaign of 1956–62 had failed to rouse a violent response, for or against.

A New Departure?

Is it possible that, after all the years of gerrymandering and discrimination, something concrete is going to be done to put relations between Catholic and Protestant in the North on a healthier footing? The electoral system is a crucial factor and it is to this area that eyes searching for hopeful signs will most intently turn. In February 1965, the Northern Ireland Boundary Commission announced that a general review of electoral boundaries would be undertaken. Maybe this could mean that the system is going to be changed. An agitation for fairer distribution of housing in Dungannon, County Tyrone, started in 1963 by the wife of a local Catholic doctor, Mrs Patricia MacCluskey, has produced a powerful offshoot in the shape of the Campaign for Social Justice in Northern Ireland. The accent now is less on the old intransigent arguments about Partition and the 'legality' of Stormont, and more on the tackling of the general problem of democratic and social justice in the self-governing state of Northern Ireland. Moreover, there are signs that Northern problems are beginning to receive closer attention in Britain itself.

Politicians, we know, however sincere in their views, are liable to be influenced by the mood of the moment. The 'official' mood is hopeful. But does it reflect a fundamental current of thought outside the political arena? I think it does. North and South of the Border there are people in responsible positions, outside politics, who are convinced that the change is real and enduring.

Among those in the South, there spring to mind men like Ernest Blythe and Dr J. F. Dempsey. Blythe, now managing director of the Abbey Theatre and a former minister for Finance in the Cumann na nGaedheal government, is a Presbyterian born in the North. For years he has been talking and writing about the need to look at the realities of the Northern situation, to accept them and then seek to make progress from that point. The signs of progress now showing themselves are only what he has been forecasting all along. Dr Dempsey—perhaps because his position as general manager of Aer Lingus enables him to rise above the obsessions of the groundlings—has for a long time been advocating a more friendly policy. In a speech to a group of fellow-accountants, he said: 'It would be well for the people in the Republic to remember that it is not a practical proposition to talk of co-operation with the people of Northern Ireland if the proposition contains any suggestion of interfering with the present constitutional position of the North'.

Dempsey on this occasion was speaking as president of the Irish Association for Cultural, Economic and Social Relations: a cross-Border association for promoting closer contacts between North and South. It was founded as long ago as 1938 as the result of discussions between Major-General Montgomery and Lord Charlemont in the North and leaders of Southern opinion like Louie Bennett, the woman trade unionist, and Professor George O'Brien of University College, Dublin. It has served as an agency for the coming together of men and women of goodwill. Its most notable contribution to the cause of better understanding between the two parts of Ireland was the survey it commissioned into group relationships in the North: *The Northern Problem* by Denis P. Barritt and Charles F. Carter, published in 1962. Albeit a little pro-Protestant, it is an objective enquiry, eschewing all propaganda motivation, and gives the best insight I know of into the nature of the problem.

Among enlightened people I contacted in the North when preparing this book, I cite three in particular: Sir Graham Larmor, William Blease and John Sayers. Sir Graham Larmor is a Northern linen magnate. He has consistently worked to improve relations between North and South, and was Dempsey's predecessor as president of the Irish Association. He told me: 'Unquestionably there is a tremendous improvement. All sensible, sane people recognise it, and are doing what they can to bring about even more progress in this matter. In my own industry, for example, we find that the South are interpreting tariff regulations in a new and intelligent way. Certainly I'd give Pope John some of the credit for the change.' Sir Graham's sentiments were echoed by William Blease, the Northern Ireland Officer of the Irish Trade Union Congress. He is widely recognised as one of the most progressive and enlightened figures in the Labour movement in the North. 'There's no question about it. There's a new spirit abroad. That's the really significant thing about the North today.'

John Sayers is the editor of the Unionist *Belfast Telegraph*, the largest and most influential paper in the North. His editorship of the *Telegraph* has been in the best traditions of journalism. Helped by the fact that he is the third member of his family to work for the paper, he began to pursue a new liberal policy before the 1958 Stormont elections. He had been political correspondent for the *Telegraph* and his experiences in this job had brought him to the conclusion that what Stormont needed was a constructive opposition party. Accordingly, during the campaign the *Telegraph* recommended Labour to its readers. Four members of the Northern Ireland Labour Party were returned. For the first time in its history Stormont had a cohesive, if not very powerful, opposition. Sayers —who is, of course, deeply wedded to the Union with Britain—has an interesting theory about the new developments. He believes that the Catholics, whom he feels are not yet taking as large a part as they might in the 'New Departure', would have no difficulty in supporting a Conservative, as opposed to a Unionist, party. If the Unionists could mutate into Conservatives in the English sense, most of the North's difficulties, he holds, would be solved. He has a high opinion of Cardinal Conway, the new head of the hierarchy. During our meeting Sayers refused to accept any special credit for his editorial line, saying that its acceptance merely shows that people were ready for such an approach.

How far this new approach will take North and South, time will tell. But at the moment of writing, enormously helpful movements are afoot in the relations between the Republic and Northern Ireland which will, I believe, have healthy repercussions on the relationships of Protestants and Catholics on both sides of the Border.

Stimulated by the Lemass–O'Neill talks, top-level discussions are taking place between the agricultural departments of the two countries, aiming at co-operative action in the spheres of veterinary surgery, marketing and agrarian development. Both governments have officially announced their intention of adopting a joint approach to tourism. Already motor traffic restrictions between North and South have been eased, and the 'Checkpoint Charley' routine at the Border, involving elaborate tryptiques and bonded cars, has disappeared. A project is afoot for common initiative in the development of power resources. This is an obvious area for co-operation. The South is running out of peat supplies, while the North has to import all the coal it uses. On its own, neither could afford a nuclear reactor; but by pooling their resources it would be feasible.

It is not possible to give further details of these developments at the time of writing. But when I started preparing material for this book at the end of 1964, the mere thought that such developments could occur at all was inconceivable. My conviction is that the change of attitude in the North is real. Although the stumbling blocks are great and old attitudes are still strongly ingrained among many, my impression is that the new spirit discernible in so many quarters is more representative of the future character of the North than the present evidences of gerrymandering and discrimination.

ENVOI

THIS book goes to press in the first days of 1966. By the time it is published, it will be clearer how Ireland intends to celebrate the fiftieth anniversary of the Rising. At the time of writing, a pessimist can find grounds for predicting an orgy of chauvinistic flag-waving, carried out against a backcloth of industrial disputes and a sharpening balance of payments crisis; in short, the grim old pattern of nationalist emotionalism obliterating concern for the state of the nation. A cynic can point to the Free Trade Agreement signed with Britain in the closing days of 1965, and comment sardonically on the Irishness of having the golden jubilee of the revolt which led to the break-up of the Union coincide with entry into a new form of Union with Britain. And an optimist can nurture the hope that, as the anniversary will fittingly be a time for remembering past ideals and saluting the nation's heroes, it will also be, no less fittingly, an occasion for the national conscience to examine itself and enquire if the Ireland of today is an Ireland that those who fought and died for Irish freedom would have considered worth fighting and dying for.

As my readers will probably hazard, I incline towards the optimistic view. Not that the pessimists and cynics lack straw for making brickbats. The advent of the 1916 anniversary has produced some deplorable pronouncements which bode ill for the future, notably from political backwoodsmen, Irish language enthusiasts and Sinn Fein extremists. In economic affairs, it is too early yet to assess the effects of the Free Trade Agreement with Britain; what is all too clear is that both countries are struggling along the same trough of economic crisis. The effects of high governmental and private spending, rising prices, mounting wage demands and a sluggish productivity-rate are probably even more immediately menacing for Ireland than for her neighbour. In 1965 they led to a rigorous credit squeeze, to price controls and to an import levy similar to that imposed by the British. All this has entailed the shelving of cherished and necessary plans for improving educational and health facilities and for revivifying the West.

The cut-back in development schemes for the poor rural areas is a bitter pill to swallow, particularly for those who hailed Whitaker and his works as marking a new era of hope for Irish countrymen and townsmen alike. A good many in Ireland are now saying that the government's plans for the rural twilight areas were more of a sop to allay local (and electoral) discontent than a serious programme of development. Exaggerated and unjust as this criticism may be, it could have a bad effect on national morale, vitiating the new air of confidence in the future which began to blow through Ireland at the end of the 'fifties. Moreover, even if the situation brightens in 1966, the effects of the stringent economy measures spotlight a new factor of enduring significance. Henceforth, and to an increasing degree, Ireland will take shape as an industrialised, urbanised society. It is already apparent that, on both sides of the Border, the poor rural areas take the same kind of subsidiary role in the thinking of planners in Dublin and Belfast as the Highlands of Scotland have taken in the thinking of planners in London.

Yet the ill wind has blown some good. The crisis measures of 1965 were followed, not by a large increase in emigration as in similar crisis periods (though the figures of emigrants did rise somewhat), but by a very hopeful move towards a national incomes policy for the industrial sector. The principles for this were set out in a report of the National Industrial and Economic Council, and were accepted by government, employers and trade unions. The details have still to be worked out, and the complete exclusion of agriculture makes it only half a policy. Nevertheless, its acceptance on such a wide front constitutes a social and economic miracle of the first order.

All the same, while the agreement on an incomes policy is a concrete achievement of great importance, it would probably be wiser to base forecasts of Ireland's immediate future less on formal policy statements than on public and private attitudes—attitudes towards work and wages, and to the four Ps: play, prayer, progress and patriotism. If, for example, the criterion of patriotism is to be governed by the values of the die-hards in the Gaelic Athletic Association, who assess a man's claim to be a true Irishman by the shape of his football, then the outlook is going to be bleak indeed. Fortunately this attitude is not representative of the country as a whole, and people generally are coming to regard it as an embarrassing anachronism. This is particularly so among young people. Here attitudes towards the country and its future are encouragingly realistic and enlightened. In debates and school magazines, on television programmes and in private conversation, the younger generation is showing itself soberly constructive both in its criticisms of present-day Ireland and in its vision of the country's future. The young people today have a wider outlook than their elders. Many of them work in England during the holidays to pay for their education; most of them are aware of the world outside Ireland; and more and more of them are recognising that, if Ireland in the future is to be as they would desire it, they themselves have to set to work in Ireland to achieve this.

Nowhere are changing attitudes of more importance than in the Church, and of all sectors of national life, none will be more affected by changes in the character of Irish society. The fall in religious vocations which has followed urbanisation in other countries has already shown signs of occurring in Ireland. Still revered, the priesthood is no longer the main gateway to social status and authority that it once was. Increasing intervention by the state in education means that poor country boys will not in such numbers as hitherto be joining the 'Brothers' or the 'Fathers'. The free education provided by the regulars will continue for a long time to come to be a very important factor in Irish education; but in the future it will no longer be the *only* form of educational opportunity for the great majority of Irish children. This and similar changes in the social role of the Church will present priests and laity alike with big, and perhaps painful, challenges to old attitudes. How these challenges will be met is perhaps the greatest single question mark hanging over Ireland's future. Happily there are signs that the Church is beginning to meet some of the challenges of the new Ireland. In the Northern diocese of Down and Conor, for instance, Bishop Philibin has introduced a new system of catechetical instruction, devised for modern needs. It is understood, furthermore, that the Irish hierarchy at the last session of the Vatican Council drew up a new scheme for salary scales and for reforming administration in all dioceses.

Admittedly, my optimism about clerical attitudes was jolted when news leaked out, as this book was in the press, that John McGahern had lost his schoolteacher job because of resentment in high places over his novel, *The Dark* (a study of adolescence). The mists *are* lifting from Irish culture, but there's still a whiff of the old miasma.

The changes in attitudes occurring in Irish politics, discussed with warm approval in chapters 5 and 12, are clearly an acid-test for determining the shape of the country's future. Yet, to be objective, one has to say that not all features of the 'new image' of Irish politics are commendable. In responding to the influence of J. F. Kennedy, some of the younger element seem to have adopted the more questionable features of American 'high pressure' politics. It will be ill for Irish politics if 'Kennedyism' comes to be identified with the practices evoked by labels like the 'Donegal Mafia'. In despondent moments, one sometimes wonders if the young lions have a tithe of the idealism which inspired the men they are succeeding. But then one thinks of the reforming, humanitarian zeal of young men like Donough O'Malley, the minister for Health, and cheerfulness breaks through.

Nor is the new spirit confined to the young for whom the past is the past. When W. T. Cosgrave died in November 1965, the strength of the political institutions which he and Kevin O'Higgins created was admirably demonstrated by the tribute paid in the Dail to the dead stateman by Sean Lemass—one of the men in the Four Courts the day that Cosgrave authorised the bombardment which began the Civil War. And some of the warmest tributes outside the Dail appeared in the editorial columns of the Irish Press group of newspapers, founded by Eamon de Valera. Cosgrave had given instructions that his coffin should go to the grave undraped by any flag. This gesture stirred people deeply, for it was a telling reminder that South and North of the Border flags have so often been used as tokens of defiance rather than of allegiance that much of their patriotic symbolism has been prostituted. It would not be the least of W. T. Cosgrave's services to Ireland if his last gesture were to stimulate a fresh recognition of what the tricolour should symbolise.

Despite all the difficulties, the move towards friendship and co-operation between South and North has continued. The Republic, for example, excluded Northern Ireland from the operation of its import levy in 1965. Yet the fresh signs of IRA activity as the country approached the anniversary of the Rising aroused forebodings for the health of the tender plant of reconciliation. Courageous and sincere as they are in their aims, one must devoutly pray that the idealism of these young men of the IRA can be directed into more constructive, peaceable channels. And where the Orangemen are concerned: surely it is fair to ask whether certain aspects of the North's present dependence on Britain should not irk them as Irishmen? In my visits around the North I found the air of bland uninvolvement just a little degrading. ('Are you having some sort of crisis down there, old boy?' 'Oh, the British levy? But, of course, it doesn't affect *us*!') Surely the Orangeman can conceive of a better destiny for himself than existence as a dependant on Britain in what the English classify as a depressed area? Given reasonable safeguards, surely it would be in the interests of the North's *self-respect* for it to be aligned more closely with the South? Such an eventuality, of course, presupposes a high degree of progress in the South.

Yet perhaps this kind of speculation is already otiose, for it is already clear that Ireland's future involves a closer relationship with Britain and with Europe. In the past, Ireland's greatest problem was that she lay too close to England for comfort or independence, yet was too far away for England completely to assimilate her. Today, however, she is near enough for friendship.

Fifty years after the Rising, mindful of what the men of 1916 died for, Ireland is striving to make herself a country which the men of today and their children will be proud to live in: a land, not of revolution, but of evolution. *Bail ó dhia ar an obair*—God bless the work!

APPENDICES

POLITICAL PARTIES 1922–65

Year	No. of seats contestable	Republican Front to 1927; thereafter Fianna Fail	Cumann na nGaedheal to 1933; thereafter Fine Gael	Labour	Farmers' Party and Clann na Talmhan	Other parties	Independents
1922	128	35	58	17	7	–	11
1923	153	44	63	14	15	–	17
1927 (i)	153	44	47	22	11	13 a	16
1927 (ii)	153	57	62	13	6	2 b	13
1932	153	72	57	7	4	–	13
1933	153	77	48	8	–	11 c	9
1937	138	69	48	13	–	–	8
1938	138	77	45	9	–	–	7
1943	138	67	32	17	14	–	8
1944	138	76	30	8	11	4 d	9
1948	147	68	31	19	7	10 e	12
1951	147	69	40	16	6	2 f	14
1954	147	65	50	19	5	3 g	5
1957	147	78	40	13	3	5 h	8
1961	144	70	47	16	2	3 i	6
1965	144	72	47	22	–	1 j	2

Details of other parties

a. 1927 (first election): National League 8, Sinn Fein 5
b. 1927 (second election): National League 2
c. 1933 Centre Party 11
d. 1944 National Labour 4
e. 1948 Clann na Poblachta 10
f. 1951 Clann na Poblachta 2
g. 1954 Clann na Poblachta 3
h. 1957 Sinn Fein 4, Clann na Poblachta 1
i. 1961 National Progressive Democrats 2, Clann na Poblachta 1
j. 1965 Clann na Poblachta 1

APPENDIX II

REPUBLIC OF IRELAND: ECONOMIC AND SOCIAL STATISTICS

1. TRADE 1929–64: VALUE AT CURRENT PRICES
(The annual Index Numbers of the volume of trade have been adjusted to include transit trade. The base is 1953 = 100.)

	Imports £000	Index No.	Exports, Re-Exports £000	Index No.
1929	61,316	86·4	47,291	118·0
1934	39,122	78·0	17,925	77·1
1944	28,531	22·4	29,917	42·9
1949	130,232	90·4	60,552	66·3
1954	179,890	97·9	115,342	102·6
1959	212,647	109·6	130,607	109·6
1964	347,815	170·0	222,394	175·2

2. EXPORTS AND IMPORTS, 1964

	Imports £ million	%	Exports £ million	%
Britain	160·5	46·1	129·8	58·4
Northern Ireland	16·0	4·6	29·2	13·1
UK Total	176·5	50·7	159·0	71·5
Other countries	171·3	49·3	63·4	28·5
Total all countries	347·8	100·0	222·4	100·0

3. ANALYSIS OF EXPORTS

	1959 £ million	1964 £ million	% Increase
Food, drink and tobacco	43·9	72·9	66
Live animals	39·1	66·7	71
Manufactures (other than food, drink and tobacco)	25·2	55·5	120
Raw materials	10·0	11·6	16
Re-Exports	12·5	15·7	26
Totals	130·7	222·4	70

These figures do not include exports from Shannon Free Airport, estimated at £14 million in 1964. Main *food and drink* exports in that year were: meat £34·4 million; dairy products £12·9 million; beverages £7·6 million; cocoa and chocolate preparations £6·9 million; fruit and vegetables £2·8 million; sugar and sugar preparations £2·2 million; fish £1·9 million. Main *live animals* exports were: cattle £54·8 million; horses, pigs, etc. £11·9 million. Main *manufactures* exports were: textiles £9·6 million; machinery £7·9 million; clothing £5·9 million; metal manufactures £4·8 million; transport equipment, ships, etc. £4·4 million; leather £3 million; footwear £2·8 million; paper £2·5 million; printed matter £2·1 million; chemicals £1·9 million.

4. GROSS NATIONAL PRODUCT

£ *million*

1958	600
1964	938
1965	1,016 (estimated)

Between 1958 and 1964, GNP in real terms (i.e. after allowing for price changes) rose by 28 per cent.

5. NATIONAL INCOME 1964

	Global Figure	
	£ *million*	%
Agriculture, forestry, fishing	167	22·0
Industry	239	31·5
Distribution and transport	119	15·7
Public administration and defence	45	5·9
Other domestic sources	158	20·8
Foreign income	39	5·1
Income from agriculture, forestry, fishing:		
wages, salaries, etc.	18	2·4
from self-employment	146	19·3
Income from other domestic sources:		
wages, salaries, etc.	404	53·3
from self-employment, etc.	160	21·1

In correlating these figures account should be taken of adjustment for stock appreciation of £9 million (1·2 per cent), which makes the total National Income in real terms £758 million.

6. REVENUE 1963–64

	£ *million*	%
Tobacco duties	33·2	18
Beer and spirits, duties and excise	21·6	12
Other sources	129·6	70
Total	184·4	100

7. STATE EXPENDITURE IN KEY SECTORS 1965–66 (estimates)

	£ *million*
Aid to agriculture	52·391
Social Welfare	38·774
Education	28·104

The figures for Social Welfare and Education do not represent the total national spending on these items. Capital expenditure (e.g. on schools) is excluded, and so is private expenditure on education in the form of school fees. Also excluded is Social Welfare expenditure financed from social insurance contributions of workers and employers, which for 1965 are estimated to amount to over £16 million. Taking into consideration the sums spent by local authorities, a tentative estimate for total expenditure on Social Welfare in 1965 would be £55 million, or 5·4 per cent of GNP. The estimated £28 million on Education represents 2·8 per cent of GNP. Of the estimated £52·4 million of expenditure on Agriculture, £33·7 million is financed out of current revenue (taxation), and £18·7 million out of the capital budget (borrowings).

8. REPRESENTATIVE WAGE RATES FOR SKILLED AND UNSKILLED WORKERS 1913–65

	Bricklayers (Dublin)		Builders' Labourers (Dublin)		Farm Labourers (National Average)
	per hour	per week	per hour	per week	per week
	s d	s d	s d	s d	s d
1913	9½	39 7	5	20 10	n.a.
1925	n.a.	n.a.	n.a.	n.a.	26 3
1931	1 10½	82 6	1 4	58 8	24 3
1935	1 9½	78 10	1 3	55 0	21 3
1939	1 10½	82 6	1 5	62 4	30 3*
1945	2 3½	100 10	1 9	77 0	40 3
1955	3 11	172 4	3 3	143 0	85 6
1965	6 4	270 11	5 6	233 9	145 3†

* 1940   † 1964

Note: In the case of building workers, normal hours of work per week were 50 in 1913, 44 in 1931, 1935, 1945 and 1955, and 44¼ in 1965.

9. WELFARE CONTRIBUTIONS AND BENEFITS

(i) *Social Insurance Contributions* (as from January 1, 1966)

	Weekly Rates	
	Male	Female
Employee	7s 4d	6s 3d
Employer	7s 4d	7s 0d

Lower contributions are payable in respect to agricultural workers, female domestic servants, soldiers and civil servants.

(ii) *Social Insurance Benefits* (as from January 1, 1966)

Weekly Rates

Contributory Old Age Pension:
basic rate	60s 0d	
married couple	107s 6d	

Widows' Contributory Pension:
widow without dependants	52s 6d	
with 1 child	68s 0d	
with 2 children	81s 0d	+ 8s for each child in excess of 2

Disability and Unemployment Benefit:
man or woman	52s 6d	
man with wife	92s 6d	
man, wife and 1 child	105s 6d	
man, wife and 2 children	118s 6d	+ 8s for each child in excess of 2

(iii) *Social Assistance Benefits* (as at August 1, 1965)

                                                    Weekly Rates

Non-Contributory Old Age Pension:
    means less than 10s a week   47s 6d
    means 10s to 20s a week   42s 6d
Non-Contributory Widows' Pension:
    means less than 10s a week   46s 0d
    with 1 child   56s 0d
    with 2 children   66s 0d + 5s for each child
                        in excess of 2

    means 10s to 20s a week   41s 0d
    with 1 child   51s 0d
    with 2 children   61s 0d + 5s for each child
                        in excess of 2

Unemployment Assistance:
  Urban Areas
    man or woman   34s 0d
    man with wife   62s 6d
    man, wife and 1 child   72s 6d
    man, wife and 2 children   82s 6d + 5s for each child
                        in excess of 2

  Rural Areas
    man or woman   28s 0d
    man with wife   54s 6d
    man, wife and 1 child   64s 6d
    man, wife and 2 children   74s 6d + 5s for each child
                        in excess of 2

10. UNEMPLOYMENT: COMPARATIVE STATISTICS 1954–65 (monthly average)

	Republic	%	Northern Ireland	%	Britain	%
1954	62,200	8·1	33,000	7·0	284,800	1·3
1955	55,000	6·8	32,300	6·8	232,200	1·1
1960	52,700	6·7	32,400	6·7	360,400	1·6
1964	48,300	5·7	32,800	6·6	380,600	1·7
1965 (July)	41,500	4·7	29,200	5·9	280,577	1·2

NORTHERN IRELAND: GROSS DOMESTIC PRODUCT 1963

	At Current Prices £ million	At Constant Prices—1958 Factor Cost £ million
Agriculture, horticulture, etc.	55·311	61·813
Mining and manufacturing	153·153	131·349
Building and contracting	27·080	24·116
Gas, electricity and water	12·350	11·625
Transport and communications	17·639	15·749
Distribution	52·760	48·404
Professional, financial and miscellaneous services	108·475	89·656
Ownership of dwellings	12·949	9·436
Government administration and defence	25·915	21·778
Totals	465·632	413·926

APPENDIX IV

SECONDARY SCHOOL PUPILS AND RELIGIOUS VOCATION IN THE IRISH REPUBLIC 1956–60

Type of School	Final Year Students	Number of Vocations
Diocesan schools	5,428	1,346
Secondary schools run by regular orders	4,395	618
Juniorates	427	265
Missionary societies	132	99
Christian Brothers	10,297	767
Lay secondary schools	937	54
Other schools	2,723	31

Diocesan schools, attended both by prospective priests and lay pupils, are under the direct administrative and financial control of the bishop. The association of lay and clerical pupils in the same classes has given these schools markedly 'progressive' characteristics. Juniorates are operated by regulars for the training of future priests.

SELECT BIBLIOGRAPHY

THERE is no lack of books dealing with Irish affairs before 1916 and with the subsequent Independence struggle and Civil War; but for events after 1923 the list becomes thinner, and the number of reputable books dwindles away to two or three between the 1920s and 1950s. For information on matters like the Shannon Scheme, the Army Mutiny, the formation of Saor Eire, the Economic War and post-war economic developments, I have had to rely mainly on interviews, newspaper reports (particularly in the *Irish Times*, the *Irish Independent* and the *Irish Press*) and a variety of pamphlets and 'occasional' publications, supplemented by private documents made available to me. The bibliography given here is by no means exhaustive; selection of books has been governed by the intention of giving those which most usefully indicate the main features of the development of Irish affairs in broad terms.

CHAPTERS 1–4
Barry, Tom, *Guerilla Days in Ireland*, Irish Press, Dublin, 1949

Béaslái, Piaras, *Michael Collins and the Making of a New Ireland*, 2 vols., Phoenix, Dublin, 1926

Beaverbrook, Lord, *Decline and Fall of Lloyd George*, Collins, London; Meredith, Des Moines, Iowa; 1963

Beckett, J. C., *Short History of Ireland*, Hutchinson, London; Hillary, New York; 1952

Breen, Dan, *My Fight for Irish Freedom*, Talbot Press, Dublin, 1924; rev. edn., Anvil Books, Tralee, 1964

Brennan, Robert, *Allegiance*, Browne and Nolan, Dublin, 1950

Bromage, Mary C., *De Valera and the March of a Nation*, Hutchinson, 1956

Callwell, C. E., *Field Marshal Sir Henry Wilson*, Cassell, London, 1927

Caulfield, Max, *The Easter Rebellion*, Muller, London; Holt, Rinehart and Winston, New York; 1963

Churchill, Winston, *The World Crisis: the Aftermath*, Thornton Butterworth, London; Scribner, New York; 1929

Clarke, Thomas J., *Leaves from an Irish Felon's Prison Diary*, Maunsel, 1962

Clarkson, J. Dunsmore, *Labour and Nationalism in Ireland*, Columbia University Press, New York, 1925

Collins, Michael, *The Path to Freedom: Arguments for the Treaty*, Martin Lester, Dublin, 1922

Connolly, James, *Labour in Irish History*, Maunsel, Dublin, 1910; *Socialism and Nationalism*, ed. Desmond Ryan, Sign of the Three Candles, Dublin, 1948; *Labour in Easter Week*, writings ed. by Desmond Ryan, Sign of the Three Candles, Dublin, 1949

Coxhead, Elizabeth, *Daughters of Erin*, Secker and Warburg, London, 1965

Crozier, Brig. Gen. Frank P., *Impressions and Recollections*, Laurie, London, 1930; *Ireland For Ever*, Cape, London, 1932

Curtiss, E., *A History of Ireland*, Methuen, London, 1960

Dail Eireann, *Minutes of the Proceedings of the First Parliament of the Republic of Ireland 1919–1921*, Stationery Office, Dublin, 1959; *Debates on the Treaty between Great Britain and Ireland, December 1921, January 1922*, Stationery Office, Dublin, 1959

Dalton, Charles, *With the Irish Brigade 1917–1921*, Davies, London, 1929

Devoy, John, *Recollections of an Irish Rebel's Youth*, Young, New York, 1929

Dwane, David T., *Life of Eamon de Valera*, Talbot Press with Fisher and Unwin, Dublin and London, 1922

Fox, R. M., *Rebel Irishwomen*, Talbot Press, Dublin, 1935; *The Irish Citizen Army*, Duffy, Dublin, 1943; *Life of Jim Larkin*, Lawrence and Wishart, London, 1957

Gallagher, Frank, *The Anglo-Irish Treaty*, Hutchinson, London, 1965

Greaves, Desmond, *James Connolly*, Lawrence and Wishart, London, 1961

Gwynn, Denis R., *Roger Casement*, Cape, London, 1930; *John Redmond*, Harrap, London, 1932

Henry, Robert Mitchell, *The Evolution of Sinn Fein*, Fisher and Unwin, London, 1920

Holt, Edgar, *Protest in Arms*, Putnam, London, 1960

Inglis, Brian, *The Story of Ireland*, Faber, London; Roy, New York; 1956

Jenkins, Roy, *Asquith*, Collins, London; Chilmark, New York; 1965

Larkin, Emmet, *James Larkin*, Routledge and Kegan Paul, London; MIT Press, Cambridge, Mass.; 1965

Le Roux, Louis, *Tom Clarke and the Irish Freedom Movement*, Talbot Press, Dublin, 1926; *Patrick H. Pearse*, Phoenix, Dublin, 1932

Lloyd George, David, *Is It Peace?*, Hodder and Stoughton, London, 1923; new edn., Gollancz, London, 1934

Lloyd George, Richard, *Lloyd George*, Muller, London, 1960

Lynch, Diarmuid, *The IRB and the 1916 Insurrection*, ed. Florence O'Donoghue, Mercier, Cork, 1947

Lyons, F. S. L., *The Irish Parliamentary Party 1890–1910*, Faber, London, 1950

Macardle, Dorothy, *The Irish Republic*, Irish Press, Dublin, 1951; Farrar, Straus and Giroux, New York, 1965

Macready, Nevil, *Annals of an Active Life*, Hutchinson, London, 1924

MacManus, M. J., *Eamon de Valera*, Talbot Press, Dublin, 1944

MacSwiney, Terence, *Principles of Freedom*, Dutton, New York, 1921

Martin, F. X., *The Irish Volunteers 1913–1915*, Duffy, Dublin, 1963; *The Howth Gun-running*, Duffy, Dublin, 1964

O'Brien, Conor Cruise, *Parnell and his Party*, Oxford University Press, London, 1953, New York, 1957; ed. *The Shaping of Modern Ireland*, Routledge and Kegan Paul, London, 1960; "Ireland and the UN", *Trinity News*, May 1964

O'Brien, William, and Ryan, Desmond, eds., *Devoy's Postbag*, Vols. I and II, Fallon, Dublin, 1953

O'Cathasaigh, P., *The Story of the Irish Citizen Army*, Maunsel, Dublin, 1919

O'Connor, Batt, *Michael Collins*, Davies, London, 1925

O'Connor, Frank, *The Big Fellow*, Nelson, London; Templegate, Springfield, Ill.; 1937

O'Donoghue, Florence, *The Story of Liam Lynch and the Republican Army 1916–23*, Irish Press, Dublin, 1952; *No Other Law*, Irish Press, Dublin, 1954

O'Faoláin, Sean, *Life of Countess Markievicz*, Cape, London, 1934; *Eamon de Valera*, Penguin, Harmondsworth, 1939

O'Hegarty, P. S., *The Victory of Sinn Fein*, Talbot Press, Dublin, 1924; *A History of Ireland Under the Union*, Methuen, London, 1952

O'Sullivan, Donal, *The Irish Free State and its Senate*, Faber, London, 1940

Pakenham, Frank, *Peace by Ordeal*, Cape, London, 1935

Pearse, Patrick H., *Collected Works*, Phoenix, Dublin, 1924

Ryan, Desmond, *James Connolly*, Talbot Press, Dublin, 1924; *Remembering Sion*,

Barker, London, 1934; *Unique Dictator*, Barker, London, 1936; *The Rising*, Golden Eagle, Dublin, 1949

Thornley, David, *Isaac Butt and Home Rule*, MacGibbon and Kee, London, 1964

White, Terence de Vere, *Kevin O'Higgins*, Methuen, London, 1948

CHAPTER 6

Aiken, Frank, *Speeches at the United Nations 1957–63*, Browne and Nolan, Dublin, published annually since 1958

De Valera, Eamon, *Peace and War: Speeches on International Affairs*, Gill, Dublin, 1944

Harrison, Henry, *The Neutrality of Ireland*, Hale, London, 1941

Hogan, V. P., *The Neutrality of Ireland in World War II*, University of Michigan Press, Ann Arbor, Mich., 1953

O'Brien, Conor Cruise, *To Katanga and Back*, Hutchinson, London, 1962; Simon and Schuster, New York, 1963

O'Sullivan, Donal, *The Irish Free State and its Senate*, Faber, London, 1940

Williams, T. Desmond, 'Irish Neutrality', articles in the *Irish Press*, Dublin, June 27 to July 17, 1953

Eire: Ireland, the weekly bulletin of the Department of External Affairs, and *Round Table*, the quarterly devoted to Commonwealth Affairs, give useful information about Ireland's external relations since the foundation of the state.

CHAPTER 7

Burke, John F., *Outlines of the Industrial History of Ireland*, Browne and Nolan, Dublin, 1950

Chubb, Basil A., *Source Book of Irish Government*, Institute of Public Administration, Dublin, 1964; with Thornley, David, 'Irish Government Observed', *Irish Times*, 1964

Farley, Desmond, *Social Insurance and Social Assistance in Ireland*, Institute of Public Administration, Dublin, 1964

FitzGerald, Garret, *State Sponsored Bodies*, Institute of Public Administration, Dublin, 1963

Hall, F. G., *The Bank of Ireland 1783–1946*, ed. George O'Brien, Hodges and Figgis with Blackwell, Dublin and Oxford, 1948

Hensey, Brendan, *The Health Services of Ireland*, Institute of Public Administration, Dublin, 1959

Kaim-Caudle, P. R., *Social Security in Ireland and Western Europe*, Economic Research Institute, Dublin, 1964

Lynch, Patrick, and Vaizey, John, *The Guinness Brewery in the Irish Economy, 1759–1876*, Cambridge University Press, London and New York, 1960

McCracken, John L., *Representative Government in Ireland*, Oxford University Press, London and New York, 1958

Nevin, Edward, *Textbook of Economic Analysis* (Irish edition), Macmillan, London, 1963

O'Connell, J. B., *Financial Administration of Ireland*, Mount Salus Press, Dublin, 1960

O'Mahoney, David, *The Irish Economy*, Cork University Press, Cork, 1962; Verry, Mystic, Conn., 1964

Official Publications:

Bunreacht na hÉireann (Constitution of Ireland), Stationery Office, Dublin

Economic Development, Stationery Office, Dublin, 1958

Reports of the Committee of Industrial Organisation, and of the National

Industrial and Economic Council, Stationery Office, Dublin
Second Programme for Economic Expansion, Stationery Office, Dublin, 1963
Statistical Abstract for 1964, Stationery Office, Dublin, 1965

CHAPTER 8

Arensberg, Conrad M., and Kimball, Solon T., *Family and Community in Ireland*,
   Harvard University Press, Cambridge, Mass., 1940
O'Brien, John, ed., *The Vanishing Irish*, McGraw-Hill, New York, 1953
Usher, Arland, *The Face and Mind of Ireland*, Gollancz, London, 1949; Devin
   Adaire, New York, 1950

Annual Reports of the Censorship of Publications Board, Stationery Office,
   Dublin

CHAPTER 9

Coffey, D., *Douglas Hyde*, Talbot Press, Dublin, 1938
Corkery, Daniel, *Fortunes of the Irish Language*, Fallon, Dublin, 1951; *The
   Hidden Ireland*, Gill, Dublin, 1951
de Fréine, Sean, *The Great Silence*, Foilseacháin Nai siúnta, Teoranta, Westport,
   1965
O'Floinn, Antathai Donnchadh, *The Integral Irish Tradition*, Gill, Dublin, 1954
Ryan, Desmond, *The Sword of Light*, Barker, London, 1939

Report of the Commission on the Restoration of the Irish Language, Stationery
   Office, Dublin, 1964
White Paper on the Irish Language, Stationery Office, Dublin, 1965

CHAPTER 10

Bieler, Ludwig, *Ireland: Harbinger of the Middle Ages*, Oxford University Press,
   London and New York, 1963; ed., *The Irish Penitentials*, Institute for
   Advanced Studies, Dublin, 1963
Blacam, Aodhde, *Gentle Ireland*, Bruce, Milwaukee, 1935
Blanchard, Jean, *The Church in Contemporary Ireland*, Clonmore and Reynolds,
   Dublin, 1963; Burns and Oates, London, 1963; Verry, Mystic, Conn., 1964
Blanshard, Paul, *The Irish and Catholic Power*, Beacon Press, Boston, Mass.,
   1953; Verschoyle, London, 1954
Brennan, Nial, *Dr Mannix*, Angus and Robertson, Sydney; Tri-Ocean, San
   Francisco; 1965
Daniel-Rops, Henri, *The Miracle of Ireland*, Clonmore and Reynolds, Dublin;
   Taplinger, New York; 1959
De Paor, Máire and Séan, *Early Christian Ireland*, Thames and Hudson,
   London, 1958
Doyle, Lynn, *The Spirit of Ireland*, Batsford, London, 1935
Gougaud, Dom Louis, *Christianity in Celtic Lands*, Sheed and Ward, London,
   1932
Lockington, Rev. W. J., *The Soul of Ireland*, Harding and More, London, 1919
MacCarthy, Michael J. Fitzgerald, *Priests and People in Ireland*, Hodges,
   Dublin, 1902
MacSuibhne, Peadar, *Paul Cullen and his Contemporaries*, 3 vols., Leinster
   Leader, Naas (vol. III, 1965)
Mould, Daphne Pochin, *Ireland of the Saints*, Batsford, London, 1953; *Irish
   Pilgrimage*, Gill, Dublin, 1955
Ryan, Rev. John, *Irish Monasticism*, Talbot Press, Dublin, 1931
Viney, Michael, *The Five Per Cent*, Irish Times, Dublin, 1965

Walsh, Rev. P. J., *William J. Walsh, Archbishop of Dublin*, Talbot Press, Dublin, 1928

The following publications have been of particular value: *The Catholic Herald*, London; *The Catholic Standard*, Dublin; *Christus Rex*, Maynooth; *Doctrine and Life*, Irish Dominican Publications, Dublin; *The Furrow*, Maynooth; *Hibernia*, Dublin; *The Irish Catholic Directory*, Dublin; *The Irish Ecclesiastical Record*, Browne and Nolan, Dublin; *The Irish Independent*, Dublin; *Studies*, Talbot Press, Dublin

CHAPTER 11

Fairfield, Letitia, *The Trial of Peter Barnes*, Hodges, London, 1953
Goertz, Herman, articles on IRA relations with Germany, *Irish Times*, August 1947
O'Donnel, Peadar, *There Will Be Another Day*, Dolmen Press, Dublin, with Oxford University Press, London; Dufour, Chester Springs, Pa.; 1963
Stephan, Enno, *Spies in Ireland*, Macdonald, London, 1962; Stackpole, Harrisburg, Pa., 1965
Stuart, Francis, 'Frank Ryan in Germany', *The Bell*, Dublin, November-December 1950

In addition to two illegal documents published by the IRA (*Resistance* and *Stephen Hayes' Confession*), the following journals have been of value: *An Phoblacht; Easter Week; Republican Congress; United Ireland; The United Irishman; The Wolfe Tone Weekly*

CHAPTER 12

Armour, W. S., *Ulster, Ireland, Britain*, Duckworth, London, 1938
Barrit, Dennis P., and Carter, Charles F., *The Northern Ireland Problem*, Oxford University Press, London and New York, 1962
Blacam, Aodh de, *The Black North*, Gill, Dublin, 1950
Blake, John W., *Northern Ireland in World War II*, Northern Ireland Stationery Office, Belfast, 1956
Colvin, Ian, *Lord Carson*, Vols. II and III, Gollancz, London, 1934
Ervine, St John Grier, *Craigavon, Ulsterman*, Allen and Unwin, London, 1949
Gallagher, Frank, *The Indivisible Island*, Gollancz, London, 1959
Gwynn, Denish, *History of Partition 1912–1925*, Browne and Nolan, Dublin, 1950
Isles, K. S., and Cuthbert, Norman, *An Economic Survey of Northern Ireland*, HMSO, Belfast, 1957
Mansergh, Nicholas, *The Government of Northern Ireland*, Allen and Unwin, London, 1936
Marjoribanks, E., *Lord Carson*, Vol. I, Gollancz, London, 1932 (continued by Colvin, Ian, *q.v.*)
O'Nualláin, Labhrás, *Ireland: Finances of Partition*, Clonmore and Reynolds, Dublin, 1952
Report of the Joint Working Party on the Economy of Northern Ireland (Hall Report), HMSO, Belfast, 1962
Shearman, Hugh, *Not An Inch*, Faber, London, 1942
Tone, Theobald Wolfe, *Autobiography*, ed. Sean O'Faoláin, Nelson, London, 1937
Wilson, Thomas, ed., *Ulster Under Home Rule*, Oxford University Press, London, 1955; *Economic Development of Northern Ireland*, HMSO, Belfast, 1965

INDEX